T0260794

Microgrid Technologies

Scrivener Publishing
100 Cummings Center, Suite 541J
Beverly, MA 01915-6106

Publishers at Scrivener
Martin Scrivener (martin@scrivenerpublishing.com)
Phillip Carmical (pcarmical@scrivenerpublishing.com)

Microgrid Technologies

Edited by

**C. Sharmeela, P. Sivaraman,
P. Sanjeevikumar,
and Jens Bo Holm-Nielsen**

Scrivener
Publishing

WILEY

This edition first published 2021 by John Wiley & Sons, Inc., 111 River Street, Hoboken, NJ 07030, USA and Scrivener Publishing LLC, 100 Cummings Center, Suite 541J, Beverly, MA 01915, USA
© 2021 Scrivener Publishing LLC
For more information about Scrivener publications please visit www.scrivenerpublishing.com.

Wiley Global Headquarters
111 River Street, Hoboken, NJ 07030, USA

For details of our global editorial offices, customer services, and more information about Wiley products visit us at www.wiley.com.

Limit of Liability/Disclaimer of Warranty
While the publisher and authors have used their best efforts in preparing this work, they make no representations or warranties with respect to the accuracy or completeness of the contents of this work and specifically disclaim all warranties, including without limitation any implied warranties of merchantability or fitness for a particular purpose. No warranty may be created or extended by sales representatives, written sales materials, or promotional statements for this work. The fact that an organization, website, or product is referred to in this work as a citation and/or potential source of further information does not mean that the publisher and authors endorse the information or services the organization, website, or product may provide or recommendations it may make. This work is sold with the understanding that the publisher is not engaged in rendering professional services. The advice and strategies contained herein may not be suitable for your situation. You should consult with a specialist where appropriate. Neither the publisher nor authors shall be liable for any loss of profit or any other commercial damages, including but not limited to special, incidental, consequential, or other damages. Further, readers should be aware that websites listed in this work may have changed or disappeared between when this work was written and when it is read.

Library of Congress Cataloging-in-Publication Data

ISBN 9781119710790

Cover image: Solar Panel Technology | Vtt Studio | Dreamstime.com
Cover design by Kris Hackerott

Set in size of 11pt and Minion Pro by Manila Typesetting Company, Makati, Philippines

Printed in the USA

10 9 8 7 6 5 4 3 2 1

Contents

Foreword

Power electronics—as a broader technology—fits into modern digital power e-grid, transport, and renewable energy. Editing a book on the current requirements and prospective scope is a challenge to qualify and accomplish according to the market requirements and end-user benefits. It is my pleasure to write a foreword to this book edited/written by my colleagues from Aalborg University, Esbjerg, Denmark and Anna University, Chennai, India—"Microgrid Technologies," which is giving viable solutions to the demands. With my read through of the book, I have identified that the content is inventive and enriched with techno-fiscals, a model for upcoming activities for the academic, researchers, and industrialists, from whom we hope the microgrids will be adapted in their work.

Microgrids are a digital power electronics innovation in new energy operation for electrical energy management with grid-connected or island mode configuration within micro-, macro-, or even nano-energy requirements. A methodical manner and straightforward presentation with all prospects, this book is made up of architectures, theories of AC and DC microgrids, sociocommercial features, energy stream and operation, renewable integration, control techniques, application of artificial intelligence, and analytical simulation examples of microgrid technologies. It is a unified contribution by international authors from Europe, India, Canada, South Africa, Egypt, and Thailand.

Critical Subjects Covered in This Volume

- *The state of the art in renewable energy system-based microgrid includes grid-connected and island structures, distributed energy storage schemes, energy and power management, load flow evaluation, protection, and coordination.*
- *Digital techniques, Internet of Things (IoT), Artificial Intelligence (AI), communications, etc. are also included.*

- *Detailed studies culminate with the analytical result for frequency regulation in a low inertia system, PSO algorithm-based UPQC controller, and power quality enhancement too.*
- *Modeling of smart meters using the most recent technologies of "game theory," "relaxation algorithm," "bi-level algorithm," and "Nikaido–Isoda formulation" for energy exchange centers and bidding strategies—a scope/look to the future digitalized microgrid in renewables is also an interesting prospect of the book.*

From an overall perspective, this book presents the fundamental concepts of modernizing the microgrids as a thirst area of more ample opportunity, and contributes to original research study findings. Therefore, this book is a handy source, offering new interest for electrical power engineers and renewable operators/state regulators.

This book is a strong addition for readers to enjoy sharing proficiency in the exciting field of microgrids. Finally, I congratulate the Editors, Contributors, and the Wiley-Scrivener Publishing, USA, for the work to bring this into reality with prompt and sharp-quality delivery.

Enjoy reading the book.

Prof. Frede Blaabjerg, Fellow IEEE
Villum Investigator Full Professor
IEEE President – Power Electronics Society
Center of Reliable Power Electronics (CORPE)
Department of Energy Technology
Aalborg University, Denmark

Acknowledgements

Foremost, thanks to the Almighty for his everlasting love throughout this endeavor.

The Acknowledgements section is always a place to appreciate the dedication, commitment, resources, and timely solution either with the digital platform or a real-time medium; timely support and bond of encouragement are vital tools for teachers and researchers from their Institution.

In these regards, we, editors, express our sincere thanks to Mr. S. Rajkumar, Executive, JLL, Bengaluru, India; Ms. A. Thaiyal Nayagi, Lecturer, Rane Polytechnic College, Trichy, India; Mr. S. Muthukumaran, Director, TECH Engineering Services, Chennai, India; Mr. K. Balaji, Sr. Electrical Engineer, Sree Nandees Technologies, Chennai, India; Mr. K. Sasikumar, Electrical Engineer, Mott MacDonald, Noida, India; Center for Bioenergy and Green Engineering, Department of Energy Technology, Aalborg University, Esbjerg, Denmark, and Department of Electrical and Electronics Engineering, College of Engineering Guindy, Anna University, Chennai, India.

We, editors, got the full support and executed the task promptly where our Institution devoted the time and liberty for enhancement with research in particular to make this book a great success.

I wish one and all who devoted time and effort for the grand success with the book.

Warm regards,
Editors

A Comprehensive Review on Energy Management in Micro-Grid System

Sanjay Kumar[1]*, R. K. Saket[2], P. Sanjeevikumar[3] and Jens Bo Holm-Nielsen[3]

[1]Electrical & Electronics Engineering Department, Centurion University of Technology and Management, Odisha, India
[2]Electrical Engineering Department, IIT (BHU) Varanasi, India
[3]Center for Bioenergy and Green Engineering, Department of Energy Technology, Aalborg University, Esbjerg, Denmark

Abstract

Since the last decades there has been a huge exploitation of non-conventional (renewable) energy resources which has increased significantly. A Micro-Grid (MG) presents an appropriate concept to integrate local resources of renewable energy with Storage System of Energy (SSE) and are synchronized to supply the customers' requirement in different circumstances. Apart from this, the Management System of Energy (MSE) has been analyzed for allocating the output power from the Distributed Generator (DG) units optimally. It also satisfies the local demand, regulates the voltage and frequency of the smart MG, and secures a flat switching between modes, connected to grid and mode of islanded operation. In this article the authors have made an outmost effort about the area of MG–MSE, evolved in the current framework, discussing the storage units and generation of MG, the importance of Electric Vehicles (EVs) as a backup unit, combined heat and power for supplying the thermal requirements, objectives function of MG-MSE and constraints of the systems and current algorithms of optimization.

Keywords: Management System of Energy (MSE), Micro-Grid (MG), Electric Vehicles (EVs), Heat and Power Combination (HPC), optimization algorithms

**Corresponding author*: kumarasanjay@gmail.com

C. Sharmeela, P. Sivaraman, P. Sanjeevikumar, and Jens Bo Holm-Nielsen (eds.) Microgrid Technologies, (1–24) © 2021 Scrivener Publishing LLC

1.1   Introduction

Previously, fossil fuel represents the popular source of electricity, creating emissions of gaseous pollutant in our environment. This led to the advent of renewable energy sources, which provided clean energy and have become the most suitable choice for mitigating the dependency on fossil fuel as it also decreases the Greenhouse effect from the atmosphere. The other natural resources included solar, wind, ocean, biomass, hydro, and geothermal, etc. and were capable of producing electrical energy.

As per the renewable global status report of 2017, the power sector is mainly concerned about the renewable technologies policy, which gives a facility of integration of it into the existing energy systems. Figure 1.1 shows the universal electricity creation until the end of 2016, and also shows that about 30.28% of the entire power is depicted by means of the renewable sources. The estimation is about 2,017 GW out of 6,660 GW the total global electrical energy capacity. Hydropower takes the 1st position in the production of RE.

Clearly, it is shown in Figure 1.2 that about 16.46% of the total power is supplied by the hydropower. It is 54.34% of the RE. The wind power follows it, which is about 7.3% of the total and 24.15% of renewable sources. Then comes Photovoltaic (PV) power (15.02% of RE), about 4.55% of total power capacity, bio-power (5.55% of RE) is about 1.7%, and others are 0.9%. But in 2016, the newly implemented renewable energy is increased by solar (PV) power (47%), wind power (15.5%) and hydropower (9) compared to 2015 [1].

Figure 1.3 shows the consumption of energy sources like natural gas, coal, renewable sources, nuclear, petroleum and other liquid fuels from

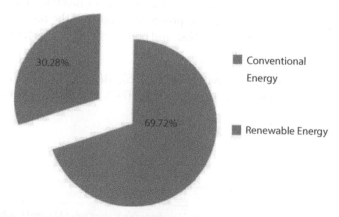

Figure 1.1 The renewable global status report.

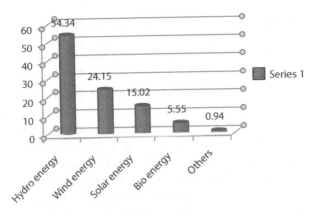

Figure 1.2 Consumption of renewable energy sources.

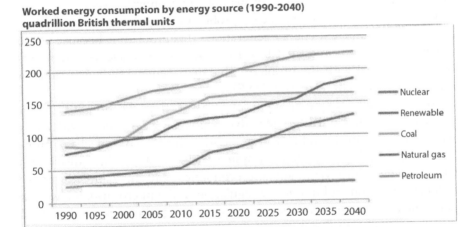

Figure 1.3 Intensification of various energy sources from 1990 to 2040.

the year 1090 to 2040 [2]. According to this, consumption of renewable sources is going to increase by 30% in the duration from 2015 to 2040.

Nowadays, maximum research is going on the utility of renewable energy. Micro-grid integration has taken the maximum concentration of researchers. A micro-grid (MG) is a distributed network that includes different possible distributed resources of energy, which can be considered as a single system, that can be optimizable, means can be balanced with generations and loads with a suitable storage system. It is also capable of doing work independently with or without connection with the utility power grid [3].

A micro-grid is a network or an association of local electrical generation resources connected through a common point known as PCC.

The micro-grid has one or more renewable generation units, conventional power generation system, the electrical storage system (ESS), the thermal storage system (TSS), electrical loads, and thermal loads. The conventional power generation system can consist of the micro turbine (MT), diesel generator set, etc. Similarly, in renewable generation units, we can make a photovoltaic (PV) generation system, wind turbines, biomass and hydrokinetic system, etc.There are two manners of operation of a micro-grid namely, connected to grid manner, and the other one is island manner. In GC mode a microgrid is in link with the conventional power grid. It is capable of participating in the energy market as a seller or buyer that can exchange energy with the utility. However, in the islanded manner, micro-grid functions as an autonomous body, as disconnected from the utility network. The island condition occurs due to several reasons such as geographical position on earth, brownout and economic issues.

Generally, the microgrids face a problem of supplying demand properly due to insufficient energy generation. This problem is because of the irregularity of loads and the RE sources [4]. So, a management system is required to deal with the problem. This management system is called a management system of energy (MSE).

The management system of energy (MSE) is the collection of different control approaches and different active, ongoing exercises along with hardware and software to mitigate the energy management objectives problems. It is a multiple functionary system. It is a system which distributes the generated power optimally and economically to the load with proper voltage regulation and frequency regulation of the micro-grid. So, we can get a smooth changeover between connected to grid manner and isolated manner of micro-grid systems, according to micro-grid components and real-time load conditions of operation. This system can be used to get high-quality power, sustainability, reliability and environmentally friendly power source.

Due to this, researchers started focusing extensively on MSE strategies for various micro-grids ranging from small home (small scale) to cities or towns (large scale) as shown in the different scales of MG of Figure 1.4.

Exploration has started on a study of the practicability of the parts of micro-grid, and it is modeled by scheduling the DGs, and forecasting the data of environmental conditions such as irradiance of sunray, speed of wind flow and water speed, forecast of energy demand and on availability optimization algorithms in the intention of cost-effective benefits with minimum impact on the atmosphere. Figure 1.5 shows the central micro-grid arrangement and components related to the energy management system. It shows that the

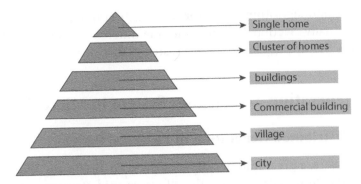

Figure 1.4 Various ranges of MG.

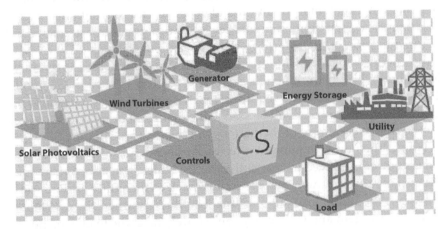

Figure 1.5 Components of micro-grid.

research is mainly focused on the resolution of different problems regarding the micro-grid by means of an energy management system.

This is a review of the different features of micro-grid and management of energy that are presented in various current topics, starting from various units of MG, synchronization of components to the recent optimization methodology with system limitations and objective functions for MSE.

Afterwards, the different configuration and components of micro-grid are deployed in Section 1.2. Here the different structures used in an energy management system with various distributed energy sources, various storage systems and different type of load or the consumer behavior are illustrated. Followed by Section 1.3, it depicts the MG–MSE and different modes of operation. Further, Section 1.4 discusses about the recent techniques and algorithms used for optimization in energy management systems. Finally, Section 1.5 concludes the different sections and further deliberates the strategy for further research in this area.

1.2 Generation and Storage System in MicroGrid

1.2.1 Distributed Generation of Electrical Power

In recent years, a great number of researchers are discussing the issues in micro-grids. Nowadays, the verities of micro-grid structures have been presented in the literature. In micro-grid the different distributed generations are utilized because of its geographical characteristic, economic benefits, environmental condition and impact on the surrounding. In Ref. [5], there is a discussion on predictive MSE with its control strategies and communication of micro-grid to the independent utility grid. A 1.5 MW wind energy associated with the battery as a storage system is analyzed. In Ref. [6] a hybrid hydrokinetic system HKT battery is used in GC mode. The surplus power of HKT is utilized for charging a battery or trade to the grid. Whether the power will be sold to the main grid or not is determined by the charge condition of the battery and the principle of the utility grid network. The power requirement of the load is provided by the HKT. The excess power is utilized to charge the storage body. Then also, if there is an excess quantity of power, that can return back to the utility grid network. However, the utility grid supplies the load directly when the distributed generation system and the battery can't entirely meet the load demand.

The universally used energy storage system is the battery. The battery system also has some limitations, as some charging and discharging current issues and unreliability according to the lifespan of the battery. So, techno-electronic indexes of micro-grid-based hybrid renewable energy resources are significantly increased by applying the distributed system of the generation with the storage system of energy [7]. Ref. [8] is a study of hybrid solar power as PV and diesel power in a distributed system supplying a load of a rural school in Ethiopia. The paper has compared the hybrid PV/Diesel distributed system with the storage system to the distributed generation system without storage as the net instantaneous rate of energy. Here a software named Homer is applied for analysis. The result was concluded that the hybrid distributed generation system with storage is having technical and economic advantages than that without storage. In Ref. [9] the authors proposed that the energy management system for hybrid micro-grid consist of photovoltaic and wind power as renewable energy sources (RES) and fuel cell (Hydrogen cell), ultracapacitor or battery as storage system of energy (SSE).

1.2.2 Incorporation of Electric Car in Micro-Grid as a Device for Backup

Nowadays the incorporation of an electric vehicle with micro-grid is viral because of its effect of low emission, inexpensive charging and decreased usage of conventional fuels. The electric car with MG can function in car-to-grid (C2G) mode or grid-to-car (G2C) mode. In Ref. [10] planned power management is proposed in the MG, including storage systems categorized into two types: regenerative fuel cell (RFC) and electric car (EV). That paper approaches with multi-goal optimization to minimize operational cost, line losses and maximise the value of energy stored in terms of RFC and EC. There are two functioning schemes planned for EC working in C2G mode to decrease the net running cost of the system. The combination of particle swarm skim of optimization as well as front and back sweep algorithm is used to solve complication, non-linear action and multidimensional property of the objective function. In Ref. [11] a large-scale electric vehicle charging station is proposed by the author, in which the required power is supplied by solar and wind power. Here both the PV and wind work with a unified MPPT technique. In Ref. [12] the author incorporated the plug-in charger of the electric vehicle in the distribution grid in both directions by using various converters. The bidirectional converters are coupled to the capacitor at the link with DC. The grid voltage may be regulated in the C2G configuration using the capacitor at the link with DC, which provides compensation for reactive power, which avoids the risk of voltage sag in the main. The mixed charging electrical car battery is used for peak load shaving and load levelling. Ref. [13] illustrates a real application of electric vehicle charging station along with a storage system of energy, which is a battery of Lithium polymer. Investigational research is done in Italy at the power and Sustainable Economic Development labs for innovative Technologies. The outcome shows the new performance of the ECs in the height of energy shaving action, as compared to the utility grid.

A resiliency-based Energy Management System of islanded operation of micro-grid is presented in Ref. [14]. Here the case studied is about micro-grid (MG) consisting of PV generation farms and WT generation farms both having storage system of energy (SSE) and distributed generation system. Based on the study, the researchers used 25 plug-in hybrid electric cars as adaptable load and supply to replicate the scheme of demand response in an optimal way, so the ECs in G2V manner are used as adaptable load, while in V2G manner is applicable as adjustable supply. Ref. [15] is a discussion on systematic energy management of a home with the smart system using PV panels as the source and plug-in EC (PEC) as storage of energy. It reduces payment for energy demand under using time tariff while supplying energy requirements to PEC and home load. A Lithium-ion battery is used in the PEC as storage and is controlled by DC–AC inverter, which allows the bidirectional flow of power. The plugs-in and plug-out of the PEC can be done once a day. The PEC mobility model is modeled by the Markov Chain model. The predictive models are used by the author to design solar power supply and home as load. The researchers proposed that the system may possibly be a significant cost savings system for the consumers. The proposed Management System of Energy manages the flow of power in between the PEC as storage, building or home as loads, and an array of PV panels and utility supply grid as supply.

1.2.3 Power and Heat Integration in Management System

The heat or thermal energy can be generated concurrently with electricity in HPC systems. The heat can be used for some other purposes such as space heating, water heating, etc. The efficiency can be enhanced with the help of HPC, in which the waste energy as heat is used for various thermal utilizations, therefore minimizing energy loss during distribution or transmission. The Cooling–Heating-Power-Combination (CHPC) is further called as tri-generation micro-grid. It is capable of providing heat, cooling and power to the consumer as required. In Ref. [16] an optimized model of a tri-generation micro-grid (CHPC) is discussed. In this case, the CHPC deals with the uncertainty of energy demand such as heating, cooling and electricity. An MSE for HPC of a GC Micro-grid optimally operates the grid and dispatches the HPC. The micro-grid supplies electrical and thermal energy requirements. In Ref. [17], the author discussed a management system of energy for HPC for a micro-grid connected to the grid, which can plan grid operation and HPC send-off optimally. The MG is taken as supply of electricity and thermal energy as required. The given methods have been concluded that V2G operation achieves a minimum rate of the objective function as compared to the operating strategies of MG with no V2G and the micro-grid with a conventional vehicle. A large-scale electric vehicle charging station is proposed in Ref. [11], where solar and wind energy is combined to supply the total power required. Here both arrays of solar panels and wind power generators work through a combined MPPT technique. The author combined the plug-in hybrid electric vehicle charger working in V2G mode with the distribution grid by the converters like rectifiers and choppers [12]. They are connected to the DC-link with the capacitor. This DC-link capacitor offers compensation of reactive power. So, this V2G charger is able to adjust the voltage of the grid by employing a capacitor at the link of dc. So, the problem of voltage drop can be avoided in the grid. This energy could be used to level the load and to shave the peak load. The authors presented an actual execution of EV charging station in the company, including an energy storing system like Li-polymer battery. The authors of Ref. [14] offered an idea about resiliency-based MSE for a micro-grid working in islanded condition. That case study was on a micro-grid consisting of PV farm, WT farm, and battery. The researchers applied 25 plug-in hybrid EC as the controllable design of supply and demand, which are optimized to show the conception of demand–supply relation. In V2G mode the plug-in EV can be considered as adjustable generation and in G2V mode the plug-in EV can be considered as adjustable demand. The authors of Ref. [15] discussed systematic management of energy for a smart home including plug-in EV (PEV) and PV panels to minimize costs during a time of use tariff, which supplies the home load and energy required to charge the PEV. A Li-ion battery is used in the PEV, which is controlled by a bidirectional converter. It allows power flow in both directions. Here the Markov Chain model is applied to design the mobility of PEV. The predictive model is used to design a home as a load and the dispersed power generation. This guaranties the cost-saving at the consumer's end. The total power flow is managed by the proposed energy management system.

1.2.4 Combination of Heat and Electrical Power System

The thermal energy also simultaneously can be generated with the electrical energy in the HPC systems, which can offer heat or thermal energy for diverse uses, like residential heating, cooling and water heating, etc. The power efficiency can be enhanced by HPC, in which the unused heat can be utilized for different heat applications, so distribution or transmission losses can be minimized. The cooling–heating-power-combination (CHPC), which is also called as tri-generation micro-grid can provide heating, cooling and electrical power to the users. In Ref. [16] it is discussed about the optimized model of tri-generation micro-grid, cooling–heating-power-combination (CHPC). In Ref. [17], the grid and HPC operation is optimally planned for MSE of HPC in GC-MG. The required electric and thermal energy can be supplied by the micro-grid.

1.3   System of Energy Management

Extensive research has been going on upon the application of an energy management system in micro-grid operated in either connected with grid network mode or isolated from grid mode. For optimal MSE the objective function has to be defined following the system constraints (mechanism and functioning mode). The MSE puts a significant impact on the environment, the life span of the generation unit and system performance. The energy management modeling is the uncertainty modeling techniques with specific objective functions and constraints [18–24].

An MSE will be able to implement in two manners, such as integrated and disintegrated. In integrated MSE there is a central controller that controls the exchange of power in MG and optimizes that with respect to market prices and security constriction. In the MG having decentralized MSE, distributed supplies and loads are having a higher degree of freedom, and it maximizes the revenue by communicating the components of MG with each other. The main aim of any MSE is to maintain the load–supply balance [25, 26].

1.3.1   Classification of MSE

According to literature, the MG energy management system is categorized into four groups:

    a. MSE based on conventional sources
    b. MSE based on SSE
    c. MSE based on DSM
    d. MSE based on Hybrid system.

1.3.1.1   MSE Based on Conventional Sources

According to this MSE during the failure of the energy storage system, the renewable energy sources are used with a backup source of energy like gas engines, diesel generators and microturbines in the MG [21].

1.3.1.2   MSE Based on SSE

The MGs face problems in managing the non-conventional sources like solar energy and wind energy because of its fluctuating nature. Often there is a variation in forecasted and real-time production of energy. SSE (storage system of energy) is the best solution to this problem. The SSE maintains a balance between energy production and consumption as load by preserving power during low-peak times and releasing power during high-peak time. Different optimization techniques are focused on improving the utilization in MG [27–29].

1.3.1.3 MSE Based on DSM

An additional way to deal with the energy unbalance in supply and load in MG is the utilization of DSM (demand-side management). The goal of this MSE technique is to match the generated power with power consumption by modifying customers' behavior or load profile [30, 31]. The DSM is divided into to categories:

i) Energy efficiency: This minimizes the consumption of power with increasing the commodities effectiveness at the demand side.
ii) Demand reaction: This (DR) changes the amount of power handling by the consumer in the response of changes in the price of electricity and encouragement payments as an aim to minimize the power expenditure during high-price hours or peak time or when the system is facing any threat in reliability.

The DR skims categorized in two ways. Such as: based on price DR and based on incentive DR [32].

1.3.1.4 MSE Based on Hybrid System

In this type, more than one of the above-mentioned types is practised together to solve MSE problems in the micro-grid [33].

1.3.2 Steps of MSE During Problem Solving

To solve a problem in micro-grid, the MSE follows some steps:

a. Prediction of uncertain parameters
b. Uncertainty modeling
c. Mathematical formulation
d. Optimization

1.3.2.1   Prediction of Uncertain Parameters

Uncertainty is the possibility of deference in real and forecasted values due to a lack of information [34]. This uncertainty in MG may be in operational parameters or in economic parameters. The operational parameters include the quantity of power generated and the quantity of power consumption. On the other hand, the economic parameter includes the effects on economic aspects such as production cost, financial growth and rate of interest, etc. [35].

The uncertain parameters can be predicted in various time ranges that are of the very small time period, a few minutes to a couple of days, which is called prediction of short term. In the prediction of mid-term, the time range is from several weeks to a few months. And in the prediction of the long term, it ranges from few months to several years [36]. The MG problems are considered for hourly intervals, so short term prediction is the best method for this.

1.3.2.2   Uncertainty Modeling

The MSE faces difficulty during decision making because of the uncertainty. That is why a verity of ways have been implemented to manage the uncertainty. Those methods are called uncertainty modeling [35]. There are some methods like stochastic method, ANN method, fuzzy method, robust optimization method and information gap decision theory [37–39].

1.3.2.3   Mathematical Formulation

The management of energy in a microgrid can be formulated mathematically as a problem of optimization with the primary aim to schedule the functionality of DGs, SSEs and loads for the short term with specific objective functions and the constraints of the components of MG. The capital cost and the operational cost are taken as the objective functions. Fuel cost, maintenance cost, start-up and short-down losses and degradation are considered as the operational cost. There are different constraints which can affect an MSE. Some cases maximum and minimum limit of the generation unit affects their safety and economic performance. The source and load balance are also a constraint that has to be taken. The rate of charging and rate of discharging of energy storage body can also be taken as a constraint. The bus voltage, feeder current, frequency, etc. are some technical constraints [40, 41].

1.3.2.4   Optimization

In the literature, there are many optimization techniques used for MSE in MGs [26]. Some examples are like (i) Heuristic approach (ii) MAS (iii) CPLEX solver (iv) SNOPT solver, etc.

1.3.3   Micro-Grid in Islanded Mode (Figure 1.6)

1.3.3.1   Objective Functions and Constraints of System

In Ref. [42] the authors have studied the micro-grid consisting of several renewable energy sources with EMS. They have taken the goal function as the cost minimization of energy, which is the net cost of RES per annual cost of the net energy produced. Now the optimization objective is subjected to various constraints, such as reliability, economic conditions and environmental conditions. The criteria of reliability can be considered as the amount of energy cannot be supplied when the amount of power demand is more than the power generation. In economic condition, all of the cost includes installation cost, running cost. The environmental constraint is about the amount of CO_2 emitted related to distributed generation system. Multi-objective optimization has been implemented by the authors of Ref. [43]. They have done the optimization for keeping power balanced in-between generation and utilisation, taking more than

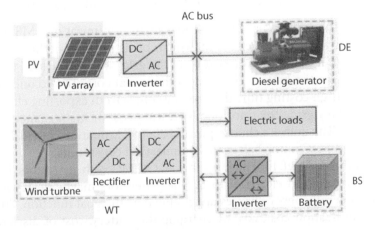

Figure 1.6 Micro-grid in Islanded mode.

one objective functions. The objective functions can be taken, such as bus voltage stability, maximum power extraction from PV panel, maximum battery protection by keeping it in a suitable range of SOC. Reduction in hydrogen consumption minimized the fluctuation.

The authors of Ref. [44] have expressed an MSE for the microgrid in standalone style such as solar power or wind power, etc. which has an objective function of cost reduction. The cost of an MG is consisting of the cost of energy injected by the distributed sources, the cost of energy storage unit like the cost of energy during charging or discharging, expenditure on the utilized energy, and the charges of penalty for undelivered power.

In Ref. [14], the authors have developed an MSE for different distributed sources like wind turbine 'WT', photovoltaic 'PV', plug-in EV 'PEV', diesel generator system 'DGS' and battery in islanded microgrid. The objective function is to make the best use of the number of adjustable loads during the islanded operation manner. The problem of optimization has been utilised to balance power. The constraints are load, limitation of the power generator and also battery specification.

In Ref. [45], the researchers have specified an idea about a cost-effective structure of thermal power plant. The goal of optimization is to decrease the cost of fuel of the thermal generators, taking consideration of the effect of the loading at the valve's point. The constraints are power balancing, power generator's limitations, and the ranges of operation of prohibited generators and its limits of ramp rate.

1.3.4   Micro-Grid Operation in Grid-Connected Mode (Figure 1.7)

1.3.4.1   Objective Functions and Constraints of the Systems

In Ref. [6], the authors have represented a cost minimization EMS of GC–HKT system with a storage system, which consists mainly of three types of costs. The energy purchasing cost from the grid satisfies the load requirement and also the battery charging is the initial cost. The second cost is during the high costing time the revenue comes from exporting electricity to the primary grid. The third one is wearing cost or maintenance cost in the system. The authors choose power balance, limitations of HKT's production and SOC of the battery as optimization constraints.

The authors in Ref. [46] have optimized GC MG with generators, Energy Storage System and electrical load. The generators maybe detachable or not. The overall energy charges are assumed as the goal function. Such as the fuel utilization cost, cost of charging the battery, cost of discharging the battery, the energy cost generated by detachable and non-detachable

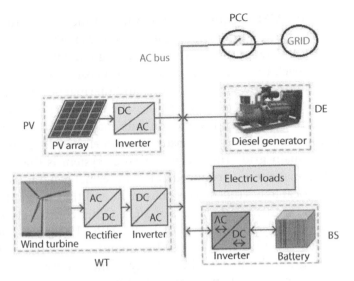

Figure 1.7 Microgrid in Grid Connected mode.

generators, the energy cost generated by trading power in between MG and the main grid network, and the cost of conveying energy demand all over the arrangement. The authors have incorporated environmental and technological factors as constraints to get the optimized result. The total quantity of energy produced by the end of the generator should be the same as the total quantity of energy at the consumption. The consumer and supplier of electricity are taken as technical constraints. Energy storage constraints include charging/discharging limitations of battery, the energy balance of battery, energy storage limitations and SOC of battery. In the end, the constraint was grid limitations that the quantity of exchanged energy in between the main grid network and MG.

The authors of Ref. [47] have given an optimized resolution for a mixed PV/WT/FC/HPC system, which is operating in the mode of grid connection. The authors have minimized the operational/running cost and maximized the system profits as system working cost includes (i) the fuel cost, (ii) the energy purchasing cost from the main gird, (iii) the installation cost of the system, (iv) the operation & maintenance cost of power generators. The authors have considered the system profits as the revenue in selling surplus energy (thermal and electrical) to the main grid when the net production of the distributed generation system go beyond the overall energy demand by the load.

The MSE for grid-connected HPC with both battery and thermal SSE, heat only boiler (HOB), thermal loads and electrical loads has evolved in Ref. [48]. This MSE technique has minimized the expenditure of the system operation. The authors have considered the expenditure of energy from HPC, HOB, CDG units, cost of importing energy from main grid and exporting back to the grid, and installation cost of different components of micro-grid. Now electrical power and thermal power balance are the main constraints for the optimization. The balancing of power guaranteed the electrical energy production and charging or discharging of the battery must be same as the consumption in electric load and energy tariff with the main grid. The thermal balance system is that when the amount of thermal energy produced at local thermal generators must be equivalent to local load (thermal) requirement and the energy (thermal) mutually shared with any other units of MGs. Other constraints are such as the capacity of the components of each MG. HPC, HOB and CDG must operate in their specified limitations. The quantity of energy exchanged with the main grid is limited by the capacity of the electric line. Also, the quantity of heat energy exchanged between two units of MG is limits with the thermal line capacity. The heat energy exchanged between thermal networks, and MGs is another constraint, which reduces thermal energy wastage when production of local thermal energy exceeds the demand of the local thermal load.

1.4   Algorithms Used in Optimizing Energy Management System

Energy management in a micro-grid is addressed by applying different approaches. All the approaches have the common aim to optimize the MG operation. Some methods are supported on linear or non-linear programming such as in Ref. [49] where a MILP is used to optimize the system. The cost function solution is obtained by linear programming, which is based on GAMS (general algebraic modeling system).

In MG, the energy obtained from RES, load demands and market rate of energy are considered as stochastic variables because of uncertainty. So, it is good to use stochastic modeling to analyze any energy management strategies. Generally, researches have gone through stochastic algorithms or metaheuristic algorithms to solve problems of optimum power balancing in MG. According to Ref. [50], in stochastic programming, the data is stochastic, and the result or solution is dependent on the collection of variables that arbitrarily generated. Recently researchers are considering that the management system of energy in micro-grids stand on the implementation of advanced technology such as collaboration of a variety of optimization technologies or improving classical algorithms, to get the most suitable solution of a problem for MSE in MG.

In Ref. [51] a multi-objective genetic algorithm was applied to a stand-alone system having an internal combustion engine and gas turbine with the PV module. In Ref. [52] the author represented a dynamic programming technique for a standalone micro-grid. The micro-grid is consisting of DG, PV panel and battery. Here the constraints of the problem are supply–load balancing and the capability of the supply generators. The main goal is to minimize the functioning cost and emission.

The authors in Ref. [53] represented a relative analysis of the various objectives of the optimization methods for MSE of standalone micro-grids. The comparison is based on linear programming and genetic algorithms. The result was found out that the controllable power consumption can reduce the cost with renewable energies.

In Ref. [54], the weight factor has been analyzed to increase the ability of PSO (Particle Swarm Optimization) technique and to balance the convergence. Even though a large amount of the internal weighted factor can create a limitation to the algorithm to discover the best possible solution locally, the convergence can be achieved at a prolonged rate. The author has recommended enhancing the PSO technique which adjusts and decreases the weight factor linearly through iterations to solve the problem. Thus, the enhanced PSO can get the optimum solution universally without fixing at local minima. This method is utilized in an MSE for hybrid power sources. In some highly developed means, the chaotic sequence is used in place of arbitrary numbers to optimize the action.

The authors in Ref. [45] have suggested CBA (Chaotic Bat Algorithm) optimize the financial send-off of the system under study. To get better performance of the BA (Bat Algorithm) to get the universal optimal solution, the chaotic sequences is applied in the primary BA. Authors of Ref. [44] have suggested Ant Colony Optimization technology for actual time functioning of MSE with a new Multi-Layer technique (MACO) in standalone micro-grid. The MACO is an enhanced version of the basic Ant Colony Optimization (ACO) algorithm. In this algorithm, the numerical quantity of levels is same as that of variables in designing on the problem and quantity of nodes in every level is equal to the numeric quantity of satisfactory values of every variable. The author investigated an MSE in Ref. [55] using a two-layer predictive control, and the degradation cost of SSE is taken as the main consideration.In Ref. [56] the author has suggested a new technology to optimize the performance of fireworks algorithm (FA) as a novel crossbreed Multi-goal-based FA and Gravitational Search Operator (MFAGSO) to resolve the non-linear trouble with several variables. There are also multiple hybrid constraints. This recommended algorithm uses gravitational explorer to lead the flash into the collection area to swap position information with optimal solutions to reach the best results.

Authors of Ref. [57] have explained an advanced algorithm called Improved Artificial Bee Colony algorithm (IABC) to get an optimized result in a hybrid grid-connected micro-grid. The author has rectified the basic ABC by generating the scrutinize bee using Gravitational Search Operator, which optimises the finding accuracy, so the universal best possible solution can be enhanced. The authors in ref. [58] have suggested a new algorithm such as Enhanced Bee Colony Optimization (EBCO), which gives a better performance of MSE for MGs with verity RESs and several SSE. EBCO operator is unlike the classical BCO, as it has the self- adaptation revulsion factor in the bee swarm, for getting the better performance of each bee swarm and that is why the finding accuracy enhances effectively in more dimensional problems.

The authors in Ref. [59] described an MSE applying Artificial Bee Colony (ABC) algorithm for an isolated MG. In Ref. [60] it proposed an MSE, which is based on utilization of fuzzy logic controller in a micro-grid that employs around 25 sets of laws. The objective function is to lower the deviation of power with maintaining battery SoC. In Ref. [61] the MSE is for an interconnected system of micro-grid using an advanced algorithm based on fuzzy logic called Mamdani algorithm. The optimization is done with the scheme combination of fuzzy logic and genetic algorithms. The authors in Ref. [62] provide an algorithm for MSE based on game theory to maximize the gain available during consumption of energy. Ref. [63] represents an adaptable neural fuzzy interference system, with the help a predictor of the echo state network. In Ref. [64] the author proposed a new approach, a Stackelberg game approach for managing the flow of energy in MG. The author of Ref. [65] suggested an MSE model for a smart micro-grid using game theory, where maximization of profit to the overall cost and satisfactory power utilization is selected as the strategy. It is a distributed energy management model.

Figure 1.8 summarizes the energy management technologies for micro-grids. Among them, some methodologies are classical techniques such as MILP, linear programming and non-linear programming. These programmings may be an excellent move towards optimization depending on the goal function and limitations. But the artificial intelligence (AI) processes are dedicated to approaches towards the situation while the classical methods come into unsatisfactory results.

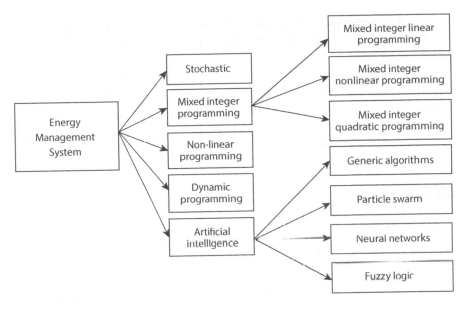

Figure 1.8 Energy management methodology.

1.5   Conclusion

This chapter discusses the amalgamation of the management system of energy in different ranges of micro-grid with numerous mechanism and diverse load type, optimizing the complete system, achieving the definite goals considering system constraints. This chapter comprehensively presents the different novelties in the area of integration of the electric car as energy supply, the setting up of thermal and power combination systems to generate simultaneously the heat and electricity to supply thermal as well as electrical requirements. And it represents the accomplishment of crossbreed optimization operators which are the excellent substitute than a single algorithm.

This literature review emphasizes on the approaches for energy management in micro-grid: islanded and connected with grid network approaches. In a further approach, optimization is done using the available information. Coordination has to be done with the grid parameters. In islanded mode, the optimization can be done with incomplete information or making a strategy to coordinate the micro-grid participants or components. Each participant optimizes its own settings. Grid-connected or centralized energy management is mostly done with metaheuristic methods. Multi-agent methods can be implemented for islanded or decentralized micro-grid.

An MSE model of a microgrid consists of a data acquisition system, monitoring and data analysis of system parameters, supervised control, and human–machine interface.

Here the review represented the methods for management depending on short term and foresight basis. The choices of grid-connected or not ensure that the designer of MG understands the balancing between cost and gain. The decentralized energy management allows greater flexibility and reliability and safety of system operation have to be considered.

References

1. REN21, *Renewables 2017 Global Status Report* (Paris: REN21 Secretariat), 2017.
2. International Energy Outlook, *US energy information administration*, September 14, 2017
3. Kirkham, ,Nightingale, D. and Koerner, T., Energy management system design with dispersed storage and generation, *Power Apparatus and Systems, IEEE Transactions on*, vol. PAS-100, no. 7, pp. 3432–3441, 1981.
4. Zheng, Y., Jenkins, B.M., Kornbluth, K., Kendall, A., Traeholt, C., Optimization of a biomass-integrated renewable energy micro grid with demand side management under uncertainty, *Appl. Energy*, 230, 836–844, 2018.
5. Syed, I. M., & Raahemifar, K., Predictive energy management, control and communication system for grid tied wind energy conversion systems, *Electric Power Systems Research*, 142, 298–309, 2017.
6. Kusakana, K., Energy management of a grid-connected hydrokinetic system under Time of Use tariff, *Renewable Energy*, 101, 1325–1333, 2017.
7. Kusakana K., Optimal scheduled power flow for distributed photovoltaic/wind/diesel generators with battery storage system, *IET Renew Power Generation*, 9(8): 916–24, 2015.
8. Giday, Z.G., Technical and economic assessment of solar PV/diesel hybrid power system for rural school electrification in Ethiopia, *International Journal of Renewable Energy Research (IJRER)*, 3(3), 735–744, 2014.
9. Thirumalaisamy, B., & Jegannathan, K., A novel energy management scheme using ANFIS for independent microgrid, *International Journal of Renewable Energy Research (IJRER)*, 6(3), 735–746, 2016.
10. Panwar, L.K., Reddy, K.S., Kumar, R., Panigrahi, B.K., & Vyas, S., Strategic Energy Management (SEM) in a micro grid with modern grid interactive electric vehicle, *Energy Conversion and Management*, 106, 4152, 2015.
11. Fathabadi, H., Novel grid-connected solar/wind powered electric vehicle charging station with vehicle-to-grid technology, *Energy*, 132, 1–11, 2017.

12. Aryanezhad, M., Optimization of grid connected bidirectional V2G charger based on multi-objective algorithm, In *Power Electronics, Drive Systems & Technologies Conference (PEDSTC)*, 2017 8th (pp. 519524), IEEE, February, 2017.

13. Sbordone, D., Bertini, I., Di Pietra, B., Falvo, M. C., Genovese, A., & Martirano, L., EV fast charging stations and energy storage technologies: A real implementation in the smart micro grid paradigm, *Electric Power Systems Research*, 120, 96–108, 2015.

14. Balasubramaniam, K., Saraf, P., Hadidi, R., & Makram, E.B., Energy management system for enhanced resiliency of microgrids during islanded operation, *Electric Power Systems Research*, 137, 133–141, 2016.

15. Wu, Z., Wang, B., & Xia, X., Large-scale building energy efficiency retrofit: Concept, model and control, *Energy*, 109, 456–465, 2016.

16. Hussain, A., Bui, V.H., Kim, H.M., Im, Y.H., & Lee, J.Y., Optimal operation of tri-generation microgrids considering demand uncertainties, *Int. J. Smart Home*, 10(10), 131–144, 2016.

17. Moradi, M.H., Hajinazari, M., Jamasb, S., & Paripour, M., An energy management system (EMS) strategy for combined heat and power (CHP) systems based on a hybrid optimization method employing fuzzy programming, *Energy*, 49, 86–101, 2013.

18. Gamarra, C., Guerrero, J.M., Computational optimiation techniques applied to micro grids planning: A review, *Renew. Sustain. Energy Rev.*, 48, 413–424, 2015.

19. Rahman, H.A., Majid, M.S., Jordehi, A.R., Kim, G.C., Hassan, M.Y., Fadhl, S.O., Operation and control strategies of integrated distributed energy resources: A review, *Sustain. Energy Rev.*, 51, 1412–1420, 2015.

20. Meng, L., Sanseverino, E.R., Luna, A., Dragicevic, T., Vasquez, J.C., Guerrero, J.M., Microgrid supervisory controllers and energy management systems: A literature review, *Renew. Sustain. Energy Rev.*, 60, 1263–1273, 2016.

21. Fathima, A.H., Palanisamy, K., Optimization in microgrids with hybrid energy systems—A review, *Renew. Sustain. Energy Rev.*, 45, 431–446, 2015.

22. Vardakas, J.S., Zorba, N., Verikoukis, C.V., A Survey on Demand Response Programs in Smart Grids: Pricing Methods and Optimization Algorithms, *IEEE Commun. Surv. Tutor.*, 17, 152–178, 2015.

23. Palizban, O., Kauhaniemi, K., Guerrero, J.M., Microgrids in active network management—Part I: Hierarchical control, energy storage, virtual power plants, and market participation, *Renew. Sustain. Energy Rev.*, 36, 428–439, 2014.

24. Korolko, N., Sahinoglu, Z., Robust Optimization of EV Charging Schedules in Unregulated Electricity Markets, *IEEE Trans. Smart Grid*, 8, 149–157, 2017.

25. Katiraei, F., Iravani, R., Hatziargyriou, N., Dimeas, A., Microgrids management, *IEEE Power Energy Mag.*, 6, 54–65, 2008.

26. Theo, W.L., Lim, J.S., Ho, W.S., Hashim, H., Lee, C.T., Review of distributed generation (DG) system planning and optimisation techniques: Comparison of numerical and mathematical modelling methods, *Renew. Sustain. Energy Rev.*, 67, 531–573, 2017.
27. Lidula, N.W.A., Rajapakse, A.D., Microgrids research: A review of experimental microgrids and test systems, *Renew. Sustain. Energy Rev.*, 15, 186–202, 2011.
28. Garcia-Gonzalez, J., Muela, R.M.R., dl Santos, L.M., Gonzalez, A.M., Stochastic Joint Optimization of Wind Generation and Pumped-Storage Units in an Electricity Market, *IEEE Trans. Power Syst.*, 23, 460–468, 2008.
29. Chen, C., Duan, S., Optimal allocation of distributed generation and energy storage system in microgrids, *IET Renew. Power Gener.*, 8, 581–589, 2014.
30. Ramin, D., Spinelli, S., Brusaferri, A., Demand-side management via optimal production scheduling in power-intensive industries: The case of metal casting process, *Appl. Energy*, 225, 622–636, 2018.
31. Behrangrad, M., A review of demand side management business models in the electricity market, *Renew. Sustain. Energy Rev.*, 47, 270–283, 2015.
32. Shayeghi, H., Sobhani, B., Integrated offering strategy for profit enhancement of distributed resources and demand response in microgrids considering system uncertainties, *Energy Convers. Manag.*, 87, 765–777, 2014.
33. Zhao, B., Xue, M., Zhang, X., Wang, C., Zhao, J., An MAS based energy management system for a standalone microgrid at high altitude, *Appl. Energy*, 143, 251–261, 2015.
34. Alavi, S.A., Ahmadian, A., Aliakbar-Golkar, M., Optimal probabilistic energy management in a typical micro-grid based-on robust optimization and point estimate method, *Energy Convers. Manag.*, 95, 314–325, 2015.
35. Soroudi, A., Amraee, T., Decision making under uncertainty in energy systems: State of the art, *Renew. Sustain. Energy Rev.*, 28, 376–384, 2013.
36. Tascikaraoglu, A., Uzunoglu, M., A review of combined approaches for prediction of short-term wind speed and power, *Renew. Sustain. Energy Rev.*, 34, 243–254, 2014.
37. Teo, K.K., Wang, L., Lin, Z., Wavelet Packet Multi-layer Perceptron for Chaotic Time Series Prediction: Effects of Weight Initialization, In *Proceedings of the Computational Science—ICCS 2001: International Conference*, San Francisco, CA, USA, 1, pp. 310–317, 28–30 May 200.
38. Al-Fattah, S.M., Artificial Neural Network Models for Forecasting Global Oil Market Volatility, *SSRN Electron. J.*, 112, 2013.
39. Amjady, N., Day-ahead price forecasting of electricity markets by a new fuzzy neural network, *IEEE Trans. Power Syst.*, 21, 887–896, 2006.
40. Fu, Q., Nasiri, A., Bhavaraju, V., Solanki, A., Abdallah, T., Yu, D.C., Transition Management of Microgrids With High Penetration of Renewable Energy, *IEEE Trans. Smart Grid*, 5, 539–549, 2014.

41. Liu, Y., Yu, S., Zhu, Y., Wang, D., Liu, J., Modeling, planning, application and management of energy systems for isolated areas: A review, *Renew. Sustain. Energy Rev.*, 82, 460–470, 2018.
42. Upadhyay, S., & Sharma, M.P., Selection of a suitable energy management strategy for a hybrid energy system in a remote rural area of India, *Energy*, 94, 352–366, 2016.
43. Han, Y., Chen, W., & Li, Q., Energy Management Strategy Based on Multiple Operating States for a Photovoltaic/Fuel Cell/Energy Storage DC Microgrid, *Energies*, 10(1), 136, 2017.
44. Marzband, M., Yousefnejad, E., Sumper, A., & Domínguez-García, J.L., Real time experimental implementation of optimum energy management system in standalone microgrid by using multi-layer ant colony optimization, *International Journal of Electrical Power & Energy Systems*, 75, 265–274, 2016.
45. Adarsh, B.R., Raghunathan, T., Jayabarathi, T., & Yang, X.S., Economic dispatch using chaotic bat algorithm, *Energy*, 96, 666–675, 2016.
46. Marzband, M., Alavi, H., Ghazimirsaeid, S.S., Uppal, H., & Fernando, T., Optimal energy management system based on stochastic approach for a home Microgrid with integrated, responsive load demand and energy storage, *Sustainable Cities and Society*, 28, 256–264, 2017.
47. Maleki, A., Hafeznia, H., Rosen, M.A., & Pourfayaz, F., Optimization of a grid-connected hybrid solar wind-hydrogen CHP system for residential applications by efficient metaheuristic approaches, *Applied Thermal Engineering*, 123, 1263–1277, 2017.
48. Hussain, A., Lee, J.H., & Kim, H.M., An optimal energy management strategy for thermally networked microgrids in grid-connected mode, *Int. J. Smart Home*, 10, 239–258, 2016.
49. Ahmad, J., Imran, M., Khalid, A., Iqbal, W., Ashraf, S.R., Adnan, M., Ali, S.F., Khokhar, K.S., Techno-economic analysis of a wind-photovoltaic-biomass hybrid renewable energy system for rural electrification: A case study of Kallar Kahar, *Energy*, 2018.
50. Blum, C., & Roli, A., Metaheuristics in combinatorial optimization: Overview and conceptual comparison, *ACM Computing Surveys (CSUR)*, 35(3), 268–308, 2003.
51. Das, B.K., Al-Abdeli, Y.M., Kothapalli, G., Effect of load following strategies, hardware, and thermal load distribution on standalone hybrid CCHP systems, *Appl. Energy*, 2018.
52. Luu, N.A., Tran, Q.T., Bacha, S., Optimal energy management for an island microgrid by using dynamic programming method, In *Proceedings of the 2015 IEEE Eindhoven PowerTech*, Eindhoven, The Netherlands, 29 June–2 July 2015.
53. Neves, D., Pina, A., Silva, C.A., Comparison of different demand response optimization goals on an isolated microgrid, *Sustain. Energy Technol. Assess.*, 2018.

54. Yu, J., Dou, C., & Li, X., MAS-based energy management strategies for a hybrid energy generation system, *IEEE Transactions on Industrial Electronics*, 63(6), 3756–3764, 2016.

55. Ju, C., Wang, P., Goel, L., Xu, Y., A two-layer energy management system for microgrids with hybrid energy storage considering degradation costs, *IEEE Trans. Smart Grid*, 2018.

56. Wang, Z., Zhu, Q., Huang, M., & Yang, B., Optimization of economic/environmental operation management for microgrids by using hybrid fireworks algorithm, *International Transactions on Electrical Energy Systems*, 27(12), 2017.

57. Roy, K., Mandal, K.K., & Mandal, A.C., Modeling and managing of micro grid connected system using improved artificial bee colony algorithm, *International Journal of Electrical Power & Energy Systems*, 75, 50–58, 2016.

58. Lin, W.M., Tu, C.S., & Tsai, M.T., Energy management strategy for microgrids by using enhanced bee colony optimization, *Energies*, 9(1), 5, 2015.

59. Marzband, M., Azarinejadian, F., Savaghebi, M., Guerrero, J.M., An optimal energy management system for islanded microgrids based on multiperiod artificial bee colony combined with markov chain, *IEEE Syst. J.*, 2017.

60. Prathyush, M., Jasmin, E.A., Fuzzy Logic Based Energy Management System Design for AC Microgrid, In *Proceedings of the International Conference on Inventive Communication and Computational Technologies (ICICCT)*, Coimbatore, India, 20 April 2018.

61. De Santis, E., Rizzi, A., Sadeghian, A., Hierarchical genetic optimization of a fuzzy logic system for energy flows management in microgrids, *Appl. Soft Comput. J.*, 2017.

62. Ma, L., Liu, N., Zhang, J., Tushar, W., Yuen, C., Energy Management for Joint Operation of CHP and PV Prosumers Inside a Grid-Connected Microgrid: A Game Theoretic Approach, *IEEE Trans. Ind. Inform.*, 2016.

63. Leonori, S., Rizzi, A., Paschero, M., Mascioli, F.M.F., Microgrid Energy Management by ANFIS Supported by an ESN Based Prediction Algorithm, In *Proceedings of the International Joint Conference on Neural Networks (IJCNN)*, Rio de Janeiro, Brazil, 8–13 July 2018.

64. Liu, N., Yu, X., Wang, C., Wang, J., Energy Sharing Management for Microgrids with PV Prosumers: A Stackelberg Game Approach, *IEEE Trans. Ind. Inform.*, 2017.

65. Mondal, A., Misra, S., Patel, L.S., Pal, S.K., Obaidat, M.S., DEMANDS: Distributed energy management using noncooperative scheduling in smart grid, *IEEE Syst. J.*, 2018.

2

Power and Energy Management in Microgrid

Jayesh J. Joglekar

MIT World Peace University, Pune, India

Abstract

The microgrid voltage management has a significant concern during unstable system condition due to limited power to frequency ratio (MW/Hz). The selection of sources for microgrid would play an essential role and power management techniques could save the microgrid from the complete blackout. The modification in the power flow controller could achieve desirable results with an appropriate position of the power flow controller.

Keywords: BESS, fuel cell, energy storage, microgrid, renewable source

2.1 Introduction

The power system in the modern world is restructured based on source, nature of load and geographical space availability. The grid size also depends on the need of society and consumers. The concept of microgrid (MG) emerges from the traditional grid. But like the traditional grid, MG has a limited area to serve and hence the transmission lines could be replaced by underground cables. Depending on the application at the consumer end, MG could be with Alternating Current or with Direct Current or mixed one. Due to limited size, capacity and consumer base, power flow in MG could be a critical issue. For the interconnected AC transmission line network, transfer capacity is an economical operational constraint. It forces to use the available infrastructure to its maximum limit. The increased usability of the transmission limit handled by the FACTS controllers. These

Email: joglekar@outlook.in

controllers are known for their applications in improving power transfer capacity as well as stability using the existing infrastructure of a transmission utility. In addition to transmission capacity enhancement and power flow control, FACTS controllers have other advantages like transient stability improvement, power oscillation damping, voltage stability and control. The transmission line capacity is enhanced by around 40 to 50% by installing a FACTS controller in comparison to conventional mechanically-driven devices, as FACTS controllers are not subject to wear and tear and require a lower maintenance [1].

2.2　Microgrid Structure

The Microgrid (MG) broadly comprises of source, load and controller, as shown in Figure 2.1. The choice of the source depends on the geographical location of MG and the type as well as the demand of the load. The emerging technologies such as fuel cell could be suitable for supplying the base load and proves advantageous over batteries. The working of a fuel cell is similar to the battery. The batteries contain the limited capacity of support chemicals. They have a fixed life cycle, but a fuel cell is supplied with fuel externally and operates continuously as long as fuel supplied. An electrolyte separates an anode and a cathode in the fuel cell. The type of fuel cell decided by electrolyte used. A fuel cell is a static energy converter from chemical to electrical energy. It is a modular, efficient and very low emission power source for a distributed system. It is clear that fuel cell is an upcoming option for conventional power generation resources [2–5]. Fuel cell produces electricity from external supplies of hydrogen fuel (on

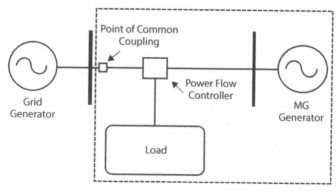

Figure 2.1 Basic structure of microgrid (MG).

the anode side) and oxidant (on the cathode side) in the presence of an electrolyte. Generally, the reactants flow in and reaction products flow out while the electrolyte remains in the cell. Fuel cells can operate almost continuously as long as the necessary fuel flows are maintained. There are different types of fuel cell based on base chemical or membrane used. Those are Phosphoric Acid Fuel Cell (PAFC), Solid Oxide Fuel Cell (SOFC), Molten Carbonate Fuel Cell (MCFC) Proton Exchange Membrane Fuel Cell (PEMFC), etc.

2.2.1 Selection of Source for DG

With multiple options available based on technology used, fuel cells became a well-known source of energy in recent years. The selection of fuel cell is broadly based on the type of application it performs. Table 2.1 shows comparison of present fuel cell technologies and suitable applications. The fuel cell is an upcoming option for power generation and hybrid power system. It ensures a reliable green power. A variety of fuel cell technologies exist and out of them, PAFC is found suitable for distributed generation.

2.2.1.1 Phosphoric Acid Fuel Cell (PAFC)

This fuel cell is a matured in technology and commercially available. PAFC has platinum or platinum alloys used as the catalyst at both electrodes. The stack consists of a repeating arrangement of anode and cathode. As the freezing point of phosphoric acid (H_3PO_4) is 40 °C, the PAFC must be kept above this temperature once commissioned, to avoid the thermal stresses. For PAFC, water cooling is used for larger power generation systems [6, 7]. The operating current densities are 150 to 400 mA/cm. The operating cell voltages are 600–800 mV. The ohmic losses in PAFC are quite small. The ability of PAFC to sustain impurity and its voltage–current and power–current characteristics makes it highly suitable for micro-grid. Figure 2.2 shows typical characteristic of PAFC plotted for 1 kW stack. Figure 2.3 shows the average cell voltage vs current density of PAFC after testing for 50 and 250 h [2].

2.2.1.2 Mathematical Modeling of PAFC Fuel Cell

The output voltage of fuel cell is given by Nernst equation as [8–11]:

$$V_{dc} = E - V_o - V_a \text{ where:} \tag{2.1}$$

Table 2.1 Fuel cell resource comparison (courtesy: DOE, US Government).

Fuel cell type	Common electrolyte	Operating temperature	Typical stack size	Efficiency	Applications	Advantages	Disadvantages
Polymer Electrolyte Membrane (PEM)	Perfluoro sulfonic acid	50–100 °C 122–212 ° typically 80 °C	<1 kW–100 kW	60% transportation 35% stationary	• Backup power • Portable power • Distributed generation • Transportation • Specialty vehicles	• Solid electrolyte reduces corrosion & electrolyte management problems • Low temperature • Quick start-up	• Expensive catalysts • Sensitive to fuel impurities Low temperature waste heat
Alkaline (AFC)	Aqueous solution of potassium hydroxide soaked in a matrix	90–100 °C 194–212 °F	10–100 kW	60%	• Military Space	• Cathode reaction faster in alkaline electrolyte, leads to high performance • Low cost components	• Sensitive to CO_2 in fuel and air Electrolyte management
Phosphoric Acid (PAFC)	Phosphoric acid soaked in a matrix	150–200 °C 302–392 °F	400 kW 100 kW module	40%	• Distributed generation	• Higher temperature enables CHP • Increased tolerance to fuel impurities	• Pt catalyst • Long start up time • Low current and power
Molten Carbonate (MCFC)	Solution of lithium, sodium, and/ or potassium carbonates, soaked in a matrix	600–700 °C 1,112–1,292 °F	300 kW–3 MW 300 kW module	45–50%	• Electric utility • Distributed generation	• High efficiency • Fuel flexibility • Can use a variety of catalysts Suitable for CHP	• High temperature corrosion and breakdown of cell components • Long start up time • Low power density
Solid Oxide (SOFC)	Yttria stabilized zirconia	700–1,000 °C 1,202–1,832 °F	1 kW–2 MW	60%	• Auxiliary power • Electric utility • Distributed generation	• High efficiency • Fuel flexibility • Can use a variety of catalysts • Solid electrolyte • Suitable for CHP & CHHP Hybrid/ GT cycle	• High temperature corrosion and breakdown of cell components • High temperature operation requires long start up time and limits

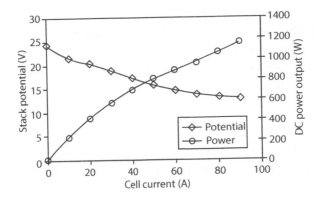

Figure 2.2 PAFC characteristics.

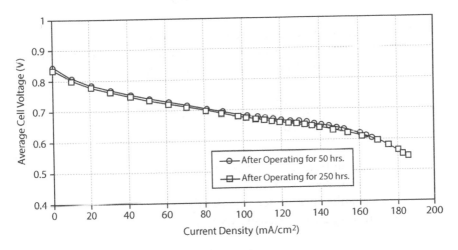

Figure 2.3 PAFC average cell voltage vs current density.

Where:

V_{dc} = Fuel cell output voltage (Volt)

E = Thermodynamic potential of fuel cell (Volt) which is expressed by:

$$E = E^0 + \frac{RT}{nF} ln \left[\frac{PH_2(PO_2)^{0.5}}{PH_2O} \right] \tag{2.2}$$

E^0 = Potential of unit cavity in fuel cell = 1.229 V

PH_2, PO_2 & PH_2O = Particle pressure of Hydrogen, Oxygen and vapor (atm)

T = Cell temperature (K)
R = Universal gas constant = 8.31441 J/mol-K
F = Faraday constant = 94,685 C/mol
n = Number of electrons participating in the reaction
V_0 = Ohmic voltage drop (Volt) which is given by:

$$V_0 = IR_{int} \qquad (2.3)$$

I   = Cell current (Amp)
R_{int} = Internal resistance between electrodes which is given by:

$$R_{int} = 0.0652 \frac{l}{0.819}$$

l = Length between two electrodes (Meter)
V_a = Summation of activation voltage drop and concentration
     voltage drop (Volt) which is expressed by:

$$V_a = \frac{RT}{\alpha nF} ln\left[\frac{i}{i_0}\right] + \frac{RT}{nF} ln\left[1 - \frac{i}{i_L}\right] \qquad (2.4)$$

α = Electron transfer co-efficient
i = Current density (A/m^2)
i_0 = Exchange current density (A/m^2)
i_L = Limiting current density (A/m^2)

$$C = \epsilon \frac{A}{l}$$

ϵ = Electrical permittivity of electrolyte
A = Effective surface area between electrodes and electrolyte
     (sq. meter). It is very large due to corrugated porous sur-
     face of the electrodes.
l = Distance between two layers of electrodes. It is very small
     (nanometer).
V_C = Voltage across the Capacitor 'C'. It is given by:

$$V_C = \left(I - C\frac{dV_C}{dt}\right)(R_a + R_c) \qquad (2.5)$$

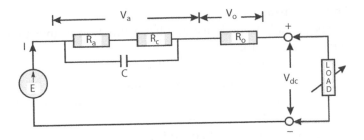

Figure 2.4 PAFC equivalent circuit.

There are three operating regions for this fuel cell. The first region is activation region where the voltage drop is due to the slowness of the chemical reactions at electrode. It is considered as R_a. The second region represents the ohmic losses due to the internal resistance of the fuel cell. It is represented by R_o. The third region represents the change in concentration of reactants as the fuel is used. It is represented by R_c. By considering these three operating regions of fuel cell, an equivalent DC circuit model is obtained as shown in Figure 2.4.

2.3 Power Flow Management in Microgrid

The transfer capacity of the existing transmission lines is an important operational constraint on interconnected A.C. transmission network. To improve this capacity of the transmission line, one has to use the FACTS controllers. These controllers are known for their applications in improving power transfer capacity and power flow control using the existing infrastructure of a transmission utility as well as improving transient stability. In addition to these controls, FACTS controllers advantageously employed for transient stability improvement, power oscillation damping and voltage stability. With the FACTS controller, the transmission line capacity can be improved by 40 to 50% as compared to conventional mechanically-driven devices. Lower maintenance required for FACTS controllers improves efficiency in operation [1].

The FACTS controllers connected to the transmission line have following basic types depending on connection:

1. Series controllers:
   It has variable impedance and has a function to inject series voltage.

2. Shunt controllers:
   It has variable impedance and has a function to inject current in the system.
3. Combined series–series controller:
   It has separate but coordinated unified (common DC bus) controllers and can compensate reactive power as well as interline transfer active power.
4. Combined series–shunt controller:
   It can inject voltage and current and has unified and coordinated real power exchange between series and shunt controllers.

The UPFC, as shown in Figure 2.5, invented in 1991, is a real-time multi-functional dynamic compensator for the AC transmission line. It can control active and reactive power as well as voltage and VAR compensation. It also can improve the power quality of the associated system. Thus UPFC can control output voltage V_o and its angle ρ ($0 \leq \rho \leq 2\pi$) [1]. The operation of UPFC depends on types of voltage source converters. The shunt converter is Static Compensator (STATCOM) and series compensator is Static Synchronous Series Compensator (SSSC) [1]. The STATCOM is a static, shunt connected compensator which can control current independent of system voltage with the help of capacitor or inductor. In UPFC,

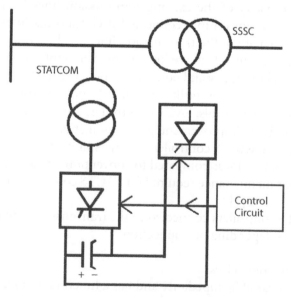

Figure 2.5 Basic UPFC.

capacitor-based current compensation considered. Hence depending on the system requirement, leading current can be injected in the system with the help of a capacitor connected to the common DC bus. It absorbs active power for charging the capacitor. So it has the role of Static Synchronous Generator (SSG) and Static VAR Generator (SVG). The SSSC is a series-connected compensator which can control series injected voltage. The magnitude of the series injected voltage is low. Still, the converter can change the voltage angle regarding sending end voltage, resulting in a change in receiving end voltage magnitude and angle depending on the system requirements.

If the compensator connected with the energy storage capacitor, then it can absorb active power too. The transmitted power P and reactive power $-jQ$ can be expressed by:

$$P - jQ = V_r \left(\frac{V_s + V_o - V_r}{jX} \right)$$

2.4 Generalized Unified Power Flow Controller (GUPFC)

The basic circuit of a GUPFC developed by Fardanesh in the year 2000 is shown in Figure 2.6. It inferred from the figure that it is a combination of UPFC and Interline Power Flow Controller (IPFC). There is one shunt

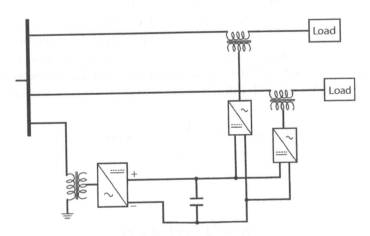

Figure 2.6 Basic GUPFC.

connected converter (STATCOM) and multiple series-connected converters (SSSC). The series converters and shunt converter are connected to a
common capacitor to form the DC bus. The shunt converters and the series
converters act as a synchronous voltage source (SVS). These converters can
generate reactive power at their terminals. Free exchange of real power is
possible because of common DC link. The real power demand is fulfilled
by shunt converter, which at the same time can absorb or supply controllable reactive power and exchange the same with series converters. The
series converters can individually inject a voltage to the appropriately connected feeder whose magnitude and phase angle can be varied to obtain
the desired voltage output. Thus the series converters act as a series compensation device. It means that the overloaded feeder lines can be balanced and any surplus power utilized by other feeders or common DC link
[1, 12, 13].

2.4.1   Mathematical Modeling of GUPFC

The basic circuit shown in Figure 2.6 is considered here for modeling. The
development is based on the fundamental frequency model of UPFC which
is presented in Refs. [14] and [15]. The basic concept of UPFC has briefly
explained already in this section. Modeling aims to determine the relationship between unified DC bus voltage and injected voltage. A three-phase,
PWM controlled voltage source inverter is typically made of six controlled
switches (GTO valves with six anti-parallel diodes) switched on and off at
very high frequency around 5 kHz. The model considered a stable voltage
condition for fundamental frequency voltage sources. One source is connected in parallel while the other connected in a series branch.

The series converters are injecting voltage and hence in the equivalent
diagram in Figure 2.7 it is represented with voltage source and modeling is
also based on this assumption [16]. The instantaneous power flowing into
shunt inverter from AC bus, neglecting transformer losses and assuming
balancing conditions with fundamental frequency, can be represented by:

$$P_{sh} = 3 \frac{a_{sh} \times V_{sh} \times v_1}{X_{sh}} \times \sin\alpha \tag{2.6}$$

Where,

$$v_1 = \sqrt{2} V_1 \sin(\omega t + \theta) \tag{2.7a}$$

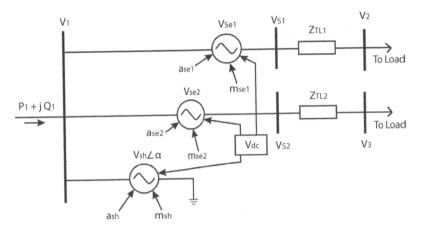

Figure 2.7 GUPFC equivalent circuit.

$$V_{sh} = \frac{1}{2\sqrt{2}} m_{sh} V_{dc} \qquad (2.7b)$$

$$m_{sh} = \frac{2\sqrt{2}\sqrt{v_{sh_d}^2 + v_{sh_q}^2}}{V_{dc}} \qquad (2.7c)$$

$$\alpha = tan^{-1}\left(\frac{v_{sh_q}}{v_{sh_d}}\right) \qquad (2.7d)$$

This model consists of two voltage sources. These voltage sources are gained from inverters connected in series and parallel. Hence amplitude modulation factors are used to calculate voltage source magnitudes as:

$$V_{sh} = k[m_{sh} V_{dc}] \qquad (2.8)$$

$$V_{se_1} = k\left[m_{se_1} V_{dc}\right] \qquad (2.9)$$

$$V_{se_2} = k\left[m_{se_2} V_{dc}\right] \qquad (2.10)$$

Where,

k = constant based on type of inverter (for six pulse converter

$= \dfrac{3}{2\sqrt{2}}$)

The power delivered by GUPFC in steady state is given by:

$$P_{se} = 3a_{se} I_{ac} V_{se} \cos\alpha \qquad (2.11)$$

Where,

$$i_{ac} = \sqrt{2} I_{ac} \sin\left(\omega t + \phi\right) \qquad (2.12a)$$

$$v_{se} = \sqrt{2} V_{se} \sin(\omega t + \phi + \alpha) \qquad (2.12b)$$

$$V_{se} = \frac{1}{2\sqrt{2}} m_{se} V_{dc} \qquad (2.12c)$$

Using line impedance for calculating voltage as shown in Equation (2.6), Equation (2.11) can be rewritten as:

$$P_{se_1} = 3 \frac{V_{s_1} \times V_2}{X_{T_1}} \times \cos\alpha_1 \qquad (2.13)$$

and

$$P_{se_2} = 3 \frac{V_{s_2} \times V_3}{X_{T_2}} \times \cos\alpha_2 \qquad (2.14)$$

Where,

P_{se_1} = Power delivered by GUPFC for first feeder (Watts)

V_{s_1} = Sending end voltage (Volts) for line 1 = $\sqrt{\left[(V_1 + V_{se_1} \times \cos\phi)^2 + (V_{se1} \times \cos\phi)^2\right]}$ (Volts)

V_{s_2} = Sending end voltage (Volts) for line 2 = $\sqrt{\left[(V_2 + V_{se_2} \times \cos\phi)^2 + (V_{se_2} \times \cos\phi)^2\right]}$ (Volts)

V_2 = Receiving end or load voltage (Volts)
$V_1 = V_{sh} = ka_{sh}m_{sh}V_{dc}$ (Volts)
$V_{se_1} = ka_{se_1}m_{se1}V_{dc}$ (Volts)
$V_{se_2} = ka_{se_2}m_{se_2}V_{dc}$ (Volts)
X_{T1}, X_{T2} = Transmission line reactance (Ω)
δ = Angle difference between V_1 and V_{s1} or V_{s2} (degree)

$$\delta_1 = tan^{-1} \frac{\left(V_{se1} \times cos\phi\right)}{\left(V_1 + V_{se_1} \times cos\phi\right)}$$

$$\delta_2 = tan^{-1} \frac{\left(V_{se_2} \times cos\phi\right)}{\left(V_2 + V_{se_2} \times cos\phi\right)}$$

ϕ = Load power factor angle (degree)
a_{sh} = Transformation ratio for shunt transformer,
a_{se} = Transformation ratio for series transformer
m_{sh} and m_{se} = amplitude modulation factors
V_{dc} = average DC capacitor voltage (Volts)
V_1 = rms voltage magnitudes of sending end voltage (Volts)
X_{sh} = shunt transformer reactance (Ω)
C = DC link capacitor value in Farad
σ_1 and σ_2 = phase shift between line currents and series inserted voltages (degree)
I_{ac1} and I_{ac2} = rms values of transmission line currents (Amp)

The resulting equation of GUPFC is considered using Equations (2.10) to (2.14) for finding out factors on which injected power depends. The resulting equation has the form given below:

$$P_{se} \propto V_{dc}^2 \times \left(sin\alpha\right) \tag{2.15}$$

Equation (2.15) is true only if a_{sh}, a_{se}, m_{sh}, m_{se}, X_T remain constant. It can be seen that series injected power by the GUPFC is controlled by DC voltage (V_{dc}) and phase angle difference between V_1 and V_{se1} (α). This means the sub-system voltage control depends on two quantities (i.e. V_{dc} and α).

2.5   Active GUPFC

The use of two SSSCs in Generalized Unified Power Flow Controller (GUPFC) is aimed at controlling active as well as reactive power. In the proposed method, GUPFC installed for the same purpose by employing active sources like fuel cells to the common DC bus instead of BESS. The system shown in Figure 2.8 where the fuel cell is embedded with GUPFC in sub-system to ensure uninterrupted supply under all fault conditions.

The heavily loaded feeders get relaxation due to impedance control and voltage profile improvement after implementation of the proposed method. The dependability of generating stations on grid power for supplying auxiliaries will be considerably reduced with improved power quality at load side with or without grid connectivity when fed with active GUPFC based sub-system [17]. Figure 2.9 shows the general outline of the proposed system.

In reasonable working conditions as sub-system sources float, the main grid supplies power to sub-system loads based on demand. Whenever there is a grid disturbance and the main grid is unable to provide additional power to the sub-system, it has to separate from the main grid at a point of common coupling (PCC). The sub-system continues supplying power to the auxiliary system of generating stations. Figure 2.10 shows the condition when sub-system source i.e., DG embedded GUPFC fulfils the demand of auxiliaries.

The proposed method is an application for generating stations. In this research work, thermal generating stations considered as it has the highest installed capacity in India [3]. Due to the grid disturbance, a generating station, usually, experiences shortfall of power for running auxiliaries. This difficulty is overcome by using the energy from the sub-system. However, the stable

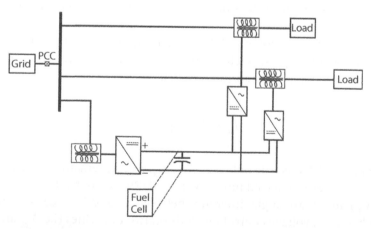

Figure 2.8 Proposed system.

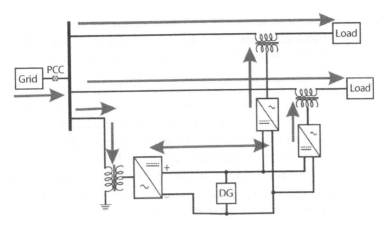

Figure 2.9 Proposed system with grid connection.

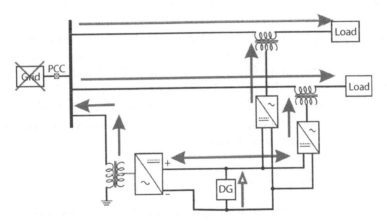

Figure 2.10 Proposed system without grid connection.

operation of the sub-system is also an issue of concern when it has a renewable, nature dependent source. The use of fuel cells can provide an uninterrupted and stable power supply if installed with proper electronic converters.

2.5.1 Active GUPFC Control System

GUPFC control system consists of the shunt converter control system and series converter control system. This control system based on the vector control approach introduced in [1]. The objective of the control system is to maintain terminal voltage using the shunt converter and injunction of the series voltage vector using the series converter. Depending on the system conditions, the series converter can inject or draw reactive power from the series element. But shunt and series converters do not share reactive power through common DC link. The control function of the shunt converter is divided into two operational modes, as listed below.

1. Power control mode: The shunt converter mainly controls reactive power (VAR) in the system. The reactive power demand decides the gate pulse of the converter, which allows current to flow. Continuous feedback closed-looped system ensures the desired current injection in the system.
2. Voltage control mode: With the help of the droop control method, the voltage regulation can be made automatically at the point of connection with reactive current regulation.

The power flow control system works for the shunt and two series compensators together. The desired active and reactive power flows (P_{s1} and Q_{S1}) are compared with the measured magnitudes (P_s' and Q_s') and error is passed through an error amplifier to produce direct and quadrature components for series connected compensating voltages (e_{2d} and e_{2q}). The magnitudes of the voltage (E_{2dq}) at the output of VSC2 and VSC3 are calculated respectively by adding relative phase angle (β_1 and β_2) [18]. The controllable range of active and reactive power flow can easily be determined with open loop control system with rated compensating voltage (E_{2dq}). The control system is illustrated in Figure 2.11.

2.5.1.1   Series Converter

Figure 2.12 shows basic control system strategy for series converters. It corrects the magnitude of the load voltage by providing corrected magnitude and angle compared with reference value. The Space Vector Pulse Width Modulation (SVPWM) helps to transfer phase voltage reference to modulation time delay cycle. The closed loop system monitors V_1 to apply appropriate corrections in the system.

Considering power demand calculation as:

$$\begin{bmatrix} p \\ q \end{bmatrix} = \begin{bmatrix} v_1 & v_2 \\ v_2 & -v_1 \end{bmatrix} \begin{bmatrix} i_\alpha \\ i_\beta \end{bmatrix}$$

Where

p = Active power demand
q = Reactive power demand

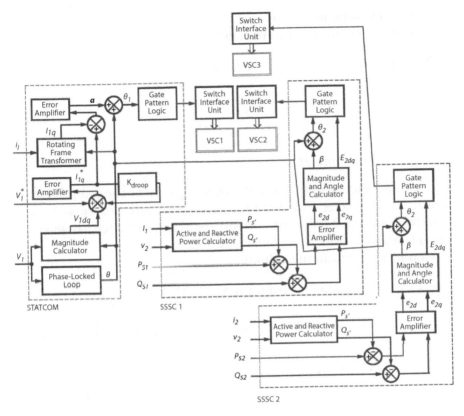

Figure 2.11 Basic control of GUPFC compensator logic.

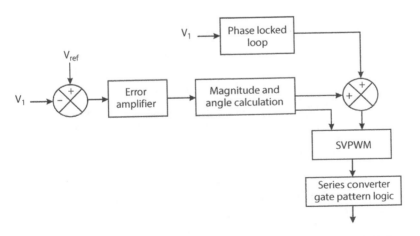

Figure 2.12 Basic control of series compensator logic.

v_1 and v_2 = Input voltage

i_α and i_β = Correction component.

The injected voltage angle can be calculated:

$$\alpha = sin^{-1} \frac{pX}{V_1 V_{s1}}$$

(2.16)

2.5.1.2 Shunt Converter

Figure 2.13 indicates shunt converter pulse logic with basic control system. The reference voltage and current are compared with desired active and reactive power demand in the circuit. The shunt converter has ability to provide source or sink for system current.

Considering transformer admittance $Y = \dfrac{1}{R+jX} = G + jB$ and bus voltage is $V\angle\delta$. The power injected using STATCOM can be shown to be [1]:

$$P = kV_{dc}^2 G - kV_{dc} V \left(G\cos(\alpha - \delta) + B\sin(\alpha - \delta) \right)$$

(2.17)

$$Q = kV_{dc}^2 B - kV_{dc} V \left(G\sin(\alpha - \delta) - B\cos(\alpha - \delta) \right).$$

(2.18)

Where,

   k = constant based on type of inverter (for six pulse converter

   $= \dfrac{3}{2\sqrt{2}}$) and $V_{dc}\angle\alpha$ is veriable input voltage for transformer.

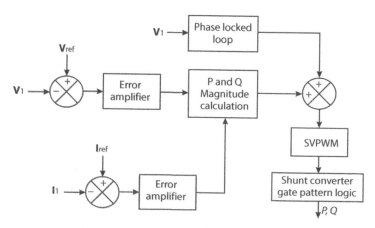

Figure 2.13 Basic control of shunt compensator logic.

2.5.2   Simulation of Active GUPFC With General Test System

The simulation study of active GUPFC system is carried out using MATLAB Simulink platform. MATLAB (matrix laboratory) is a multi-optional numerical computing environment and programming language. It is developed by MathWorks Inc. MATLAB allows matrix manipulations, plotting of functions and data, implementation of algorithms, creation of user interfaces and interfacing with programs written in other languages, including C, C++, Java, Fortran and Python. An additional package, Simulink, adds graphical multi-domain simulation and Model-Based Design for dynamic and embedded systems. The simulations carried out with the following conditions and assumptions:

1. Hardware: Intel Core i5 2,450 M CPU, 2.5 GHz, 4 GB RAM with Win 7, 64 bit OS.
2. Software: MATLAB Simulink (7.10.0.499) 2010a release
3. Simulation time: 3.00 s
4. Simulation solver: ode23tb (stiff/TR-BDF2)
5. Simulation type: Variable step
6. Simulation relative tolerance: 1e−3: 0.001

The active GUPFC is simulated for the simplified general test system as shown in Figure 2.14. The test system parameters presented in the Appendix. With a grid connection, the system uses power for load feeders, whereas the system without grid connection continues to supply power to TPS auxiliaries using active GUPFC. Hence a load of TPS auxiliaries is always taken care of by active GUPFC.

The system illustrated above is simulated for two phases to a ground fault with phases A and B (R and Y) and phases B and C (Y and B) using MATLAB Simulink. The simulation conducted without GUPFC, with GUPFC and with active GUPFC for common test conditions. The combined result is plotted with load voltage against time and illustrated in Figure 2.15. The sequence of events is as shown in Table 2.2.

2.5.3   Simulation of Active GUPFC With IEEE 9 Bus Test System

With IEEE 9 bus test model, as shown in Figure 2.16, various fault conditions such as three-phase to ground fault and single-phase to ground fault are simulated with and without grid connection using MATLAB simulation, as illustrated in Figure 2.17. The results are presented for test cases

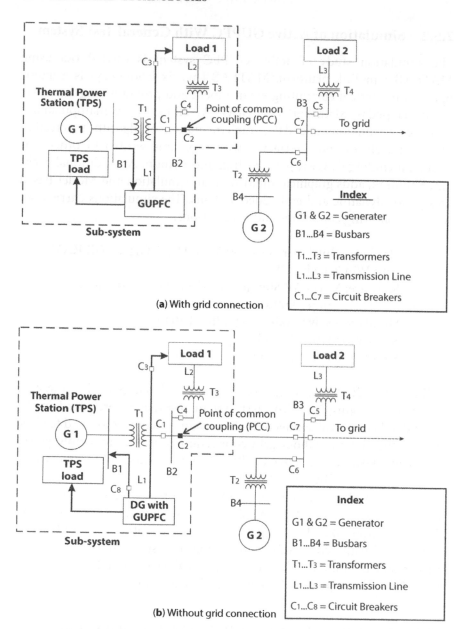

(a) With grid connection

(b) Without grid connection

Figure 2.14 Simplified test system.

with and without GUPFC, with and without fuel cell (distributed generation) and with active GUPFC. Three-phase to ground fault shown from 1.0 to 1.5 s on time axis whereas single phase to ground fault shown between 2.0 and 2.5 s on time axis.

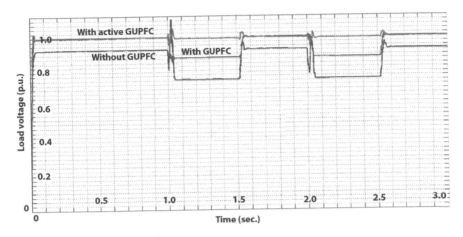

Figure 2.15 Test system simulation.

Table 2.2 Test system simulation events.

S. No.	Time (s)	Event
1	0.00	Start
2	1.00	Fault on A and B phases
3	1.02	CB opens (disconnect sub-system from main system)
4	1.50	Fault Clear
5	1.52	CB close (connects sub-system to main system)
6	2.00	Fault on B and C phases
7	2.02	CB opens (disconnect sub-system from main system)
8	2.50	Fault Clear
9	2.52	CB close (connects sub-system to main system)
10	3.00	End

2.5.3.1   Test Case: 1—Without GUPFC and Without Fuel Cell

Figure 2.18 shows the load voltage profile when the system is under intentional islanding condition. A healthy working condition between 0.0 and 1.0 s, the load voltage observed as 1 pu. A three-phase to ground fault initiated between 1.0 and 1.5 s. A sudden drop in voltage occurs at 1.0 s and then a spike due to intentional islanding is seen at the instant of

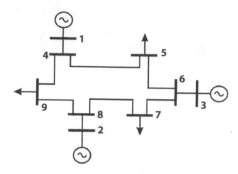

Figure 2.16 IEEE 9 bus system.

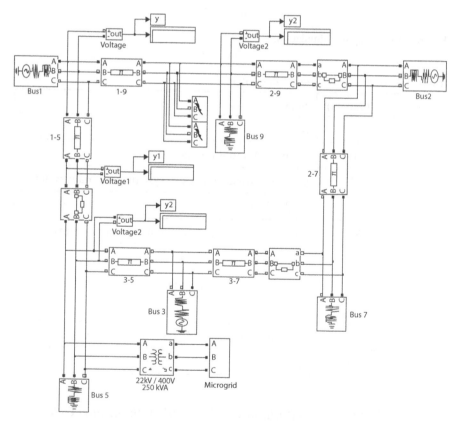

Figure 2.17 IEEE 9 bus test system MATLAB simulation model.

1.0 s. After the occurrence of fault at 1.02 s generator at bus number 3 and load at the bus no. 5 get islanded from the main system. During islanding conditions (i.e. between 1.02 and 1.5 s), the load voltage rises to 1.25 pu. The load voltage becomes normal to 1.0 pu when the islanded part of the

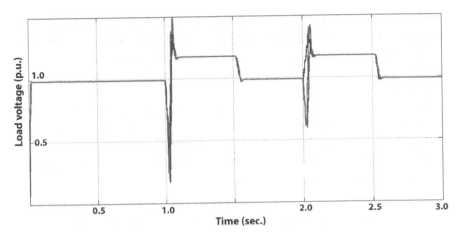

Figure 2.18 Load voltage profile in test case-1.

system reconnected with the main system at 1.5 s and remains at 1.0 pu till t = 2.0 s.

During the single-phase to ground fault (i.e. between 2.0 and 2.5 s), the load voltage rises to 1.25 pu due to the intentional islanding of the generator at the bus no. 3 and load at the bus no. 5. The voltage profile improves due to the islanding of a balanced system.

2.5.3.2   Test Case: 2—Without GUPFC and With Fuel Cell

Figure 2.19 shows an improved load voltage profile compared to similar intentional islanding conditions described in Section 2.5.3.1. During

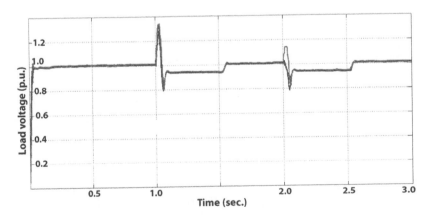

Figure 2.19 Load voltage profile in test case-2.

three-phase to ground fault (i.e. between 1.0 and 1.5 s), a voltage spike observed at the switching of intentional islanding of load at an instant of 1.0 s. The load voltage settles to 0.95 pu thereafter during the three-phase fault. The load voltage attains 1 pu during the healthy condition during 1.5 to 2.0 sec.

At 2.0 s phase to ground fault occurs on phase A. The voltage spike is encountered at this instant due to switching of intentional islanding. During the single-phase to ground fault (i.e. between 2.0 and 2.5 s), the load voltage is around 0.95 pu. After clearing of single-phase to ground fault, the load voltage becomes 1 pu.

2.5.3.3   Test Case: 3—With GUPFC and Without Fuel Cell

Figure 2.20 shows the load voltage profile in intentional islanding condition with GUPFC and without fuel cell. At normal healthy working conditions between 0.0 and 1.0 s, the load voltage observed around 1 pu. A three-phase to ground fault observed between 1.0 and 1.5 s. After the occurrence of fault at 1.02 s generator at the bus no. 3 and load at the bus no. 5 get islanded from the main system. A spike due to switching seen at the instant of 1.0 s. During islanding conditions (i.e. between 1.02 and 1.5 s), the load voltage rises to around 1.1 pu. The load voltage gets normalized to 1 pu when islanded part of the system reconnected with the main system (i.e. between 1.5 and 2.0 s) During the single-phase to ground fault (i.e. between 2.0 and 2.5 s), the load voltage rises to around 1.1 pu due to the intentional islanding of the generator at the bus no. 3 and a load at the bus no. 5. The voltage profile improves due to the islanding of a balanced system.

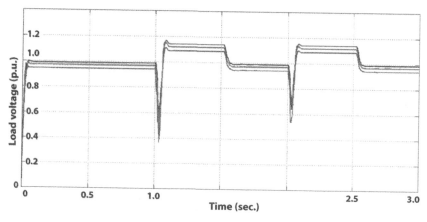

Figure 2.20 Load voltage profile in test case-3.

2.5.3.4   Test Case: 4—With GUPFC and With Fuel Cell

As shown in Figure 2.21 with GUPFC and fuel cell in the system under intentional islanding condition, load voltage observed is 1 pu with a healthy system (i.e. between 0.0 and 1.0 s). A brief spike due to switching observed at the instant of fault (i.e. at 1.0 s). The load voltage rises to around 1.1 pu during three-phase to a ground fault between 1.0 and 1.5 s but minor unbalance is observed. The improvement in the load voltage is due to the presence of fuel cells and GUPFC. After clearing of the fault at 1.5 s the load voltage becomes normalized to 1 pu.

The load voltage again rises to 1.1 pu and remains constant during the single-phase to ground fault (i.e. during 2.0 to 2.5 s) with a brief switching spike at the instant of 2.0 s. After clearing of the fault, the load voltage becomes normalized to 1 pu.

2.5.3.5   Test Case: 5—With Active GUPFC

Figure 2.22 shows the load voltage profile with an active GUPFC based sub-system. The load voltage remains constant during the entire simulation period. The intentionally islanded load has almost constant voltage. The brief spikes observed during switching in the system at 1.0 and 2.0 s. The fuel cell embedded GUPFC improves the load voltage profile during the three-phase to ground fault and single-phase to ground fault. The GUPFC, as compared to previous test cases, receives power for improving load voltage profile during fault due to fuel cell connected to its common DC bus. The load voltage profile using active GUPFC during

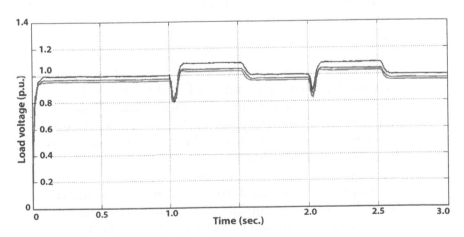

Figure 2.21 Load voltage profile in test case-4.

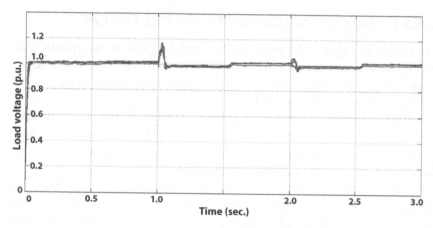

Figure 2.22 Load voltage profile in test case-5.

intentional islanding condition shows almost constant load voltage of 1 pu during the simulation.

By examining different test cases, it can be seen that load voltage remains constant with active GUPFC. The percentage load voltage deviation from the rated load voltage calculated as:

$$\%Load\ voltage\ deviation = \frac{\left(V_{rated} - V_{actual}\right)}{V_{rated}} X100 \qquad (2.19)$$

Figure 2.23 illustrates the graph of percentage load voltage deviation from the rated value of 1 pu in line to ground fault and Figure 2.24 illustrates for three-phase to ground fault.

The observations are listed below:

1. The system without GUPFC and without fuel cell shows maximum percentage deviation of load voltage under the non-islanding condition and intentional islanding connection with rated load voltage of 1 pu. It observed that the percentage variation in intentional islanding conditions is less than that of non-islanded conditions.
2. The system without GUPFC and with fuel cell shows improvement in the load voltage profile in intentional-islanding connection but fails to maintain load voltage profile with the non-islanding condition during the fault.

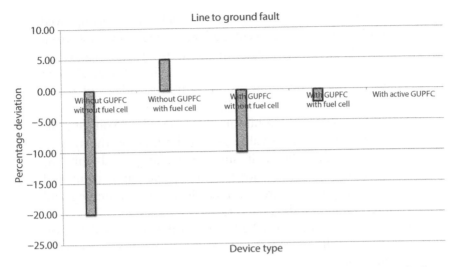

Figure 2.23 Summary of simulation: Percentage load voltage deviation from rated value for line to ground fault.

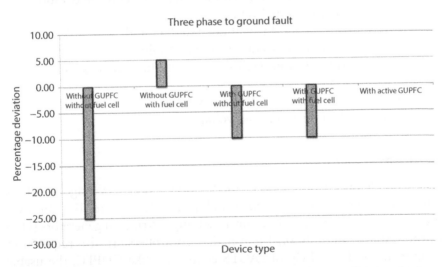

Figure 2.24 Summary of simulation: Percentage load voltage deviation from rated value for three phase to ground fault.

3. The system with GUPFC and without fuel cell shows improvement in load voltage profile during 27a fault in intentional islanding condition but with the non-islanded condition, the load voltage deviation in this system matches the system without GUPFC and without fuel cell.

4. The system with GUPFC and with fuel cell shows improved results and lower percentage load voltage deviation from rated load voltage during the fault. The percentage deviation of the load voltage is minimum in intentional islanded system operation compared to the non-islanded system.

5. The system with active GUPFC i.e. GUPFC embedded with the fuel cell shows minimum percentage load voltage deviation from its rated value during the fault on the system. The most probable fault, single phase to ground fault, has minimum percentage load voltage deviation as compared to three-phase to ground fault during non-islanding and intentional islanding conditions.

6. The graphs in Figures 2.23 and 2.24 illustrate the deviation of load voltage from rated value under different network situations.

7. The load voltage in 'without GUPFC and without fuel cell' and 'with GUPFC and without fuel cell' shows maximum deviation from rated value.

8. The load voltage in 'without GUPFC and with fuel cell' shows medium deviation from rated value.

9. The system in 'with GUPFC and with fuel cell' has a lower deviation.

10. The load voltage in 'with active GUPFC' has the lowest deviation from the rated load voltage.

2.5.4 Summary

Due to fault on any component of the power system, voltage profile is affected; and hence power stability and quality deteriorate. The improvement in stability is not possible only by adding distributed generators (DG) in the system, but additional power flow controllers are also required to support it. With the help of FACTS controllers like GUPFC, the usable capacity of the transmission line improves and it can be flexibly loaded with larger limits depending on the system conditions. GUPFC fails to control power flow when capacitor charging power becomes unavailable due to fault. If GUPFC is present in the intentionally separated sub-system, then the charging of the capacitor is an additional load on the sub-system, which becomes sensitive due to the small power number (MW/Hz). The performance of GUPFC depends on the amount of charge on its capacitor, which depends on the connection to the energy source. It is, therefore, necessary that a generation embedded with the GUPFC system is needed.

2.6   Appendix General Test System

The part of MAC 24 system considered a comprehensive test system. The original MAC 24 system diagram is shown in Figure 2.25. It is available in MiPower software as a standard test system. Table 2.3 shows network parameters.

2.6.1   IEEE 9 Bus Test System

The nine bus test system referred from MATPOWER program. After solving DC load flow for the test system, the simulation model obtained using graph theory. The bus numbers 4, 6, 8 were deleted from the simulation model as these buses were neither connected to generator nor to load. The original nine bus system and its data shown in Figure 2.26. Table 2.4 shows the branch data of IEEE 9 bus system.

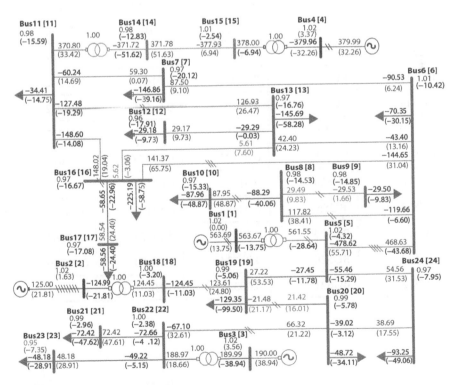

Figure 2.25 MAC 24 network diagram.

Table 2.3 MAC 24 network parameters.

From	To	R (pu)	B (pu)	B/2 (pu)
BUS15	BUS14	0.00430	0.04770	0.63700
BUS7	BUS11	0.02444	0.12226	0.10272
BUS12	BUS13	0.01321	0.06608	0.05552
BUS13	BUS11	0.00314	0.01570	0.05275
BUS13	BUS16	0.00578	0.02891	0.02429
BUS16	BUS11	0.00247	0.01239	0.04164
BUS16	BUS17	0.00248	0.01239	0.01041
BUS5	BUS6	0.00450	0.02251	0.30260
BUS6	BUS7	0.03716	0.18586	0.15616
BUS6	BUS13	0.05169	0.25856	0.21723
BUS6	BUS16	0.01530	0.07655	0.57882
BUS6	BUS8	0.01239	0.06195	0.20822
BUS8	BUS9	0.00363	0.01817	0.06107
BUS8	BUS10	0.00330	0.01652	0.05552
BUS18	BUS19	0.00537	0.02685	0.09022
BUS19	BUS5	0.01263	0.06319	0.21237
BUS19	BUS20	0.01131	0.05658	0.19016
BUS20	BUS24	0.01982	0.09913	0.08328
BUS24	BUS5	0.02494	0.12473	0.10480
BUS22	BUS23	0.03633	0.18173	0.15269
BUS22	BUS20	0.01734	0.08674	0.29149
BUS22	BUS21	0.00330	0.01652	0.01388

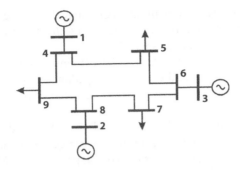

Figure 2.26 IEEE 9 bus test system.

Table 2.4 IEEE 9 bus test system branch data.

fBus	tBus	r	x	B	z
1	4	0	0.0576	0	0.0576
4	5	0.017	0.092	0.158	0.0935
5	6	0.039	0.17	0.358	0.17
3	6	0	0.0586	0	0.0586
6	7	0.0119	0.1008	0.209	0.1015
7	8	0.0085	0.072	0.149	0.0725
8	2	0	0.0625	0.25	0.0625
8	9	0.032	0.161	0.306	0.1641
9	4	0.01	0.085	0.176	0.0855

References

1. Hingorani, N.G. and Gyugyi, L., *Understanding FACTS*, IEEE Press and John Wiley Inc., 1 ed., 2000.
2. Basu, S., *Recent Trends in Fuel Cell Science and Technology*, New Delhi, India: Anamaya Publishers, Copublished by Springer, 2007.
3. C.E.A. India, *Report on review of performance of thermal power stations 2009–10*, p. VII, September 2010.
4. Secretariat, *Renewable energy technologies: Cost analysis series—hydropower*, IRENA working paper, vol. 1, June 2012.
5. Nayak, *Energetica India: cost economics of solar kwh*, January/February 2012.

6. Ignacio, J., Zamora, I., Martin, J.S., Aperribay, V. and Egua, P., Hybrid fuel cell technologies for electrical microgrids, *Electrical Power System Research*, vol. 80, pp. 993–1005, September 2010.

7. E.T.S. Inc., *Fuel Cell Handbook*, U.S. Department of Energy, seventh ed., 2004.

8. Yoon, K.H., Jang, J.H. and Cho, Y.S., Impedance characteristics of a phosphoric acid fuel cell, *Journal of Materials Science*, vol. 17, pp. 1755–1758, 1998.

9. Jia, J., Li, Q,. Wang, Y,. Cham, Y.T. and Han, M., Modeling and dynamic characteristic simulation of a proton exchange membrane fuel cell, *IEEE Transactions on Energy Conversion*, vol. 24, pp. 283–291, March 2009.

10. Tanni, M.A. and Iqbal, M.T., Modeling and control of a grid connected PAFC system, *International Journal of Energy Science*, vol. 4, pp. 69–76, July 2014.

11. Nehrir, M. and Wang, C., *Modeling and Control of Fuel Cell: Distributed Generation Applications*, New Jersey, USA: IEEE Press, Wiley Publication, 2009.

12. Kazemi and Karimi, E., The effect of interline power flow controller (IPFC) on damping inter-area oscillations in the interconnected power systems, *Proceedings of IEEE ISIE 2006*, July 9–12, 2006, Montreal, Quebec, Canada, pp. 1911–1915, July 2006.

13. Diez-Valencia, V. and Jacobson, D., Interline power flow controller (IPFC) steady state operation, *Proceedings of the 2002 IEEE Canadian Conference on Electrical and Computer Engineering*, pp. 280–284, 2002.

14. Uzunovic, E. and Reeve, J., Fundamental frequency model of unified power flow controller, *Proceedings of the North American Power Symposium (NAPS)*, pp. 275–282, 1998.

15. Schauder, C.D. and Mehta, H., Vector analysis and control of advanced static VAr compensator, *IEE Proceedings—C*, vol. 140, pp. 299–306, July 1993.

16. Zhang, X.-P., Handschin, E. and Yao, M., Modeling of the generalized unified power flow controller (GUPFC) in a nonlinear interior point OPF, *IEEE Transactions on Power Systems*, vol. 16, pp. 367–373, August 2001.

17. Santander, Combined Operation of UPQC and fuel cell with common DC bus, *International Conference on Renewable Energies and Power Quality*, March 2008.

18. Sen, K.K. and Sen, M.L., *Introduction to FACTS Controllers: Theory, Modeling, and Applications*, Wiley-IEEE Press, September 2009.

3

Review of Energy Storage System for Microgrid

G.V. Brahmendra Kumar and K. Palanisamy*

School of Electrical Engineering, Vellore Institute of Technology, Vellore, India

Abstract

The high penetration of renewable energy resources (RES) will give an impact on the electric power system (EPS) operation due to intermittent and uncertain features of RES. Hence, Microgrid (MG) is one of the promising solutions to attain power reliability and sustainable energy deployment by combining different RES, distribution sources, and loads. The fluctuating nature of RES will be smoothed with an energy storage system (ESS) and delivers high power quality. However, the available ESS technology is facing challenges due to several problems such as management, sizing, charging and discharging characteristics, life cycle, and reliability. The ESS management for the effective operation of MG remains challenging in modern EPS networks. The integration of two or more ESS can increase the reliability, and stability, overcomes the power quality issues, and obtains excellent features in one specific application. This chapter describes the classification of present and advanced ESS technologies stated on the formation of energy and materials, its features, capacity, and process of evaluation. Hence, the optimal energy management system and advanced ESS topology can be the best option for future enhancement to cost reduction and enhance the overall efficiency of the system. The significant contribution of this chapter is the comprehensive study of choosing future ESS to achieve the sustainable improvement of MGs.

Keywords: Microgrid, energy storage system, renewable energy resources, power management, power electronic system, power system network, trends, and challenges

*Corresponding author: kpalanisamy@vit.ac.in

C. Sharmeela, P. Sivaraman, P. Sanjeevikumar, and Jens Bo Holm-Nielsen (eds.) Microgrid Technologies, (57–90) © 2021 Scrivener Publishing LLC

3.1   Introduction

The two main factors for the increased use of electricity and energy consumption over the last few decades are rapid growth in the global population and a change in consumer habits. The manufacturing, transportation, and construction sectors make up a significant part of the total electricity consumption. In 2050 global energy demand will be more than double, and by the end of the 20th century, more than triple. Technological developments in existing energy networks with conventional methods will not be enough to meet this demand sustainably [1]. Since their negative effects on climate (global warming, loss of layers of ozone, ozone concentrations at ground level, emissions, acid rain, etc.) and the increasing fossil fuels depletion, the use of energy-efficient technologies, clean and RESs, etc., should be preventive steps in processes for energy production to consumption [2].

At the time of generation, energy is consumed. The right electricity must always be given to meet the changing demand. The reliability and efficiency of the power supply would suffer from an imbalance among supply and demand. In addition, the production of electricity is typically situated far away from consuming sites [3]. The cost of construction and wasted energy are increased by long transmission lines. Nevertheless, the situation is complicated by regular and seasonal variations in RESs. Short-term and long-term storage is considered among the most effective methods for solving these problems [4].

Energy storage means energy production in various styles, which can be used to carry out some useful operations in the future [5]. The resources that can be transported and processed will open new horizons for business stakeholders. It is difficult to store electricity. In general, electrical energy storage needs to be transformed into another type of energy [6]. Improving energy storage is crucial if energy efficiency is to be increased. One of the keys to progress in storing energy is both to find new materials and to understand how new and existing materials work. Energy can be stored through numerous approaches, for example, chemical, mechanical, electrical, and heat systems. Such approaches include pumped hydro storage, latent heat, and phase-change materials dependent thermal-based ESSs that are extensively analyzing and also easily applicable [7].

ESS and RE systems are becoming widely supported alternatives [8]. ESS helps in many ways to incorporate renewables and maintains a decent power balance during the energy crisis. This ensures that the overall system reliability has an essential impact by stored energy for the period of off-peak hours with low costs [9]. ESS also promotes energy integration. In Ref. [10], information was examined regarding applications of ES technology. The poor battery life cycle has been described as the most important barrier for ESSs to prevent MG growth.

For the ESS in MGs, several important considerations exist. The architecture of the ESS in MG appliances is at the center of attention with efficient control of ESS, charging and discharge, power electronic interfaces, and conversion process, reliability, and safety from risks [11]. Figure 3.1 describes the effect of the power system network of an energy storage facility. In an EPS network, the selection and control of ESS and power services significantly lessen the deviations. ESS can offer a variety of benefits for energy systems, such as increased deployment and improved economic efficiency in renewable energy [12]. Energy saving is also critical for electrical systems, enabling load and peak shaving, frequency control, power oscillation damping, and improved performance quality and reliability, as shown in Figure 3.2. This chapter aims to present the significance of current ESSs, identify challenges and obstacles, and provide suggestions for further progress, application areas, unique characteristics, and partial comparisons.

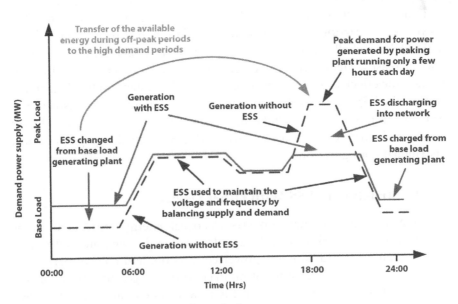

Figure 3.1 Load demand outline with ESS [11].

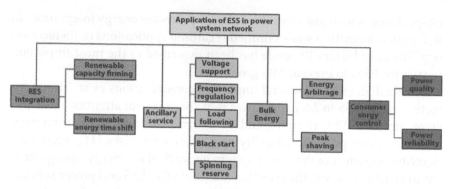

Figure 3.2 Application of ESS in a power system network [13].

3.2 Detailed View of ESS

This section describes the overview of ESS configurations, structures, and its classifications.

3.2.1 Configuration of ESS

The ESS technology for the MG application is presented in Figure 3.3. In the aggregated system, the power delivery from DER to the PCC link is maintained constant, and the total ESS capacity can be used to soften the power flow variations in the system. The design and regulation of large scale ESS are challenging, whereas the capacity of ESS rises, system cost also increases. Hence, the small-scale ESS and DERs can be utilized to achieve the effective and reliable operation of the system. In the distributed system, the ESSs are directly associated with several interfaced distribution sources [9]. However, the regulation of power flow and reduction of losses in power electronic interfaces for DER and ESS is a challenging option in a distributed configuration.

3.2.2 Structure of ESS With Other Devices

The ESS is a device that converts electrical energy into chemical or mechanical energy. However, storage devices can be separated into three stages, such as central storage, power conversion, and control parts. The energy is stored after transformation in central storage; the power conversion operates as interlink between the power system and central storage

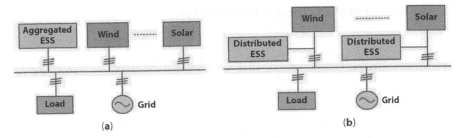

Figure 3.3 (a) Aggregated system and (b) Distributed system.

with the bi-directional transfer. In the control part, the process of charge or discharge is controlled by the usage of sensing and regulating devices. The ESS is not an ideal source of supply; it always suffers from losses in each stage of the storing process [11]. The ESS configuration with other devices is shown in Figure 3.4.

The energy generation, loss, and output of the device is given in the following equations,

$$E_{out} = E_{gen} - \Delta E_{loss} \tag{3.1}$$

$$\Delta E_{loss} = \Delta E_{charge} + \Delta E_{discharge} + \Delta E_{stored} \tag{3.2}$$

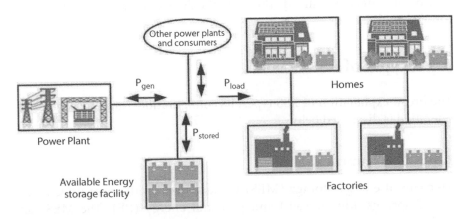

Figure 3.4 ESS configurations with other devices.

The total storage efficiency is formulated as,

$$\eta_{stored}^{total} = \frac{E_{out}}{E_{gen}} = \eta_{stored} \times \eta_{charge} \times \eta_{discharge} \tag{3.3}$$

$$\eta_{stored} = \frac{E_{stored}}{E_{charge}} ; \eta_{charge} = \frac{E_{stored}^*}{E_{stored}} ; \eta_{discharge} = \frac{E_{stored}^*}{E_{discharge}} \tag{3.4}$$

Where, η_{charge}, $\eta_{discharge}$, and η_{stored} are the efficiency of the charge, discharge and storage intervals. ΔE_{loss}, ΔE_{charge}, $\Delta E_{discharge}$ and ΔE_{stored} are the total energy loss, charge, and discharge, storage losses. E_{stored}^*, and E_{stored} are the stored, and existing energy of the central stage and also E_{out}, E_{gen}, E_{charge}, and $E_{discharge}$ are the energy of the output, generated, charge and discharge intervals, respectively.

3.2.3   ESS Classifications

In recent days, various ESSs have been developed, and the ESS is an essential element in a MG as it minimizes the power fluctuations and deals with severe imbalance challenges amongst the supply side and demand side. The detailed classification of ESS is reviewed in the following sections. ESS can be classified as mechanical, chemical, electrical, hybrid, and thermal ESSs such systems categorized as a battery, FES, CAES, SC, and hydrogen storage devices based on the process and formation of materials utilized. These are the devices more commonly used for MG applications.

3.3   Types of ESS

The broad explanation of ESS types, its configurations, and the process of operation is discussed below.

3.3.1   Mechanical ESS

Mechanical energy storage (MES) works based on the pressurized gas, forced springs, kinetic (KE) and potential energy (PE). The MES can easily distribute the energy for mechanical works whenever it required. The MES mainly classified as FES, PHS, and CAES technologies [14].

The PHS has mostly contributed systems in the world among the three systems based on its storage capacity and life cycle. It also has some constraints, such as capital cost, complexity in implementation, and the impact on the environment. Hence, the PHS is limited to future developments [15]. The detailed explanation of the three systems in Figure 3.5 is discussed below.

3.3.2   Flywheel ESS

The FES can be categorized as high and low-speed machines. The configuration of flywheel based ESS is shown in Figure 3.6. It works on mechanically stored energy to KE from rotor mass rotating at higher speeds. The stored KE in FES is relevant to the speed and inertia. The stored energy is used to smooth the working of machines, and the faster rotates flywheel can store more energy [16]. The high-speed FES contains a composite disk with low speed and high inertia. Thus, the stored energy changes in a

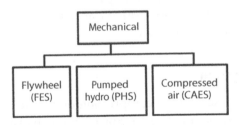

Figure 3.5 Types of Mechanical ESS.

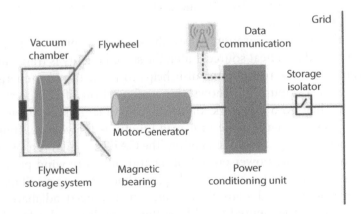

Figure 3.6 Flywheel based ESS configuration.

square with angular momentum. The stored energy is salvaged by reducing the speed of a flywheel over decelerating torque and reverting KE to the electrical motor, this can be worked as a generator. The small speed FES has a steel disk comparatively low inertia and high speed, and the speed about less than 10000 rpm machines takes into account as low-speed FES, which is most widely held in industries. The FES reserves the electrical energy in the spinning mass. Hence, the total FES stored energy is given as [17],

$$E_{FES} = \frac{1}{2} J \times \omega^2 \tag{3.5}$$

$$J = m \times r^2 \tag{3.6}$$

Where E_{FES}, J, m, ω, and r^2 are the stored energy in FES, moment of inertia, mass, angular velocity, and radius of the flywheel, respectively. The FES has some limitations as low energy density, high cost, and high self-discharge. The high-speed FES system can reduce the cost and discharge with development technology [18].

3.3.3   CAES System

The CAES works based on the compression of air and stores the pressure energy. The turbine is operated to convert the expansion of compressed gas into mechanical energy. During the lower demand, the excess power drives as a generator, and it works as a series of compressors to bring in air into the storage unit. The storage unit will deliver this energy into the underground reservoir.

When the power generation is low, the stored compressed air is delivered and heated by a heat source. Later, the stored energy is transmitted to the turbine, and the recuperator unit helps to reuse the heat energy that gets wasted [7]. Figure 3.7 shows the configuration of compressed air-based ESS. The CAES can work for small-scale to large-scale power units. It mainly serves as large-scale unit grid functions for voltage, frequency control, load shifting, and peak shaving. The CAES has high response time, and it can soften the power output of on and off-shore wind plants [19]. But it has a limitation for a large-scale plant that choosing a suitable location with underground natural caverns. An advanced adiabatic CAES plant has been implemented to address this issue. It has also faced lower

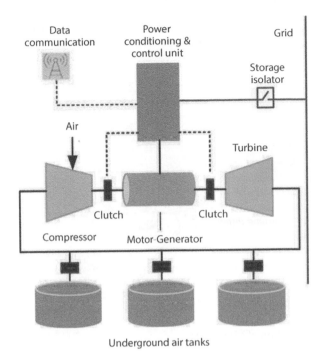

Figure 3.7 Structure of compressed air based ESS.

discharge efficiency issues. To solve all these issues related to CAES, a combined heating, cooling, and power system was studied [20].

3.3.4   PHS System

The PHS system works based on the water flow between the two different head reservoirs to compensate for the peak demand of supply. The energy can be stored and delivered at a large-scale level is possible with PHS systems. The PHS is associated with RES, such as solar and wind power, which can produce more stable power within the EPS network [21]. The PHS system is illustrated in Figure 3.8. The excess energy is used for storage during the lower demand, and it can deliver during peak demand whenever it required. During off-peak periods, the pumped turbine rotates and transfers the water to the high head storage reservoir. Hence, the storage water is used to generate electricity during peak periods or peaks in demand from consumers [22]. The PHS is characterized as closed, semi-open, and open loop systems. In a closed-loop, the PHS contains the two basins, which are divided through a vertical distance; neither it is associated with the surplus

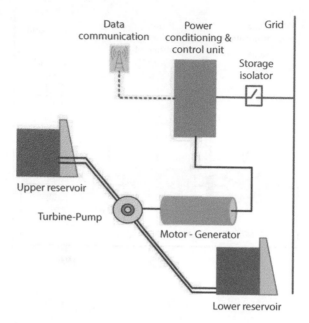

Figure 3.8 configuration of PHS system.

water body. In a semi-open system, the PHS is separated by one in which an artificial basin and another is river impoundment with steady water flow. The open-loop or pumped back system comprises the continuous water flow over the upper and lower basin/reservoirs [23].

3.3.5   CES Systems

CES systems can store the energy for long intervals. The stored energy is in the form of atoms, and molecules that can be transferred within the system by means of chemical reactions. The material is converted into another substance in the cycle of a chemical reaction.

The commonly utilized CE fuels are in the dominant energy source wherein both energy transportation and electricity generation such as hydrogen, diesel, natural gas, and liquid petroleum gas (LPG). By using the heat engine as a prime mover, these chemicals are easily converted to ME and TE and then electrical energy. In contrast, the stored chemical energy is released for direct electricity production during chemical transfer reactions. All of these, hydrogen technology is mostly used in applications due to its ability to store a higher amount of electrical energy. Hence, the CES

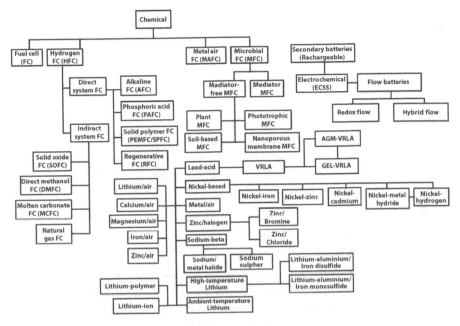

Figure 3.9 Detailed classification chemical based ESS.

system is quite suitable for a large volume of energy storage and for greater intervals. The detailed classification of chemical-based ESS (CES) is shown in Figure 3.9 [24].

3.3.6 Hydrogen Energy Storage (HES)

Hydrogen storage is mostly used in industrial applications because it is an emission-free electricity generation. HES deliver only water vapour into the atmosphere when it burns. As compared to other hydrocarbon fuels, HES burns faster, and it has a high energy density by weight (142 kJ/Kg), and lower energy density by volume. HES can be categorized as physical and material-based storage. Gas-based storage consists of a high-pressure tank (350–370 bars), and the hydrogen boiling point is −252.8 °C. Thus, the liquid-based hydrogen storage needs cryogenic methods of cooling. The material storage can be done with chemical hydrogen, metal hydride, and sorbent materials. HES system works by adsorption on the solid surface or by absorption within solids [25]. The HES system function diagram is shown in Figure 3.10. It consists of a storage tank, electrolyzer/ electrochemical converter, and fuel cell. An electrolyzer helps to split the water molecule into hydrogen and oxygen and thus generate electricity.

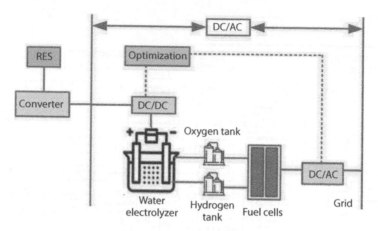

Figure 3.10 Functional diagram of HES.

Three types of electrolyte technologies are used, such as alkaline, solid electrolyte, and polymer electrolyte membranes (PEM). In these, the alkaline technology is mostly used because it is developed technology and low material cost. PEM is a high-power density device, but it has a higher material cost. The alkaline and PEM efficiency ranges are between 62 and 82%. The oxide electrolyte efficiency range is about to 86%, but it faces several issues due to corrosion, closures, and thermal cycling [26]. The chemical reaction of HES is given below,

$$2H_2O + O_2 \leftrightarrow 2H_2O + e^-$$ (3.7)

The application of HES in low-voltage MG is performed well in [27]. The HES requires the significant potential to support the MG and aggregators in practical use when a wide range of RES is employed. To address several issues, it requires an ideal material and is a challenge option for the utilization of this technology. HES system is better preferred for load-shifting applications, but it is a costly method, and efficiency is an essential criterion to develop this technology.

3.3.7 Battery-Based ESS

The CE in the active material is converted into electrical energy. Chemical reaction completes this conversion process in electrochemical storage systems (ECSS), and energy is retained for a specific voltage and time as electrical current. The voltage and current levels are created by the series or parallel cell connections. Many new electrode substances and electrolytes were tested and suggested cost improvement, life-cycle, battery safety, the density of energy, and power. The functional diagram of battery-based ESS is presented in Figure 3.11. Ref. [24] provides a study of ECSSs including flow batteries (FBs), lithium-ion batteries (Li-ion), sodium–sulfur and related nickel–cadmium (Ni–Cd), nickel-metal hydride (Ni–Mh), lead-acid, and zebra batteries. Some of these ECSSs also provide performance data for SCs and lithium-ion batteries.

In ECSS, lithium batteries perform an enormously important role among the several types of batteries due to their high specific power and energy density. In terms of usable energy capacity, a charged Li-air battery produces a source of energy for electric vehicles competing with gasoline. During discharge, the basic battery chemistry is the lithium metal electrochemical oxidation at anode and the removal of oxygen from the cathode liquid [28]. The properties, merits, and demerits of modern battery-based ESS are presented in Table 3.1. Several technical challenges need to be tackled before Li-air batteries attained the high efficiency and become commercially feasible: design of cathode structures, optimizing the composition of the electrolyte, and elucidation of complex chemical reactions during charging and discharge. Li-air battery's most important advances and the key limiting factors, as well as their current knowledge of chemistry were outlined in [29]. The Li-ion battery is a kind of Li battery used as an electrode material by an interrelated lithium compound. Ref. [30] reviews and compares the stored energy in Li-air batteries and lithium–sulfur (Li–S) batteries and discusses the challenges of cell operation and improvement. These say that while both batteries give better energy density than Li-ion batteries and can

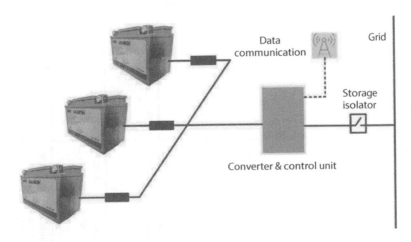

Figure 3.11 Typical view of battery-based ESS.

Table 3.1 Properties, merits, and demerits of modern battery-based ESS [6].

Battery type	Capital cost ($/kWh)	Cycle efficiency (%)	Energy density (Wh/L.)	Self-discharge (%/day)	Discharge time	Response time	Life time (Yrs)	Merits	Demerits
Lead-acid	250–400	80–90	60–90	0.1–0.2	<4 h	ms	<20	Capital cost is low. Mature technology.	Required high maintenance. Cycling time is low. Low power and energy density. The performance is poor at lower temperatures.
Li-ion	600–3,900	80–97	250–500	0.1–0.3	<1 h	ms	<15	Quick response time. Life cycle efficiency is high. Energy and power density is high.	Cost is high. Life cycle depends on the level of discharge. Depth of Discharge (DoD) has an impact on life.
Ni-Cd	800–2,500	60–85	60–180	0.2–0.7	<5 h	ms	15-20	Mature technology. Strong and reliable.	Impact on the environment. High cost. Energy density is low.
Sodium-Sulphur	300–600	75–85	150–350	Low	<6 h	ms	<15	Self-discharge is low. Rated capacity is high. Energy density is high. Highly recyclable.	Operating cost is high. Temperature control devices are needed.
Vanadium redox (VRB)	160–1,100	65–85	15–40	Low	<8 h	<10 min	<10	Faster response. Efficiency is high.	Lower energy and power densities. Construction is complex.

be even more cost in terms-competitive than Li-ion batteries. However, before they can reach markets, detailed research on the fundamental chemistry included in Li–O$_2$ and Li–S cells is required.

3.3.8   Electrical Energy Storage (EES) System

EES system works based on the electrical energy storage capacity to generate electricity, and it delivers to the load for usage when required. The energy is stored in the form of an electrical or magnetic field through SC or SMES. EES can be classified into capacitors, SC and SMES are shown in Figure 3.12 below. The capacitors are used to high current applications but only for transient intervals due to their lower generation capacity. The SMES can be used for the exits of power plants to smooth the power output, in which it is used to provide peak energy consumption. Instead of capacitors, SC offers high capacity storage in a small package. The EPS is facing challenges related to integrating the transmission and distribution network with RES [31]. The EES is the solution for mitigating the issues facing with EPS network and helps to maintain the load balancing, power quality improvement, operating the EPS, and for MG support.

3.3.8.1   Capacitors

The capacitor can store the electricity by direct method mostly. It consists of metal plates, which can separate by a non-conducting material termed

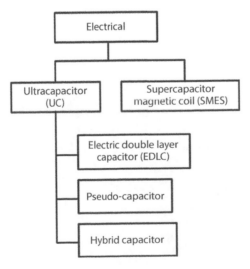

Figure 3.12 Classifications of EES.

as a dielectric. One plate can be charged from a direct current source with electricity, and another plate is already included in it as an opposite sign charge. The surface of stored energy can be a metal electrode or plastic film. The capacitor can work only transient periods because it is a low energy density device, but it has high power density and deliver high currents to the system.

3.3.8.2 Supercapacitors (SCs)

SCs can store the EE amongst two conducting electrodes and also named as UCs and EDLCs. It is an alternative solution for capacitors because SCs have no chemical reactions. SC can be used for high power applications, and it has a long-life cycle for charging or discharging conditions up to a million times as compared with conventional battery.

The high surface area carbon-coated material is used for SCs, so increases the SC energy density [32]. The pulse load is used for EPS applications (communication and spacecraft technology); therefore, it creates disturbances in MG networks. Thus, the SC is used to proper power balancing and fast response for the smoothing of the EPS network. The SC application can be applicable for islanded and grid-connected operation modes to maintain the proper power balance in normal and faulty circumstances, explained in [33]. Figure 3.13 shows the functional diagram of the SC storage system. The efficiency of SC is between 84 and 97%, but the self-discharge rate is high (up to 40% per day). To overcome these issues,

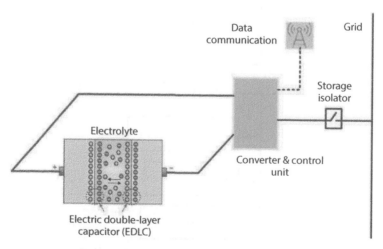

Figure 3.13 Functional diagram of SC-based ESS.

researchers focus on developing several new technology-based materials such as carbon, graphene, and ultra-small Si nanoparticles.

3.3.9 SMES

Superconductive Magnetic Energy Storage (SMES) systems operate based on the theory of electrodynamics. The magnetic field stored energy is generated in a superconducting coil by the direct current flow, which is remained beyond its critical superconducting temperature. Superconductive material is cryogenically cooled, and by discharging the coil, and the stored energy can be discharged back into the network [34]. The typical view of SMES illustrates in Figure 3.14. The amount of energy stored in the coil is W_{LS},

$$W_{Ls} = \frac{1}{2}LI^2 \qquad (3.8)$$

Where L denoted the coil's inductance, I is the current flowing through the coil. SMES devices are defined as two types such as SMES high temperature (HTS) operating at about 70K and SMES low temperature (LTS) operating at about 7K. Compared to HTS system, the LTS system performance and technology is more matured. This approach has a rapid

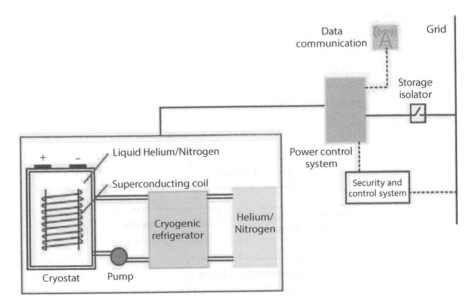

Figure 3.14 Typical view of SMES.

reaction to conditions that are constrained to a few milliseconds in charge and discharge.

In addition, this device has high energy density (4 kW/l) and also high efficiency (95–98%) with an estimated 30-year long lifetime. It is possible to express the stored energy in SMES systems as follows: SMES systems are suitable for commercial use within the range of 0.1– 10 MW. The potential is set to increase about 100 MWh in the subsequent decade with the advancement of technology. However, the cost of installing the SMES system remains high ($10,000/kWh) because of its cooling system complexity and coil material [7]. In fact, frequent shifts in this technology's operating current cause SMES unstable. This issue has been solved in Ref. [35]. In UPSs, SMES technology is mostly applicable and enhances the quality of power. Because of the flexible features, it provides in the exchange of real and reactive power, and it has to become popular for MG applications [36]. Current SMES technology statistics are based on decreasing coil costs and cooling systems and make this appliance that is extremely desirable to customers. In addition, to improve storage capacity, a hybrid SMES system could be technologically advanced [37].

3.3.10   Thermal Energy Storage Systems (TESS)

The TES process can be divided as follows: sensible heat (SHS), latent heat (LHS), absorption, and adsorption is presented in Figure 3.15 below [38].

TES systems are suited for storing heat or cold for further use in a storage medium under various circumstances such as temperature, and location [39]. TES systems are significant for heavy industrial and residential uses, including space and process heating/cooling, processing of hot water, and electricity generation. The functional diagram of TESS is presented in Figure 3.16.

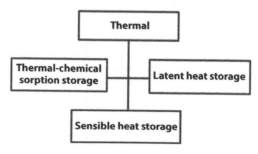

Figure 3.15 Types of thermal-based ESS.

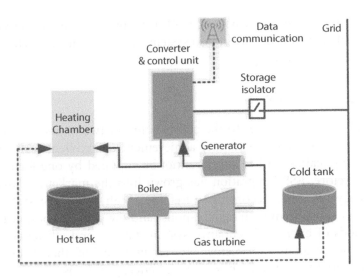

Figure 3.16 Functional diagram of TESS.

3.3.10.1   SHS

Sensible heat storage in the process contributes to changes in temperature. The particular heat capacity and the weight of the medium will use to determine a storage system's capacity. The storage medium may be liquid, solid, or solid filler material in different phases [40].

3.3.10.2   Latent

Unlike sensible heat storage, latent heat will not be sensed by temperature change. The use of phase-change materials (PCMs) is used as ES devices for LHS [41]. In the latent heat cycle, thermal conductivity (k) is a crucial element. In addition, during the phase transition, density and enthalpy are essential as they evaluate the volumetric storage capacity. Available for usage in LHS systems are organic (paraffin), inorganic, and bio-based PCM (salt hydrates) [40].

3.3.10.3   Absorption

One of indirect ways to store heat is this form of thermo-chemical storage. The heat is often not processed as SHS or LHS directly but through a physicochemical process. For this method, absorption and adsorption are two clear cases that absorb and release heat, respectively, in charge and discharge mode. The significant benefit of sorption energy storage is the high energy density (approx. 1,000 MJ/m³), ensuing in a smaller volume of material [42]. Several absorption systems work as heat pumps that allow both cooling and heating.

3.3.10.4   Hybrid ESS

Hybrid ESS (HESS) states to the combination of two or more ESSs used for the gain of each ESS for the achievement of excellent features in a specific application. All features cannot be supplied by one form of the ESS. Therefore, ESS integration has grown into the market for advanced technology, like MG. According to Ref. [43], high-power ESS systems are helpful for short-term with high response and the slow response with longer periods of energy. To enhance system stability and efficiency and to reduce energy quality problems, MG requires an ESS that incorporates the functionality of the high power and energy systems. The configuration of a hybrid ESS is shown in Figure 3.17. HESS is a more complicated management strategy than a single ESS, involving multiple aspects, such as charging/discharging features, response time, power-sharing, life cycle, and performance. Several researchers used numerous techniques to investigate this new development for energy storage. The HESS literature review shows that battery/SC [44], battery/SMES [45], battery/FC [46], FC/SC [47], SC/RFB [48] integration is possible for applications with a MG system. The technology battery/SC is now very commonly used and popular. In comparison with the battery-only system, the HESS has enhanced in

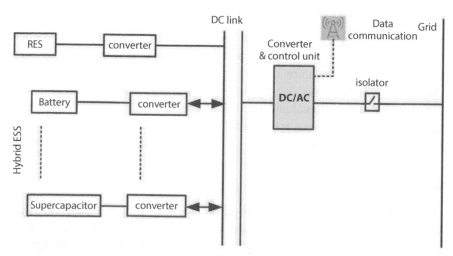

Figure 3.17 Typical Hybrid ESS.

frequency stabilization performance for use in MG. The battery life cycle in this application is extended by protecting high-frequency charge or discharge cycles and for peak currents.

3.4   Comparison of Current ESS on Large Scale

The comprehensive analysis of different large scale ESS parameters, merits, and demerits are provided in Table 3.2.

3.5   Importance of Storage in Modern Power Systems

ESS is a significant part of the power system in the following circumstances without additional capacity.

3.5.1   Generation Balance and Fluctuation in Demand

Electric demand as well as generation, fluctuates in the nature of a power system. The demand change depends on the characteristics of end-user usage. The penetration of RE is one of the main sources of erratic output fluctuation. Frequent demand and generation fluctuation affect grid stability and complicate the management of the network. Hours of hydrogen or gas plants are typically run due to its rapid synchronization capabilities during high electrical demand. However, hydropower supply is limited for many reasons, and operating gas systems for high demand periods would cause practical difficulties and add to this requirement. Nonetheless, the supply of hydroelectric power plants is limited because of several factors, and operational gas plants would pose practical difficulties and increased costs in terms of demand. The performance of thermal plants is smaller for low load and outcomes in an inexpensive process [49]. There is a provision of minimum demand for the maintenance of economic production. Over time of generation, ESS will serve as a load without waste of energy and work as a generator during high demand hours to ensure the generation and load balance.

3.5.2   Intermediate Penetration of Renewable Energy

RESs are being used to increase rapidly. Intermittent design of RES contributes to uncontrolled grid stability and intermittent generation. Whenever

Table 3.2 Merits and demerits of various storage devices [25].

Storage type	Power density (kW/m³)	Energy density (kWh/m³)	Cycle efficiency (%)	Lifetime (Cycles)	Merits	Demerits
FES	40–2,000	20–400	80–95	800–10⁵	Large potential for conservation of power. Requirement for small areas. No emissions. Matured technology.	Issues of noise and security. High cost per energy storage unit.
CAES	0.2–10	0.2–2	60–90	>10⁴	Capacity is high. Cost per kWh is low. Power electronic converter requirement is low.	Issues of safety and leakage. Need for cavities under the surface. It needs fuel.
PHS	0.1–1.5	0.2–2	65–85	>0.5 × 10⁴	Life cycle is longer. Storage capacity is high. Mature technology.	Storage is centralized. Potential impact on the climate. Cost is high.
HES	>500	500–3,000	75–90	>1,000	Environmental impacts are low. Distributed storage and other uses of hydrogen generated.	Efficiency is low. Investment cost is high. Power electronic converters are required to control. Difficulty to maintain the stable load.

(Continued)

Table 3.2 Merits and demerits of various storage devices [25]. (*Continued*)

Storage type	Power density (kW/m³)	Energy density (kWh/m³)	Cycle efficiency (%)	Lifetime (Cycles)	Merits	Demerits
SC	>10,000	1–35	90–95	<10⁶	Power density is high.	Issues of safety. Cell interdependence. Environmental impacts. Life cycle is reliant on cell voltage imbalances and maximum voltage thresholds.
SMES	300–4,000	0.2–6	80–95	>10⁵	Faster response. High reliability and efficiency. Life expectancy, which is independent of the duty cycle.	Cost is high. Larger magnetic fields are required.
TES	>500	500–3,000	75–90	>1,000	Capital cost is low. Energy density is high. Self-discharge is low.	Cycle efficiency is low.

the energy is available, ESS will store and discharge the energy to make output continuous. ESS can function as a buffer for RES and grid to minimize grid intermission [49].

3.5.3   Use of the Grid

ESS provides the power system with stored energy during peak hours and reduces transmission congestion caused by overload. This will enhance the transmission network life and decrease investments in transmission capacity [50].

3.5.4   Operations on the Market

In a decentralized system, generator companies (Gencoms) are penalized for differing from the planned generation. This will improve the longevity of the transport infrastructure and decrease investment under transmission capacity. To escape this penalty levied by the regulatory authorities, Gencoms are enforced to buy high-cost energy from gas stations [51]. Improved RES penetration increases grid frequency, and increased demand reduces grid frequency.

3.5.5   Flexibility in Scheduling

In order to avoid violations from regulators, Gencoms must sustain the grid frequency in the quantified band. The reduction in energy purchasing cost during peak hours of demand is one of ESS's major contributions. This helps Gencoms keep the power system running efficiently during peak load hours. Ancillary services can meet energy storage costs in similar ways [52].

3.5.6   Peak Shaving Support

The "peak-shaving" is called energy management during peak hours. This can be accomplished by higher unit costs over peak hours and the limiting consumption of energy over peak hours. Peak demand is typically fulfilled with the aid of high-cost energy from gas plants, and much coordination and preparation are required. On the other hand, during high demand, the Gencoms-installed ESS can discharge the stored energy and the consumption of energy [49].

3.5.7   Improve the Quality of Power

The ESS can provide improved voltage and frequency management by matching load and demand changes in the system. It can also monitor the power flow and control area error of the connecting line [49].

3.5.8   Carbon Emission Control

ESS will provide electricity for peak demand hours and therefore reduce the process of high-hour gas/diesel plants. ESS can also assist large penetration of RES and minimize the dependence of fossil fuels, and also reduces a certain degree of carbon emissions. Whereas ESS can provide high demand hours with electricity, the operation of gas/diesel peak hour plants can be reduced. ESS can also support massive RES penetration and reduce fossil fuel reliance [50]. ESS will reduce energy cuts by offering a spinning reserve for high demand time. Through keeping the power supply continuous at the consumer level, ESS will improve power reliability.

3.5.9   Improvement of Service Efficiency

ESS will reduce energy consumption by offering a spinning reserve for a time of high demand. By preserving the continuity of electricity supply at the consumer end, ESS will increase the efficiency of power [51].

3.5.10   Emergency Assistance and Support for Black Start

Immediate energy can also be supplied with the minimal start time to help in situations of emergency and black start [51].

3.6   ESS Issues and Challenges

ESS technology's current situation and HESS implementation will overcome many of the problems that the previous technology has faced, such as performance and storage capacity. In view of BESS technology, lack of appeal due to calendar aging, and cyclical aging, the potential for further developed technology to be applied for future MG technologies [53]. Work is now concentrated on the scale, price, protection, or efficient energy management of the network. In the selection of materials, power electronic interfaces, energy balance among the ESS and MG, and protection for this technology can be established as a key issues and challenges.

3.6.1   Selection of Materials

The most important considerations for the ESS system are material quality, material costs, and the supply of raw materials. The storage device life cycle is determined by materials. Many storage materials have been addressed in different storage systems and their production methods, for example, hydraulic, thermal, carbon, gravity, electromagnetic, and electrochemical equipment. In most cases, the choice of material is not optimal. The output of high-quality ESS materials with a key contribution must be discussed for further production of ESS in the MG application [54]. The materials can be heavily dependent on charging and discharging properties, life cycle, efficiency, energy and power density, and corrosion. Existing large storage ESS systems are still costly, which are FES, PHS, and SMES, battery with lithium-ion, NaS, and FBs. In addition, the hybrid ESS consists of super-capacitor/battery, provides a large ES space but can continue to improve the performance of this HESS system [55]. This allows the ESS material selection to be driven in MG applications with increased energy efficiency and reliability by cost-effective, long-term modern technologies.

3.6.2   ESS Size and Cost

Sizing and cost are relatively high for various ESS technologies. If the size improves, the cost increases as well. Volume is based on the energy and power rating [56], as reviewed in various studies on CAES, FES, HES, and TES and BESS capacity. The cost of energy per unit is also a significant energy factor, and it includes the costs of installation and maintenance. Cost is contingent on the stored equipment, life cycle, power, charging/discharging rate, and DoD [44]. While the cost of various ESSs is high and safe and effective in different categories, ESS is an indispensable alternative to MG. In the near future, there are many limitations to soothing voltage and oscillation levels of the single ESS of MG, despite the expected price decrease for some new technologies (for instance Li-ion, FB, Ni–Cd, or Ni–Zn) and evaluating existing storages such as PHS, CAES, FES, HES and TES. Therefore, HESS is built with technological advancements in the fields of energy arbitration, voltage support, peak shaving, and time-shifting to incorporate more systems in order to ensure an efficient operation [11]. With its integration of battery/SC, battery/SMES, battery/flywheel, CAES/SC, and FC/SMES, and CAES/flywheel, storage capacity can be increased, which helps in decrease the plant overall size and costs by preventing the addition of more storage systems independently [45]. It also contributes considerably to rising storage life expectancy. Thus, it can be a significant challenge to RE and conventional networks for a widespread energy storage program to align the capacity to lower costs and increase reliability [57].

3.6.3 Energy Management System

The optimization in power distribution in the ESS technology for MG applications is possible through distributing the power of the energy management system (EMS). Some ESS, such as the CAES, and Li-ion batteries, are models for large integration, whereas medium-scale energy management is effective in TES, SMES, FBs, and fuel cells [31]. In order to design an effective EMS, the minimum device loss and SOC control will play a vital role in maximizing the output and retaining the future demand reserve [58], respectively. In addition, HESS can handle energy fluctuations, which enhance power efficiency and reduce the maximum rate of change of active power. The topology of battery/SC HESS is a good alternative for ongoing developments. Therefore, an EMS that improves overall efficiency and reduces costs can optimize advanced ESS control for MG appliances with reliable and stable features.

3.6.4 Impact on the Environment

Environmental impact studies have already shown that the emissions of greenhouse gas or other industrial pollutants have decreased as RESs increase. Fossil fuel combustion (CAES) and magnetic field (SMES), as well as recyclable materials and/or processed chemicals during production and disposal period, are causing environmental hazards. HESS should incorporate intermittent renews in the power grid so that fuel consumption and toxic emissions can be reduced [59]. Although RES production is 100% expensive [60], the researchers are aiming to reduce the cost of RES installation and maintenance for sustainable development.

3.6.5 Issues of Safety

ESS protection is the prerequisite for current MG applications. Different factors must be addressed adequately to ensure safe and secure processes, such as life cycle, material magnetic properties, temperature, short-circuit issues, and overcharge/discharge features of ESS. Temperature control mechanism is required for the devices as CAES, TES, and NaS batteries; SC is subject to high self-discharge rates; FCs need corrosive safety with lower and higher temperatures; lead-acid batteries requisite daily operation maintenance; and overcharging and over-discharging protection are required in Li-ion batteries [61]. Recent research can concentrate on solving these problems in order to make the system extremely user-friendly.

3.7   Conclusion

An ESS is one of the supporting systems in the future for smart grid designs. ESSs may encourage the integration of RESs by removing the changes in their electric power output. ESSs can encourage system stability and provide other auxiliary installations, including load follow-up, black start, and spinning reserve. In addition, ESSs can help offset peak loads, thereby reducing generator failures. A significant contribution to compensating for peak loads can be the sum of stored energy. This can raise the installed capacity of base generation units, which is also a major factor in price and energy usage.

The ESS seemed to be crucial to managing the complexity of new technology, evolving consumer habits, behaviours, shifting power generation processes, and changing supply networks over the last decade. In addition, it can make various grid functioning improvements, such as reliability, fast response, load matching ability, and so on. Key resource problems such as sustainability and environmental protection are aimed at diversifying energy sources and increasing the use of RES. Despite the short and long-term variability in RESs, the variance in energy generation involves some critical steps. Through their easy handling, reliability, consistency, and flexibility, energy storage is important to improve electric power grid system response capacity.

Effective storage of energy can compensate for precisely the difference between short-term and long-term levels of energy generation and consumption. The reliability and performance of power distribution systems will be improved by all of these developments. Some criteria for the correct selection of the ESS are investment costs, integrated design, power, energy density, electricity and energy levels, life cycles, response times, and efficiency. Therefore, the difference of use should be taken into account, either static or compact. For compact devices, energy storage capacity takes precedence.

This chapter shows that hybrid ESS is extremely attractive for MG applications in ensuring decent performance with reliable deployment.

This analysis addressed many causes, problems, and possible solutions and recommendations for ESSs of the following generation in MG implementations, which can lead to updating and enhancing existing ESS at an advanced level for academics, researchers and industries. Therefore, the main involvement of the chapter is the detailed analysis of various ESS integrations in MG applications to give the developed ESSs and their potential implementation in the MG network a thorough insight.

Acknowledgment

This work is supported by the Department of Science and Technology (DST), Government of India (GOI) with the project grant SR/FST/ETI-420/2016(C) under FIST scheme.

References

1. Nault, R.M., Basic research needs for solar energy utilization, Report of the basic energy sciences workshop on solar energy utilization, Argonne Natl Lab, 18–21, 2005. http://www.sc.doe.gov/bes/reports/files/SEU_rpt.pdf.
2. Guney, M.S., Evaluation and measures to increase performance coefficient of hydrokinetic turbines. Renewable and Sustainable Energy Reviews, 15(8), 3669–3675, 2011. https://doi.org/10.1016/j.rser.2011.07.009.
3. Zakeri, B., and Syri, S., Electrical energy storage systems: A comparative life cycle cost analysis. Renewable and Sustainable Energy Reviews, 42, 569–596, 2015. https://doi.org/10.1016/j.rser.2014.10.011.
4. Kumar, G.V.B., Kumar, G.A., Eswararao, S., and Gehlot, D., Modelling and Control of BESS for Solar Integration for PV Ramp Rate Control, 368–374, 2018. https://doi.org/10.1109/ICCPEIC.2018.8525173.
5. Solutions, E., *Electricity Storage: Technologies, impacts, and prospects*, (September) 2015.
6. Guney, M.S., and Tepe, Y., Classification and assessment of energy storage systems. Renewable and Sustainable Energy Reviews, 75, 1187–1197, 2017. https://doi.org/10.1016/j.rser.2016.11.102.
7. Amirante, R., Cassone, E., Distaso, E., and Tamburrano, P., Overview on recent developments in energy storage: Mechanical, electrochemical and hydrogen technologies, Energy Conversion and Management, 132, 372–387, 2017. https://doi.org/10.1016/j.enconman.2016.11.046.
8. Olivier, J.G.J., Janssens-Maenhout, G., Muntean, M., and Peters, J.A.H.W., Trends in global CO2 emissions: 2016 Report, PBL Netherlands Environ, Assessment Agency, The Hague, The Netherlands, Tech. Rep. 103425, 1–86, 2016.

9. Tan, X., Li, Q., and Wang, H., Advances and trends of energy storage technology in Microgrid, International Journal of Electrical Power and Energy Systems, 44(1), 179–191, 2013. https://doi.org/10.1016/j.ijepes.2012.07.015.

10. Katsanevakis, M., Stewart, R.A., and Lu, J., Aggregated applications and benefits of energy storage systems with application-specific control methods: A review, Renewable and Sustainable Energy Reviews, 75, 719–741, 2017. https://doi.org/10.1016/j.rser.2016.11.050.

11. Rohit, A.K., and Rangnekar, S., An overview of energy storage and its importance in Indian renewable energy sector: Part II—Energy storage applications, benefits and market potential, Journal of Energy Storage, 13, 447–456, 2017. https://doi.org/10.1016/j.est.2017.07.012.

12. Kumar, G., Sarojini, R., Palanisamy, K., Padmanaban, S., Holm-Nielsen, Large Scale Renewable Energy Integration: Issues and Solutions, Energies 2019, 12, 1996. https://doi.org/10.3390/en12101996.

13. Palizban, O., and Kauhaniemi, K., Energy storage systems in modern grids – Matrix of technologies and applications, Journal of Energy Storage, 6, 248–259, 2016. https://doi.org/10.1016/j.est.2016.02.001.

14. Aneke, M., and Wang, M., Energy storage technologies and real life applications—A state of the art review, Applied Energy, 179, 350–377, 2016. https://doi.org/10.1016/j.apenergy.2016.06.097.

15. Luo, X., Wang, J., Dooner, M., and Clarke, J., Overview of current development in electrical energy storage technologies and the application potential in power system operation, Applied Energy, 137, 511–536, 2015. https://doi.org/10.1016/j.apenergy.2014.09.081.

16. Amiryar, M.E., and Pullen, K.R., A Review of Flywheel Energy Storage System Technologies and Their Applications, Applied Sciences, 286, 1–21, 2017. https://doi.org/10.3390/app7030286.

17. Sebastian, R., and Alzola, R.P., Flywheel energy storage systems: Review and simulation for an isolated wind power system, Renewable and Sustainable Energy Reviews, 16, 6803–6813, 2012. https://doi.org/10.1016/j.rser.2012.08.008.

18. Mousavi, S.M.G., Faraji, F., Majazi, A., and Al-haddad, K., A comprehensive review of Flywheel Energy Storage System technology, Renewable and Sustainable Energy Reviews, 67, 477–490, 2017. https://doi.org/10.1016/j.rser.2016.09.060.

19. Zhao, P., Wang, J., and Dai, Y., Thermodynamic analysis of an integrated energy system based on compressed air energy storage (CAES) system and Kalina cycle, Energy Conversion and Management, 98, 161–172, 2015. https://doi.org/10.1016/j.enconman.2015.03.094.

20. Yao, E., Wang, H., Wang, L., Xi, G., and Maréchal, F., Thermo-economic optimization of a combined cooling, heating and power system based on small-scale compressed air energy storage, Energy Conversion and Management, 118, 377–386, 2016. https://doi.org/10.1016/j.enconman.2016.03.087.

21. Menéndez, J., Ordóñez, A., Álvarez, R., and Loredo, J., Energy from closed mines: Underground energy storage and geothermal applications, Renewable and Sustainable Energy Reviews, 108, 498–512, 2019. https://doi.org/10.1016/j.rser.2019.04.007.
22. Beevers, D., Branchini, L., Orlandini, V., Pascale, A. De, and Perez-blanco, H., Pumped hydro storage plants with improved operational flexibility using constant speed Francis runners, *Applied Energy*, 137, 629–637, 2015. https://doi.org/10.1016/j.apenergy.2014.09.065.
23. Al-hadhrami, L.M., Rehman, S., and Alam, M., Pumped hydro energy storage system: A technological review, Renewable and Sustainable Energy Reviews, 44, 586–598, 2015. https://doi.org/10.1016/j.rser.2014.12.040.
24. Koohi-Fayegh, S., Rosen, M.A., A review of energy storage types, applications and recent developments, Journal of Energy Storage, 27, 101047, 2020. https://doi.org/10.1016/j.est.2019.101047.
25. Niaz, S., Manzoor, T., and Hussain, A., Hydrogen storage: Materials, methods and perspectives, Renewable and Sustainable Energy Reviews, 50, 457–469, 2015. https://doi.org/10.1016/j.rser.2015.05.011.
26. Ehsan, S., and Wahid, M.A., Hydrogen production from renewable and sustainable energy resources: Promising green energy carrier for clean development, Renewable and Sustainable Energy Reviews, 57, 850–866, 2016. https://doi.org/10.1016/j.rser.2015.12.112.
27. Konstantinopoulos, S.A., Anastasiadis, A.G., Vokas, G.A., Kondylis, G.P., and Polyzakis, A., Optimal management of hydrogen storage in stochastic smart microgrid operation, *International Journal of Hydrogen Energy*, 43(1), 490–499, 2018. https://doi.org/10.1016/j.ijhydene.2017.06.116.
28. Nitta, N., Wu, F., Lee, J.T., and Yushin, G., Li-ion battery materials: present and future. Biochemical Pharmacology, 18(5), 252–264, 2015. https://doi.org/10.1016/j.mattod.2014.10.040.
29. Thackery, M.M., Wolverton. C., and Isaacs. E.D., Electrical energy storage for transportation-appraoching the limits of and going beyond, lithium-ion batteries, Energy & Enivironmental science, 5(7), 7854, 2012. https://doi.org/10.1039/c2ee21892e.
30. Bruce, P.G., Freunberger, S.A., Hardwick, L.J., and Tarascon, J.-M., Li–O2 and Li–S batteries with high energy storage, 11, 19–30, 2012. https://doi.org/10.1038/NMAT3191.
31. Chen, H., Ngoc, T., Yang, W., Tan, C., Li, Y., and Ding, Y., Progress in electrical energy storage system: A critical review, Progress in Natural Science, 19(3), 291–312, 2009. https://doi.org/10.1016/j.pnsc.2008.07.014.
32. Farhadi, M., and Mohammed, O., Energy Storage Technologies for High-Power Applications, IEEE Transactions on Industry Applications, 52(3), 1953–1961, 2016. https://doi.org/10.1109/TIA.2015.2511096.
33. Habib, H.F., Mohamed, A.A.S., Hariri, M. El, and Mohammed, O.A., Utilizing supercapacitors for resiliency enhancements and adaptive microgrid

protection against communication failures, *Electric Power Systems Research*, 145, 223–233, 2017. https://doi.org/10.1016/j.epsr.2016.12.027.

34. Wagner, L., Overview of energy storage methods, 2007. ⟨http://www.moraas-sociates.com/publications/0712%20Energy%20storage.pdf⟩

35. Gong, K., Shi, J., Liu, Y., Wang, Z., Ren, L., and Zhang, Y., Application of SMES in the Microgrid Based on Fuzzy Control, IEEE Transactions on Applied Superconductivity, 26(3), 1–5, 2016. https://doi.org/10.1109/TASC.2016.2524446.

36. Molina, M.G., Mercado, P.E., Power Flow Stabilization and Control of Microgrid with Wind Generation by Superconducting Magnetic Energy Storage, IEEE Transactions on Power Electronics, 26(3), 910–922, 2011. https://doi.org/10.1109/TPEL.2010.2097609.

37. Pan, A.V, Macdonald, L., Baiej, H., and Cooper, P., Theoretical Consideration of Superconducting Coils for Compact Superconducting Magnetic Energy Storage Systems, *IEEE Transactions on Applied Superconductivity*, 26(3), 1–5, 2016. https://doi.org/10.1109/TASC.2016.2533564.

38. Electrical energy storage, White paper, International Electrotechnical Commission, Geneve, 2011. https://www.iec.ch/whitepaper/energystorage/

39. Cabeza, L.F., Martorell, I., Miro, L., Fernandez, A.I., Barreneche, C., Introduction to thermal energy storage (TES) systems, A volume in Woodhead Publishing Series in Energy, 1–28, 2015. https://doi:10.1533/9781782420965.1.

40. Pfleger, N,. Bauer, T., Martin, C., Eck, M., and Wörner, A., Thermal energy storage—Overview and specific insight into nitrate salts for sensible and latent heat storage, Beilstein J Nanotechnology, 6, 1487–1497, 2015. https://doi:10.3762/bjnano.6.154.

41. Pelay, U., Luo, L., Fan, Y., Stitou, D., and Rood, M., Thermal energy storage systems for concentrated solar power plants, Renewable and Sustainable Energy Reviews, 79, 82–100, 2017. https://doi.org/10.1016/j.rser.2017.03.139.

42. Bales, C., Thermal Properties of Materials for Thermo-chemical Storage of Solar Heat, IEA Solar Heating and Cooling Programme, 1–20, 2005.

43. Hemmati, R., and Saboori, H., Emergence of hybrid energy storage systems in renewable energy and transport applications—A review, Renewable and Sustainable Energy Reviews, 65, 11–23, 2016. https://doi.org/10.1016/j.rser.2016.06.029.

44. Jing, W., Hung, C., Wong, W.S.H., and Wong, M.L.D., Dynamic power allocation of battery-supercapacitor hybrid energy storage for standalone PV microgrid applications, *Sustainable Energy Technologies and Assessments*, 22, 55–64, 2017. https://doi.org/10.1016/j.seta.2017.07.001.

45. Li, J., Antony. M., Zhang, M., and Yuan, W., Analysis of battery, lifetime extension in a SMES-battery hybrid energy storage system using a novel battery lifetime model, Energy, 86, 175-185, 2015. http://dx.doi.org/10.1016/j.energy.2015.03.132.

46. Khaligh, A., Li, Z., Battery, Ultracapacitor, Fuel Cell, and Hybrid Energy Storage Systems for Electric, Hybrid Electric, Fuel Cell, and Plug-In Hybrid

Electric Vehicles: State of the Art, IEEE Transactions on Vehicular Technology, 59(6), 2806–2814, 2010. https://doi.org/10.1109/TVT.2010.2047877.

47. Martin, I.S., Ursu, A., and Sanchis, P., Integration of fuel cells and supercapacitors in electrical microgrids: Analysis, modelling and experimental validation, International Journal of Hydrogen Energy, 38, 11655-11671, 2013. https://doi.org/10.1016/j.ijhydene.2013.06.098.

48. Etxeberria, A., Vechiu, I., Camblong, H., and Vinassa, J., Comparison of three topologies and controls of a hybrid energy storage system for microgrids, Energy Conversion and Management, 54(1), 113–121, 2012. https://doi.org/10.1016/j.enconman.2011.10.012.

49. Staff Paper on Introduction of Electricity Storage System in India, Central Electricity Regulatory Commission New Delhi, 2017.

50. India Energy, GoI, User Guide for India's 2047 Energy, Electrical Energy Storage, 2017. http://indiaenergy.gov.in/iess/docs/Storage %20Documentation.pdf.

51. Rampersadh, N., Davidson, I.E., Grid Energy Storage Devices, IEEE PES-IAS PowerAfrica, 121–125, 2017.

52. Serban, E., Ordonez, M., & Pondiche, C., Voltage and Frequency Grid Support Strategies Beyond Standards, IEEE Transactions on Power Electronics, 32(1), 298–309, 2017. https://doi.org/10.1109/TPEL.2016.2539343.

53. Karanasios, E., Ampatzis, M., Phuong, H., and Kling, W.L., A Model for the Estimation of the Cost of Use of Li-Ion batteries in residential storage applications integrated with PV panels, 49th International Universities Power Engineering Conference (UPEC), 1–6, 2014. https://doi.org/10.1109/UPEC.2014.6934739.

54. Lichtner, S. Advanced Materials and Devices for Stationary Electrical Energy Storage Applications, U. S. Department of Energy, 2010.

55. Vazquez, S., Lukic, S. M., Galvan, E., Franquelo, L.G., and Carrasco, J.M., Energy Storage Systems for Transport and Grid Applications, IEEE Transactions on Industrial Electronics, 57(12), 3881–3895, 2010. https://doi.org/10.1109/TIE.2010.2076414.

56. Alsaidan, I., Khodaei, A., and Gao, W., A Comprehesive Battery Energy Storage Optimal Sizing Model for Microgrid Applications, IEEE Transactions on Power Systems, 33(4), 3968–3980, 2018. https://doi.org/10.1109/TPWRS.2017.2769639.

57. Berkel, K. Van, Rullens, S., Hofman, T., Vroemen, B., Steinbuch, M., Topology and Flywheel Size Optimization for Mechanical Hybrid Powertrains, IEEE Transactions on Vehicular Technology, 63(9), 4192–4205, 2014. https://doi.org/10.1109/TVT.2014.2312646.

58. Jiang, W., Zhang, L., Zhao, H., Huang, H., and Hu, R., Research on power sharing strategy of hybrid energy storage system in photovoltaic power station based on multi-objective optimisation, IET Renewable Power Generation, 10, 575–583, 2016. https://doi.org/10.1049/iet-rpg.2015.0199.

59. Halabi, L.M., Mekhilef, S., Olatomiwa, L., and Hazelton, J., Performance analysis of hybrid PV/diesel/battery system using HOMER: A case study

Sabah, Malaysia, Energy Conversion and Management, 144, 322–339, 2017. https://doi.org/10.1016/j.enconman.2017.04.070.

60. Somma, M. Di, Yan, B., Bianco, N., Graditi, G., Luh, P.B., Mongibello, L., and Naso, V., Operation optimization of a distributed energy system considering energy costs and exergy efficiency, Energy Conversion and Management, 103, 739–751, 2015. https://doi.org/10.1016/j.enconman.2015.07.009.

61. Lippert, M., Li-ion energy storage takes microgrids to the next level, Reinforced Plastics, 17(4), 159–161, 2016. https://doi.org/10.1016/j.ref.2016.07.001.

4

Single Phase Inverter Fuzzy Logic Phase Locked Loop

Maxwell Sibanyoni, S.P. Daniel Chowdhury* and L.J. Ngoma

Department of Electrical Engineering, Tshwane University of Technology (TUT), Pretoria, South Africa

Abstract

This chapter presents the implementation of a Fuzzy Logic Control (FLC) in the Loop Filter of the Second Order Generalized Integrator Phase Locke Loop (SOGI PLL) which improves the performance of the PLL instead of the conventional Proportional Integral Control in the Loop Filter. The performance of the proposed SOGI FLC PLL is evaluated against other PLL models simulated in Matlab/Simulink. The results reveal that the use of the FLC improves the performance of the SOGI PLL, it has better performance which is less overshoot and quicker settling time than the other PLL models simulated.

Keywords: Solar PV, single phase grid, inverter, maximum power point, maximum power point tracking, time step

4.1 Introduction

Conventionally residential grid connected solar photovoltaic (PV) systems were designed to disconnect from the grid when the grid has disturbances such as voltage sags. The solar PV systems were expected to trip within specific time constrains. This operating mode cannot offer the required reliability, stability and availability required by the modern distribution networks which are having a large penetration of renewable energy sources, mainly single phase solar PV systems [1].

---

*Corresponding author: spchowdhury2010@gmail.com

C. Sharmeela, P. Sivaraman, P. Sanjeevikumar, and Jens Bo Holm-Nielsen (eds.) Microgrid Technologies, (91–120) © 2021 Scrivener Publishing LLC

Solar Photovoltaic Inverters need to be able to operate under faults such as noise, low voltage ride and harmonics. Phase angle and frequency control are an essential part of the solar inverter synchronization within grid specifications. Phase Locked Loop (PLL) is the predominantly used synchronization topology in three phase and single phase solar inverters. Most PLL structures implement PI control in their Loop Filter however PI control has disadvantages such the control parameters are obtained through trial and error based procedures. Earlier research has focused mainly on improving the performance of the Phase Detector (PD) component of the PLL structure while this chapter focuses on improving the Loop Filter (LF).

In this chapter a Fuzzy Logic Control in the Loop Filter of the Second Order Generalized Integrator PLL (SOGI PLL) is modeled in Matlab/Simulink. Multiple PLL synchronization techniques are studied and modeled in Matlab/Simulink to gain insight on the operation of various PLL techniques. The stability issues likely to arise from the proposed synchronization model are analyzed on the models simulated in Matlab/Simulink for a single phase system.

In the following sections, descriptions of the various elements that make up a complete single-phase photovoltaic (PV) generator system suitable for connecting to the grid system are presented and their suitability to modeling are evaluated. The well-known models in Matlab/Simulink are interfaced with the photovoltaic generator to complete the single-phase connected grid system. To prove how valid the chosen approach is, the simulation results of the voltage and current waveforms and the harmonic content are compared with results from field measurement. The results of the photovoltaic generator with Maximum Power Point Tracking (MPPT) are compared with the generator without a MPPT system incorporated. The MPPT enables the PV generator to produce continuous maximum power most of the time. The MPPT continuously finds the voltage at maximum point or the current to enable maximum power to be produced.

4.2 PLL Synchronization Techniques

The traditional control strategy applied to the single phase converter system includes two cascaded loops: an inner current loop which is responsible for power quality issues and current protection and an outer voltage control loop. In this case, it is possible to add control methods into the inner loop in single-phase systems in grid fault mode operations to support the grid [2]. The overall structure of a single-phase grid-connected PV system is given in Figure 4.1 [2].

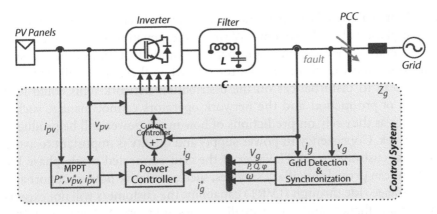

Figure 4.1 Overall control structure of a single-phase grid-connected PV system.

Grid tied power tuning systems all depend on the efficient operation of the synchronization technique used, therefore synchronization to the utility grid is an important aspect for applications such as active power filters, dynamic voltage restorers, uninterruptible power supplies, and distributed power generation and storage systems. Phase, amplitude and frequency of the utility voltage are critical information for the operation of the grid-connected inverter systems [3]. The operation of such systems needs to be instantaneous and the data accusation needs to be precise. The synchronization process needs to comply with the local and international regulatory standards or specifications. To ensure that the system generates correct reference signals the detection of the phase angle, amplitude and frequency of the utility voltage needs to be quick and accurate. A diverse range of synchronization topologies have been presented in recent years. Zero crossing detection based method which has a time delay slightly greater than half grid period and is able to obtain the grid frequency fast and accurate even with big noise [4]. Kalman filtering, digital Fourier transform and its modifications, recursive weighted least squares estimation algorithms, artificial neural networks, the methods based on the concept of adaptive notch filter, and phase-locked loop (PLL)-based algorithms, are among the existing synchronization techniques [5]. Due to their simplicity, robustness and effectives, synchronization techniques based on PLL have gained more interest in single phase systems [2, 6].

Conventionally residential grid connected solar PV systems were designed to disconnect from the grid when the grid has disturbances such as voltage sags. The solar PV systems were expected to trip within specific time constrains. This operating mode cannot offer the required reliability, stability and availability required by the modern distribution networks which are having a large penetration of renewable energy sources mainly single phase solar PV systems. With a large penetration of single phase grid connected PV systems, an operation mode that allows the PV system to suddenly disconnect from the grid when there is a small grid fault could lead to disturbances on the distribution network. This could lead to loss of production and the network operators cannot manage such a network as they rely on predictions of how much power will be produced each week. Consistency in power supply and quality is important to avoid faults at customer level. However, if the grid-connected single-phase PV systems can provide ancillary services, such as reactive power support and low-voltage ride through (LVRT) capability, the customers will not experience many flickers and power quality issues anymore. Network operators will be willing to have more PV integration into their grids. Due to the infinite nature of solar energy, solar PV systems have a higher prospect of penetrating the electrical energy market. Technological advancements that are currently on going mean that PV systems will become more smart and easier to manage. More capabilities and functionality of the PV systems are being developed.

The basic structure of any PLL consists of three blocks: a phase detector (PD), a loop filter (LF) and a voltage controlled oscillator (VCO) [7]. The input of the PLL is a continuous time sinusoidal signal or the zero crossing signals which is compared with output of the VCO in the PD. The high order harmonics in the phase error can be filtered out with the LF and the output modifies the frequency of the VCO. The feedback action is such that the phase error is forced to zero. When zero error is achieved, the input signal is sampled exactly at zero crossings and the PLL is locked [8]. All PLLs have this basic structure and differ mainly through the various methods in the implementation of the PD. The basic structure of the PLL is given in Figure 4.2 [8].

Single phase PLL synchronization topologies mainly differ in the phase detector design. There are a number of techniques to generate the

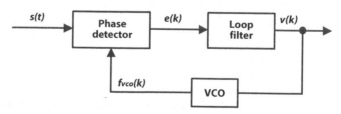

Figure 4.2 Basic structure of the PLL.

orthogonal voltage and each topology has its own advantages and disadvantages. The common methods used in the technical literature make use of the transport delay block, Hilbert transformation, Inverse Park transformation. However, these methods have one or more of the following shortcomings: frequency dependency, high complexity, nonlinearity, poor or no filtering. Therefore, more attention should be paid on single-phase PLL systems [5].

Four typical single-phase PLL topologies described in this dissertation are the T/4 Delay PLL, PLL based on Inverse Park Transform (IPT-PLL), Enhanced PLL (EPLL) and Second Order Generalized Integrator based PLL (SOGI-OSG). The former two methods are trying to build a d_q system by incorporating an Orthogonal Signal Generator system, while EPLL and SOGI-OSG methods are based on the combinations of adaptive filters with a sinusoidal multiplier and an Orthogonal Signal Generator (OSG) system, respectively [9]. Other single-phase PLL solutions and none PLL methods have been reviewed to achieve the goal of developing a better synchronization method that will best suit the South African grid requirements.

4.2.1 T/4 Transport Delay PLL

A T/4 Transport Delay PLL uses a T/4 delay block set to one fourth of the number of samples contained in one cycle of the fundamental frequency, to generate the quadrature signal to obtain the d_q components when the nominal grid frequency time period is represented by T. The park transform is then used to detect the phase which is defined as:

$$\begin{bmatrix} v_d \\ v_q \end{bmatrix} = \begin{bmatrix} cos\hat{\theta} & sin\hat{\theta} \\ -sin\hat{\theta} & cos\hat{\theta} \end{bmatrix} \begin{bmatrix} v_\alpha \\ v_\beta \end{bmatrix} \tag{4.1}$$

Where $\Delta\theta = \theta - \hat{\theta}$ is the detected phase error, and $\hat{\theta}$ is the locked phase. In steady state conditions the error $\Delta\theta$ is small [2]. The T/4 Delay PLL topology is not suitable due to its susceptibility to the input grid conditions. It does not provide the required robustness during voltage sags or frequency variations. In other words, the frequency variation is a challenge to the robustness of T/4 Delay PLL technique. Below is the structure of the T/4 delay PLL Figure 4.3 [2].

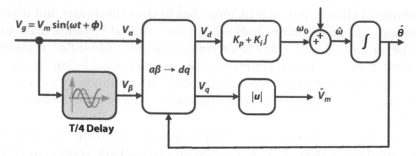

Figure 4.3 Structure of the T/4 delay PLL.

4.2.2   Inverse Park Transform PLL

The Inverse Park Transform $(d_q \rightarrow \alpha\beta)$ is made up of $(d_q \rightarrow \alpha\beta)$ and $(\alpha\beta \rightarrow d_q)$ blocks. It consists of two Low Pass Filters which feedback the outputs of the Direct Park Transform $(\alpha\beta \rightarrow d_q)$ as shown in Figure 4.4 [10]. The Inverse Park is defined as [11]:

$$
\begin{bmatrix} v_\alpha \\ v_\beta \end{bmatrix} = \begin{bmatrix} cos\hat{\theta} & -sin\hat{\theta} \\ sin\hat{\theta} & cos\hat{\theta} \end{bmatrix} \begin{bmatrix} v_d \\ v_q \end{bmatrix}
\tag{4.2}
$$

The Inverse Park Transform PLL is easy to implement but the Low Pass Filters require accurate tuning. The Inverse Park Transform performs better than the T/4 Delay PLL when it comes to harmonic rejection due to its structure having two Low Pass Filters. However the only draw down of the Inverse Park Transform is its dependence on the Low Pass Filter as defined by [2]:

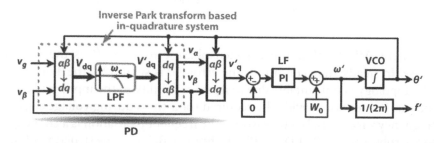

Figure 4.4 Inverse Park Transform based PLL.

$$\begin{bmatrix} v_\alpha \\ v_\beta \end{bmatrix} = \begin{bmatrix} \dfrac{w_c(s)}{s^2 + w_c(s) + w'^2} \\ \dfrac{w_c w'}{s^2 + w_c(s) + w'^2} \end{bmatrix} v_g \qquad (4.3)$$

v_g is the input grid voltage.

4.2.3   Enhanced PLL

The Enhanced PLL (EPLL) is made up of an Adaptive Notch Filter and a sinusoidal multiplier in the PD section of the PLL. The Adaptive Notch Filter and sinusoidal multiplier are then combined with the traditional structure of the PLL (LF and VCO). The Enhanced PLL technique is different from other synchronization techniques because it generates a 90° shift of the input signal without generating a quadrature signal. The locked phase $\hat{\theta}$ and the detected phase error ε are used by the Adaptive Filter to approximate the amplitude of the input voltage v_i [9]. The output of the Adaptive Filter $\hat{v}_i$ that is required when all the PLL parameters are adequately tuned is defined as:

$$\hat{v}_i = \hat{V}_m sin\hat{\theta} \qquad (4.4)$$

The filter parameters are tuned by automatic repetitive computation

$$\hat{V}_m(k+1) = \hat{V}_m(k) + \Delta\hat{V}_m(k) \qquad (4.5)$$

Where $\hat{V}_m$ is the approximated amplitude of the input voltage, k is the iterating number and $\Delta\hat{V}_m$ is the correction term whose function is to minimize the quadrature estimate of the objective function. From Equation (4.4) it can be seen that the output signal $\hat{v}_i$ is locked in phase θ and amplitude. The stability and settling time response of the EPLL is solely dependent on the control parameter k_a which gives too many emphases on tuning the control parameter k_a [2]. The structure of the Enhanced PLL is shown in Figure 4.5 below [10].

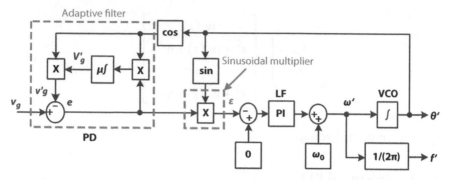

Figure 4.5 Enhanced PLL.

4.2.4 Second Order Generalized Integrator Orthogonal Signal Generator Synchronous Reference Frame (SOGI-OSG SRF) PLL

The Second Order Generalized Integrator Orthogonal Signal Generator PLL (SOGI-OSG) is made up of two adaptive filters. The SOGI-OSG generates two orthogonal signals v_α and v_β. v_α is in phase and has the same amplitude as the grid input voltage. v_β has 90° phase shift from the input voltage but has the same amplitude [12]. The transfer functions of the SOGI block are defined as:

$$G_\alpha(s) = \frac{v_\alpha}{v_i}(s) = \frac{kw_o s}{s^2 + kw_o s + w_o^2} \tag{4.6}$$

$$G_\beta(s) = \frac{v_\beta}{v_i}(s) = \frac{kw_o^2}{s^2 + kw_o s + w_o^2} \tag{4.7}$$

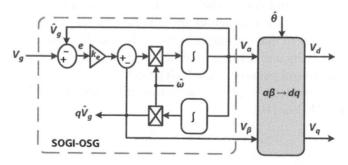

Figure 4.6 Phase Detector of the SOGI PLL.

Where v_i is the grid voltage and w_o is the grid nominal frequency. The orthogonal signals generated by the SOGI-OSG are fed through to the LF and the VCO of the PLL [13]. The structure of the PD of the SOGI PLL is given in Figure 4.6 [2].

4.2.5   Cascaded Generalized Integrator PLL (CGI-PLL)

In Refs. [14, 15] a Cascaded Generalized Integrator PLL with fixed gain parameters is presented. A Cascaded Generalized Integrator PLL consists of two blocks of second order generalized integrator in cascaded form which is connected to a synchronous reference frame PLL as shown in Figure 4.7 [15].

The cascaded generalized integrator PLL is able to remove the dc offset because the dc gain in the transfer functions of both v_α and v_β is zero therefore the dc offset will not show on the embedded synchronous reference frame PLL. The transfer functions for the orthogonal voltages are as follows:

$$G_{\alpha,c}(s)=\frac{v_\alpha}{v_g}(s)=\frac{(kw_os)^2}{(s^2+kw_os+w_o^2)^2} \tag{4.8}$$

$$G_{\alpha,c}(s)=\frac{v_\beta}{v_g}(s)=\frac{k^2w_o^3s}{(s^2+kw_os+w_o^2)^2} \tag{4.9}$$

Where v_α and v_β are the orthogonal voltages from the grid voltage. v_g is the grid voltage, k is the gain and w_o is the nominal fundamental frequency of the grid voltage.

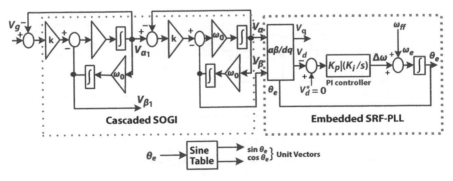

Figure 4.7 Cascaded Generalized Integrator PLL (CGI-PLL).

Each second order generalized integrator subsystem reduces harmonic distortion from the systems, therefore the total harmonic distortion of less than 1% is achieved. The system achieves total harmonic distortion of less than 1% by determining the highest bandwidth that gives a total harmonic distortion of 1% or less.

4.2.6 Cascaded Delayed Signal Cancellation PLL

In Refs. [14, 16] a Cascaded Delayed Signal Cancellation PLL (CDSC-PLL) is presented which is able to compensate for wider range of harmonics and current imbalances without too much computational burden and less complexity. The structure of the CDSC-PLL is shown in Figure 4.8 [16]. The CDSC-PLL consists of a cascaded connection of delayed cancellation blocks which achieves the requirement of unwanted harmonic attenuation by using a delayed operation principle that makes it possible to separate different frequencies that occur in the same time space. The Delayed Signal Cancellation operator transfer function is given by

$$v_{\alpha\beta}^h(t) = \frac{1}{2}\left(v_{\alpha\beta}^h(t) + e^{-j\theta_r}v_{\alpha\beta}^h\left(t - \frac{T}{n}\right)\right)$$

(4.10)

$$v_{\alpha\beta}^h(t) = Gv_{\alpha\beta}^h(t)$$

(4.11)

G represents the harmonic gain, T represents the fundamental period and is the chosen rotational vector.

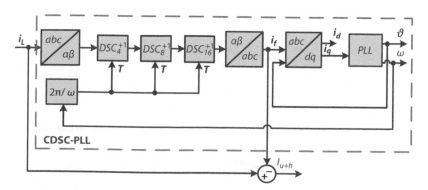

Figure 4.8 Cascaded Delayed Signal Cancellation Phase Locked Loop (CDSC-PLL).

$$G = \frac{1 + e^{-j}(\theta_r + \theta_n)}{2} \qquad (4.12)$$

$$G = Ge^{j\theta} \qquad (4.13)$$

The Cascaded Delayed Signal Cancellation method achieves the attenuation of unwanted harmonics by making the harmonic gain equal to zero for all instances except for when the harmonic order is equal to the targeted harmonic order for which then results in a harmonic gain of unity.

$$\theta_r = -\frac{2\pi h^*}{n} \qquad (4.14)$$

h Represents the harmonic order and h^* represents the targeted harmonic order

$$G = \frac{Cos(\theta_r + \theta_n)}{2} \qquad (4.15)$$

$$\varnothing = -\frac{\theta_r + \theta_n}{2} \qquad (4.16)$$

In order to eliminate unwanted harmonic, the harmonic gain $G = 0$ in Equation (4.15) then $n = 2(h - h^*)$.

4.3   Fuzzy Logic Control

Fuzzy logic is a control systems theory that is based on artificial intelligence (AI), with its application varying from various control systems, estimation systems, identification, and optimization systems. Fuzzy logic control like a human operator depends on a base of knowledge and its knowledge relies on a set of linguistic if-then rules. Linguistic variables are used to implement the if-then rules. Fuzzy logic rules are designed from numerical variables which must be converted to linguistic variables. When systems are too complicated for standard model based control techniques and the systems have non-linear characteristics, fuzzy logic control (FLC) is the best solution as it is able to handle systems that do not have precise data points defined. Fuzzy logic control handles systems that have vagueness and uncertainty. Using fuzzy logic control systems have the following advantages:

- A mathematical or analytical model of the system to be controlled is not needed
- Is able to operate nonlinear systems,
- Is able to tolerate with inaccuracies and noise in the system to be controlled.

In general, FLC consists of several components, namely the establishment of fuzzy sets, followed by determining membership functions, then setting fuzzy rules in line with the membership functions and lastly then defuzzification. As shown in Figure 4.9 [17], the fuzzification section is relying on the data from the membership function, the inference engine gets its control settings from the rule base whilst defuzzification relies on the membership function output.

The fuzzifier transforms crisp inputs to linguistic variables using membership functions which are kept in the fuzzy knowledge base. The fuzzy output of the inference engine is turned into binary values by means of the membership functions that are homogenous to the ones used by the fuzzifier. What makes fuzzy logic control more significant from other control systems is its ability to convert imprecise input data into desired outputs. Therefore, the fuzzy logic system is regarded to be a nonlinear mapping of an input into a real number.

Mamdani and Sugeno or r Takogi–Sugeno–Kang Method are there two widely used fuzzy inference systems [18]. The Mamdani fuzzy system rule consequent is based on fuzzy sets while the Takogi-Sugeno (TS) uses different linear functions of input variables as rule consequent. Almost all the

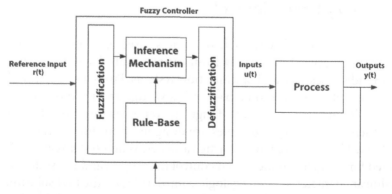

Figure 4.9 Basic Structure of Fuzzy Logic Controller.

practical Takagi-Sugeno fuzzy systems use linear functions in rule consequent, which is crucial to their practicality and usefulness. This is because when a nonlinear rule consequent is used, properly choosing the structure and parameters of the rule consequent becomes extremely difficult. Advantages of Mamdani method are it is well enhanced to human input and has widespread acceptance. The aspect of variables monitored during simulations decides the values of the variables and the membership functions are assigned off-line. The control rules are represented by a set of chosen fuzzy rules.

Fuzzy logic control is chosen as the preferred method because it is best suited for systems that have unpredictability such as solar PV systems due to the unpredictability of the sun. Fuzzy logic systems are easier to implement because they use natural language and require less mathematical computation compared to other systems. Fuzzy logic systems provide quicker responses and they require less cost as compared to other control systems for the same application [19]. Fuzzy logic control is chosen over PI control systems as PI control uses fixed proportional and integral gain which cannot automatically change when the grid experiences sudden disturbances [20].

4.4   Fuzzy Logic PLL Model

The structure of the Fuzzy Logic Control scheme consists of three main functions. Fuzzification function which relies on data from the membership function, the inference engine function which gets its control settings from the rule base and defuzzification function which relies on the membership function output.

4.4.1   Fuzzification

The membership function values are allocated to linguistic variables using five fuzzy subsets named: Negative Big (NB), Negative Medium (NM), Zero (Z), Positive Medium (PM) and Positive Big (PB). The signals e and Δe are selected as inputs to FLC in some cases as shown in Figures 4.10 to 4.15. The membership function values which use 3 fuzzy subsets named: Negative Big (NB), Medium (M) and Positive Big (PB) are shown in Figure 4.11. Membership function values which use 5 fuzzy subsets are shown in Figure 4.15.

The signal e is the output of the alpha-beta to d_q transform block which is then added with a zero, the signal Δe is the change in error in the sampling period of time. In the first stage, the crisp variables of errors are converted into fuzzy variables using the triangle shape as shown in Figure 4.11, and each fuzzy variable is a member of the subsets with a degree of membership varying between −250 and 250.

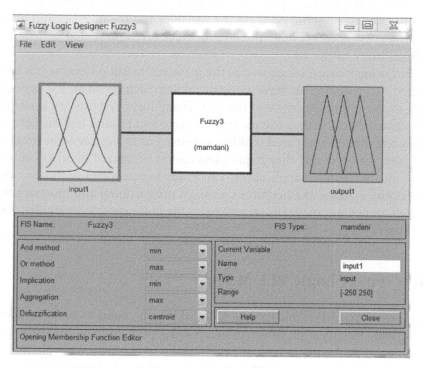

Figure 4.10 Single input and single output Fuzzy Logic Control Structure.

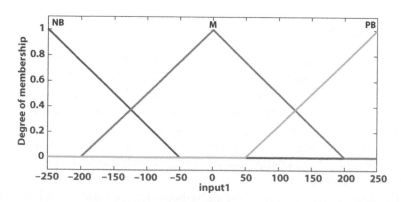

Figure 4.11 Single input Membership function.

4.4.2   Inference Engine

The inputs converted into fuzzy values are transmitted to the interface engine which is made up of fuzzy rule base and fuzzy implication

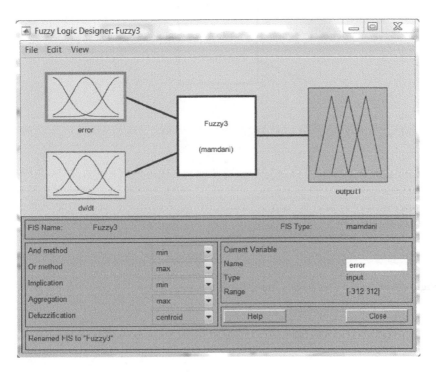

Figure 4.12 3 × 3 Fuzzy Logic Control Structure.

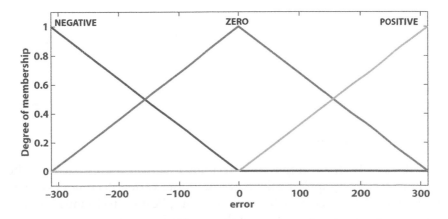

Figure 4.13 Membership function of 3 × 3 fuzzy set.

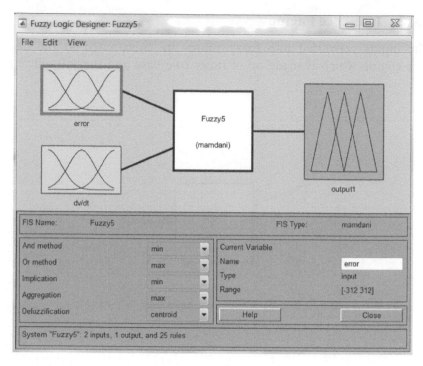

Figure 4.14 5 × 5 Fuzzy Logic Control Structure.

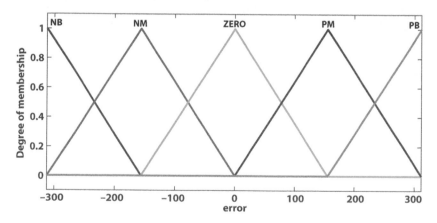

Figure 4.15 Membership function of 5 × 5 fuzzy set.

sub-blocks. The fuzzy implication technique is then used to achieve the output fuzzy set by applying the fuzzy rule base. Various techniques can be applied for this process such as max-min implication technique. Figures 4.16 to 4.18 show the rules-base of the designed system.

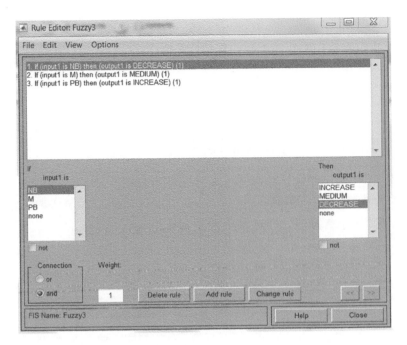

Figure 4.16 Rule base for single input fuzzy set.

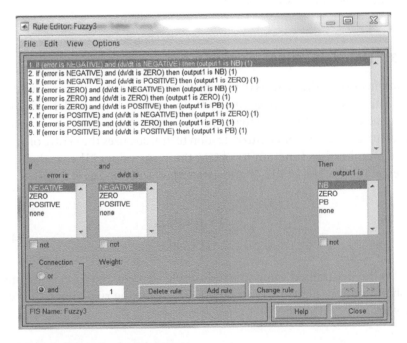

Figure 4.17 Rule base for 3 × 3 fuzzy set.

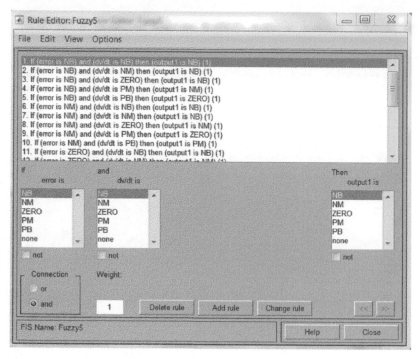

Figure 4.18 Rule base for 5 × 5 fuzzy set.

4.4.3   Defuzzification

Defuzzification is the process of interpreting the inference engine output into real values. The fuzzy centroid method is the commonly used defuzzification technique however there are many various other defuzzification techniques in literature. The centroid defuzzification technique uses the centre of gravity of the membership function to obtain the crisp values. The mathematical representation of the centre of gravity method is defined as [16, 21]

$$X^* = \frac{\int x.\mu_c(x)dx}{\int \mu_c(x)dx} \tag{4.17}$$

X^* is the defuzzified value, x is the sample element and $\mu_c(x)$ is the membership function. Figure 4.19 to Figure 4.21 show the rule-viewers for each fuzzy set.

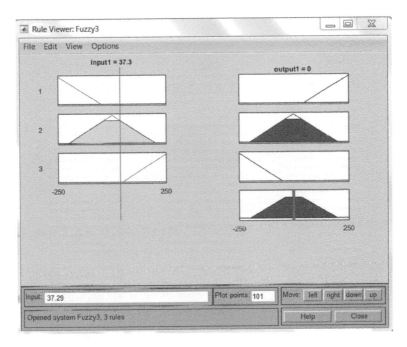

Figure 4.19 Rule viewer for single input fuzzy set.

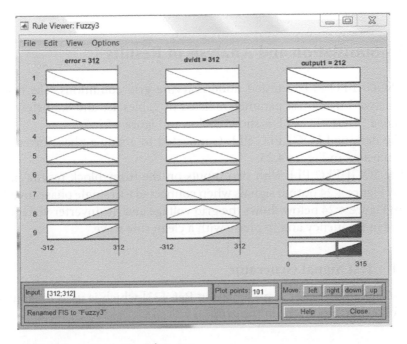

Figure 4.20 Rule viewer for 3 × 3 fuzzy set.

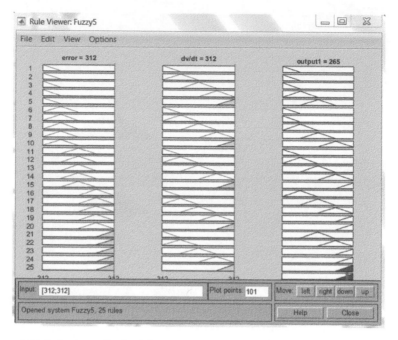

Figure 4.21 Rule viewer for 5 × 5 fuzzy set.

4.5   Simulation and Analysis of Results

The SOGI FLC PLL is tested under varying grid conditions. The results are analyzed using test parameters listed in Tables 4.1 and 4.2 below. The designed SOGI FLC PLL is shown below in Figure 4.22.

The designed SOGI FLC PLL Connected to a single phase inverter is shown below in Figure 4.23.

The SOGI FLC PLL with two inputs on the fuzzy block results in the below Figure 4.24 output signals when connected to a single phase inverter. From Figure 4.24 below shows the grid voltage and the inverter voltage are locked in frequency and in phase with a clean sine wave.

4.5.1   Test Signal Generator

A test signal generator is presented in Ref. [23] which is used to simulate the following conditions in the grid:

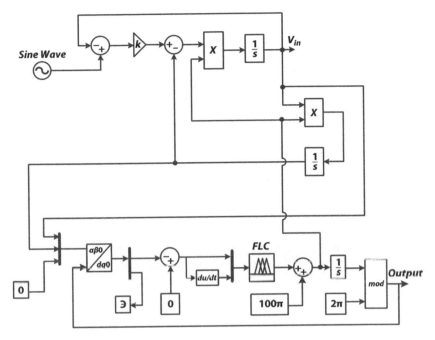

Figure 4.22 SOGI two inputs and one output FLC PLL structure.

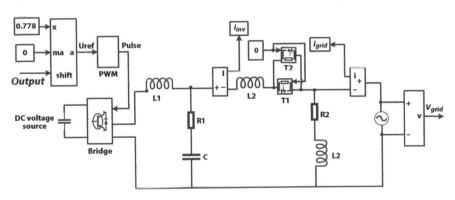

Figure 4.23 SOGI two inputs and one output FLC PLL connected to a single phase inverter.

- Harmonic interference
- Periodic pulses
- Noise

Figure 4.25 shows the test signal generator which is developed in Matlab/ Simulink [23] and Figure 4.26 shows the test signal generator connected to

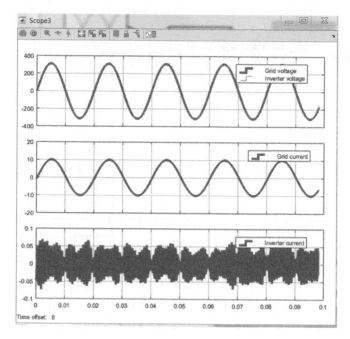

Figure 4.24 (a) Inverter output voltage compared with grid voltage, (b) Grid current, (c) Inverter output current.

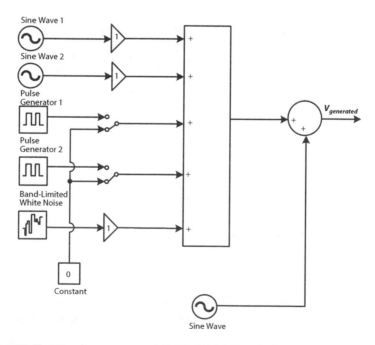

Figure 4.25 Test signal generator modelled in Matlab/Simulink.

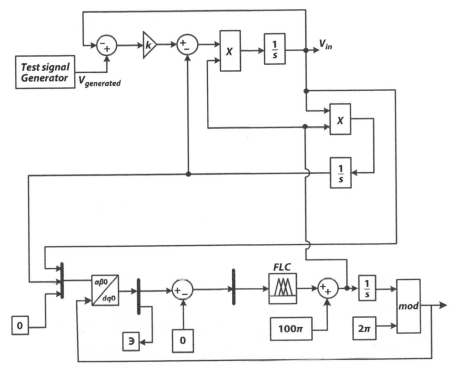

Figure 4.26 Test signal generator connected to SOGI FLC PLL.

the developed SOGI FLC PPL model to demonstrate the performance of the SOGI FLC PLL under various fault conditions in the network.

4.5.2 Proposed SOGI FLC PLL Performance Under Fault Conditions

4.5.2.1 Test Case 1

On the initial test case, the SOGI FLC PLL is examined on its ability to lock on a pure sinusoidal waveform. The test signal generator outputs from the harmonics, pulse interference and all noise are disabled. The generated PLL output voltage and the input grid voltage are in phase. Figure 4.27 below shows the grid voltage and the generated SOGI FLC PLL output voltage. It takes less than 1 cycle for the generated signal to be synchronized with the grid signal. The synchronization takes place at 15 ms. The voltage error which is produced from the difference between the grid signal and the generated signal settles at 30 ms to zero error.

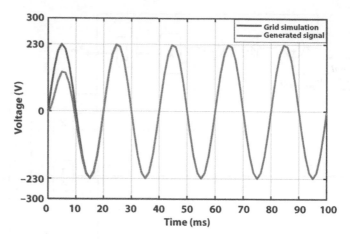

Figure 4.27 SOGI FLC PLL under no fault condition.

4.5.2.2   Test Case 2

On the second test case, a signal that has 5% third harmonic (150 Hz) and 6% fifth harmonic (250 Hz) is added to the fundamental sinusoidal wave, there is no phase shift added, the equations for this input signal is presented in Equation (4.19). Figure 4.28 reflects the behaviour of the SOGI FLC PLL which indicates that their input grid voltage and the PLL output voltage are in phase. The zero crossing in the first harmonic is not affected by the higher harmonics and zero crossing occurs at 10 ms. The voltage error which is produced from the difference between the grid signal and the generated is 20 V.

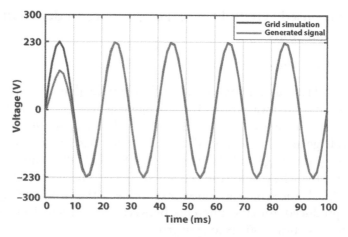

Figure 4.28 SOGI FLC PLL under 3rd and 5th harmonic conditions.

$$w = 2\pi f = 2\pi\ 50 \tag{4.18}$$

$$y(t) = \sin(wt) + 0.05\sin(3wt) + 0.06\sin(5wt) \tag{4.19}$$

4.5.2.3   Test Case 3

In this case, a phase shift is added to the harmonics which were added in test case 2 above. This addition of the phase is reflected by Equation (4.20) below. Figure 4.29 shows that the SOGI FLC PLL has the ability lock on the signal and there is no shift on the generated output of the PLL. At 10 ms the first harmonics experience the zero cross which is similar to the result in test case 2. The voltage error which is produced from the difference between the grid signal and the generated is 20 V.

$$y(t) = \sin(wt) + 0.05\sin\left(3wt + \frac{\pi}{2}\right) + 0.06\sin\left(5wt + \frac{\pi}{2}\right) \tag{4.20}$$

4.5.2.4   Test Case 4

Periodic pulses are added to the system which have the same time period as the input signal. Two pulses are introduced to the system with parameters listed in Table 4.1 below [23]. The resultant output of the SOGI FLC PLL shows that the pulses introduced to the system have no effect on the zero crossings as shown in Figure 4.30. At 10ms the first zero cross occurs.

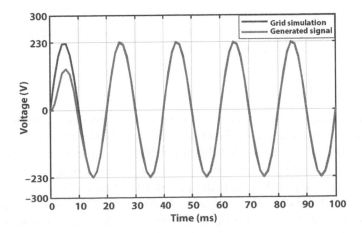

Figure 4.29 SOGI FLC PLL under 3rd and 5th harmonic with phase shift condition.

Table 4.1 Test parameters for test case 4.

	Positive pulse	Negative pulse
Amplitude	0.4	−0.4
Width	0.5 ms	0.5 ms
Delay	0.5 ms	10.5 ms
Period	20 ms	20 ms

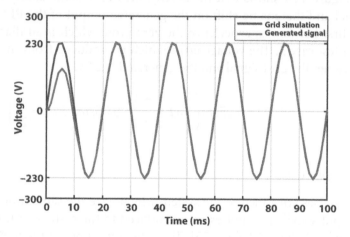

Figure 4.30 SOGI FLC PLL under pulse interference.

It takes less than 1 cycle for the generated signal to be synchronized with the grid signal. The synchronizations take place at 15 ms. The voltage error which is produced from the difference between the grid signal and the generated signal settles at 30 ms to zero error.

4.5.2.5   Test Case 5

This case is implemented in the same way as test case 4, the parameters for the two pulses are listed in Table 4.2 below [23]. The resultant output of the SOGI FLC PLL shows that the pulses have no effect on the zero crossings as shown in Figure 4.31 which reflect an improvement from the result found in Ref. [23]. In Ref. [23] the pulses listed below cause multiple zero crossings and the PLL does not lock. At 10 ms the first zero cross occurs. The voltage error which is produced from the difference between the grid signal and the generated signal settles at 30 ms to zero error.

Table 4.2 Test parameters for test case 5.

	Positive pulse	**Negative pulse**
Amplitude	−0.2	−0.2
Width	0.1 ms	0.1 ms
Delay	0.5 ms	10.5 ms
Period	20 ms	20 ms

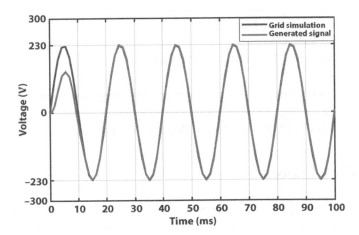

Figure 4.31 SOGI FLC PLL under modified pulse interference.

4.5.2.6   Test Case 6

The final test case involves the introduction of white noise to the system. The white noise is introduced at a maximum Total Harmonic Distortion of 8%. The SOGI FLC PLL has the ability to lock on the input signal and the PLL is not affected by the introduction of the while noise while in Ref. [23] the white noise causes multiple zero crossings which reflects a design improvement. It takes less than 1 cycle for the generated signal to be synchronized with the grid signal. The synchronizations take place at 15 ms. At 10 ms the first zero cross occurs as presented in Figure 4.32. The voltage error which is produced from the difference between the grid signal and the generated signal settles at 30 ms to zero error.

The designed SOGI FLC PLL has been tested for THD up-to 8% which demonstrates that the SOGI FLC PLL can be able to operate under cases of 20% PV integration in decentralized strategy, 50% PV integration in decentralized

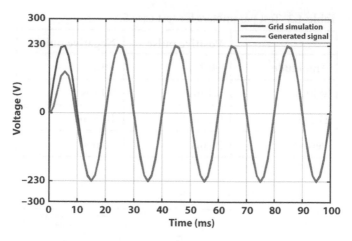

Figure 4.32 SOGI FLC PLL under noise interference.

strategy, 100% PV integration in a centralized strategy, 100% wind integration in centralized strategy, a combination of 100% wind integration in centralized strategy and 100% PV integration in decentralized strategy [22].

4.6   Conclusion

This chapter concludes that the SOGI FLC PLL has the ability to handle the harmonics, noise and pulse interferences presented in the network. The SOGI FLC PLL is able to operate under such faulty conditions while having a better settling time compared to other PLL techniques discussed in Section 4.2 which proves that the designed model is capable to meet and exceed the grid requirements of the South African national grid. Tests were undertaken in accordance to the EN50160 standard which the South African national grid code on renewable energy sources. The designed PLL model when connected to a single phase inverter produces the best sine wave synchronization.

Acknowledgment

The authors of this chapter would like to thankfully acknowledge the Tshwane University of Technology, Pretoria, South Africa for enabling the authors to conduct and complete the research culminating to research outputs such as this chapter.

References

1. Lakshmanan, S.A., Jain, A. and Rajpurohit, B.S., Grid Voltage Monitoring Techniques for Single Phase Grid Connected Solar PV system, in *Proc. 2014 IEEE 6th India International Conference on Power Electronics*, pp. 1–6.
2. Yang, Y., Blaabjerg, F. and Zou, Z., Benchmarking of Grid Fault Modes in Single-Phase Grid-Connected Photovoltaic Systems, *IEEE Transactions on Industry Applications*, vol. 49, pp. 2167–2176, October 2013.
3. Lubura, S., Šoja, M., Lale, S. and Ikić, M., Single-phase phase locked loop with DC offset and Noise rejection for Photovoltaic Inverters, *IET Power Electronics*, vol. 7, pp. 2288–2299, September 2014.
4. Xiong, L., Zhuo, F., Liu, X., Zhu, M., Chen, Y. and Wang, F., Research on Fast Open-loop Phase Locking Scheme for Three-phase Unbalanced Grid, in *Proc. 2015 IEEE Applied Power Electronics Conference and Exposition*, pp. 1672–1676.
5. Ciobotaru, M., Teodorescu, R. and Agelidis, V.G., Offset rejection for PLL based Synchronization in Grid-connected Converters, in *Proc. 2008 Twenty-Third Annual IEEE Applied Power Electronics Conference and Exposition*, pp. 1611–1617.
6. Golestan, S., Monfared, M., Freijedo, F.D. and Guerrero, J.M., Dynamics Assessment of Advanced Single-Phase PLL Structures, *IEEE Transactions on Industrial Electronics*, vol. 60, pp. 2167–2177, June 2013.
7. Dong, D., Wen, B., Boroyevich, D., Mattavelli, P. and Xue, Y., Analysis of Phase-Locked Loop Low-Frequency Stability in Three-Phase Grid-Connected Power Converters Considering Impedance Interactions, *IEEE Transactions on Industrial Electronics*, vol. 62, pp. 310–321, January 2015.
8. Geng, H., Sun, J., Xiao, S. and Yang, G., Modelling and Implementation of an All-Digital Phase-Locked-Loop for Grid-Voltage Phase Detection, *IEEE Transactions on Industrial Informatics*, vol. 9, pp. 772–780, May 2013.
9. Yang, Y. and Blaabjerg, F., Synchronization in Single-Phase Grid-Connected Photovoltaic Systems under Grid Faults, in *Proc. 2012 3rd IEEE International Symposium on Power Electronics for Distributed Generation Systems*, pp. 476–482.
10. Yang, Y., Hadjidemetriou, L., Blaabjerg, F. and Kyriakides, E., Benchmarking of Phase Locked Loop based Synchronization Techniques for Grid-Connected Inverter Systems, in *Proc. 2015 9th International Conference on Power Electronics-ECCE Asia*, pp. 2167–2174.
11. Kamouny, K.E., Lakssir, B., Hamedoun, M., Benyoussef, A. and Mahmoudi, H., Simulation, Testing and Implementation of a Phase Locked Loop Used to Control a PV-Micro-Inverter, in *Proc. 2017 International Renewable and Sustainable Energy Conference*, pp. 1–5.
12. Panda, S.K. and Dash, T.K., An Improved Method of Frequency Detection for Grid Synchronization of DG Systems During Grid Abnormalities, in

Proc. 2014 International Conference on Circuits, Power and Computing Technologies, pp. 153–157.

13. Kulkarni, A. and John, V., A Novel Design Method for SOGI-PLL for Minimum Settling Time and Low Unit Vector Distortion, in Proc. 2013 *IECON 2013—39th Annual Conference of the IEEE Industrial Electronics Society*, pp. 274–279.

14. Sibanyoni, M. and Chowdhury, S.P., Synchronization strategy for single phase inverters for feeding renewable energy in South African National Grid, in *Proc. 2017 52nd International Universities Power Engineering Conference*, pp. 1–4.

15. Kulkarni, A. and John, V., Design of a Fast Response Time Single-Phase PLL with DC Offset Rejection Capability, in *Proc. 2016 IEEE Applied Power Electronics Conference and Exposition*, pp. 2200–2206.

16. Wang, J., Konikkara, D.D. and Monti, A., A Generalized Approach for Harmonics and Unbalanced Current Compensation through Inverter Interfaced Distributed Generator, in *Proc. 2014 IEEE 5th International Symposium on Power Electronics for Distributed Generation Systems*, pp. 1–8.

17. Haiyunnisa, T., Alam, H.S. and Salim, T.I., Design and Implementation of Fuzzy Logic Control System for Water Quality Control, in *Proc. 2017 2nd International Conference on Automation, Cognitive Science, Optics, Micro Electro-Mechanical System, and Information Technology*, pp. 98–102.

18. Gambhir, J. and Thakur, T., Modeling and Control of Large Wind Farm based on DFIG using classical PI and Fuzzy logic controller (FLC), in *Proc. 2017 International Conference On Smart Technologies For Smart Nation*, pp. 454–459.

19. Jurenoks, A. and Novickis, L., Fuzzy Logic Control Method for Autonomous Heating Systems in Energy Efficient Homes, in *Proc. 2017 2nd International Conference on Integrated Circuits and Microsystems*, pp. 236–240.

20. Al-Toma, A.S., Taylor, G. A., Abbod, M. and Pisica, I., A Comparison of PI and Fuzzy Logic Control Schemes for Field Oriented Permanent Magnet Synchronous Generator Wind Turbines, in *Proc. 2017 IEEE PES Innovative Smart Grid Technologies Conference Europe*, pp. 1–6.

21. Arifur, R.S., *Novel controls of Photovoltaic (PV) solar farms*, Ph.D. dissertation, Dept. Electrical and Computer. Eng., Univ. Western, London, 2012.

22. Shafiullah, G.M. and MT Oo, A., Analysis of Harmonics with Renewable Energy Integration into the Distribution Network, in *Proc. 2015 IEEE Innovative Smart Grid Technologies*, pp. 1–6.

23. Stastny, L., Mego, R., Franek, L. and Bradac, Z., Zero Cross Detection Using Phase Locked Loop, *International Federation of Automatic Control*, vol. 49, pp. 294–298, October 2016.

5

Power Electronics Interfaces in Microgrid Applications

Indrajit Sarkar

Department of Electrical Engineering, MNNIT Allahabad, Prayagraj, India

Abstract

Microgrid concept came into existence with the use of Distributed Renewable Energy Resources (DRERs) like wind, solar, geothermal, micro hydro turbines, biomass, Fuel-cell and other energy resources. It uses such energy resources with Energy Storage System, to form a small-scale self-sustained power distribution network. Applications of microgrids are for towns, shopping malls, remote military bases, remote research locations, villages, islands etc. i.e. powering remote locations where local generations are available but is outreach of utility grid. However, interfacing such energy resources with microgrid is challenging without power electronics, because the type of outputs from these DRERs are not suitable for standard household and industrial consumers, and for the utility grid. Power electronics plays the interfacing role and controls the power flow by converting the outputs of DRERs to suitable forms for the consumers. These power converter interfaces between the energy sources and the consumer to transform the variable input to high quality output suitable for the consumers. With the advancement of state of art in converter technologies, power semiconductor devices and fast processing DSPs, the use of power electronics become further justified for such applications. Here, an overview of power converter topologies and their control techniques used in microgrid applications presented in details.

Keywords: AC microgrid, DC microgrid, hybrid microgrid, power electronic converters

---

Email: indrajit@mnnit.ac.in

C. Sharmeela, P. Sivaraman, P. Sanjeevikumar, and Jens Bo Holm-Nielsen (eds.) Microgrid Technologies, (121–144) © 2021 Scrivener Publishing LLC

5.1 Introduction

The idea of establishing microgrid has become popular by utilizing the renewable energy sources like solar PV, wind energy resources, hydrogen or fuel cell energy resources, biomass, etc. as an alternative to the rapidly depleting fossil fuel resources and for the growing environmental concern. For hydrogen or fuel cell energy resources it is to be noted that they are not truly renewable, however their abundant availability with less polluting characteristics made them an alternative energy resource to the fossil fuel resources. The four key components of a microgrid are the consumers or the loads, the distribution network, DRERs and the ESS to form a small scale low voltage power distribution network. It is a self-sustained local grid with DRERs as the key energy sources for the electrical power generation. In microgrid application, ESS plays an important role, because due to intermittent nature of DRERs, there is a need for electrical energy storage system to improve the system reliability and availability [1].

Though a microgrids is capable of operating independently in islanded mode (not connected to the utility grid or to any other microgrid), for economic and reliable operation, it can be operated in interconnected mode as well. In interconnected mode, a microgrid exchanges power with the utility grid or with other neighboring microgrids. Therefore, for establishing microgrids with such power flow control capabilities, the power electronics converters with power flow control capability are used in building the interfaces for the interconnections, which not only secure cost-effective and reliable interfacing, but enables the microgrids to control the power flow very effectively.

5.2 Microgrid Classification

According to microgrid architecture, microgrids can be classified into AC microgrid, DC microgrid and hybrid microgrid. AC microgrid can be further subdivided into high frequency AC (HFAC) microgrid and line frequency AC (LFAC) microgrid. The classification of microgrids is presented in Figure 5.1 [2].

5.2.1 AC Microgrid

The typical architecture of a power electronics based AC microgrid is shown in Figure 5.2. In AC microgrid, the main bus is AC in which all the

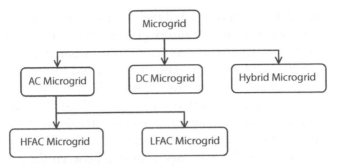

Figure 5.1 Classification of microgrids.

loads, energy resources and the ESS are connected through power electronics interfaces.

In Figure 5.2, only two renewable energy sources are shown, the solar PV and the wind energy, and both the sources are equipped with power electronics converters with unidirectional power flow capability to interface with the microgrid. For solar PV, the DC output from the PV is first converted into higher DC voltage (with maximum power point tracking

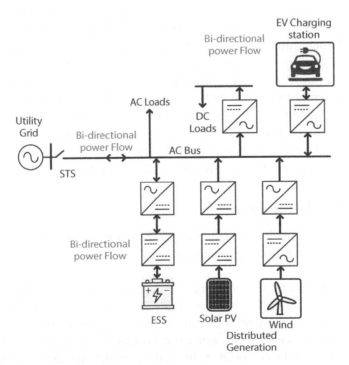

Figure 5.2 The typical configuration of an AC microgrid.

(MPPT) control) and then converted into three-phase or single-phase AC to supply to the loads or to the utility grid. Similarly, for the wind generators, the variable AC output from the wind turbine generator is first converted into DC and then the same is converted into suitable AC to feed to the microgrid. In AC microgrid, since the main bus is AC, therefore it can be connected directly to the utility grid using a static transfer switch (STS) without employing any power electronic interface (for line frequency AC microgrid) as shown in Figure 5.2. The advantage of a grid connected microgrid is the exchange of power between the grid and the microgrid. When there is surplus power generation in the microgrid, the microgrid can supply the surplus power to the grid, whereas when there is a deficit of power or in case of contingencies in the microgrid, the grid can supply power to the microgrid, hence bi-directional flow of power takes place between the grid and the microgrid for a grid connected microgrid. Further, it is to be noted in Figure 5.2 that, for DC loads or for the Electric Vehicle (EV), the AC is converted into DC and then step-down to suitable DC using DC–DC converter. The interfacing converters connecting the EV and the ESS are of bi-directional in nature to enable the bi-directional flow of power between the EV or the ESS and the microgrid.

As presented in Figure 5.1, the AC microgrids can be further classified into high frequency AC microgrid and power or line frequency AC microgrid, and then subdivided into single-phase or three-phase AC microgrids. High frequency AC microgrids (400/500 Hz) are popular for aircraft applications and for remote military bases, because with higher operating fundamental frequency, the size of the filter components get reduced and hence the compact design of the power electronics converters can be achieved. This is at the cost of higher operating losses and need for an extra AC to AC converter for integrating the microgrid with the conventional utility grid whose nominal frequency is 50 or 60 Hz.

5.2.2   DC Microgrids

DC microgrid with low voltage DC as the main bus is popular over AC microgrid due to following advantages.

i.   DC microgrids are significantly more efficient with DRERs,
ii. Low voltage DC is considerably safer than high voltage AC,
iii. Conductor size in DC microgrid is slightly increased (for same power level, not proportional to reduction in DC voltage level), as DC utilizes the complete conductor cross section without any skin affect,

iv. DC lighting needs lesser Watt/surface area than AC lighting (around 40% space saving),

v. There is ease of power flow control in DC by controlling the current flow direction and keeping the voltage polarity unaltered,

vi. Synchronization is not required,

vii. The complexity of the system much reduced with reduced number of power electronic converters.

The typical power structure of a DC microgrid is shown in Figure 5.3. In DC microgrid, the main bus is DC and loads, DRERs are connected to the main bus using power electronics interfaces. In Figure 5.3, two renewable energy resources, solar and wind are connected to the main bus using DC–DC, AC–DC converters respectively which is comparatively simpler than the connections in AC microgrid as shown in Figure 5.2. Unlike AC microgrid, it can be seen here that only one converter is used for each one of them. Similarly, for the EV charging there is a bi-directional DC–DC converter. One additional bidirectional DC–AC converter can be seen to be necessary in DC microgrid to connect the microgrid with the utility grid. The few application examples of DC microgrids are

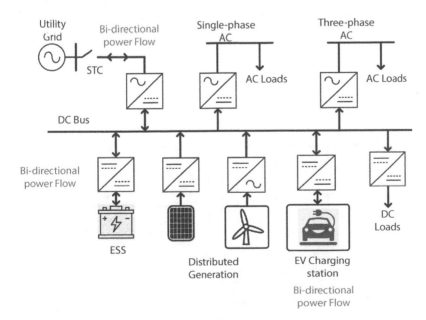

Figure 5.3 Typical power structure of a DC microgrid.

i. Electric vehicle charging stations
ii. Shipboard power systems
iii. Power supply for telecommunication systems
iv. Office buildings and commercial facilities.

5.2.3 Hybrid Microgrid

Hybrid microgrid structure is a hybrid between AC and DC microgrids as shown in Figure 5.4 and has the characteristics of both AC and DC microgrids. It can be seen in Figure 5.4 that it has both the AC and the DC buses for integrating DRERs and supplying power to the loads. Both the AC and DC buses have their own loads, storage systems and DRERs. Therefore, hybrid microgrid structure is much more versatile than AC or DC microgrids. As shown in Figure 5.4, there is an AC–DC converter between the AC bus and the DC bus (not present in AC or DC microgrids) to control the flow of power between the AC and DC buses. Therefore, a hybrid microgrid can be treated as an interconnected DC, AC microgrids, where the control of power flow is achieved by using controlled power electronics converters.

The idea of hybrid microgrid is to expand the existing distribution network by integrating a variety of DRERs into it. For example, the DC bus present in the hybrid microgrid is used to integrate the DRERs with DC outputs, the ESS, the fuel cell and the DC loads, whereas the AC bus is

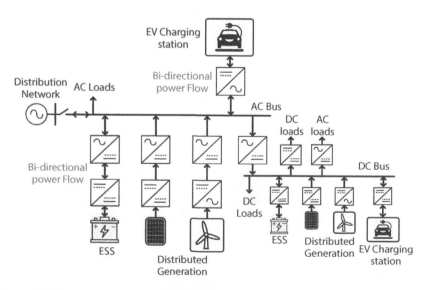

Figure 5.4 The power structure of hybrid microgrid.

connected to the utility grid and supplying power to the AC loads. However, both the buses suitable for integrating any type of DRERs depending on their availability using power electronics converters. Therefore, presence of both the AC and DC bus provides the degree of freedom for connecting the loads and integrating the DRER units. However, stable and reliable operation of such hybrid microgrid with coordinated protection is still is a research focus.

5.3   Role of Power Electronics in Microgrid Application

In early days, with diesel engine driven AC generator based microgrids, there were no use of power electronics components as the generator was the only source of electrical power and was fed directly to the AC loads. However, with the advent of use of DRERs in microgrid applications, the role of power electronics became significant since power electronics is the only technology using which the different forms of electrical energy generated from DRERs can be converted into suitable AC or DC electrical energy for the standard household and industrial consumers, and for integrating with the utility grid [2-7]. For example, the output from solar PV is DC at some voltage level (depending on PV array and the insolation level). The output from wind generator is three-phase variable AC. Moreover, for optimum utilization of the renewable resources, we need controlled power electronics converter as interface between the source and the consumer. Power electronics further helps in efficient and optimum control of the appliances. Therefore, with the use of controlled power electronics converters, the

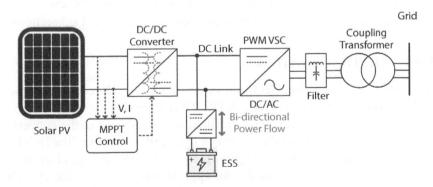

Figure 5.5 Grid connected PV application: The DC–DC converter interface with MPPT control.

reliable operation of microgrid with high quality output power is achieved. The key power electronics converters used in microgrid application are presented in the following sections.

5.4   Power Converters

As mentioned earlier, power electronics technology plays a key role in establishment of microgrid. To describe the role of power electronics in integrating DRERs, two examples are presented in Figures 5.5 and 5.6, where integrating solar and wind power with the utility grid using power electronics interfaces are presented respectively.

For solar PV, the DC output is converted into stable DC using a DC–DC converter with MPPT tracking, and then it is converted into single- or three-phase AC using a DC–AC Voltage Source Converter (VSC). The energy storing element i.e. the battery is connected to the DC-link using a bi-directional DC–DC converter to compensate for the intermittent nature of PV power. The battery supplies power to the load when PV power is not sufficient, and gets charged when surplus power is available from the PV.

For wind energy extraction, the three-phase variable AC output from the wind generator is first converted into DC, and then the same DC is converted into three-phase AC as shown in Figure 5.6(a). This is the state of art for the Squirrel Cage Induction Generator (SCIG) or Permanent Magnet Synchronous Generator (PMSG). Whereas, for Wound Rotor Induction Generator (WRIG), a back–back converters is used as shown in Figure 5.6(b). In this case, the cost and size of the converter is much less compared to the previous case in which rated power converters are employed. Therefore, power electronics is the only viable technology with which the integration of loads and the DRERs with microgrid becomes feasible. Different types of power electronics converters are discussed in detail in next subsections.

5.4.1   DC/DC Converters

The common use of power electronics converter is DC–DC converter which is also known as DC transformer. In DC–DC converters, the input DC voltage is converted into DC voltage at different voltage level at the converter output with or without isolation between the input and output. The DC–DC converters are used in DC microgrid to convert the DC voltage of the main DC bus to dc voltage level suitable for applications. Moreover, the DC–DC converter pays the role for extracting power from the energy sources at maximum power point called Maximum Power Point (MPPT) tracking.

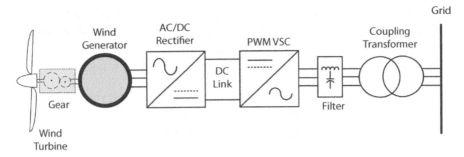

Figure 5.6 (a) Wind generator of Squirrel Cage Induction Generator or Permanent Magnet Synchronous Generator.

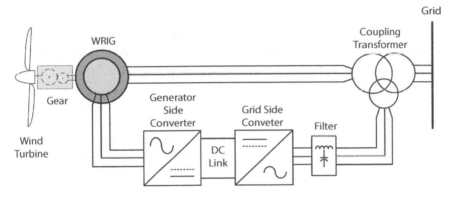

Figure 5.6 (b) Wound Rotor Induction Generator with back–back converters.

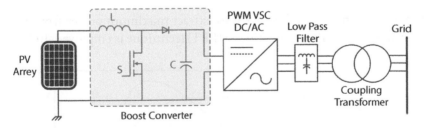

Figure 5.7 Application of boost converter in grid connected PV application.

In DC–DC converters, the power flow between the input and output could be either unidirectional or bi-directional, and are discussed each one of them one by one.

5.4.2   Non-Isolated DC/DC Converters

The power circuit diagram shown in Figure 5.7 is to convert the low voltage DC output of the PV panel into power frequency AC to feed the solar power to the utility grid. For connecting a solar inverter to the utility grid at voltage level of 400 V, the DC-link voltage of the inverter should be around 1,000 V. However, since the output voltage from a single PV panel is around 40 V, therefore, 1,000 V DC can be achieved in following ways.

- Stepping up the input DC voltage i.e. the DC-link voltage by connecting multiple PV modules in series,
- By using a step-up line frequency transformer at the DC–AC converter output,
- By connecting few PV modules in series, and then stepping up the DC voltage level using a step-up DC–DC converter or boost converter.

The typical power circuit diagram of a grid connected PV application using boost converter is shown in Figure 5.7. Here the DC voltage output from PV array is step up into high voltage DC using the boost converter and then converted into PWM AC using the PWM VSC. The PWM AC is then filtered using a low pass filter before connecting to the utility grid using a coupling transformer. In this application, there are two power electronics interfaces, the DC–DC boost converter which boosts or step up the DC voltage keeping the MPPT and the DC–AC PWM VSC converter which converts the DC into PWM AC.

5.4.2.1 Maximum Power Point Tracking (MPPT)

Due to low efficiency of solar PV, to extract maximum power from it, the Maximum Power Point Tracking (MPPT) technique is employed. In MPPT

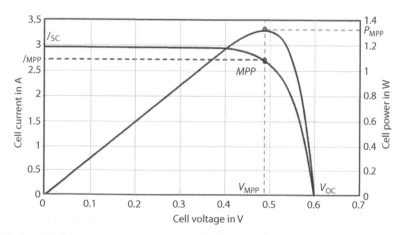

Figure 5.8 Typical I–V and P–V curves of a solar PV module.

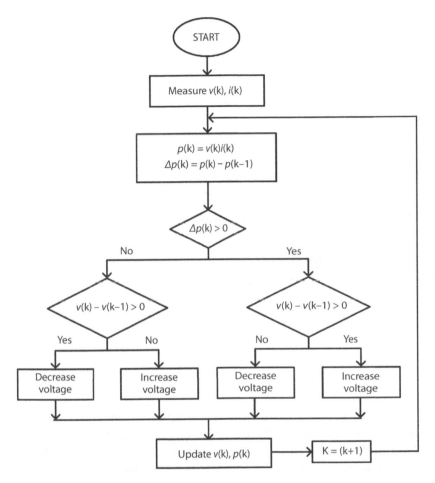

Figure 5.9 Flow chart of Perturb and Observe MPPT algorithm.

technique, the maximum power is extracted from the source by following the maximum power point in the I–V characteristics of the PV module as shown in Figure 5.8 [12, 13]. In Figure 5.7, it is achieved using the boost converter by varying the duty ratio using any of the MPPT algorithms. Few popular MPPT algorithms are as follows:

- Constant voltage method,
- Perturb and Observe method,
- Constant current method.

The flowchart for the Perturb and Observe MPPT technique is shown in Figure 5.9 and the typical voltage and current waveforms are shown in Figure 5.10.

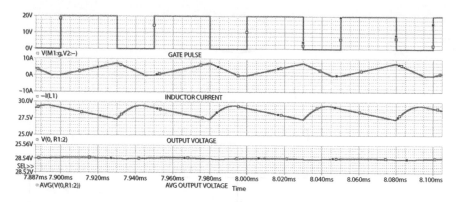

Figure 5.10 Boost converter voltage and current waveforms.

For the boost converter operating in continuous conduction mode, the expression for the output voltage and current is given by

$$V_o = \frac{V_i}{(1-d)} \tag{5.1}$$

$$I_o = (1-d)I_i \tag{5.2}$$

Where, (V_i, I_i), (V_o, I_o) are the voltage, current sets of the input and output stages respectively, and d is the duty ratio (t_{ON}/T) of switch S.

The interleaved boost converter shown in Figure 5.11 can reduce the output ripple by increasing the effective switching frequency by interleave action, therefore minimizes output and input capacitor filter sizes. The interleaved boost converter is used for medium and high power applications.

Similarly, the step-down DC–DC converter i.e. buck converter power circuit is sown in Figure 5.12 [8, 9]. In this topology, the input high voltage DC is converted into low voltage DC without any isolation between the input and the output. For the buck converter operating in continuous conduction mode, the expression for the output voltage and current are given by

$$V_o = dV_i \tag{5.3}$$

$$I_o = \frac{Ii}{d} \tag{5.4}$$

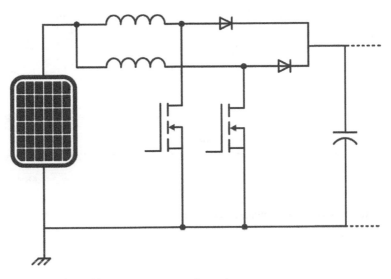

Figure 5.11 Interleaved boost converter configuration.

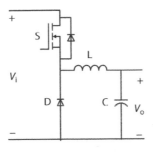

Figure 5.12 Non-isolated step-down DC–DC converter.

The typical waveforms of voltage and current in buck converter are shown in Figure 5.13.

The buck-boost converter which is a cascade connection of buck and boost converters is shown in Figure 5.14. It features voltage step-up and step-down capabilities of the input voltage depending on the operating duty ratio.

The expression for the output voltage and current in continuous conduction mode for a buck-boost converter is given by

$$V_o = \frac{d}{(1-d)} V_i \tag{5.5}$$

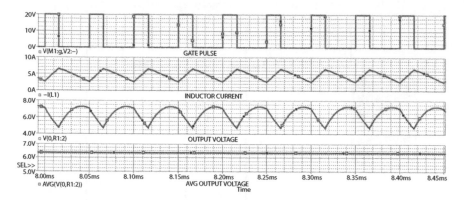

Figure 5.13 Buck converter voltage and current waveforms.

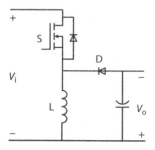

Figure 5.14 Buck-boost converter configuration.

$$I_o = \frac{(d-1)}{d} I_i \tag{5.6}$$

Therefore, buck-boost is a useful DC–DC converter by which the output voltage can be varied greater than or less than the input voltage by varying the duty ratio d from greater than to less than 0.5. Hence, d less than 0.5 is the boost operation and greater than 0.5 is the buck operation.

The converters discussed in this section are capable of stepping up or down or both the input DC voltage at the converter output. However, their application is limited only to the applications not require any isolation between the input and the output. Further, there is no possibility of power fed back from the output to the input i.e. don't have bi-direction power flow capability. The DC–DC converters discussed in next section provides isolation between the input and the output, and then few converters with bi-directional power flow capability are also discussed.

5.4.3 Isolated DC/DC Converters

DC–DC converters with galvanic isolation between the input and the output are also available for DC–DC conversion applications, and known as isolated DC–DC converters. Commonly used isolated DC–DC converters are Flyback converter, Push–pull converter, Full-bridge and Half-bridge converter as shown in Figures 5.15 (a), (b), (c) and (d) respectively [8, 9].

For low power applications, the Flyback converter is preferred, whereas for medium and high power applications the Push–pull, Half-bridge and Full-bridge converters are preferred. The transformer presented in these configurations is used to provide the galvanic isolation and helps to attain the required output DC voltage level using adequate turns ratio. One key point to be noted in these converter configurations is that that due to the presence of diodes at the converter output, there is no possibility of flow of

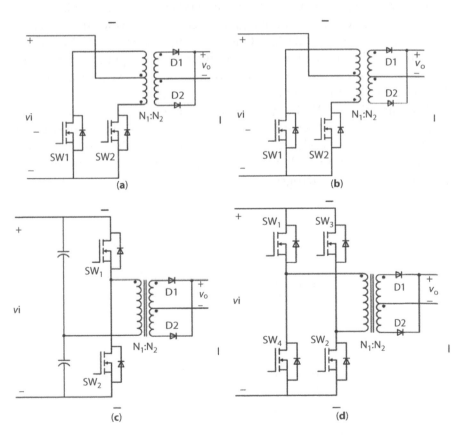

Figure 5.15 Isolated DC–DC converters: (a) Flyback, (b) Push–pull, (c) Half-bridge, (d) Full-bridge.

power from the output to the input and hence they are unidirectional in nature.

In Push–pull, Half- and Full-bridge converters, diodes are connected to the center tapping point of the secondary winding of the center tap transformer similar to full wave rectifier circuit with two diodes. Similarly, the output can be converted using diode bridge rectifier without using the center tap transformer similar to full-bridge diode bridge rectifier circuit.

Another popular DC–DC converter with high frequency isolation link is shown in Figure 5.16. Since, both the input and the output are equipped with active H-bridges, hence this configuration is known as the Dual Active Bridge (DAB) configuration. The input DC is first converted into high frequency AC using the input H-bridge, and then the high frequency AC in stepped up or down using the isolation transformer. Finally the high frequency AC is converted into DC by the output stage H-bridge. DAB configuration is very popular in present day and can be used for high power applications. Due to presence of high frequency transformer, the DAB converter features compact design. One important feature of DAB converter is there is bi-directional flow of power between the input and the output. Therefore, such converter configuration can be employed for integrating ESS with the DC microgrid or for charging discharging EV.

A bi-directional EV charging converter topology present in charging station or in EV mobile charger is shown in Figure 5.17. This converter can operate in both the modes, charging the EV which is the boost mode and discharging the EV in buck mode, therefore can be employed for interfacing EV with the DC microgrid.

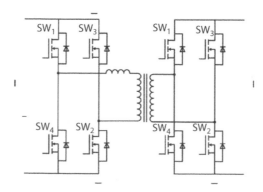

Figure 5.16 DAB converter for isolated DC–DC conversion.

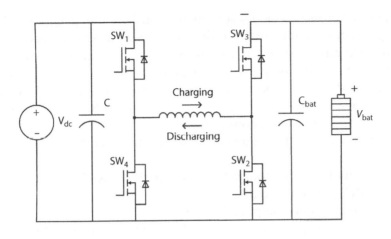

Figure 5.17 EV charging using bi-directional DC–DC converter.

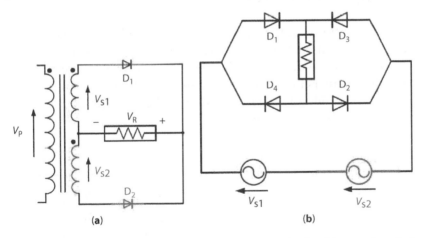

Figure 5.18 Full wave diode rectifier circuits: (a) using two diodes, (b) using four diodes.

5.4.4   AC to DC Converters

In this section, the converters used for AC to DC conversion are discussed starting from the most basic AC to DC converters using diode rectifiers. The most commonly used diode rectifiers are shown in in Figure 5.18 [8-11]. Figure 5.18 (a) shows the full wave diode rectifier using two diodes and one center tap transformer; whereas Figure 5.18 (b) shows the full wave diode bridge rectifier using four diodes. Rectifier with two diodes is more efficient than the rectifier with four diodes as only one diode is conducting at a time, whereas two diodes are simultaneously conducting for the diode bridge rectifier circuit. However, double the peak inverse voltage and the use of uncommon center tap transformer is disadvantages of the previous rectifier circuit. The output voltage waveform of a diode bridge rectifier with and without DC link capacitor filter is shown in Figure 5.19. With the presence of filter capacitor, peaky current is drawn by the rectifier from the source during capacitor charging.

The following are the features of diode rectifier circuits.

- Simple, robust, compact and economic conversion,
- Reliable and efficient,
- Uncontrolled output DC voltage
- Non-regenerative i.e. power flow from the DC side to AC side is not possible,
- Injecting lower order harmonics into the AC source,
- Requirement of large input and output filers,

For medium power applications, three-phase diode bridge rectifier with three diode legs is used. For high power applications, to meet the input current harmonic standard, high pulse rectifiers like 12-pulse rectifier with two 6-pulse rectifiers in series is used with a complex phase-shifting transformer and input filter in order to minimize the lower order current harmonics from the input line current.

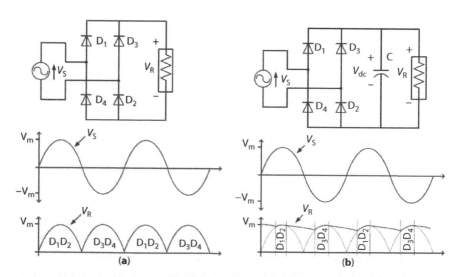

Figure 5.19 Output voltage waveforms: (a) without, (b) with DC-link capacitor.

To enable regeneration and to improve the input line current profile, PWM rectifier or active rectifier shown in Figure 5.20 is used for applications requiring high quality input current with power factor correction as well as to regulate the DC-link voltage. However, the use of six active switches leads to more complex structure and the control compared to diode rectifier circuits. Moreover, due to PWM action at high switching frequency, the switching losses are more in this converter and hence make it less efficient than diode rectifier circuits.

Other topologies for converting AC into DC without and with isolation are shown in Figure 5.21. In Figure 5.21 (a), the AC is first converted into controlled DC and then the same is further converted into application specific DC voltage using the output DC–DC converter. Therefore, such AC–DC converters are useful for integrating ESS and EV with the AC microgrid. Similarly, the AC–DC converter using PWM rectifier and DAB with high frequency isolation link capable of bi-directional power flow is shown in Figure 5.21 (b), which also useful for AC microgrid for integrating ESS and EVs.

5.4.5   DC to AC Converters

The converters converting DC into AC are useful in DC microgrid for converting the DC bus voltage into three-phase or single-phase AC to fed to the AC loads and for interconnecting to the utility grid. These are called Voltage Source Converter or Voltage Source Inverter (VSC/VSI). Three VSC configurations with single-phase and three-phase output are shown in Figure 5.22 [10, 11], in which the converters shown in Figure 5.22 (a) and (b) has single-phase output (half-bridge and full-bridge respectively) whereas, the voltage source converter presented in Figure 5.22 (c) has three-phase output. The converter shown in Figure 5.22 (c) is the most versatile VSC

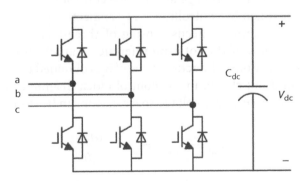

Figure 5.20 PWM rectifier or active rectifier.

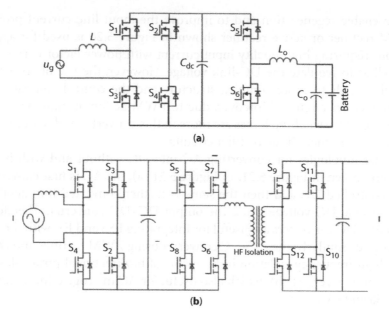

Figure 5.21 EV charging using bi-directional AC–DC converters: (a) without, (b) with isolation.

configuration and used for most of the grid connected PV applications for integrating PV to the utility grid.

For medium-voltage high power applications, the Neutral Point Clamped (NPC) multi-level converter shown in Figure 5.22 (d) is preferred due to reduced filer size requirement and can be realized without series connection of low voltage switches.

The typical control strategy of a PWM VSC in d–q reference frame using PI controllers is shown in Figure 5.23 [14-16]. Here, the reactive power and the DC-link voltage are the two control parameters and independently controlled by controlling v_{qf}, v_{df} respectively.

This control technique needs sensing of three-phase voltage, current and the θ_f (position of the rotating reference frame) for the abc-dq and dq-abc transformations. The actual value of θ_f is obtained using Phase Lock Loop (PLL) and not shown in the control block diagram. In stator reference frame, the three-phase voltage space vector can be expressed as

$$v_{abc}^{con} = v_{abc} + ri_{abc} + L\frac{di_{abc}}{dt} \qquad (5.7)$$

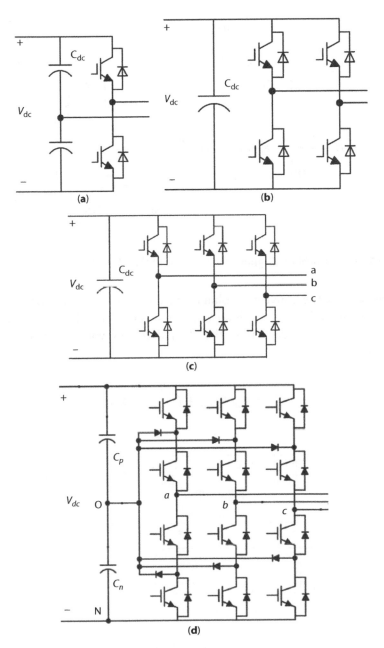

Figure 5.22 PWM VSC for converting DC to AC. (a) Single-phase half-bridge, (b) single-phase full-bridge, (c) three-phase, (d) Neutral Point Clamp (NPC) inverter.

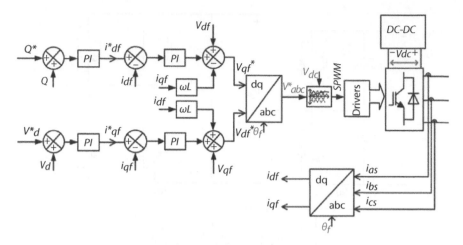

Figure 5.23 Control block diagram of three-phase VSC in d–q reference frame.

where, v_{abc}^{con} is the converter voltage space vector, v_{abc} is the load voltage space vector and i_{abc} is the load current space vector. In synchronously rotating d–q reference frame, the d- and q-axes voltage equations are expressed as

$$v_{df}^{con} = v_{df} + ri_{df} + L\frac{di_{df}}{dt} - \omega Li_{qf} \tag{5.8}$$

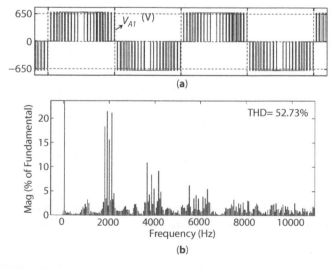

Figure 5.24 (a) PWM output voltage waveform, (b) the harmonic spectrum.

$$v_{qf}^{con} = v_{qf} + ri_{qf} + L\frac{di_{qf}}{dt} + \omega Li_{df} \tag{5.9}$$

where, v_{df}^{con}, v_{qf}^{con} are d- and q-axes converter voltages, v_{df}, v_{qf} and i_{df}, i_{qf} are the d–q load voltages, currents obtained from abc-dq transformations respectively. Therefore, the i_{df}^*, i_{qf}^* generated by the PI controllers from the Q^* and v_d^* commands further processed using Equations (5.8) and (5.9) to get the required v_{df}^{con}, v_{qf}^{con}.

For modulation of the converter, the two most popular methods are Sine PWM (SPWM) technique with injected third-harmonic (for better DC-link utilization) and the Space Vector PWM (SVPWM). The typical PWM output voltage waveform using carrier phase-shifted PWM technique and the corresponding FFT are shown in Figure 5.24.

5.5   Conclusion

Microgrid technology is a viable option for utilizing the DRERs and for which power electronics technology has proven to be the superior compared to other technologies. In this chapter, the brief introduction to different types of microgrids is presentedand their features are discussed. The features of various power electronics converters like DC–DC, DC–AC, AC–DC which are useful for power electronics based microgrid are further discussed in detail. It is justified that the power electronics technology found to be the most promising solution for establishment of future microgrid technology.

References

1. Hatziargyriou N., Asano H., Iravani R., & Marnay C., Microgrids, *IEEE Power Energy Magazine.*, 6(4), 78–94, 2007.
2. Xiongfei, W., Josep, G.M., Frede, B. & Zhe, C., A Review of Power Electronics Based Microgrids, *Journal of Power Electronics*, 12(1), 181–192, 2012.
3. Blaabjerg, F., Chen, Z., & Kjaer, S.B., Power electronics as efficient interface in dispersed power generation systems, *IEEE Transaction Power Electronics*, 19, 1184–1194, 2004.
4. Wenlong, J., Chean, L.H., Shung, W.W.H., Wong, M.L.D., Battery-supercapacitor hybrid energy storage system in standalone DC micro-grids: a review, *IET Renewable Power Generation.*, 11(4), 461–469, 2016.

5. Nababan, S., Muljadi, E., & Blaabjerg, F., An overview of power topologies for micro-hydro turbines, *3rd IEEE International Symposium on Power Electronics for Distributed Generation Systems (PEDG)*, 737–744, 2012.

6. Chen, Z., Guerrero, J.M., & Blaabjerg, F., A review of the state of the art of power electronics for wind turbines, *IEEE Transaction Power Electronics*, 24(8), 1859–1875, 2009.

7. Fu, Q., Montoya, L.F., Solanki, A., *et al.*, Microgrid generation capacity design with renewables and energy storage addressing power quality and surety, *IEEE Transaction on Smart Grid*, 3(4), 2019–2027, 2012.

8. Mohan, N., Undeland, T.M., & Robbins, W.P., *Power electronics: Converters, applications, and design*, New York: Wiley, 1995.

9. Muhammad, R.H., *Power electronics: devices, circuits, and applications*, New Jersey: Pearson, 1993.

10. Bose, B.K., *Modern Power Electronics and AC Drives*, Prentice Hall, 2002.

11. Bin, W., *High Power Converters and AC Drives*, Wiley, 2006.

12. Koutroulis, E., Kalaitzakis, K. & Voulgaris, N.C., Development of a micro controller based, photovoltaic maximum power point tracking control system, *IEEE Transactions on Power Electronics*, 16(1), 46–54, 2001.

13. Kamarzaman, N.A., & Tan, C.W., A comprehensive review of maximum power point tracking algorithms for photovoltaic systems, *Renewable and Sustainable Energy Reviews*, 37, 585–598, 2014.

14. Carrara, G., Gardella, S., Marchesoni, M., Salutari, R., Sciutto, G., A new multilevel PWM method: A theoretical analysis, *IEEE Transaction Power Electronics*, 7(3), 497–505, 1992.

15. Kazmierkowski, M.P., Malesani, L., Current control techniques for three-phase voltage-source PWM converters: a survey, *IEEE Transaction Power Electronics.*, 45(5), 691–703, 1998.

16. Peng, F.Z. and Lai, J.-S., Generalized instantaneous reactive power theory for three-phase power systems, *IEEE Transactions on Instrumentation and Measurement*, 45(1), 293–297, 1996.

6

Reconfigurable Battery Management System for Microgrid Application

Saravanan, S.[1], Pandiyan, P.[2*], Chinnadurai, T.[3], Ramji, Tiwari.[1], Prabaharan, N.[4], Senthil Kumar, R.[1] and Lenin Pugalhanthi, P.[1]

[1]Department of EEE, Sri Krishna College of Technology, Coimbatore, India
[2]Department of EEE, KPR Institute of Engineering and Technology, Coimbatore, India
[3]Department of ICE, Sri Krishna College of Technology, Coimbatore, India
[4]School of Electrical & Electronics Engineering, SASTRA Deemed University, Thanjavur, India

Abstract

Battery packs are formed by the interconnection of a greater number of battery cells. These battery packs are used in many electrical and electronics applications like sustainable energy systems, robotics, electric/hybrid vehicles and energy storage system in microgrid and smart grids. As a result, battery-based applications require a well-designed battery pack. Most of the research articles deal with the protection circuit, cell-balancing approach and battery management system. Nowadays, researchers are looking into reconfigurable based battery pack design to overcome the issues faced by the traditional system and conjunction with battery management systems like safety problems, low reliability, less energy efficiency and short lifetime. The most important characteristics of a reconfigurable battery management system are the arrangement of battery dynamically reconfigured concurrently depending upon the current status of battery cells using switching control according to load demand. Numerous research articles pertaining to reconfigurable battery pack techniques have been designed and implemented in real-time that makes the cell balancing condition at the time of charging/discharging cycle and also offer the fault-tolerant capability. This proposed chapter gives an overview of the reconfigurable battery system along with its challenges.

Keywords: Reconfigurable, battery management system, cell imbalance, state of health, state of charge, rate discharge effect, rate recovery effect, sensors

Corresponding author: pandyyan@gmail.com

C. Sharmeela, P. Sivaraman, P. Sanjeevikumar, and Jens Bo Holm-Nielsen (eds.) Microgrid Technologies, (145–176) © 2021 Scrivener Publishing LLC

6.1 Introduction

In recent years, the requirement of power generation is improving to greater extent to meet the required demand. The effect of environmental factors and rise in economy relating non-renewable energy sources-based power generation enables to look into sustainable energy sources-based power generation. Solar PV, fuel cells and wind are the renewable energy sources which have been deemed clean, inexhaustible, unlimited, and environmentally friendly. This forces the power industries to generate power through renewable energy sources and to realize their required demand partially. The government policies are also insisting on the same. The renewable energy sources like photovoltaic (PV), wind energy, hydro and fuel cells are not available to harness the energy for the entire day which directs towards the implementation of the energy storage system [1].

Currently, researchers are focusing mainly on the smart ways to use the batteries. The variety of optimization algorithms, scheduling method, and control techniques have been extensively studied to enhance the performance of the batteries so that it accomplishes complete operation automatically and improves the lifespan of the battery. Batteries are available in different sizes. Based on the applications, a few numbers of batteries are assembled together as a battery pack to meet the required load demand. Every battery exhibits numerous non-linear characteristics, it enables performance degradation. The performance improvement of the battery pack is the major confronting issue for the researchers. In order to fulfill the safety and reliability issues, battery packs are usually employed by the management system which takes care of monitoring the charging/discharging status and health status of the battery packs [2].

Static Battery management system (S-BMS) or traditional BMS are constructed using more of cells/batteries connected in fixed arrangement configuration such as series, parallel or a combination of these two to satisfy the requirement of load current and voltage. This method of battery management employed in harsh environments leads to reflect its individual cell characteristics because of uneven temperature gradient profile across the battery pack, non-uniform aging patterns or differences in their manufacturing tolerances [3]. Therefore, unbalancing in battery/cell occurs which in turn reduces the usage of entire battery pack. Thought of going for second time usage of battery packs, it creates furthermore complexity because of small difference in characteristics of every individual batteries would have been manifold at the first life of final stage. The optimization of S-BMS has been carried out using different scheduling techniques. The scheduling technique reported in Ref. [4] considers the charging-discharging time periods for scheduling whereas utilizing the battery behaviors like rate capacity effect and recovery effects are considered in Ref. [5]. These scheduling algorithms are preferred mostly for small scale battery management systems such as mobile devices as well as laptops. This method is not suitable for large scale battery management system. A promising solution is so called a reconfigurable battery management system (R-BMS), which overcomes the issues faced in traditional BMS and also applicable for large scale applications. Dynamic load conditions required applications like EVs are predominately works with this R-BMS in better way. The unique features of R-BMS are full utilization of battery pack, high fault tolerance and provide extended lifetime.

In this chapter, modeling of battery cell along with its characteristics and overview of the existing R-BMS topologies have been discussed. An overview of real-time implementation in design aspects and thermal management system of the battery is also addressed. Furthermore, various challenges to be faced in every sub-block which are to be anticipated at the time of real-time implementation, thus giving the directions towards the future research scopes.

6.2   Individual Cell Properties

In this section, the battery properties like the modeling of the cell, State of Health (SoH), State of Charge (SoC), battery life, rate discharge effect and recovery effects are discussed.

6.2.1   Modeling of Cell

Developing the accurate battery modelling gives the exact characteristics under various situations. In this section, summary of few commonly adopted methods are discussed.

6.2.1.1   Second Order Model

Generally prepared second order electrical modelling with the two set of coupled resistor and capacitor (RC) pair with a single resistor in series is reported in Ref. [6] and as shown in Figure 6.1. In this method, one RC pair is dedicated to short term instantaneous response and the other one is used for long-term as well as the slow response of voltage (v) and current (i) of batteries. But most of the cases, only one RC pair (i.e., single time constant) is commonly employed to simulate the long-term slow response characteristics of the batteries.

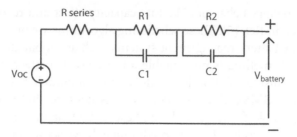

Figure 6.1 Battery equivalent electric circuit.

Where, R_{series} denotes the internal or series resistance, R_1C_1 pair is responsible for short term response, R_2C_2 pair is dedicated long term response for characterizing the real time batteries and V_{oc} denotes the battery open circuit voltage.

Consider the state variables are voltage drop across R_1C_1 pair (V_1), the voltage drop across R_2C_2 pair (V_2) and SoC. Therefore, the dynamic behavior of the battery using state-space model is given in Eq. (6.1).

$$\begin{bmatrix} \dot{v}_1 \\ \dot{v}_2 \\ \dot{SoC} \end{bmatrix} = \begin{bmatrix} -\dfrac{1}{R_1C_1} & 0 & 0 \\ 0 & -\dfrac{1}{R_2C_2} & 0 \\ 0 & 0 & 0 \end{bmatrix} \begin{bmatrix} v_1 \\ v_2 \\ SoC \end{bmatrix}$$

$$+ \begin{bmatrix} \dfrac{1}{C_1} \\ \dfrac{1}{C_2} \\ -\dfrac{1}{3,600C} \end{bmatrix} \bullet i + E.v_n \tag{6.1}$$

Where, C represents battery rated storage capacity in ampere-hours. v_n & E denote the noise and system matrix.

6.2.2 Simplified Non-Linear Model

First order battery modelling with non-linear characteristics is discussed in Ref. [7]. This modeling is widely used and adopted in MATLAB/Simulink.

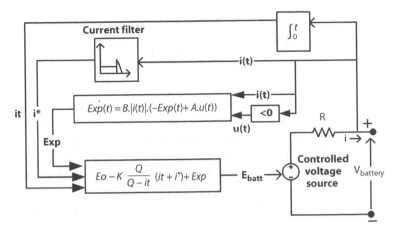

Figure 6.2 Implantation of battery model in MATLAB/Simulink.

The work presented in Ref. [8] deals about models of different variety of batteries, Li-Ion based battery modeling is discussed here. The charging as well as discharging analytical equation of Li-Ion battery is represented by Eqs. (6.2) and (6.3) respectively.

$$V_{battery} = V_{OC} - R.i - K\frac{C}{it - 0.1.C}.i^* - K\frac{C}{C - it}.it + A.\exp(-B.it) \quad (6.2)$$

$$V_{battery} = V_{OC} - R.i - K\frac{C}{C - it}.(it + i^*) + A.\exp(-B.it) \quad (6.3)$$

where, V_{oc}, R, i, i^*, C, K and it are the open circuit voltage, internal resistance, current, filtered current, total capacity, resistance or polarization constant and used capacity respectively. A as well as B represents the amplitude of the exponential zone and inverse time constant. The discharge equation pertaining to Li-Ion battery implemented using MATLAB-Simulink model is depicted in Figure 6.2.

6.3 State of Charge

Measuring the quantity of charge in a battery with respect to its rated storage capacity is termed as State of Charge (SoC). It does not have a unit and commonly measured by the digital representation of 1/0—fully charged/discharged. The battery SoC at time t with storage capacity is denoted by Eq. (6.4) as follows

$$SoC = SoC_i - \frac{1}{3{,}600C} \int_0^t i(\tau)d\tau \qquad (6.4)$$

where, SoC_i represent the storage the capacity of the battery at initial stage and i denotes the current. The current value is taken as positive while the battery is charging whereas negative when it is discharging.

Estimation of SoC is being difficult because of the listed issues such as unknown SoC at initial condition, sensor noise and fading of battery total capacity. The degradation of battery capacity over entire charge–discharge cycles and also self-discharge is the main factors restrict the estimation of SoC inaccurate value.

6.4   State of Health

Measuring the quantity of battery charging with respect to the exactly designed battery storage capacity is called as State of Health (SoH). In general, poor batteries are recognized using SoH only. This is also not having unit and commonly represented in the range of 0 (Not possible to store charge anymore), 1 (Ability to store charge upto specific rate capacity) or 0–100%. For instance, SoH represented by 0.8 means that 0.8 ampere-hours for a rated battery capacity of 1 ampere-hour. The battery capacity is reduced due to charging-discharging cycles as well as ageing. Therefore, it is necessary to track the value of SoH of a battery because it informs exactly regarding the actual battery capacity.

The various impedance (Z) based SoH measurement is reported in Ref. [9]. Alternative methods to estimate SoH are self-discharge rate, internal impedance/resistance method, the capability of accepting a charge, charge–discharge cycles, etc. Due to the problem conditions, the methods used for estimating SoH can also utilized to find SoC also. But these methods are specifically used for nickel–cadmium and lead-acid batteries. The Coulomb based counting the cycle is used for SoH measurement is discussed in Ref. [10].

6.5   Battery Life

Degrading of battery capacity is a generally happening event which reduces SoH or decreases the battery storage capacity. The factors pertaining to reduce the degradation of battery are metal deposition at the time of over-charging, electrolytes decomposition process and deposition of a film on electrodes [11]. These factors are considered for modeling in general any-how it mainly depends on the type of chemistry occurs in the battery. SoH is used to quantify the left behind the capacity of the battery. Even though, measuring the endurance of battery is also important. Counting the cycle is generally used method to specify the capacity degrading process at the time of battery life cycle. An entire procedure for charging as well as dis-charging of the battery is termed as a cycle. In general, an endurance of the battery is to quantify the rest of the capacity after a specific cycle count.

The capacity degradation primarily depends on film deposition on the electrode caused due to oxidation of the cell according to the study reported in Ref. [12]. The film growth process is represented in Eq. (6.5).

$$\frac{\partial \delta}{\partial t} = \frac{i_k M}{L \alpha \rho F} \tag{6.5}$$

Where, i_k denotes the rate of current flow reaction and δ is the film thick-ness [12], M, α, ρ, L denote the constant of any particular battery. The fast charging (load current is higher) tends to fast degradation of battery capac-ity which directs to decrease the counting of a cycle. Hence, algorithms should be designed in such a way that maximizes the endurance of battery life with respect to cycle count by means of high capacity (SoH) as possible.

6.6 Rate Discharge Effect

A common factor that happens in all variety of battery is the rate of dis-charge effect, which proved by Peukert's law. If the discharge (current) effect is increased this makes the reduction of output energy in the battery. Due to the restriction of the inner electrochemical process in the battery, this causes the rate of discharge effect

$$C_p = I^k t \tag{6.6}$$

Where, Cp—the rate of storage capacity (A-h), I—current (A), and t—operating time (h). Assume that this effect is nil, then the operating time will be $t = Cp / I$, which is denoted as $k = 1$ in Eq. (6.6). In particle, all batteries operating time is $t < Cp / I$ because of $k > 1$. The above property clearly shows that by reducing the current of individual batteries which increases its operating period.

6.7   Recovery Effect

The recovery effect is the most common thing that occurs in all the batteries. After discharge, the battery will become ideal which makes the voltage recovery done by the electrochemical reactions. If the discharge rate increases, this leads to the voltage drop in the battery. The above issue has overcome, by giving some rest to the battery which also extends its lifetime. The mathematical representation of the recovery effect is given below Eq. (6.7).

$$F_R : C_d \times t_d \times t_r \rightarrow V_{OUT} \tag{6.7}$$

Where F_R—recovery effect, C_d—discharge rate, t_d—discharge time, t_r—rest time and V_{OUT}—output voltage.

6.8   Conventional Methods and its Issues

A single cell or battery is not sufficient to meet the load demand so that a grouping of cells or battery requires solving the problem. Variety of grouping of batteries is done depending upon the specific load requirements such as higher current, higher voltage or higher power. The three types of topologies are followed in traditional battery management system as follows:

- Series connected
- Parallel connected
- Series-Parallel connected
  - Serially connected configuration
  - Parallelly connected configuration

Figure 6.3 depicts the four varieties of topologies realized in the traditional system. Every cell connected in specific configuration undergoes degradation in different level irrespective of the connection pattern.

6.8.1   Series Connected

Figure 6.3 (a) shows a series connection-based topology for the battery pack. According to Kirchhoff's voltage law, the total voltage is obtained through sum of the individual cell voltage in the battery storage system. In this arrangement, an enormous quantity of current is drawn for charging/discharging which in turn to diminish the life span of the battery and may

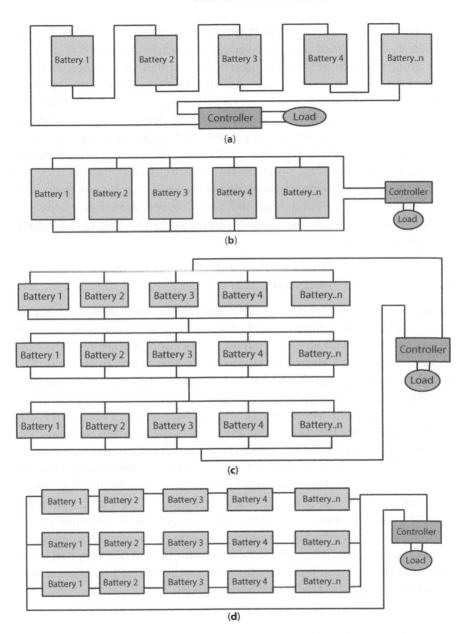

Figure 6.3 Existing topologies: (a) Series connection, (b) parallel connection, (c) PCC, (d) SCC.

start damaging the physical structure. Cell equivalence is to be considered to overcome these issues pertaining to series connection.

As a cell with less SoH or a faulty cell is available in a series connection leads to discharge very fast than the other group, without considering the load requirement. Therefore, maximum working time is reduced. Due to the series connection of cells, a variety of internal resistance of any cell in a group tends to not much difference because of total resistance is the sum of the individual resistances. But in this series connection topology, variation in SoC/voltage in every cell is possible. This voltage imbalance amongst the cells leads to over-discharge and may also tend to damage permanently [13]. The active and passive method of balancing is available for series connection is reported in Ref. [14]. The external fault occurs in series connections are open circuit or short circuit. The open circuit fault in series connection topology makes the series connection ineffective whereas a short circuit fault leads to a rise in current drawing capacity and rapid change in temperature, finally directs to malfunction of the battery management system.

6.8.2   Parallel Connected

Figure 6.3 (b) illustrates the parallel connection-based battery pack topology. This method is more suitable for the energy storage system which draws more current. Due to the parallel connection arrangement, the existence of one faulty cell in a group creates unsafe to rest of the cells. The healthy cells in a group should balance the faulty cell lower output current relentlessly and thus reducing the life span.

Due to the parallel connection, charging/discharging of every cell is differ in tiny changes because of its internal resistance. While the operation of parallel connected battery connection, this directs a huge variation in current drawing capacity for every cell. Due to the parallel connection, the voltage across each cell is the same. This brings to self-balanced architecture forever and makes the same State of Charge (SoC) for each individual cell [15]. In contrast to series connection arrangement of cells, open circuit fault does not affect the regular operation however creates a burden to the rest of the cells in a group whereas short circuit fault makes very bad situation due to single fault tends to whole system damage or thermal runaway because of creating cascade connection of cells.

6.9   Series-Parallel Connections

A grouping of series and parallel connected cells are needed in order to improve the operating voltage and battery capacity. Series-parallel based topology comes into the category when both voltage and currents are to be improved.

The two different configurations of this topology are illustrated in Figure 6.3 (c) Parallel connected configuration (PCC) and Figure 6.3 (d) Series connected configuration (SCC). Inside a battery pack, the parallel string of cells is connected in a series manner to construct a parallel connected configuration. Due to parallel interconnection of each cell, self-balance by itself, there are fewer requirements for an external cell-balancing circuit. But the cell-balancing for module level is definitely needed. This unique characteristic is the most viable solution for higher capacity and higher current applications. The shortcomings of parallel-connected configuration are fault due to open circuit and leakage current. The short circuit fault occurs when the leakage current goes beyond the certain level which also directs into a similar type of faults in the rest of the parallel connected cells. The failure caused by the open-circuit is that it limits the power transferred from the energy storage system to load [16].

The series connection makes to improve voltage rating whereas parallel connection leads to enhance the current rating in SCC. This type of SCC is absolutely needed to satisfy the high voltage requirement and it also not possible for constructing a single battery to fulfil the high voltage applications like gird storage systems and electric vehicles etc. The extraordinary attention is to be taken when comes to the assembling of parts, maintenance and servicing of such SCC due to its higher operating voltage. In order to, increase the capacity of SCC by means of including 'n' number of series connected batteries in parallel to keep the operating voltage constant. The battery pack module level cell-balancing happens at the time of rest period because of their interconnection in parallel. However, the cells inside the battery pack are not balanced. This leads to the implementation of very complicated intra SCC based cell balancing circuit [16]. The defect may occur in the series-connected configuration are open or short circuit. The open-circuit directs to enhance more stress on the rest of the cells connected in a string. In the other hand, short circuit leads to total failure owing to thermal runaway. SCC is more prone to open circuit fault whereas less prone to short circuit fault.

6.10   Evolution of Battery Management System

Reducing the health degradation and improving the operating time of battery are the most challenging issue. Variety of algorithms is developed for discharging has been carried out previously. In order to improve the operating time, capacity rate and recovery effects are used in most of the methods. This section discusses about the optimization methods implemented for BMS, R-BMS and comparison also made for the methods to be discussed.

6.10.1   Necessity for Reconfigurable BMS

Nowadays, Static-Battery Management System (S-BMS) is broadly employed in large scale application like electric vehicles, energy storage in smart grids, independent power grids for homes and robotics. The optimal utilization of battery packages is required for higher operating time as well as increasing battery life. Increasing the operating time of battery cells by utilizing fully is done through scheduling algorithm. Scheduling algorithm requires more than an actual number of battery cells because it depends on the backup battery cells to meet up the demand when one of the battery cells is switched off. Adding extra battery cells in small scale application is possible solution whereas it is impossible to implement for large scale applications due to the complexity of the circuit and cost. In addition, the scheduling algorithm is easily implemented in a single battery package whereas module level scheduling creates more computation complexity owing to different parameters like SoH, SoC of every module and load demand [17]. In scheduling algorithm, problems occurring due to non-linear characteristics of the battery are not exactly focused. Hence optimum solution cannot be possible in this scenario.

Voltage regulators are used in S-BMS to keep the voltage level constant when discharging as well as it offers multiple voltage output. For providing multiple voltage output, DC–DC converters are employed and efficiency of the converters depends on output and input voltage level in the form of voltage regulators. If the input voltage to the regulators is less than the operating voltage leads to more power loss, in turn, reduce the efficiency. Therefore, dealing with this issue by means of a voltage regulator is not a feasible solution. The fault tolerant is the primarily significant need for a large-scale battery management system. Currently, the scheduling algorithm selects the particular cells in BMS is carried out when it is in working condition but there are no actions are taken against to remove the cell permanently once it is faulty or over discharging from the particular cell. This issue is overcome by incorporating the reconfigurability in BMS. In this section, various topologies available for R-BMS are discussed in detail. The re-configuration with BMS improves the following features like increase in operating time, fault tolerance and improvement in efficiency.

6.10.2   Conventional R-BMS Methods

On the other hand, a Reconfigurable Battery Management System (R-BMS) utilizes the batteries that are connected automatically in battery packs through switching logic control to meet the necessary demand and change in their inherent characteristics such as voltage, withstanding capacity and so on. This topology produces less power loss compared with power converters to satisfy the preferred load curve. There are various reconfigurable topologies are available in the literature [18]. The topologies are 1) First design, 2) Series topology, 3) Self X topology, 4) Dependable Efficient Scalable Architecture (DESA), 5) Genetic algorithm-based topology, 6) Graph-based topology and 7) Power tree-based topology.

6.10.2.1   First Design

Figure 6.2 shows the First design which is more preferred to fulfil the power requirement in minimum value through changing the voltage of each battery cell dynamically by considering the non-linearity characteristics of each individual battery. This reconfiguration method adopts any of the arrangement such as series, parallel and series-parallel topology by controlling the switches to meet the load demand. This design obeys the basic concept like the same voltage in the parallel circuit and same current in series circuit.

The hardware model is developed with reconfiguration done for each cell using 5-control switches as depicted in Figure 6.4 which works to create a variety of configuration. Every battery/cell in the battery packages is arranged in series or parallel to the nearby cell or desperate entirely from the pack is called Full reconfigurability. Consider the two modules connected in SCC topology reported in Ref. [19] taken as an example. In this topology, the total battery pack goes below a rated voltage, the SCC turn out to be in series connection to improve the voltage level. The switches are opened or closed in order to realize the proposed reconfiguration arrangement. The complete pack is utilized for a second time only when the rated voltage is reached another time. The operating time and capacity are improved by 14.58 and 28.5% respectively adopting this reconfiguration topology.

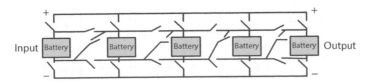

Figure 6.4 First design having 5 switches per cell.

6.10.2.2   Series Topology

Series topology-based reconfiguration in Figure 6.5 exploits the battery usage completely. This results in more operating time, improvement in reliability and enhanced tolerant capability to failures of single/multiple battery cells. Each cell with two controllable switches which makes a series connection or bypass the connection as shown in Figure 6.3. The battery cells in a pack automatically reconfigured in a series manner when the threshold voltage is reached nearby to keep the voltage at the required level. In the same way, the cells are connected in bypass in charging mode while it initiates to overcharge to avoid the requirement of cell balancing.

The safety pertaining to the battery pack in real-time is ensured through the sensors' data in this topology. This topology reported in Ref. [20] produce the maximum energy capacity of 66.7% even at the time of worst battery failure situations and gives the maximum efficiency of 98% under maximum load by taking power dissipations of switches into consideration.

6.10.2.3   Self X Topology

Figure 6.6 gives an idea about Self X based reconfigurable method. Here, X means that Reconfiguration, balance, healing and optimization of battery cells. The 'N' cells are connected in parallel as a single string which

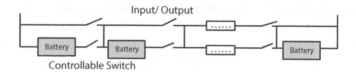

Figure 6.5 A series-connected reconfigurable battery pack.

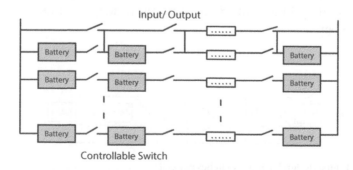

Figure 6.6 A Self-X reconfigurable multi-cell battery pack.

is isolated or connected by means of individual switches. The number of strings 'M' is connected in a series manner which is bypassed through a single switch per string. Therefore, totally M × (N + 1) switches are needed to implement this arrangement as depicted in Figure 6.6. The hybrid battery model reported in Ref. [21] is used for real-time application because of less computation time, higher accuracy in prediction of SoC. This method comprises of three sections namely cell pack, switching circuit as well as the BMS. The model based SoC estimation is carried out in BMS through current, cell voltage and temperature. This reconfiguration method along with an optimal scheduling technique allows finding out the exact faulty battery cells from the connected topology and also makes the fault-tolerant based management system with less number of switches.

The limitation of this topology is that it does not permit two cells of the similar string in series or two cells of dissimilar strings to be connected in parallel. The strings are chosen according to the current demand and SoC. The optimum value of current and voltage obtained from the control module by means of the following trade-offs,

1. The output voltage should be chosen in order to work the DC-DC converter at retaining maximum efficiency as well as higher voltage gain.
2. Each the cell should be utilized only when its rated capacity meets the load demand.

Dynamic reconfiguration is used to separate the faulty cells by healing those cells. The dynamic reconfiguration with this topology using an optimum scheduling algorithm [21] produces a fault tolerant system with minimum quantity of switches.

6.10.2.4   Dependable Efficient Scalable Architecture Method

DESA reconfiguration (Figure 6.7) of the battery management system is implemented where the integration and controlling of large-capacity battery packs application with less number of switches using Controller Area Network (CAN) bus for making communication between local and global battery management system. The global and local BMS based on monarchy relationship [22] in which the instructions from global BMS are accomplished through local BMS. The necessity for a local controller is the smallest amount in a fully centralized systems because the global controller works on higher speed in switching configurations as well as in fault detections using monitoring the individual cells performance directly

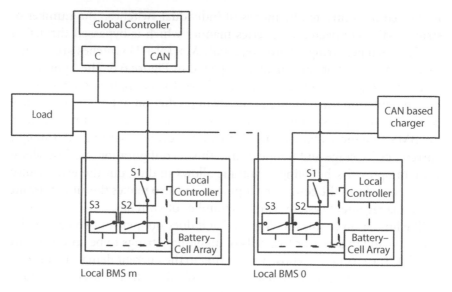

Figure 6.7 Schematic diagram of DESA.

and controlling the switches according to the load demand. In the case of large battery pack applications, the computational complexity due to the global controller is enormously high and therefore DESA based centralized topology works better in that situation.

The major disadvantage of this method is that the total battery management system will get failure if a fault takes place in either local or global battery management side. A logical switch configuration based algorithm discussed along with DESA architecture is employed through a global controller to direct a local controller using three array level switching namely parallel switch (S1—P-Switch), series switch (S2—S-Switch) and bypass switch (S3—B-Switch) as illustrated in Figure 6.7. This DESA topology works on the principle that neither CAN bus nor global controller fails [22]. The entire system gets failure when the fault occurs in any of these two components of DESA because of communication issues.

DESA with derived cost model has the capability to generate cost effective battery pack. This topology proved that improving reliability, saving cost and reducing the service cost in the order of 2×, 7× and 4.2× times respectively compared to traditional battery models.

6.10.2.5   Genetic Algorithm-Based Method

The well-established dynamic reconfigurable method using genetic algorithm-based topology is depicted in Figure 6.8. This reconfiguration

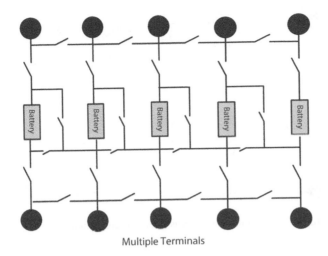

Multiple Terminals

Figure 6.8 Genetic algorithm based topology.

technique has two important goals which are to reconfigure the battery management is in an online to get the information regarding faulty batteries and provide the numerous output voltage terminals. The syntactic and semantic bypassing mechanism based genetic algorithms are used to generate configuration. In case of syntactic bypassing mechanism, the switching or bypassing of the cell from series to parallel as well as vice versa when no fault happens and the faulty cell is isolated [23]. In the other hands, the semantic bypassing mechanism directs meaningful to the syntactic mechanism by means of taking decisions that which group of cells in a string should be utilized at the time of operation in such a way that every cell maintain the constant voltage at the terminals and degrades all the cells at the similar rate.

Furthermore, this genetic algorithm along with scheduling provides optimum utilization of every cell in a battery pack. This work is established with six switches which enhance the fault tolerance the capability of BMS and to prevent the use of DC–DC converter for providing dissimilar voltage terminals.

6.10.2.6   Graph-Based Technique

A graph-based algorithm to reconfigure the battery management system shown in Figure 6.9 is the most suitable technique for satisfying the load requirements in real-time. In a traditional system, ineffective voltage regulators are used whereas multi-terminal output terminals are provided in

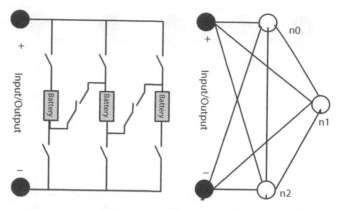

Figure 6.9 Graph based topology and paths as graph representation.

case of reconfiguration battery management system. Two switches per battery pack and three switches per battery cell are used in graph-based technique is as shown in Figure 6.9.

Higher efficiency obtained using the effective scheduling of charging/discharging and resting time in a proper way [24]. The performance degradation of battery packs occurs due to unbalanced cell in a battery pack and SOH of the rest of the cells. In most of the literature, the SoH factor is not addressed effectively expect the study carried out in Ref. [25]. The paper proposed in Ref. [25] deals about two algorithms such as Full-SHARE algorithm (SoH Aware RE-configuration algorithm) as well as Partial-SHARE algorithm with graph based approach is used to achieve for fully and partially reconfigurable battery packs. The simulation and experimental evaluation report that Full- and Partial-SHARE algorithm produces 10–30% more capacity compared to the SOH-oblivious system. The proposed algorithm performs well even with harsh cell imbalance conditions and increases the battery pack capacity in the range of 10–60% [26].

6.10.2.7 Power Tree-Based Technique

The power tree model based reconfiguration system is visualized in the form of an inverted tree in which the overall battery pack considered as root and individual sub-block pack considered as leaves. The overall capacity of battery packs are divided into sub-packs consists of series (Ns) and parallel (Np) combinations which are defined as the division of (Ns × Np) packs into a set of 'n' sub-packs (Nsi × Npi), where, i = 1,2,3,...n. The atomic node is defined as the division is carried out till the value which is

Table 6.1 Comparison of various reconfigurable topologies properties.

S. No.	Reconfiguration topology types	No. of switches used	Operating response	Computational difficulty	Hardware difficulty
1.	First Design	5	Low	High	High
2.	Series	2	Medium	Low	Low
3.	Self-X	2	Medium	Low	Medium
4.	DESA	Nil	High	Medium	Medium
5.	Genetic Algorithm	6	High	High	High
6.	Graph	3	High	High	Low
7.	Power Tree	3	High	High	High

indivisible. However, the number of divisions is limited by power range level. This division-based algorithm has features such as fast power real-location (FPR) and fast failure recovery (FFR). The number of additional cells is reduced to produce an optimum number for a stipulated time period (T) using A* heuristics search [27] in power tree-based topology.

This re-configurability topology is not having a direct relationship with the number of switches used. Therefore, it is not the best method so far. The multi-chemistry-based energy storage systems are capable of producing high power and high energy to the load [28] by means of taking into consideration of various cell chemistry properties apart from the methods mentioned above. In the next method, distributed R-BMS reported in Ref. [29] claims that increased reliability, scalability, the possibility of adding/disconnecting the modules and failure identification controller to detect a single battery pack rather than the entire module. Due to distributive nature, maintenance and replacement is easy compared to traditional BMS. The performance of the power tree is better than with other reconfigurable topologies are illustrated in Table 6.1.

6.11   Modeling of Reconfigurable-BMS

The major goal of R-BMS is increasing the reliability of cell faults and efficiency of the battery packs. For constructing the R-BMS requires a greater number of passive circuit elements of switches. This leads to enlarging the complexity issues and affects the reliability and predictability of the system. The testing at that design phase enables the designer to think of real-time implementation in the easiest way. To implement this technique, R-BMS is to be considered as a Cyber Physical Systems (CPS). CPS is a method in which modelling of a variety of components as modules or blocks and tests the integration of the modules. The simulation of designed R-BMS with CPS creates the platform to identify the major issues like failure of cells and switches, responses to load variation, reconfiguration speed and other parameters at the time of design phase itself. In addition to it, extra features to be included in R-BMS can be done through updating the modular part alone.

The real-time embedded system which collects the data directly from the physical environment is referred to as time-dependent data. This data should be processed further to take a decision for generating the actuation signals. The actuation signal is very simple in case of small scale networked embedded systems. On the other hand, issues such as stochastic behavior and timing variability [30] occur in large scale application. In R-BMS, the time dependent data sensed in real-time is the foremost action to be done for constructing battery reconfiguration system. The differential equation is preferred due to the collected data in continuous time. The realization of reconfiguration in BMS is carried out by means of actuating the switches in predefined specific condition. For example, each cell comprises of two definite states in series connected topology in which one state is being used to make a series connection in the network and another is used to bypass from the network. This approach reveals that predefined unique set of patterns for each configuration of R-BMS topology and different switching states for the configuration used. From this statement, R-BMS is considered as Finite State Machine (FSM) and each state is regarded as a single configuration. Therefore, the reconfiguration-based modeling techniques work on the input of real-time sensors data as a function of the differential equation and actuate the switches in a discrete set of values in R-BMS for changing the state from one to another. Thus, the entire system is modelled in hybrid in nature which consists of both continuous and discrete characteristics.

6.12   Real Time Design Aspects

Reconfiguration in a BMS controls every cell module. Therefore, performance, robustness and fault tolerance of CPS should be evaluated. R-BMS is divided into three modules such as sensing module, decision control module and actuation module. Getting stable data is the biggest challenging task in the sensing module. For calculating the SOH and SOC of each battery pack or cell is the most difficult task due to its non-linear characteristics, which creates further complexity by adding the reconfigurability feature. The next module is the control module in which a variety of algorithms and techniques are tested for improving the decision-making capability in a smart way to handle any hard situation. The actuation module is the last module comprises of switches in which configuration of cell or battery modules are controlled. This stage is the difficult task where the control signals from the decision control module to be realized in a manner which neither the load nor the battery packs are affected to ensure the safe working condition. Some of the challenging factors faced to implement the R-BMS like thermal issues and circuit safety are discussed in the review paper [31]. This section deals about the various challenging factors to be considered while designing stage itself in R-BMS. There are sensing module stages, decision control stage and actuating signal generation stage.

6.12.1   Sensing Module Stage

In this module, sensors design and development for sensing the different parameters pertaining to battery management and its deployment are focused. In addition, an efficient way to recover the data from the sensor modules is also carried out in this section. Sensors data from sensors are playing a vital role to maintain the BMS to operate within the control limits and produce the optimized output. Design of sensing circuit with fault detection for each battery pack increases the circuit complexity and reliability. This directs to rapidly affect the computational tasks involved in turn results in a decrease in overall simplicity. Therefore, for better improvement trade-off the parameters are essential. If the number of sensing circuits for each battery is decreased in order to decrease the circuit complexity leads to poor battery fault detection and also choosing the specific battery to meet the required load demand. Hence, the benefit of adding the reconfiguration feature in a BMS will not be solved. For implementing a large scale BMS, researchers [32] adopted the best sensing technique in which sensors are chosen to acquire data by means of heuristics and acts accordingly. The same technique has to be utilized to realize the R-BMS also.

6.12.2   Control Module Stage

This is the heart of the R-BMS in which algorithm is employed to characterize the reliability, scalability and re-configurability features. The algorithm implemented in this control module should provide the assurance to utilize each cell fully in the particular battery package in effective manner and structured way. From the literature survey, the following are the design features used in control module.

6.12.2.1   Health Factor of Reconfiguration

First of all, to verify whether the reconfiguration with the proposed algorithm gives the optimum outcomes or not is the major goal for implementing the R-BMS. Depending upon the load demand, the cell configuration should be chosen to produce the best result. Consider the following example to clarify the above-mentioned factor. In order to meet the load of 50 V with (10 × 1) or (10 × 2) Lithium based cells of the mean voltage value of 5 V per cell. Here, 10 represents the number of cells in a pack and 1 & 2— denotes the current handling capacity of each pack respectively. According to the load current requirement, one of the battery packs is to be assigned. In case, load demands 1 A in the whole sum, the algorithm should choose a 10 × 1 battery pack whereas load requires more than 1 A in total (less than 2 A), 10 × 2 battery pack will be the desired choice by the algorithm due to the fact that cell degrades its health performance while more than its rated capacity being drawn. Therefore, defining the health factor is the basic requirement for each configuration of R-BMS according to load demand. Most of the existing algorithms in the literature fail to address this Health factor. Implementing the smart algorithms with health-factor will be the future scope of research in the area of R-BMS.

6.12.2.2   Reconfiguration Time Delay and Transient Load Supply

R-BMS employs to meet the load demand with no delay at any circumstances. In dynamic reconfiguration of battery packages, two challenging issues such as re-configuration time delay and transient load supply [33] are in front to distribute the power in an uninterrupted way. Re-configuration time in R-BMS is defined as the minimum time required for creating a new arrangement of cell configuration. The system performance degrades specifically for large scale dynamic reconfiguration of battery packs in which every sensor available in the system operates uninterrupted way. It requires the fastest response in reconfiguration at the time of load changes, over discharge and any battery fault conditions. The reusing the last used switch configuration leads to produce very less reconfiguration time [34]. Coordinated switching based on agile reconfiguration is the future scope of research to reduce the reconfiguration time.

The other factor influences the large scale dynamically reconfiguration system is to supply the load current at reconfiguration time. For example, consider the following case is that the load demand varies from 200 V (high voltage), 4 to 100 V, 8 A (high current) and reconfiguration time of 1 min. For meeting the load current of 8 A in a single minute is not an easy task. To overcome this issue, the secondary power supplies based on supercapacitor is the best option to meet up the transient load currents. This is also scope for extending the research in the field of the battery management system.

6.12.3   Actuation Module

The hardware pertaining to R-BMS such as processors, switches and cells comes under this section. Most of the operations carried out in this module only. If the actions are taken in the wrong manner, it leads to failure of the entire R-BMS. Some of the design features with respect to this module is explained as follows.

6.12.3.1   Order of Switching

The optimization technique discussed in Section 6.3 deals about the rules and algorithms to choose a few numbers of cells or battery packs depending upon its specifications. Even though, the order of switching is not discussed so far. Order of switching is essential in R-BMS because inappropriate manner of switching sequence may lead to an unfavorable fault like a short circuit. Consider the battery pack consists of four cells (C1, C2, C3 and C4) with four switches arranged for reconfiguration as depicted in Figures 6.10 to 6.12.

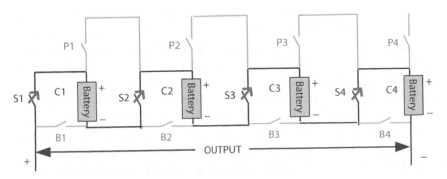

Figure 6.10 4S configuration-based order of switching.

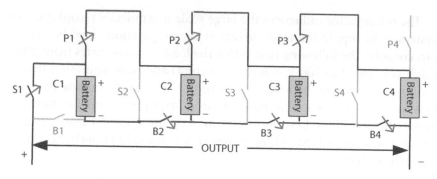

Figure 6.11 4S to 4P configuration-based faults occurring switches.

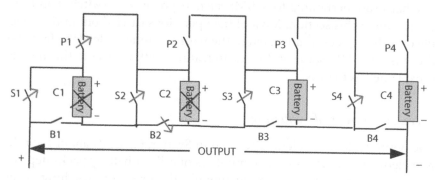

Figure 6.12 4P configuration-based order of switching.

The 4S configuration where all series switches are in ON state is depicted in Figure 6.10 and fault occurring switches where series switches are in OFF state is shown in Figure 6.11. The parallel configuration (4P) configuration of switches with ON state is illustrated in Figure 6.12. In order to have a reliable load condition, there must be transition from 4S configuration to 4P configuration. Thus, the S_2, S_3 and S_4 switches are changed to OFF state and then P_1, $[P_2 \, B_2]$, $[P_3 \, B_3]$ and B_4 are toggled to ON state. If S_2 and P_1 are in ON state, then cell C_1 is short circuited. Similarly, if S_2 and B_2 are in ON state, then C_2 is short circuited. In order to have smooth switching system, the need for derivative of switch dependency is must for dynamic reconfiguration. The chances of a short circuit are high when the system is connected in series configuration which can be seen in Figure 6.11. Thus, to avoid this conflict, the series switch should be in OFF state before parallel switch or bypass switch is switched ON. Thus, it can be stated that the serial switch is dependent on both parallel switch and bypass switch. Whereas, the bypass switch and parallel switch are not dependent on each other. Thus, an analysis of switching dependency is required to reduce the transition time and short circuit faults which in turn increases the reliability and efficiency of the battery reconfiguration system.

6.12.3.2   Stress and Faults of Switches

The performance of the reconfigurable battery pack highly depends on the switches which are highly sensitive in nature. The type of switch, position of switch plays an essential role in the performance of the battery system. Solid state switches are highly recommended over electromechanical relays for its reliability and safety. Because of electromechanical relays constitute of high voltages and arcs which affects the performance of the battery system. The only disadvantage of the solid-state switch is high power consumption. Generally employed solid state power electronic switches are MOSFET and IGBTs. Based on the requirement and applications, the types of switches are considered for the system. Generally, for high power application, IGBT switches are used whereas for high frequency application, MOSFETs are considered. The major drawback of the switches is its switching loss and voltage stress due to prolonged ON–OFF state. And moreover, to turn ON and OFF, the additional driver circuit is required which consumes the power. Thus, by using an optimal number of switches, the load on the system will be reduced and also the switching loss will also be reduced. Thus, to enhance the efficiency, enhanced—MOSFET with high depletion layer is generally used in the high power application.

The efficiency of the BMS highly depends on the switching loss. The power delivers by RBMS is high when compared to SBMS but the loss due to switches affects the system reliability. Thus, to increase the efficiency of the system such losses should be considered which is caused due to conduction and also by switching transient. The exact power loss as well as efficiency of the particular R-BMS topology is difficult to determine because of no standard on-off time for different switches employed over each cell. The switching in R-BMS is mainly depends on few factors such as the current flowing through the switches, the individual cell voltage, the voltage across it and the operating time of various modes which is highly unpredictable. Thus, a comparison of the previous topology is not possible unless the system has the same battery parameters and configuration of the standard test condition. In Ref. [21], the authors have configured Series topology and self X topology. The losses incurred due to switching are not enormous concern for the transition period between ON state to OFF state is approximately 30 min for implementing the application. But when as large battery packs are considered for the application, the switching loss may increase. Similarly, in Ref. [22], the authors implemented DESA disused about the switching losses caused by the system in the entire process of the conversion.

Thus, an in-depth analysis is required to build an R-BMS topology to enhance its efficiency. Providing a good trade-off between flexibility and efficiency, the number of switches is calculated in an optimized way. In order to increase the flexibility of the system, the number of switches is increased thus tends to enhance the switching losses. Since the reliability of Reconfigurable BMS are highly dependent on switching faults, analysis of faults such as "open" and "short" should be rapid to avoid any further serious faults. To identify single switch open circuit faults, short circuits, post short circuits and rest of the unknown faults happening in eclectic drive of EVs is carried out by a neural network technology, trained by a machine learning approach is reported in Ref. [35].

6.12.3.3   Determining Number of Cells in a Module

Reconfiguration of the battery management system does not overcome all the short comes of conventional BMS such as extended time and cell parameters. In order to estimate the available operational time, analysis of a number of healthy cells in the battery system is required [23]. Thus, to cope up with the problem of low operating time caused due to unhealthy cell, both scheduling and reconfigurable methods is must enhance the operating time as well as providing the backup cell. Thus, to maintain the longer functional period and operating time of the battery packs in R-BMS needs backup cells requirement compared to traditional systems. Additionally, exact quantity of backup cells needed by scheduling methods to that of the number of working cells in conventional BMS. Whereas, in RBMS the number of backup cells required is less than that of a number of the working cell, since they reconfigure themselves to provide extra time and also to reduce the cost and size of the overall system.

Thus, it is essential to analysis the optimized BMS which determines the number of cells required, operating time and cost of the system. The optimization can be done by analyzing the failure cell rate, load demand and failure or mismanagement of sensing devices. The optimization of the BMS system will increase the efficiency and reliability of the system without increasing the size and cost of the system.

6.13   Opportunities and Challenges

6.13.1   Modeling and Simulation

Graph model based reconfigurable battery system has few drawbacks. In this model, connectivity is one of the major issues in which out-degree connectivity to be found is not in a straightforward manner. The solution for this issue possibly lies in between conservative connectivity extremes along with spatial neighborhoods and all-to-all connectivity. Variety of connectivity architecture with exact constraints makes much understanding and also clarifies the advantages of more flexible systems. There is no integrated framework available for simulation of BMS till now. Therefore, developing software dedicated only for BMS is required with an increasing research interest in this area. Nowadays, researchers are developing simulation work by themselves using single battery modeling and constructing the design manually. This approach tends to rise in time requirement and short of a general framework for creating group effort in an easy manner.

6.13.2   Hardware Design

Hardware development is not explored very well. Two types of hardware design exist in practice. One which dedicated only for a single load with three switches per cell and the second one which is employed for more than one load with six switches per cell. The number of switches may be reduced from six by giving up a few loads. The number of loads is restricted in most of the practical applications. For considering the electric vehicle application, drive motor alone requires high voltage and rest of the secondary appliances operates on low voltage in the range of 12 V. The reconfigurability or modular based battery management system is preferred for large scale applications. One of the field study reports [36] proved that approximately 8% of the entire weight devoted to switches and associated elements. Depending upon the level of reconfigurability, this value can be increased.

6.13.3   Granularity

Granularity is also having an avenue in BMS. In case of small-scale applications, reconfiguration of each battery or cell is possible. However, it is not feasible in case of large-scale applications. Therefore, re-configuration is applicable only for modules (fixed number of batteries is connected in some configuration) not single batteries or cells. This makes the researchers think to solve the following problematic questions such as how much reconfiguration flexibility should be considered and what must be the size of the fixed configuration module? In addition, the query may take place to design a module whether it may be SCC, PCC or hybrid of both.

6.13.4 Hardware Overhead

Evaluation of hardware, overhead is an added issue coupled with granularity. The switches with least switching losses of 1% are available for implementing R-BMS, rather than switching losses supported practical aspects are also to be considered for analysis. In general, these switches are needed for the specific works and resources because of the major issues such as control circuit size, overall losses incurred by different battery configuration and cost. The performance of switches plays on a vital role in overall system reliability which is also an equally important issue. Although, R-BMS deals specifically about the cell or battery failure, it is not explored about if the switches get failure. The switch failure should be carefully analyzed for implementing in real time due to its quantity being used and importance on the reliability of the system. The extensive work to be done in this area particularly discusses the identifying the switch failure types, detection, forecasting of failure and impacts on the integration of R-BMS.

6.13.5 Intelligent Algorithms

There is possibility to enhance the small-scale stand-alone appliances such as tablets, smart watches and phones etc rather than large-scale applications. For extracting the battery tradeoffs in the best way to boost the operation time by creating high-level polices and having flexible batteries. These personal electronics gadgets are already equipped with extraordinary features like personal scheduling, motion tracking and so on. This information may be used to define the best policy automatically for each individual user. The user's information pertaining to their daily schedule and subsequent action makes the researchers build a smart intelligent algorithm to perform fast or slow charging depending upon the situation prevailing at the time. The future research gives the scope in the area of improving battery performance using high-level information.

6.13.6 Distributed Reconfigurable Battery Systems

The distributed re-configurable battery management system is an attractive research area as discussed in Ref. [37]. Currently, R-BMS works for centralized control which causes a bottleneck in the large-scale real-time control system. Due to the upcoming smart cells with communication and tracking performance to realize the distributed control network discussed in Ref. [38]. The design of smart cells available in present is performing the distributed control actions which are restricted to fixed connection topology. This directs to validate the capability of smart cells in R-BMs to maximize the overall performance is also a new research area to be explored.

6.14   Conclusion

This chapter gives an overview of the various optimization techniques existed so far to implement the reconfigurable battery management system in the best way. The discussion about the characteristics of the individual cell or battery is modeled using first or second-order approximation and measures the parameters such as SoC, SoH, battery life, rate discharge effect and rate recovery effect to check the healthiness of the battery are presented. An outline of traditional battery connection arrangement, cell imbalance, and faults pertaining to it are presented to choose the one for the required application. The evolution of dynamically reconfigurable battery management system from a conventional battery management system is also reported well to opt for it. The real-time design aspects along with challenges and opportunities also explained for creating interest to the budding researchers in the field of the reconfigurable battery management system.

References

1. Muhammad, S., Rafique, M.U., Li, S., Shao, Z., Wang, Q., Liu, X., Reconfigurable Battery Systems: A Survey on Hardware Architecture and Research Challenges, *ACM Trans. Design Autom. Electron. Syst. (TODAES)*, *24*(2), 1–27, 2019.
2. Nehrir, M.H., Wang, C., Strunz, K., Aki, H., Ramakumar, R., Bing, J., Salameh, Z., A review of hybrid renewable/alternative energy systems for electric power generation: Configurations, control, and applications, *IEEE trans. Sustain. energy*, *2*(4), 392–403, 2011.
3. Ji, F., Liao, L., Wu, T., Chang, C., Wang, M., Self-reconfiguration batteries with stable voltage during the full cycle without the DC–DC converter, *J. Energy Storage*, 28, 101213, 2020.
4. Lin, N., Ci, S., Wu, D., Guo, H., An Optimization Framework for Dynamically Reconfigurable Battery Systems, *IEEE Trans. Energy Conver.*, *33*(4), 1669–1676, 2018.

5. Rao, R., Vrudhula, S., Rakhmatov, D., Analysis of discharge techniques for multiple battery systems, In *Proceedings of the 2003 International Symposium on Low Power Electronics and Design, 2003. ISLPED'03*, pp. 44–47, 2003.

6. Chen, M., Rincon-Mora, G.A., Accurate electrical battery model capable of predicting runtime and IV performance, *IEEE Trans. Energy Convers.*, 21(2), 504–511, 2006.

7. Tremblay, O., Dessaint, L.A., Experimental validation of a battery dynamic model for EV applications, *World elect. Veh. J.*, 3(2), 289–298, 2009.

8. Kim, T., Qiao, W.A., hybrid battery model capable of capturing dynamic circuit characteristics and nonlinear capacity effects, *IEEE Trans. on Energy Convers.*, 26(4), 1172–1180, 2011.

9. Huet, F., A review of impedance measurements for determination of the state-of-charge or state-of-health of secondary batteries, *J. Power Sources*, 70(1), 59–69, 1998.

10. He, L., Yang, Z., Gu, Y., Liu, C., He, T., Shin, K.G., SoH-aware reconfiguration in battery packs, *IEEE Trans. Smart Grid*, 9(4), 3727–3735, 2016.

11. Zou, C., Hu, X., Wei, Z., Wik, T., Egardt, B., Electrochemical estimation and control for lithium-ion battery health-aware fast charging, *IEEE Trans. Ind. Electron.*, 65(8), 6635–6645, 2017.

12. Rong, P., Pedram, M., An analytical model for predicting the remaining battery capacity of lithium-ion batteries, *IEEE Trans. Very Large Scale Integration (VLSI) Syst*, 14(5), 441–451, 2006.

13. Han, W., Zhang, L., Battery cell reconfiguration to expedite charge equalization in series-connected battery systems, *IEEE Robotics and Auto. Letters*, 3(1), 22–28, 2017.

14. Cao, J., Schofield, N., Emadi, A., Battery balancing methods: A comprehensive review, In *2008 IEEE Vehicle Power and Propulsion Conference*, pp. 1–6, 2008.

15. Gong, X., Xiong, R., Mi, C.C., Study of the characteristics of battery packs in electric vehicles with parallel-connected lithium-ion battery cells, *IEEE Trans. Indus. App.*, 51(2), 1872–1879, 2014.

16. Plett, G.L., Klein, M.J., Simulating battery packs comprising parallel cell modules and series cell modules, In *Proc. of EVS*, pp. 1–17, 2009.

17. Chowdhury, P., Chakrabarti, C., Static task-scheduling algorithms for battery-powered DVS systems, *IEEE trans. Very large scale integration (VLSI) Syst.* 13(2), 226–237, 2005.

18. Viswanathan, V., Palaniswamy, L.N., Leelavinodhan, P.B., Optimization techniques of battery packs using re-configurability: A review, *J. Energy Storage*, 23, 404–415, 2019.

19. Alahmad, M., Hess, H., Mojarradi, M., West, W., Whitacre, J., Battery switch array system with application for JPL's rechargeable micro-scale batteries, *J. Power Sources*, 177(2), 566–578, 2008.

20. Kim, T., Qiao, W., Qu, L., A series-connected self-reconfigurable multicell battery capable of safe and effective charging/discharging and balancing

operations, In *2012 Twenty-Seventh Annual IEEE Applied Power Electronics Conference and Exposition (APEC)*, pp. 2259–2264, 2012.

21. Kim, T., Qiao, W., Qu, L., Power electronics-enabled self-X multicell batteries: A design toward smart batteries, *IEEE Trans. Power Electron.*, 27(11), 4723–4733, 2012.

22. Kim, H., Shin, K.G., DESA: Dependable, efficient, scalable architecture for management of large-scale batteries, *IEEE Trans. Ind. Inform.*, 8(2), 406–417, 2011.

23. Kim, H., Shin, K.G., On dynamic reconfiguration of a large-scale battery system, *IEEE Real-Time and Embedded Technology and Applications Symposium*, pp. 87–96, 2009.

24. He, L., Gu, L., Kong, L., Gu, Y., Liu, C., He, T., Exploring adaptive reconfiguration to optimize energy efficiency in large-scale battery systems, *Real-Time Systems Symposium*, pp. 118–127, 2013.

25. He, L., Gu, Y., Zhu, T., Liu, C., Shin, K.G., HARE: SoH-aware reconfiguration to enhance deliverable capacity of large-scale battery packs, In *Proceedings of the ACM/IEEE Sixth International Conference on Cyber-Physical Systems*, pp. 169–178, 2015.

26. He, L., Yang, Z., Gu, Y., Liu, C., He, T., Shin, K.G., SoH-aware reconfiguration in battery packs, *IEEE Trans. Smart Grid*, 9(4), 3727–3735, 2016.

27. Rios, L.H.O., Chaimowicz, L., A survey and classification of A* based best-first heuristic search algorithms, In *Brazilian Symposium on Artificial Intelligence*, pp. 253–262, 2010.

28. Zimmermann, T., Keil, P., Hofmann, M., Horsche, M. F., Pichlmaier, S., Jossen, A., Review of system topologies for hybrid electrical energy storage systems, *J. Energy Storage*, 8, 78–90, 2016.

29. Steinhorst, S., Shao, Z., Chakraborty, S., Kauer, M., Li, S., Lukasiewycz, M., Wang, Q., Distributed reconfigurable battery system management architectures, In *Asia and South Pacific Design Automation Conference (ASP-DAC)*, pp. 429–434, 2016.

30. Derler, P., Lee, E.A., Vincentelli, A.S., Modeling cyber-physical systems, *Proceedings of the IEEE*, 100(1), 13–28, 2011.

31. Ci, S., Lin, N., Wu, D., Reconfigurable battery techniques and systems: A survey, *IEEE Access*, 4, 1175–1189, 2016.

32. Kim, H., Shin, K.G., Efficient sensing matters a lot for large-scale batteries, In *IEEE/ACM Second International Conference on Cyber-Physical Systems*, pp. 197–205, 2011.

33. He, L., Gu, L., Kong, L., Gu, Y., Liu, C., He, T., Exploring adaptive reconfiguration to optimize energy efficiency in large-scale battery systems, In *IEEE 34th Real-Time Systems Symposium*, pp. 118–127, 2013.

34. Jin, F., Shin, K.G., Pack sizing and reconfiguration for management of large-scale batteries, In *IEEE/ACM Third International Conference on Cyber-Physical Systems*, pp. 138–147, 2012.

35. Masrur, M.A., Chen, Z., & Murphey, Y., Intelligent diagnosis of open and short circuit faults in electric drive inverters for real-time applications, *IET Power Electron.*, 3(2), 279–291, 2010.
36. Song, C., Energy informatization and internet-based management and its applications in distributed energy storage system, *Proceedings of the CSEE*, 35(14), 3643–3648, 2015.
37. Steinhorst, S., Shao, Z., Chakraborty, S., Kauer, M., Li, S., Lukasiewycz, M., Wang, Q., Distributed reconfigurable battery system management architectures, In *Asia and South Pacific Design Automation Conference (ASP-DAC)*, pp. 429–434, 2016.
38. Steinhorst, S., Lukasiewycz, M., Narayanaswamy, S., Kauer, M., Chakraborty, S., Smart cells for embedded battery management, In *IEEE International Conference on Cyber-Physical Systems, Networks, and Applications*, pp. 59–64, 2014.

7

Load Flow Analysis for Micro Grid

P. Sivaraman[1*], Dr. C. Sharmeela[2] and Dr. S. Elango[3]

[1]Leading Engineering Organisation, Chennai, India
[2]Anna University, Chennai, India
[3]Coimbatore Institute of Technology, Coimbatore, India

Abstract

Micro grid is defined as Distributed Energy Resources (DER) and interconnected loads with clearly defined electrical boundaries that act as a single controllable entity with respect to the grid as per IEEE std 2030.7-2017. Micro grid can connect and disconnect from the grid to enable the operation in both grid connected and islanding operations. That is micro grid can operate both in grid connected and islanded modes of operation. Whenever micro grid is in islanded mode, it will work as an autonomous system without distribution grid power supply. Whenever micro grid operates in grid connected mode, power flows bi-directionally between the distribution grid and micro grid at the Point of Interface (PoI) or Point of Common Coupling (PCC). So, it is essential to conduct the power system analysis during the planning/design stage of micro grid for different loading conditions for safe and reliable operation. This chapter discuss the load flow analysis for micro grid with example of 5 MW. Modeling and simulation of 5 MW micro grid is performed in ETAP software.

Keywords: Micro grid, load flow analysis, point of interface (PoI), ETAP, Distributed Energy Resources (DER), Point of Common Coupling (PCC)

7.1 Introduction

The consumption of electric power is growing day by day due to various factors like standard of living, industrial evolution, etc. [13], [14], [15], [16]. Micro grid is defined as Distributed Energy Resources (DER) and interconnected loads with clearly defined electrical boundaries that act as a single

Corresponding author: psivapse@gmail.com

C. Sharmeela, P. Sivaraman, P. Sanjeevikumar, and Jens Bo Holm-Nielsen (eds.) Microgrid Technologies, (177–196) © 2021 Scrivener Publishing LLC

controllable entity with respect to the grid as per IEEE std 2030.7-2017 [3]. Micro grid can connect and disconnect from the grid to enable the operation in both grid connected and islanding operations. That is micro grid can operate both in grid connected and islanded modes of operation. Micro grid controller plays an important role in micro grid system [1]. It shall have energy management system and real time control functions that operates in following conditions both grid connected and islanded modes of operation

- Automatic transfer from grid connected mode to islanding mode
- Reconnection and resynchronization from islanded mode to grid connected mode
- Optimization of both real and reactive power generation and consumption by energy management system
- Grid support
- Ancillary services, etc.

7.1.1   Islanded Mode of Operation

Whenever micro grid is in islanded mode of operation, it will work as an autonomous system without distribution grid power supply [6], [8], [9]. In this mode of operation, fault in transmission or distribution grid shall not propagate into the micro grid [1].

7.1.2   Grid Connected Mode of Operation

Whenever micro grid is in grid connected mode of operation, power flows bi-directionally between the distribution grid and micro grid at the Point of Interface (PoI) or Point of Common Coupling (PCC) [4], [7]. In this mode of operation, transmission or distribution grid fault propagate into the micro grid leading to reduction of voltage.

The grid connected micro grid system shall have the following technical requirements to be met at the PoI as per IEEE std 2030.9-2019 [2]. These technical requirements are following

- Low Voltage Ride Through (LVRT)
- High Voltage Ride Through (HVRT)
- Frequency Ride Through (FRT)
- Anti-islanding operation
- Power quality requirement
- Import and export of real and reactive power

So, it is essential to conduct the power system analysis for different loading conditions of micro grid for safe and reliable operation [5]. This chapter discuss the load flow analysis for micro grid with example of 5 MW.

7.2   Load Flow Analysis for Micro Grid

The micro grid has the combination of power sources, energy storage systems and loads. It operates either in grid connected or islanded mode of operation. There is a bidirectional power flow between the micro grid and distribution grid in grid connected mode. So, it is essential to check the system performance for various system operating conditions during micro grid planning/designing/expansion time [1]. The typical operating conditions are,

i.   Minimum and maximum loading conditions
ii.   Minimum and maximum generation of DER
iii.   Energy storage system in working condition and maintenance
iv.   With and without connection to distribution grid.

The objective of load flow analysis is used to find the following parameters for various operating conditions of the micro grid [11], [12].

i.   Voltage profile at various buses
ii.   Tap selection and settings of transformers
iii.   Loading of the components and/or circuits
iv.   Real and reactive power losses in the micro grid
v.   Real and reactive power flows in various branch circuits
vi.   Sizing of reactive power compensation devices like capacitor banks, STATCOM, etc.
vii.   Micro grid performance during emergency conditions/operations.

7.3   Example

The micro grid system consists of solar PV system, battery energy storage system, loads and distribution grid. The rating details of micro grid are tabulated in Table 7.1.

The Single Line Diagram (SLD) of micro grid system considered for the analysis is shown in Figure 7.1.

Table 7.1 Rating of micro grid.

S. No.	Description	Capacity
1	Solar PV system AC capacity (MW)	5
2	Battery energy storage system (MW/MWh)	4.95/10
3	Aggregated loads (MW) at 0.85 power factor	4.5

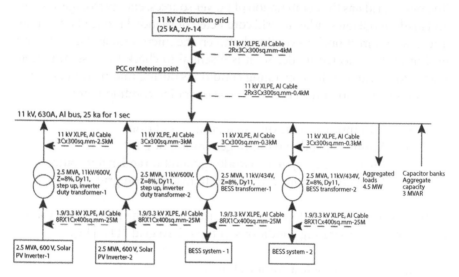

Figure 7.1 SLD of micro grid system.

7.3.1   Power Source

The micro grid has two power sources. One is external grid power source and another one is internal power source within the boundary of micro grid. It has the aggregated installed capacity of solar PV system of 5 MW. The name plate details of solar inverter are listed in Table 7.2.

7.4   Energy Storage System

The aggregated installed capacity of Battery Energy Storage System (BESS) is 4.95 MW at UPF with 10 MWh. The name plate details of BESS inverters are listed in Table 7.3.

Table 7.2 Name plate details of solar inverter.

S. No.	Input/output	Description	Values
1	Input (DC)	Startup voltage (V)	900
		MPPT voltage (V)	900 to 1,450
		Rated input current (A)	3,200
		Maximum DC power (kWp)	3,750
2	Output (AC)	Rated output power (kW) at UPF	2,500
		Rated output current (A)	2,400
		Nominal voltage (V)	600
		Frequency (Hz)	50
		Current THD (%) at rated power	less than 3
		Efficiency (%)	99.25

Table 7.3 Name plate details of BESS inverters.

S. No.	Description		Values
1	Battery side (DC)	DC voltage (V)	634 to 1,000
		Minimum DC voltage (V)	614
		Maximum DC voltage (V)	1,100
		Maximum DC current (A)	3,960
2	Grid side (AC)	Maximum AC power (kVA)	2,475
		Maximum AC current (A)	3,292
		Nominal AC voltage (V)	434
		Frequency (Hz)	50
		Current THD (%) at rated power	less than 3
		Efficiency (%)	98.6

7.5   Connected Loads

The aggregated load (including residential loads, commercial customer loads and agricultural loads) is 4.5 MW operating at 0.85 power factor at 11 kV voltage level.

7.6   Reactive Power Compensation

The capacitor banks are used for reactive power compensation at 11 kV voltage level. The aggregated capacity of capacitor banks installed in micro grid is 3 MVAR.

7.7   Modeling and Simulation

The SLD of micro grid shown in Figure 7.1 is modeled in ETAP simulation software is shown in Figure 7.2.

The various operating conditions of this micro grid are listed in Table 7.4.

7.7.1   Case 1

The operating conditions of micro grid are as follows

- ✓ Micro grid system is connected with distribution grid
- ✓ Solar PV system 1 is delivering rated power

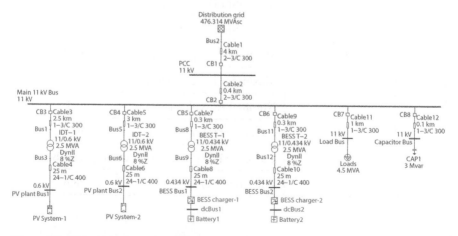

Figure 7.2 SLD of micro grid in ETAP.

Table 7.4 Various operating conditions of micro grid.

| Case | Solar PV system | | BESS System | | Loads | Capacitor banks | Distribution grid |
	System 1	System 2	System 1	System 2			
Case 1	Working at its rated capacity	Working at its rated capacity	Charging	Charging	Working at full load	Working at its rated capacity	Connected
Case 2	Working at its rated capacity	Working at its rated capacity	Out of service	Charging	Working at full load	Working at its rated capacity	Connected
Case 3	Working at its 50% capacity	Working at its 50% capacity	Out of service	Out of service	Working at 50% load	Working at its 50% capacity	Connected
Case 4	Working at its 50% capacity	Working at its 50% capacity	Charging	Dis-charging	Working at full load	Working at its 90% capacity	Dis-Connected
Case 5	Working at its 50% capacity	Working at its 50% capacity	Dis-charging	Out of service	Working at full load	Working at its 90% capacity	Dis-Connected

✓ Solar PV system 2 is delivering rated power
✓ BESS system 1 is in charging mode
✓ BESS system 2 is in charging mode
✓ Loads are drawing the full load power
✓ Capacitor bank delivering rated reactive power.

The bus voltage, real power and reactive power of case 1 are listed in Table 7.5.

From Table 7.5, the solar PV systems 1 and 2 are delivering the rated power of 2.5 MW at unity power factor. The voltage profile at various buses is within ±3% voltage tolerance from nominal voltage. Both BESS systems 1 and 2 are charging at 2.425 MW at unity power factor.

The circuit loadings (real power, reactive power, PF, voltage drop, real power losses and reactive power losses) of case 1 are listed in Table 7.6.

From Table 7.6, total real power losses are 244.32 kW and total reactive power losses are 876.81 kVAR.

7.7.2   Case 2

The operating conditions of micro grid are as follows

✓ Micro grid system is connected with distribution grid
✓ Solar PV system 1 is delivering rated power
✓ Solar PV system 2 is delivering rated power

Table 7.5 Bus voltage, real power and reactive power.

Bus ID	Voltage (%)	Real power (MW)	Reactive power (MVAR)	Current (A)
PCC	99.16	3.867	0.265	205.20
Main 11 kV Bus	99.08	8.758	3.208	494.10
Capacitor Bus	99.10	0.000	2.946	156.00
Load Bus	98.51	3.802	2.356	238.30
PV plant Bus1	100.79	2.500	0.000	2,387.00
PV plant Bus2	100.90	2.500	0.000	2,384.00
BESS Bus1	97.08	2.425	0.000	3,324.00
BESS Bus2	97.08	2.425	0.000	3,324.00

Table 7.6 Circuit components loading.

ID	Real power (MW)	Reactive power (MVAR)	Current (A)	PF (%)	% Voltage drop	Real power loss (kW)	Reactive power loss (kVAR)
BESS T-1	2.465	0.206	131.1	99.65	1.65	32.836	197
BESS T-2	2.465	0.206	131.1	99.65	1.65	32.836	197
Cable1	3.898	0.287	205.2	99.73	0.84	31.284	22.073
Cable2	3.867	0.265	205.2	99.77	0.08	3.128	2.207
Cable3	2.464	−0.199	130.2	−99.68	0.6	15.743	11.108
Cable4	2.5	0	2,387	100	0.13	3.259	4.739
Cable5	2.464	−0.198	130	−99.68	0.71	18.847	13.298
Cable6	2.5	0	2,384	100	0.13	3.252	4.728
Cable7	2.467	0.208	131.1	99.65	0.08	1.917	1.353
Cable8	2.432	0.009	3,324	100	0.25	6.321	9.21

(Continued)

Table 7.6 Circuit components loading. (*Continued*)

ID	Real power (MW)	Reactive power (MVAR)	Current (A)	PF (%)	% Voltage drop	Real power loss (kW)	Reactive power loss (kVAR)
Cable9	2.467	0.208	131.1	99.65	0.08	1.917	1.353
Cable10	2.432	0.009	3,324	100	0.25	6.321	9.21
Cable11	3.823	2.371	238.3	84.98	0.57	21.11	14.895
Cable12	0	2.946	156	0	0.02	0.905	0.638
IDT-1	2.496	−0.005	2,387	−100	0.98	32.36	194
IDT-2	2.496	−0.005	2,384	−100	0.98	32.285	194
Total						244.32	876.81

✓ BESS system 1 is out of service
✓ BESS system 2 is in charging mode
✓ Loads are drawing the full load power
✓ Capacitor bank delivering rated reactive power.

The bus voltage, real power and reactive power of case 2 are listed in Table 7.7.

From Table 7.7, the solar PV systems 1 and 2 are delivering the rated power of 2.5 MW at unity power factor. The voltage profile at various buses is within ±3% voltage tolerance from nominal voltage. BESS system 1 kept as out of service and 2 is charging at 2.425 MW at unity power factor.

The circuit loadings (real power, reactive power, PF, voltage drop, real power losses and reactive power losses) of case 2 are listed in Table 7.8.

From Table 7.8, total real power losses are 171.41 kW and total reactive power losses are 640.49 kVAR.

7.7.3   Case 3

The operating conditions of micro grid are as follows

✓ Micro grid system is connected with distribution grid
✓ Solar PV system 1 is delivering its 50% rated power
✓ Solar PV system 2 is delivering its 50% rated power
✓ BESS system 1 is out of service

Table 7.7 Bus voltage, real power and reactive power.

Bus ID	Voltage (%)	Real power (MW)	Reactive power (MVAR)	Current (A)
PCC	99.71	1.405	0.018	73.97
Main 11 kV Bus	99.68	6.299	2.999	367.4
Capacitor Bus	99.7	0	2.982	157
Load Bus	99.11	3.812	2.362	237.5
PV plant Bus1	101.38	2.5	0	2,373
PV plant Bus2	101.5	2.5	0	2,370
BESS Bus2	97.7	2.425	0	3,302

Table 7.8 Circuit components loading.

ID	Real power (MW)	Reactive power (MVAR)	Current (A)	PF (%)	% Voltage Drop	Real power loss (kW)	Reactive power loss (kVAR)
BESS T-2	2.464	0.204	130.3	99.66	1.64	32.421	195
Cable1	1.409	0.02	73.97	99.99	0.29	4.066	2.869
Cable2	1.405	0.018	73.97	99.99	0.03	0.407	0.287
Cable3	2.464	-0.197	129.4	-99.68	0.59	15.558	10.978
Cable4	2.5	0	2,373	100	0.13	3.221	4.683
Cable5	2.465	-0.196	129.3	-99.68	0.71	18.627	13.143
Cable6	2.5	0	2,370	100	0.13	3.214	4.672
Cable9	2.466	0.205	130.3	99.66	0.08	1.893	1.335
Cable10	2.432	0.009	3,302	100	0.25	6.241	9.093
Cable11	3.832	2.377	237.5	84.98	0.57	20.954	14.785
Cable12	0	-2.982	157	0	0.02	0.916	0.646
IDT-1	2.496	-0.005	2,373	-100	0.98	31.981	192
IDT-2	2.496	-0.005	2,370	-100	0.98	31.907	191
Total						171.41	640.49

✓ BESS system 2 is out of service
✓ Loads are drawing the 50% load power
✓ Capacitor bank delivering 50% of its rated reactive power.

The bus voltage, real power and reactive power of case 3 are listed in Table 7.9.

From Table 7.9, the solar PV systems 1 and 2 are delivering the 50% of their rated power of 1.252 MW at unity power factor. The voltage profile at various buses is within ±3% voltage tolerance from nominal voltage. BESS system 1 kept as out of service and 2 is charging at 2.425 MW at unity power factor.

The circuit loadings (real power, reactive power, PF, voltage drop, real power losses and reactive power losses) of case 3 are listed in Table 7.10.

From Table 7.10, total real power losses are 81 kW and total reactive power losses are 321.44 kVAR.

7.7.4   Case 4

The operating conditions of micro grid are as follows

✓ Micro grid system is disconnected with distribution grid
✓ Solar PV system 1 is delivering its 50% rated power
✓ Solar PV system 2 is delivering its 50% rated power
✓ BESS system 1 is in charging mode
✓ BESS system 2 is in discharging mode

Table 7.9 Bus voltage, real power and reactive power.

Bus ID	Voltage (%)	Real power (MW)	Reactive power (MVAR)	Current (A)
PCC	99.61	1.903	0.011	100.3
Main 11 kV Bus	99.57	4.379	1.497	243.9
Capacitor Bus	99.58	0	1.487	78.4
Load Bus	99.29	1.907	1.182	118.6
PV plant Bus1	100.52	1.252	0	1,198
PV plant Bus2	100.58	1.252	0	1,197
BESS Bus2	97.59	2.425	0	3,306

Table 7.10 Circuit components loading.

ID	Real power (MW)	Reactive power (MVAR)	Current (A)	PF (%)	% Voltage Drop	Real power loss (kW)	Reactive power loss (kVAR)
BESS T-2	2.464	0.204	130.5	99.66	1.65	32.498	195
Cable1	1.91	0.016	100.3	100	0.39	7.473	5.273
Cable2	1.903	0.011	100.3	100	0.04	0.747	0.527
Cable3	1.243	−0.05	65.35	−99.92	0.31	3.968	2.8
Cable4	1.252	0	1198	100	0.07	0.822	1.185
Cable5	1.243	−0.05	65.31	−99.92	0.37	4.756	3.355
Cable6	1.252	0	1197	100	0.07	0.821	1.183
Cable9	2.466	0.205	130.5	99.65	0.08	1.897	1.339
Cable10	2.432	0.009	3,306	100	0.25	6.256	9.115
Cable11	1.912	1.186	118.6	84.99	0.28	5.228	3.688
Cable12	0	−1.487	78.4	0	0.01	0.228	0.161
IDT-1	1.251	−0.001	1,198	−100	0.57	8.156	48.937
IDT-2	1.251	−0.001	1,197	−100	0.57	8.146	48.877
Total						81.00	321.44

✓ Loads are drawing the full load power
✓ Capacitor bank delivering 90% of its rated reactive power.

The bus voltage, real power and reactive power of case 4 are listed in Table 7.11.

From Table 7.11, the solar PV systems 1 and 2 are delivering the 50% of their rated power of 1.252MW at unity power factor. The voltage profile at various buses is within ±3% voltage tolerance from nominal voltage. BESS systems 1 is in charging and 2 is discharging at 2.425 MW at unity power factor.

The circuit loadings (real power, reactive power, PF, voltage drop, real power losses and reactive power losses) of case 4 are listed in Table 7.12.

From Table 7.12, total real power losses are 69.58 kW and total reactive power losses are 218.47 kVAR.

7.7.5   Case 5

The operating conditions of micro grid are as follows

✓ Micro grid system is disconnected with distribution grid
✓ Solar PV system 1 is delivering its 50% rated power
✓ Solar PV system 2 is delivering its 50% rated power

Table 7.11 Bus voltage, real power and reactive power.

Bus ID	Voltage (%)	Real power (MW)	Reactive power (MVAR)	Current (A)
BESS bus 1	100	1.008	0.032	1,341
BESS Bus2	102.08	2.425	0	3,160
Bus2	100	0	0	0
Capacitor Bus	100.85	0	2.746	142.9
Load Bus	100.26	3.829	2.373	235.8
Main 11 kV Bus	100.83	4.865	2.745	290.8
PCC	100	0	0	0
PV plant Bus1	101.77	1.252	0	1,183
PV plant Bus2	101.83	1.252	0	1,183

Table 7.12 Circuit components loading.

ID	Real power (MW)	Reactive power (MVAR)	Current (A)	PF (%)	% Voltage Drop	Real power loss (kW)	Reactive power loss (kVAR)
BESS T-1	1.014	0.066	52.92	99.79	0.69	5.349	32.094
BESS T-2	2.419	−0.008	3,160	−100	0.94	29.689	178
Cable1	0	0	0	0	0	0	0
Cable3	1.243	−0.049	64.55	−99.92	0.31	3.871	2.731
Cable4	1.252	0	1,183	100	0.07	0.801	1.155
Cable5	1.243	−0.049	64.51	−99.92	0.37	4.64	3.274
Cable6	1.252	0	1,183	100	0.07	0.801	1.154
Cable7	1.015	0.066	52.92	99.79	0.03	0.312	0.22
Cable8	1.009	0.034	1,341	99.94	0.11	1.03	1.494
Cable9	2.39	−0.186	124.7	−99.7	0.07	1.733	1.223
Cable10	2.425	0	3,160	100	0.24	5.715	8.326
Cable11	3.85	2.388	235.8	84.98	0.56	20.665	14.581
Cable12	0	−2.746	142.9	0	0.02	0.759	0.536
IDT-1	1.251	−0.001	1,183	−100	0.57	7.957	47.743
IDT-2	1.251	−0.001	1,183	−100	0.57	7.948	47.686

Table 7.13 Bus voltage, real power and reactive power.

Bus ID	Voltage (%)	Real power (MW)	Reactive power (MVAR)	Current (A)
PCC	100	0	0	0
Main 11 kV Bus	99.66	3.833	2.682	246.4
Capacitor Bus	99.68	0	2.683	141.3
Load Bus	99.1	3.811	2.362	237.5
PV plant Bus1	100.61	1.252	0	1,197
PV plant Bus2	100.67	1.252	0	1,196
BESS bus 1	100	1.369	0.136	1,830

✓ BESS system 1 is in discharging mode
✓ BESS system 2 is kept out of service
✓ Loads are drawing the full load power
✓ Capacitor bank delivering 90% of its rated reactive power.

The bus voltage, real power and reactive power of case 5 are listed in Table 7.13.

From Table 7.13, the solar PV systems 1 and 2 are delivering the 50% of their rated power of 1.252 MW at unity power factor. The voltage profile at various buses is within ±2% voltage tolerance from nominal voltage. BESS system 1 is in discharging at real power of 1.369 MW and reactive power of 0.136 MVAR.

The circuit loadings (real power, reactive power, PF, voltage drop, real power losses and reactive power losses) of case 5 are listed in Table 7.1.4

From Table 7.14, total real power losses are 60.77 kW and total reactive power losses are 184.38 kVAR.

7.8   Conclusion

Micro grid can operate both in grid connected and islanded modes of operation. Whenever micro grid is in islanded mode, it will work as an autonomous system without distribution grid power supply. Whenever micro grid operates in grid connected mode, power flows bi-directionally

Table 7.14 Circuit components loading

ID	Real power (MW)	Reactive power (MVAR)	Current (A)	PF (%)	% Voltage Drop	Real power loss (kW)	Reactive power loss (kVAR)
BESS T-1	1.367	-0.139	1,830	-99.49	0.18	9.955	59.731
Cable1	0	0	0	0	0	0	0
Cable3	1.243	-0.05	65.29	-99.92	0.31	3.961	2.794
Cable4	1.252	0	1,197	100	0.07	0.82	1.182
Cable5	1.243	-0.05	65.25	-99.92	0.37	4.747	3.349
Cable6	1.252	0	1,196	100	0.07	0.819	1.181
Cable7	1.357	-0.199	72.2	-98.94	0.04	0.581	0.41
Cable8	1.369	-0.136	1,830	-99.51	0.12	1.916	2.787
Cable11	3.832	2.377	237.5	84.98	0.57	20.959	14.788
Cable12	0	-2.683	141.3	0	0.02	0.742	0.523
IDT-1	1.251	-0.001	1,197	-100	0.57	8.141	48.847
IDT-2	1.251	-0.001	1,196	-100	0.57	8.131	48.788
Total						60.77	184.38

between the distribution grid and micro grid at the Point of Interface (PoI) or Point of Common Coupling (PCC). So, it is essential to conduct the power flow analysis during the planning/design stage of micro grid for different loading conditions for safe and reliable operation. This chapter discussed the load flow analysis for micro grid with example of 5 MW.

References

1. IEEE Std 2030.9-2019, *IEEE recommended practice for the planning and design of the microgrid.*
2. IEEE Std 2030.8-2018, *Testing for micro grid controllers provides the testing procedures for micro grid controller.*
3. IEEE Std 2030.7-2017, *IEEE standard for specification of micro grid controllers.*
4. Nikkhajoei, H. and Iravani, R., Steady state model and power flow analysis of electronically coupled distributed resource units, *IEEE Trans. Power Del.,* Vol 22, No.1, pp.721–728, Jan 2007.
5. Wang, C. and Nehrir, MH., Analytical approaches for optimal placement of distributed generation sources in power systems, *IEEE Trans. Power Syst.,* vol. 19, no. 4, pp. 2068–2076, Nov. 2004.
6. Weisbrich, A.L., Ostrow, S.L. and Padalino, J.P., WARP: a modular wind power system for distributed electric utility application, *IEEE Trans. Ind. Appl.,* vol. 32, no. 4, pp. 778–787, Jul./Aug. 1996.
7. Hatziadoniu, J., Lobo, A.A., Pourboghrat, F. and Daneshdoost, M., A simplified dynamic model of grid-connected fuel-cell generators, *IEEE Trans. Power Del.,* vol. 17, no. 2, pp. 467–473, Apr. 2002.
8. Nikkhajoei, H. and Iravani, R., A matrix converter based micro-turbine distributed generation system, *IEEE Trans. Power Del.,* vol. 20, no. 3, pp. 2182–2192, Jul. 2005.
9. Katiraei, F., Iravani, M.R. and Lehn, P.W., Micro-grid autonomous operation during and subsequent to islanding process, *IEEE Trans. Power Del.,* vol. 20, no. 1, pp. 248–257, Jan. 2005.
10. Liu, S., Wang, X., Liu, P.X., Impact of communication delays on secondary frequency control in an islanded Microgrid, *IEEE Transactions on Industrial Electronics,* 62(4), 2021–2031, 2015.
11. IEEE Std 399—1997, *IEEE recommended practice for industrial and commercial power system analysis.*
12. IEEE Std 3002.2—2018, *Recommended practice for conducting load-flow studies and analysis of industrial and commercial power systems.*
13. P. Sivaraman, C. Sharmeela and D. P. Kothari, "Enhancing the voltage profile in distribution system with 40 GW of solar PV rooftop in Indian grid by 2022: a review" 1st International conference on Large scale grid integration renewable energy in India, September, 2017, New Delhi, India.

14. Sivaraman, P., and Sharmeela, C. (2020). Introduction to electric distribution system. In Baseem Kahn, Hassan Haes Alhelou & Ghassan (Eds.), *Handbook of Research on New Solutions and Technologies in Electrical Distribution Networks*, (pp. 1–31). Hershey, PA: IGI Global.
15. Sivaraman, P., and Sharmeela, C. (2020). Solar Micro-Inverter. In J. Zbitou, C. Pruncu, & A. Errkik (Eds.), *Handbook of Research on Recent Developments in Electrical and Mechanical Engineering* (pp. 283–303) Hershey, PA: IGI Global.
16. C. Sharmeela, Sivaraman, P., and S. Balaji (2020). Design of Hybrid DC Mini Grid for Educational Institution: Case Study, Lecture Notes in Electrical Engineering, 580, pp. 125-134.

8

AC Microgrid Protection Coordination

Ali M. Eltamaly[1], Yehia Sayed Mohamed[2], Abou-Hashema M. El-Sayed[2] and Amer Nasr A. Elghaffar[2,3]*

[1]Electrical Engineering Department, Mansoura University, Mansoura, Egypt
[2]Electrical Engineering Department, Minia University, Minia, Egypt
[3]Testing and Commissioning Department, Alfanar Company, Riyadh, Saudi Arabia

Abstract

A Microgrid is mainly uses to supply the local resource which is an unreliable or very small source, also it can be used to support the national grid during emergency cases. The protection and control techniques in the microgrid are considered as the highlight points which increase the reliability and independently to use the microgrid system. The faults in the linked microgrid with the utility grid can affect to damage the renewable generation, increase the thermal stresses on system equipment and affect the stability of the main grid, if the fault is not cleared immediately. For this purpose, this chapter aims to describe the optimum protection logic to be enabled with the microgrid depending on the advanced protection and control techniques to save the reliable and security system. Using the directional overcurrent protection function with the Over-Head Transmission Line (OHTL) to the utility grid can prevent the false operation during the fault into the parallel OHTL. The proposed analysis in this chapter has been simulated with OHTL 115 kV, 60 H.Z to describe the operating characteristics of using the distance protection function and the using of the multi-curves overcurrent protection function depending on the advanced protection numerical relay.

Keywords: Microgrid, protection system, high voltage, numerical relays

8.1 Introduction

There is no doubt that the electrical power system consists of the technological foundation of industrial societies and is the essential driver

---

Corresponding author: amernasr70@yahoo.com

C. Sharmeela, P. Sivaraman, P. Sanjeevikumar, and Jens Bo Holm-Nielsen (eds.) Microgrid Technologies, (197–226) © 2021 Scrivener Publishing LLC

of the world financial matters. Although, the electrical systems are designed to provide the most elevated level of development, unanticipated issues are continually experienced, requiring the plan of increasingly proficient and reliable systems dependent on novel innovations [1]. Hence, day by day, the electrical grid in the world must be growing with new substations related to increasing of the demand power and the increasing of the life slander. Electricity is playing now a high importance for everyone, so it's important to reach a high accurate design system to save a stable power sources to the consumers. Among the new technologies that support the power system stability, microgrid has been representing an important technology for solving the challenge for feeding the remote loads, critical industrial and military needs. In the last decades years, the world focused to increase the Distributed Energy Resources (DERs) which directly leads to improving the reliability of the power system which greatly enhanced the development of the microgrids. A microgrid system can be defined as a small-scale electric grid to provide efficient and flexible techniques for embedded energy production. However, the small compact grid that operates individual or with the utility grid can be known as a microgrid, which depends on the renewable energy sources or generators [2]. Due to the fact that fossil fuel is a fading source, the world researchers are trying to utilize the renewable energy sources that can operate in multi-sources of Distributed Generations (DGs) units as a wind turbine, photovoltaic system, which consist of a microgrid system as shown in Figure 8.1. For this reason, the developing countries have taken good progress for using the microgrids [3]. Generally, OHTL is used as a link between two busbars in the power system, which also can be used to connect between the microgrid and the utility grid, so it considered as one of the important parts to save the microgrid reliable continuously. But, it's not economical to design high-cost OHTL that fails at an abnormal condition, so using the protection system can provide a secure and more stable system. The faults in the microgrid can happen due to a lot of cases such as insulation failure, mechanical problems, electrical and thermal disturbance. Researchers applied more studies and use multi-methods to find the fault instantaneously, for example, using the Instantaneous Angular Speed (IAS) [4], cross-correlation k-nearest neighbor [5], S-transform and pattern recognition [6], neural network related to adaptive linear design [7] ΔV-I locus method [8], and Wave-Let Network [9]. The wavelet approach method is the better method due to the accurate value detection, operating pickup and trip time.

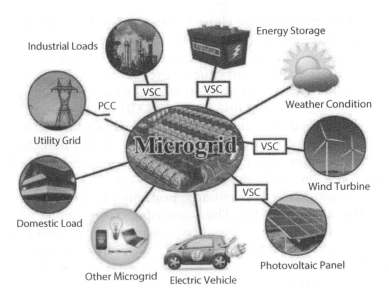

Figure 8.1 A sample of islanding microgrid design.

Furthermore, it can be used for analyzing the complex protection models [10]. The electrical faults as the short circuit can either be symmetrical or unsymmetrical fault. The symmetrical is a 3-phase short circuit which occurs by 5% of the total percentage faults in the power system. The other faults are named as the unsymmetrical faults that are one line to ground (L-G), which occurs by 85% from the faults, line with line fault (LL) which occurs by 10% from the total percentage faults in the power system. Faults occur at insulation fail or any abnormal weather condition. Hence, it's important to use the required protection system to find the fault with high response to isolate the fault zone for saving the system insecure and stability condition [11]. The basic operation logic of the protection system is depending on the fault current, voltage value and their locations. The accurate event recorder and the simplification of changing the setting in the numerical relays are the main contributions that encouraged the world to uses and utilize the Intelligent Electronic Devices (IEDs) functions. One of the main contributions of using the numerical protection relays is the facility to communicate with the substation automation system through IEC 61850 protocol which can cover and transmit all the alarms and the load values to the control entre. The distance protection system is used to save the OHTL more secure to prevent from isolation system during the fault out of the protection zone, that can classify to forward and reverse zone. The Directional Over Current (DOC) time delay setting is used with OHTL protection system to prevent the protection system false operation at the fault into the opposite direction. There are some solutions can use to decrease the system interruption after isolating the fault zone as using the Automatic Bus Transfer Scheme (ABTS) techniques depending on the advanced control relay, using the Auto-Recloser (AR) function in the protection relay to normalize the system after transient fault, using the Supervisory Control Acquisition Data Automation (SCADA) fast decision to maintain the system [12]. Regarding this discussion, this chapter introduces the optimum protection function to save the microgrid in a safe condition. The proposed operation sample for using the protection function with the microgrid has been validated with distance protection system by the FREJA Win software to lay the distance reach scheme which applied by the secondary injection with the intelligent electronic device.

8.2   Fault Analysis

The Microgrid idea has attracted attention as an answer for broadening and decentralizing the distribution system, supervising and control ability. Where the microgrid can be associated with the MV grid or independently. So, studying the faults and how to overcome the un-preferred conditions in the microgrid can enhance the microgrid operation and security to be able to link with the national distribution network without affecting on the

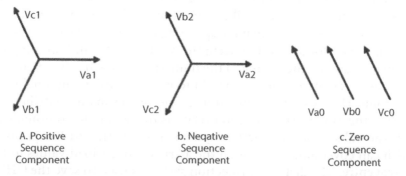

Figure 8.2 Analyzing electrical component in positive, negative and zero sequence.

utility grid. To analyze the fault, the simulation system composed of three components: positive, negative, zero sequences, can simplify the analyzing system as shown in Figure 8.2. The positive sequence is the clockwise sequence for voltage and current known as "abc", the negative sequence is the opposite rotation for voltage and current known as "cba" and the zero sequence find the voltage and current phase angle between the phases is zero degrees.

8.2.1 Symmetrical Fault Analysis

The voltage value is zero at 3-phase symmetrical fault, the symmetrical fault analysis and the sequence diagram can be discussed as shown in Figures 8.3 and 8.4 respectively, where the currents in each sequence can found by the equations below:

$$I_{a0} = 0 \tag{8.1}$$

$$I_{a2} = 0 \tag{8.2}$$

$$I_{a1} = \frac{1 \angle 0}{Z_1 + Z_f} \tag{8.3}$$

So, Equation (8.3) can be written as the equation below during the fault impedance Z_f is zero.

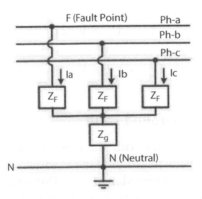

Figure 8.3 Symmetrical fault diagram.

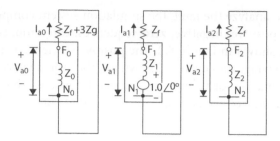

Figure 8.4 Three-Phase symmetrical fault sequence diagram.

$$I_{a1} = \frac{1\angle 0}{Z_1}$$

$$\begin{bmatrix} I_{af} \\ I_{bf} \\ I_{cf} \end{bmatrix} = \begin{bmatrix} 1 & 1 & 1 \\ 1 & a^2 & a \\ 1 & a & a^2 \end{bmatrix} \begin{bmatrix} 0 \\ I_{a1} \\ 0 \end{bmatrix} \tag{8.4}$$

By replacing the parameters using Equation (8.4)

$$I_{af} = \frac{1\angle 0}{Z_1}, I_{bf} = \frac{1\angle 240}{Z_1}, I_{cf} = \frac{1\angle 120}{Z_1}$$

Also, the voltage value can be found as:

$$V_{af} = V_{bf} = V_{cf} = 0 \tag{8.5}$$

$$V_{a0} = V_{a1} = V_{a2} = 0 \tag{8.6}$$

8.2.2   Single Line to Ground Fault

During failing one conductor with the ground, the fault is known as an un-symmetrical single line to ground fault as shown in Figure 8.5, where at the fault point (F) the fault impedance is Z_f. This fault can be described as shown in Figure 8.6 for the sequences in the un-symmetrical fault diagram [13–15]. The positive sequence currents, negative-sequence currents and zero sequence currents can be calculated by following Equation (8.7):

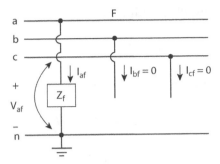

Figure 8.5 Single line-to-ground fault diagram.

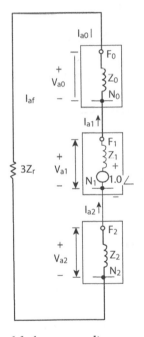

Figure 8.6 Single line-to-ground fault sequence diagram.

$$I_{a0} = I_{a1} = I_{a2} = \frac{1 \angle 0}{Z_0 + Z_1 + Z_2 + 3Z_f} \qquad (8.7)$$

$$\begin{bmatrix} I_{af} \\ I_{bf} \\ I_{cf} \end{bmatrix} = \begin{bmatrix} 1 & 1 & 1 \\ 1 & a^2 & a \\ 1 & a & a^2 \end{bmatrix} \begin{bmatrix} I_{a0} \\ I_{a1} \\ I_{a2} \end{bmatrix}$$

Where, by analyzing Ph-a fault current;

$$I_{af} = I_{a0} + I_{a1} + I_{a2} \tag{8.8}$$

Also, Equation (8.8) can be written as:

$$I_{af} = 3I_{a0} + 3I_{a1} + 3I_{a2} \tag{8.9}$$

$$V_{af} = I_{af}Z_{af} \tag{8.10}$$

And, the phase fault voltage is:

$$V_{af} = 3Z_f I_{a1} \text{ , And, } V_{af} = V_{a0} + V_{a1} + V_{a2}$$

$$V_{a0} + V_{a1} + V_{a2} = 3Z_f I_{a1} \tag{8.11}$$

So, by obtaining the sequence currents and voltages:

$$
\begin{bmatrix} V_{a0} \\ V_{b1} \\ V_{c2} \end{bmatrix} =
\begin{bmatrix} 0 \\ 1\angle 0 \\ 0 \end{bmatrix} -
\begin{bmatrix} 1 & 1 & 1 \\ 1 & a^2 & a \\ 1 & a & a^2 \end{bmatrix}
\begin{bmatrix} I_{a0} \\ I_{a1} \\ I_{a2} \end{bmatrix} \tag{8.12}
$$

By solving Equation (8.21);

$$V_{a0} = -Z_0 I_{a0} \tag{8.13}$$

$$V_{b1} = 1 - Z_1 I_{a1} \tag{8.14}$$

$$V_{c2} = - Z_2 I_{a2} \tag{8.15}$$

8.2.3　Line-to-Line Fault

The line to line fault is considered as one of the unsymmetrical faults as shown in Figure 8.7. At the fault point (F), the fault impedance is Z_f. This fault can be simplified as drawn by the sequences network shown in Figure 8.8 [13]. The characteristic fault impedance is directly affecting the fault currents, where at zero impedance the fault current will be a maximum value. So, from Figures 8.7 and 8.8, the fault can analyzed by the following equations.

$$I_{af} = 0, I_{bf} = -I_{cf} \qquad (8.16)$$

$$V_{bc} = ZI_{bf}$$

$$I_{a0} = 0$$

$$I_{a1} = -I_{a2} = \frac{1\angle 0}{Z_1 + Z_2 + Z_f} \qquad (8.17)$$

At the fault impedance is zero;

$$I_{a1} = -I_{a2} = \frac{1\angle 0}{Z_1 + Z_2} \qquad (8.18)$$

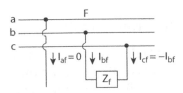

Figure 8.7 Line to line fault diagram.

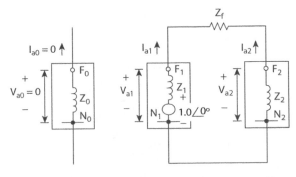

Figure 8.8 Line-to-line fault sequence diagram.

And the fault currents for Ph-b and Ph-c are:

$$I_{bf} = -I_{cf} = \sqrt{3}\, I_{a1} \angle -90$$

Also, the voltage can analyze by the following equations;

$$V_{af} = V_{a1} + V_{a2} = 1 + I_{a1}(Z_2 - Z_1)$$

$$V_{bf} = a^2 V_{a1} + a V_{a2} = a^2 + I_{a1}(a\, Z_2 - a^2 Z_1)$$

$$V_{cf} = a V_{a1} + a^2 V_{a2} = a + I_{a1}(a^2\, Z_2 - a Z_1)$$

Finally, the voltages equations are:

$$V_{ab} = V_{af} - V_{bf} \tag{8.19}$$

$$V_{bc} = V_{bf} - V_{cf} \tag{8.20}$$

$$V_{ca} = V_{cf} - V_{af} \tag{8.21}$$

8.2.4   Double Line-to-Ground Fault

The double line to ground fault is considered an unsymmetrical fault with the three-phase currents not equalized during the fault as shown in Figure 8.9, where at the fault point (F) the fault impedance is (Z_f) and the line to ground impedance is Z_g [13–15].

The observed analysis equations from Figure 8.9:

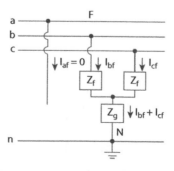

Figure 8.9 Double line-to-ground fault diagram.

$$I_{af} = 0 \tag{8.22}$$

$$V_{bf} = (Z_f + Z_g)I_{bf} + Z_g I_{cf} \tag{8.23}$$

$$V_{cf} = (Z_f + Z_g)I_{cf} + Z_g I_{bf} \tag{8.24}$$

And the sequence currents can be obtained as:

$$I_{a0} = 0$$

$$I_{a1} = \frac{1\angle 0}{(Z_1 + Z_f) + \dfrac{(Z_2 + Z_f)(Z_0 + Z_f + 3Z_g)}{(Z_2 + Z_f) + (Z_0 + Z_f + 3Z_g)}} \tag{8.25}$$

$$I_{a2} = -\left[\frac{(Z_0 + Z_f + 3Z_g)}{(Z_2 + Z_f) + (Z_0 + Z_f + 3Z_g)} \right] I_{a1} \tag{8.26}$$

$$I_{a0} = -\left[\frac{(Z_2 + Z_f)}{(Z_2 + Z_f) + (Z_0 + Z_f + 3Z_g)} \right] I_{a1} \tag{8.27}$$

An alternative method is,

$$I_{af} = 0 = I_{a0} + I_{a1} + I_{a2} \tag{8.28}$$

$$I_{a0} = -(I_{a1} + I_{a2}) \tag{8.29}$$

During the very small fault impedance and ground impedance, so Z_f and Z_g can be neglected. So, the sequences components are driven by the below equations.

$$I_{a1} = \frac{1\angle 0}{(Z_1 + Z_f) + \dfrac{(Z_2)(Z_0)}{(Z_2) + (Z_0)}} \tag{8.30}$$

$$I_{a2} = -\left[\frac{(Z_0)}{(Z_2) + (Z_0)} \right] I_{a1} \tag{8.31}$$

$$I_{a0} = -\left[\frac{(Z_2)}{(Z_2)+(Z_0)}\right]I_{a1}$$

$$(8.32)$$

So, fault currents for Ph-b and Ph-c are:

$$I_{bf} = I_{a0} + a^2 I_{a1} + a I_{a2}$$

$$(8.33)$$

$$I_{cf} = I_{a0} + a I_{a1} + a^2 I_{a2}$$

$$(8.34)$$

The summation current through the neutral can be found by the Equation (8.35) below:

$$I_n = 3 I_{a0} = I_{bf} + I_{cf}$$

$$(8.35)$$

Finally, the phase voltage can be obtained as shown in the bellow equations which driven from the sequence diagram as shown in Figure 8.10.

$$V_{af} = V_{a0} + V_{a1} + V_{a2}$$

$$(8.36)$$

$$V_{bf} = V_{a0} + a^2 V_{a1} + a V_{a2}$$

$$(8.37)$$

$$V_{cf} = V_{a0} + a V_{a1} + a^2 V_{a2}$$

$$(8.38)$$

8.3   Protection Coordination

One of the microgrid facility to operate online with the main grid or individual. The faults can occur in the microgrid or in the utility distribution

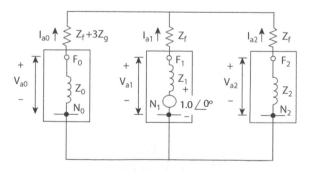

Figure 8.10 Double line-to-ground fault sequence components.

system. Hence, the protection system should coordinate to protect both sides. Using the IED numerical relay can cover the required protection function depending on the voltage value, the current and their angles in the protected part. The selecting of the optimum protection function is depending on the operating voltage and the rated current in the protected part. in order to, at the low voltage and low current, it's better to use the Miniature Circuit Breaker (MCB) which uses up to 63 A rated current. And at the low voltage with high rated current, the Molded Case Circuit Breaker (MCCB) is the optimum selection which can use up to range 2,500 A. In another hand, the protection functions to be used to protect the high voltage lines which can be used with the microgrid can be summarized as.

8.3.1   Overcurrent Protection

The overcurrent protection is used to sense the overload current or the fault current, to isolate the fault zone instantaneous or after the delay time. The definite time overcurrent is using to isolate the protected zone at the value of current greater than the setting value. But, the optimum setting for the overcurrent protection function to adjust with the operation characteristics curves as Normally Inverse (NI), Very Inverse (VI), Moderately Inverse (MI), Long Inverse (LI), Standard Inverse (SI), Extremally Inverse (EI), and so on [16]. The using curves are used to trip the fault fast with the high current value, which can prevent the false protection operation during load starting current. The below equations are used to calculate the IEC standard inverse curves.

$$(\text{Standard Inverse})T_P = TD * \left(\frac{0.14}{M^{0.02} - 1} \right) \tag{8.39}$$

$$(\text{Very Inverse})T_P = TD * \left(\frac{13.5}{M - 1} \right) \tag{8.40}$$

$$(\text{Extremely Inverse})T_P = TD * \left(\frac{80}{M^2 - 1} \right) \tag{8.41}$$

$$(Long - Time\ Inverse)T_P = TD * \left(\frac{120}{M - 1} \right) \tag{8.42}$$

$$(Short-Time\ Inverse)T_p = \text{TD} * \left(\frac{0.05}{M^{0.04} - 1} \right) \qquad (8.43)$$

Where, T_p is the trip time delay by second, TD is the time-dial setting, and M is the applied multiples of the setting current. By using the Equations (8.56)–(8.60), we can draw the operation characteristic curves under different currents as shown in Figure 8.11 for the IEC SI curve which is driven by Equation (8.39). Also, the ANSI inverse curve can be uses for overcurrent protection setting with the numerical protection relays, the ANSI delay trip time is determined by the Equation (8.44) which uses with all ANSI curves by different values as mentioned in Table (8.1) [16–19].

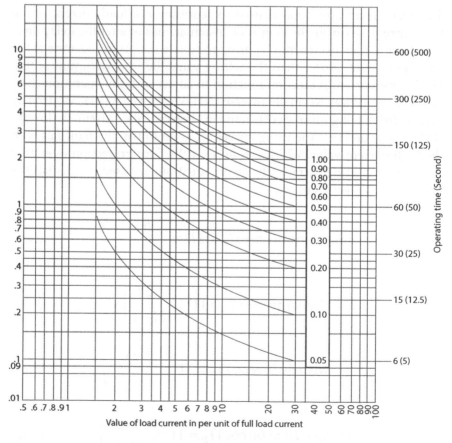

Figure 8.11 IEC Standard Inverse (SI) operating curve.

Table 8.1 ANSI inverse curves constant values.

ANCI curve type	A	B	C	D	E
ANSI Normally inverse curve	0.0274	2.2614	0.3	−4.1899	9.1272
ANSI extremely inverse curve	0.0399	0.2294	0.5	3.0094	0.7222
ANSI Very inverse curve	0.0615	0.7989	0.34	−0.284	4.0505
ANSI Moderately inverse curve	0.1735	0.6791	0.8	−0.08	0.1271

$$T_{P(ANSI)} = \text{Dial} * \left(A + \frac{B}{\left[\dfrac{I_{Inj}}{I_{Setting}} - C \right]} + \frac{D}{\left[\dfrac{I_{Inj}}{I_{Setting}} - C \right]^2} + \frac{E}{\left[\dfrac{I_{Inj}}{I_{Setting}} - C \right]^3} \right)$$

$$(8.44)$$

Where, $T_{P(ANSI)}$ is the operating trip time by second, Dial: is the multiplying factor, I_{Inj}: the input current, $I_{Setting}$: pickup relay setting value and A,B,C,D: constant values related to the ANCI curve type as shown in Table (8.1).

8.3.2 Directional Overcurrent/Earth Fault Function

Nowadays, with the existence of the electric grid and the power system becoming more complex, the protection system is a highly important part of the power system. With the developments of the protection relay, the numerical devices are the high step point that affected the accuracy of the protection system. The utilizing of the directionality function can prevent the wrong operation, by operating in the forward or reverse value as required depending on the current and voltage value and the polarization angle. The directionality torque function is depending on the phase shift of the current angle related to the voltage angle, so the directional protection relay needs to feed on the line current and voltage transformers secondary sides. The torque angle for the directional phase to ground fault setting is shown in Figure 8.12 and the phase to phase fault torque angle is shown in Figure 8.13 [19, 20]. The directional protection function is requiring to calculate the positive (+Ve), negative (−Ve) and zero sequence component, that are common for all direction protection relays.

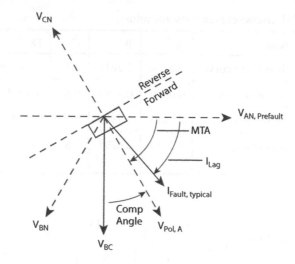

Figure 8.12 Directional characteristics for phase to ground fault.

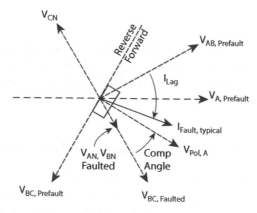

Figure 8.13 Directional characteristics for double line to ground fault.

For direction overcurrent protection or direction earth fault protection, the voltage polarization is reference for estimating the fault direction by judging the current phasor. The residual voltage can be determined by Equations (8.45) to (8.53) below:

$$|V_{res}| = \sqrt{\left(V_{resR}^2 + V_{resX}^2\right)} \tag{8.45}$$

$$\theta_{Res} = \cot\left(V_{resX} / V_{resR}\right) \tag{8.46}$$

Where, $V_{resR} = V_{Ar} + V_{Br} + V_{Cr}$, $V_{ResX} = V_{Ax} + V_{Bx} + V_{Cx}$ (8.47)

$$V_{Ar} = |V_A| COS\ \theta_A$$ (8.48)

$$V_{Br} = |V_B| COS\ \theta_B$$ (8.49)

$$V_{Cr} = |V_C| COS\ \theta_C$$ (8.50)

$$V_{Ax} = |V_A| Sin\ \theta_A$$ (8.51)

$$V_{Bx} = |V_B| Sin\ \theta_B$$ (8.52)

$$V_{Cx} = |V_C| Sin\ 0_C$$ (8.53)

The residual current can be determined by the Equations (8.54) to (8.62) below:

$$|I_{res}| = \sqrt{\left(I_{resR}^2 + I_{resX}^2\right)}$$ (8.54)

$$\theta_{Res} = cot\left(I_{resX} / I_{resR}\right)$$ (8.55)

Where, $I_{resR} = I_{Ar} + I_{Br} + I_{Cr}$, $I_{ResX} = I_{Ax} + I_{Bx} + I_{Cx}$ (8.56)

$$I_{Ar} = |I_A| COS\ \theta_A$$ (8.57)

$$I_{Br} = |I_B| COS\ \theta_B$$ (8.58)

$$I_{Cr} = |I_C| COS\ \theta_C$$ (8.59)

$$I_{Ax} = |I_A| Sin\ \theta_A$$ (8.60)

$$I_{Bx} = |I_B| Sin\ \theta_B$$ (8.61)

$$I_{Cx} = |I_C| Sin\ \theta_C$$ (8.62)

The operating angle rages can be determined by the below Equations (8.63) and (8.64).

$$Limit_1 = \theta_{res} + MTA + 90 \tag{8.63}$$

$$Limit_2 = \theta_{res} + MTA - 90 \tag{8.64}$$

Where, MTA is the maximum effect protection element angle. Finally, at the fault condition happens, the protection relay will compare the residual current and the polarization voltage to the limit operating angle to take the trip decision during the result reached to the setting value to send the trip command to isolate the protected zone.

8.3.3   Distance Protection Function

The main trustful points with electrical customers are to provide a secure and reliable power system. The numerical protection relay functions can support the protection system to detect the fault in very low time delay with an accurate selectivity to isolate the fault zone. In addition, using the distance protection function to protect the transmission line between the microgrid and the utility grid, can enhance the quality of fault detection [21]. The distance protection characteristic is reliant the load impedance, that can be operated in Quadrilateral, Mho, Offset Mho,

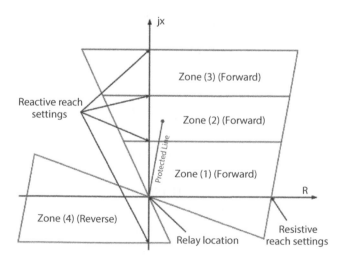

Figure 8.14 Typical distance protection quadrilateral operation settings.

etc. Figure 8.14 shows an example of a typical quadrilateral operation setting for OHTL distance protection function. The setting is adjusted to define the fault location, which classifies to multi-zone. Figure 8.15 shows a typical distance protection setting for the forward zones, where

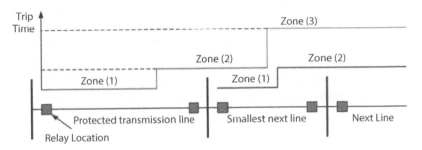

Figure 8.15 Distance protection logic.

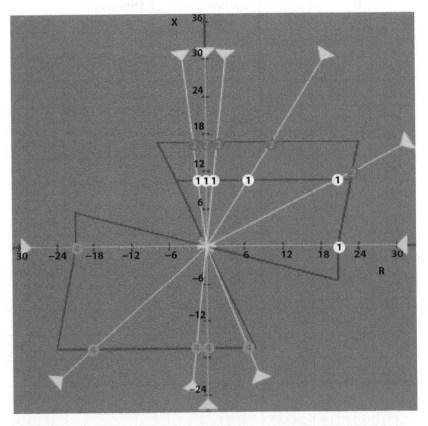

Figure 8.16 The quadrature distance protection test graph for phase to ground fault.

Zone-1 operates without time delay at the relay measured impedance in Zone-1 area that covers 80% of line length. Zone-2 operates with a time delay between 200 and 400 ms at the relay measured impedance in Zone-2 area that covers the total of the protected line and 20% in the next smallest OHTL connected to the next busbar. Also, Zone-3 operates with a time delay between 400 and 800 ms at the relay measured impedance in Zone-3 area, that covers total line length and 50 percentage of the smallest line connected to the next busbar [21–23]. The distance protection function can simulate the secondary injection with the numerical protection relay to shows the operating trip time and the covered area to ensure the protection relay can operate if required to isolate the fault

Table 8.2 The quadrature distance test result values for phase to ground simulation.

X (Ω)	R (Ω)	Z (Ω)	Z phase angle	Zone	Difference percentage	Remark
0.000	20.860	20.860	0.0	1	0.2%	ACCEPT.
10.493	6.557	12.374	58.0	1	0.4%	ACCEPT.
16.265	10.164	19.179	58.0	2	0.8%	ACCEPT.
10.547	0.000	10.547	90.0	1	0.2%	ACCEPT.
16.399	0.000	16.399	90.0	2	0.3%	ACCEPT.
10.490	20.588	23.106	27.0	1	0.4%	ACCEPT.
11.798	23.154	25.987	27.0	2	0.2%	ACCEPT.
−16.406	0.000	16.407	270.0	4	0.3%	ACCEPT.
10.548	1.109	10.606	84.0	1	0.2%	ACCEPT.
16.349	1.719	16.439	84.0	2	0.5%	ACCEPT.
−16.324	−1.715	16.415	264.0	4	0.6%	ACCEPT.
0.000	−20.890	20.891	180.0	4	0.1%	ACCEPT.
−16.436	6.343	17.618	291.1	4	0.2%	ACCEPT.
10.525	−1.310	10.606	97.1	1	0.3%	ACCEPT.
16.313	−2.031	16.439	97.1	2	0.6%	ACCEPT.
−16.473	−18.214	24.559	222.2	4	0.1%	ACCEPT.

zone. The simulation example has been validated with 115 kV OHTL using the FREJA kit for secondary injection and with numerical protection relay. The instrument transformers for CT ratio and VT ratio setting are 1,600/1 A and 115 KV/115 V respectively. Figure 8.16 shows the result sheet for the quadrature distance protection test graph for the phase to ground fault simulation. Table (8.2) shows the phase to ground simulation test result. Figure 8.17 shows the distance trip time test graph for the phase to ground fault, and Table (8.3) shows the test result trip time values for a phase to ground fault simulation. Figure 8.18 and Table (8.4) show the test graph for unsymmetrical quadrature distance protection and the simulation test result respectively for the phase to phase fault simulation. Figure 8.19 and Table (8.5) show the distance trip time test graph and test result trip time values respectively for a double line to ground fault simulation.

8.3.4   Distance Acceleration Scheme

Using the fiber optical cable for communication between the two-end numerical protection relay can uses for accelerating the trip scheme

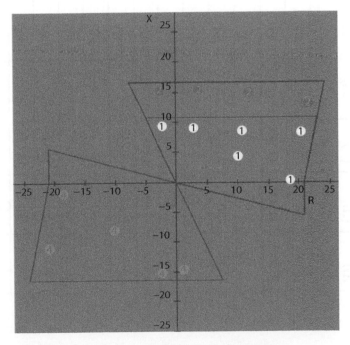

Figure 8.17 Distance trip time test graph for phase to ground fault.

Table 8.3 Test result trip time values for phase to ground fault simulation.

X (Ω)	R (Ω)	Z (Ω)	Z phase angle	Adjusted time	Operating time	Time different %	Zone	Remark
15.142	−2.571	15.359	99.7	0.400	0.428	7.2%	2	ACCEPT.
15.428	4.000	15.939	75.5	0.400	0.430	7.6%	2	ACCEPT.
15.000	12.000	19.210	51.4	0.400	0.431	8.0%	2	ACCEPT.
13.142	21.714	25.382	31.2	0.400	0.432	8.1%	2	ACCEPT.
8.285	20.571	22.177	22.0	0.050	0.028	21.3	1	ACCEPT.
8.571	11.000	13.945	38.0	0.050	0.025	25	1	ACCEPT.
9.000	3.142	9.533	70.8	0.050	0.025	20.7	1	ACCEPT.
9.286	−2.000	9.499	102.2	0.050	0.028	21.3	1	ACCEPT.
0.285	18.857	18.860	0.9	0.050	0.032	23.8	1	ACCEPT.
−14.714	1.285	14.770	275.0	1.200	1.228	2.4%	4	ACCEPT.
−15.428	−2.285	15.597	261.6	1.200	1.229	2.4%	4	ACCEPT.
−11.000	−20.857	23.580	207.9	1.200	1.225	2.2%	4	ACCEPT.
−2.000	−18.571	18.679	186.2	1.200	1.235	3.0%	4	ACCEPT.
−8.142	−10.142	13.006	218.8	1.200	1.222	1.9%	4	ACCEPT.
4.285	10.285	11.142	22.7	50	0.024	21.0	1	ACCEPT.

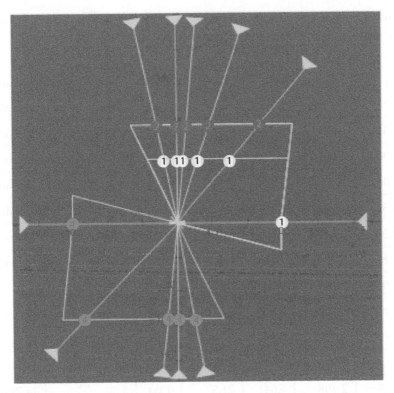

Figure 8.18 The quadrature distance protection test graph for double line to ground fault.

between the microgrid and the utility grid is high data transmission rate as shown in Figure 8.20. The operation logic to accelerate the trip time to be instantaneous is depending the start initiation of zone (2) with receiving signal from the remote relay, where during the fault in zone (2) for protection relay in microgrid it will be zone (1) fault for protection relay in the utility grid. The acceleration logic is describes as shown in Figure 8.21 for numerical protection relay MICOM-P546 [24]. The acceleration scheme uses to isolate the transmission line instantaneously at the fault happen in zone-2 between the microgrid and the main grid due to the basic scheme for zone-2 is between 200 and 400 ms [25, 26].

8.3.5   Under/Over Voltage/Frequency Protection

The electric consumer is searching for a stable and reliable power system. The disturbances in the power system as over/under voltage or over/under frequency, are directly affecting the microgrid quality which

Table 8.4 The quadrature distance test result values for double line to ground simulation.

X (Ω)	R (Ω)	Z (Ω)	Z phase angle	Zone	Difference percentage	Remark
5.273	5.273	8.204	50.0	0.3%	1	In Zone
8.235	8.235	12.812	50.0	0.2%	2	In Zone
0.000	0.000	6.250	90.0	0.6%	1	In Zone
0.000	0.000	9.795	90.0	0.3%	2	In Zone
−1.331	−1.331	6.407	102.0	0.4%	1	In Zone
−2.082	−2.082	10.018	102.0	0.3%	2	In Zone
10.407	10.407	10.407	0.0	0.4%	1	In Zone
−1.028	−1.028	9.844	264.0	0.4%	4	In Zone
0.000	0.000	9.727	270.0	0.8%	4	In Zone
1.730	1.730	9.961	280.0	0.2%	4	In Zone
−10.429	−10.429	10.430	180.0	0.2%	4	In Zone
2.108	2.108	6.641	71.5	0.2%	1	In Zone
3.250	3.250	10.242	71.5	0.9%	2	In Zone
0.662	0.662	6.329	84.0	0.2%	1	In Zone
1.030	1.030	9.853	84.0	0.3%	2	In Zone
−9.340	−9.340	13.539	226.4	0.3%	4	In Zone

leads to damage the electric equipment and the control system. Hence, it's important to justify the protection coordination to save the microgrid system by continuously monitor the system voltage. By enabling the protection voltage function to supervise the system voltage during over/under the nominal value in the safe limit, to trip and isolate the microgrid during abnormal value [3, 27]. Also, due to the unbalance between the generation grid and the load value, the generation governor control will operate to regulate the system, which direct effect on the frequency value that can damage the loads if the governors failed to regulate the system, hence, it's significant to utilize the frequency protection function

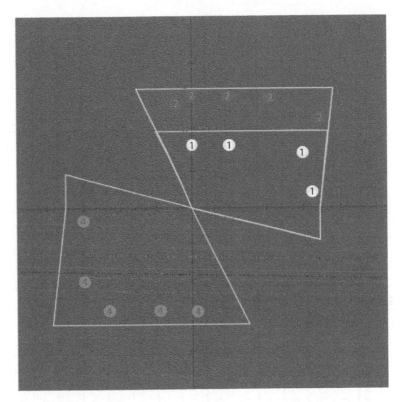

Figure 8.19 Distance trip time test graph for double line to ground fault.

to isolate the protected zone during the frequency value out of the limit frequency value.

8.4   Conclusion

The microgrid has traditionally performed a coordinated set of loads, distributed generation and energy storages. In this way, the microgrid is basically an integrated power system which is possible to synchronize to be in-service with the utility grid or in a separate system. In this chapter, the protection of microgrid is introduced. The protection system depending on the numerical protection relay can improve the distribution network reliability and save the microgrid in normal operation. The general faults in the transmission system are occurred by the damage in the insulation that can case open conductor which named a series fault and short circuit fault which named as shunt faults, with a note, the shunt fault is the

Table 8.5 Test result trip time values for double line to ground fault simulation.

X (Ohm)	R (Ohm)	|Z| (Ohm)	Z phase angle	Time setting	Trip time	Time tol. %	Diff. time %	Zone	Remark
8.657	−1.371	8.765	99.0	0.400	0.434	10.0%	8.7%	2	ACCEPT.
9.342	0.000	9.342	90.0	0.400	0.433	10.0%	8.5%	2	ACCEPT.
9.257	2.914	9.705	72.6	0.400	0.437	10.0%	9.5%	2	ACCEPT.
8.828	7.971	11.895	48.0	0.400	0.434	10.0%	8.6%	2	ACCEPT.
7.457	10.457	12.844	35.5	0.400	0.434	10.0%	8.6%	2	ACCEPT.
4.542	9.000	10.082	26.8	0.050	0.027	50 ms	22.7	1	ACCEPT.
5.228	3.171	6.115	58.8	0.050	0.031	50 ms	19.0	1	ACCEPT.
5.228	0.085	5.229	89.1	0.050	0.034	50 ms	15.5	1	ACCEPT.
1.286	9.858	9.941	7.5	0.050	0.028	50 ms	21.9	1	ACCEPT.
−8.742	0.514	8.758	273.4	1.200	1.234	5.0%	2.9%	4	ACCEPT.
−8.742	−2.828	9.189	252.1	1.200	1.236	5.0%	3.0%	4	ACCEPT.
−8.657	−6.942	11.097	231.3	1.200	1.232	5.0%	2.7%	4	ACCEPT.
−6.171	−8.914	10.842	214.7	1.200	1.232	5.0%	2.7%	4	ACCEPT.
−1.200	−9.085	9.164	187.6	1.200	1.228	5.0%	2.4%	4	ACCEPT.

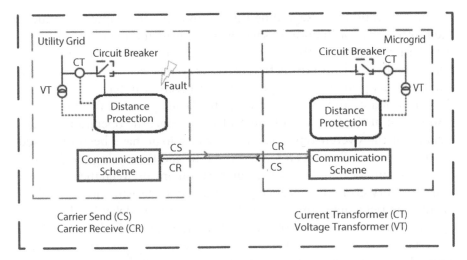

Figure 8.20 The distance accelerating scheme for OHTL between the microgrid and the utility grid.

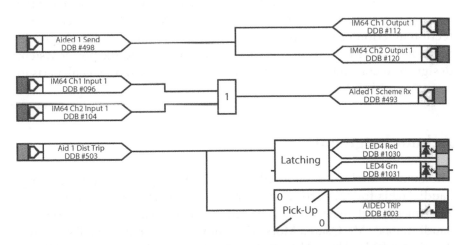

Figure 8.21 Programing the acceleration scheme by the numerical protection relay MICOM P546.

most and famous fault. The symmetrical 3-phase fault in the transmission system is occurred by 5% of the total percentage faults. The other faults occurred at 85%, 10% for the line to ground fault, the line to line fault from the total faults respectively. The fault analysis is an important way to design the optimum protection system and to calculate the required setting to isolate the fault zones without before damage the system that discussed in this chapter in Section 8.2. Regarding this discussion, this chapter introduced the protection coordination to save the microgrid and the utility grid system during the faults in the transmission line or the generation part. Using overcurrent time delay setting to protect the system can save the microgrid and the utility grid, but by supporting the protection system with enabling the directionality function can prevent the false operation for the protection system at the fault out of the protection zone, the operation characteristics of the overcurrent and directionality logic have been discussed in this chapter in Sections 8.3.1 and 8.3.2. In addition, using the distance protection function to classify the transmission line between the microgrid and the utility grid. The distance protection characteristics are depending on the line percentage impedance, the distance-time delay is adjusted to operating in instantaneous trip at the fault in a zone (1) which is 80% of the total protected line, and the remaining length is covered by distance zone (2) and the delay time can be instantaneous with carrier receives a signal from the remote relay which discussed and simulated in this chapter in Section 8.3.3. Also, it's important to protect the microgrid loads by over voltage and under voltage protection function to save the loads in the normal operating voltage. Moreover, using the over/under frequency protection function can save the critical loads as discussed in this chapter in Section 8.3.4. Finally, from this chapter, we recommend the power system designers to consider the numerical protection relays to protect all parts in the microgrid system.

Acknowledgment

The authors wish to acknowledge Alfanar Testing and Commissioning, Saudi Arabia for supporting to complete this research. Specially thanks to Mr. Amer Abdullah Alajmi (General Manager, Alfanar Engineering Service, Saudi Arabia), Mr. Osama Morsy (Executive Manager, Alfanar T&C, Saudi Arabia) and Mr. Abou Al Ez M. Hamed (Eastern Area Manager, Alfanar T&C, Saudi Arabia).

References

1. Eltamaly, A.M., Y. Sayed Mohamed, Y., El-Sayed, A.H.M. *et al.*, Adaptive static synchronous compensation techniques with the transmission system for optimum voltage control, *Ain Shams Engineering Journal*, 2020, https://doi.org/10.1016/j.asej.2019.06.002

2. Maitra, A., *et al.*, Microgrid controllers: expanding their role and evaluating their performance, *IEEE Power Energy Mag.*, 15(4), 41–49, 2017.

3. Aghdam, F.H. and Kalantari, N.T., Distributed Energy Resources and Microgrid Infrastructure. Springer Book chapter, *Microgrid Architectures, Control and Protection Methods, Power Systems*, 2020, https://doi.org/10.1007/978-3-030-23723-3_4

4. Lie, B., Zhang, X. and Wu, J., New procedure for gear fault detection and diagnosis using Instantaneous angular speed, *Mechanical Systems and Signal Processing* 85, 2017.

5. Dasguptaa, A., Debnath, S. and Das, A., Transmission line fault detection and classification using cross-correlation and k-nearest neighbor, *International Journal of Knowledge-based and Intelligent Engineering Systems*, 19, pp: 183–189, 2015, DOI 10.3233/KES-150320.

6. Mishra, M., Routray, P. and Rout, P.K., A Universal High Impedance Fault Detection Technique for Distribution System Using S-Transform and Pattern Recognition, *Technol Econ Smart Grids Sustain Energy*, pp: 1:9, 2016, DOI 10.1007/s40866-016-0011-4.

7. Tung, D.D. and Khoa, N.M., A Novel Algorithm of Directional Overcurrent Protection Relay Based on Adaptive Linear Neural Network, *Int. J. Electron. Electr. Eng.*, 2016, doi: 10.18178/ijeee.4.6.494-499.

8. Cai, W., Gu, R., Li, M. and Shi, L., *Online fault detection technology of distribution transformer based on ΔU-I locus method*, November, 2016, DOI: 10.13296/j.1001-1609.hva.2016.11.028.

9. Silva, K., Souza, B.A. and Brito, N.S.D., Fault Detection and Classification in Transmission Lines Based on Wavelet Transform and ANN, *IEEE Transactions on Power Delivery* 21(4): 2058–2063, November 2006 with 168 reads, DOI: 10.1109/TPWRD.2006.876659.

10. Prasad, A. and Belwin Edward, J., Application of Wavelet Technique for Fault Classification in Transmission Systems, *2nd International Conference on Intelligent Computing, Communication & Convergence (ICCC-2016)*, Procedia Computer Science 92, pp: 78–83, 2016.

11. Ali, M., Eltamaly, *et al.*, HVDC over HVAC Transmission System: Fault Conditions Stability Study, *International Journal of Research Studies in Electrical and Electronics Engineering*, 5(1), pp. 24–37, 2019. DOI: http://dx. doi. org/10.20431/2454-9436.0501004

12. Bakar, A.H.A., *et al.*, The study of directional overcurrent relay and directional earth-fault protection application for 33 kV underground cable system in Malaysia, *Electrical Power and Energy Systems* 40, 113–119, 2012.

13. Santam, J., *Analysis of power systems under fault conditions*, Master of Science, In Electrical and Electronic Engineering at California State University, Sacramento, 2011.

14. Gupta, A., Chandran, S.V. and Bhat, S.S., Simultaneous fault analysis, *International Conference on Power, Automation and Communication (INPAC), India*, 2014, DOI: 10.1109/INPAC.2014.6981131.

15. Han, R. and Zhou, Q., Data-driven solutions for power system fault analysis and novelty detection, *11th International Conference on Computer Science & Education (ICCSE)*, 2016, ISBN: 978-1-5090-2218-2, DOI: 10.1109/ICCSE.2016.7581560.

16. Instruction manual: SEL-710 Relay, code: 20130726, 2013.

17. ABB Network Partner, ANSI numbers and IEEE Standard Electric Power System Device Function Numbers acc. to IEEE C.37.2–1991. 1MRB520165-Ben, July 1998.

18. Legrand, *Breaking and protection devices, Power Guide 2009*, Book 05, Legrand, 2009.

19. Girgis, A.A. and Johns, M.B., A Hybrid Expert System for Faulted Section Identification, Fault Type Classification and Selection of Fault Location Algorithms, *IEEE Power Engineering Review*, 2002, Online ISSN: 1937-4208, PP: 978–985.

20. Horak, J., Directional Overcurrent Relaying (67) Concepts, *59th Annual Conference for Protective Relay Engineers*, 2006, DOI: 10.1109/CPRE.2006.1638701.

21. Eltamaly, A.M., Elghaffar, A. N. A., Modeling of distance protection logic for out-of-step condition in power system, *Electrical Engineering*, 11/2017, DOI:10.1007/s00202-017-0667-3

22. Mohajeri, A., Seyedi, H., Sabahi, M., Optimal setting of distance relays quadrilateral characteristic considering the uncertain effective parameters, *Int. J. Electr. Power Energy Syst.*, 73, 1051–1059, 2015, doi:10.1016/j.ijepes.2015.06.011.

23. Eltamaly, A., *et al.* Advanced Control Techniques for Enhancing the Power System Stability at OOS Condition, Insight—*Energy Science*, Volume 2 Issue 1, 2019, doi: 10.18282/i-es.v2i1.89.

24. Elbaset, A.A., Sayed, Y., Elghaffar, A.N.A., IEC 61850 Communication Protocol with the Protection and Control Numerical Relays for Optimum Substation Automation System, *Journal of Engineering Science and Technology Review*, 13 (2), 2020, DOI: 10.25103/jestr.132.01

25. Han, M., Guo, H., Crossley, P., EEE 1588-time synchronization performance for IEC 61850 transmission substations, *Electrical Power and Energy Systems*, 107, pp: 264: 272, 2019. https://doi.org/10.1016/j.ijepes.2018.11.036.

26. Ali, N.H. and Eissa, M.M., Accelerating the protection schemes through IEC 61850 protocols, *Electrical Power and Energy Systems*, 102, pp: 189: 200, 2018. https://doi.org/10.1016/j.ijepes.2018.04.035.

27. Carlos, A., Miguel Castilla, *Microgrid Design and Implementation*, Book Springer, 2019, https://doi.org/10.1007/978-3-319-98687-6

9

A Numerical Approach for Estimating Emulated Inertia With Decentralized Frequency Control of Energy Storage Units for Hybrid Renewable Energy Microgrid System

Shubham Tiwari*, Jai Govind Singh and Weerakorn Ongsakul

Department of Energy, Environment, and Climate, School of Environment, Resources and Development, Asian Institute of Technology, Pathum Thani, Thailand

Abstract

This chapter addresses the issue of frequency stability in a low inertia islanded microgrid with high renewable energy sources (RESs) penetration. To mitigate this, a robust decentralized control strategy is used, enabling various RESs i.e. battery systems, supercapacitors, and fuel cells to provide ancillary service for frequency restoration. Further, a mathematical formulation is proposed to estimate and quantify the emulated inertia in microgrid by the static renewable sources. To evaluate the performance of the proposed methodology, a microgrid having a conventional synchronous generator, solar photovoltaics, fuel cells acting as generating units is modeled. Moreover, battery and supercapacitors are integrated into the system as ancillary service providers. The performance of the controller is determined by simulating the system response for multiple uncertainties. The effectiveness of the controller is demonstrated graphically, as well as with mathematical validation by using the proposed numerical approach for quantifying inertia. This article will ensure that a decentralized approach enabling all generators to dispatch the active power support, will not only regulates the frequency nadir points but also reduces the need of active power in doing so. Thus, reducing the electrical stress on each unit responsible for providing support to the microgrid against the high penetration of RESs.

Keywords: Primary frequency control, inertia emulation, decentralize control in microgrid, energy storage, fuel cells, supercapacitors, ancillary services

Corresponding author: tiwariucestudy@gmail.com

C. Sharmeela, P. Sivaraman, P. Sanjeevikumar, and Jens Bo Holm-Nielsen (eds.) Microgrid Technologies, (227–254) © 2021 Scrivener Publishing LLC

9.1   Introduction

There are immeasurable efforts to move the world on the paths of sustainability. Due to growing irreversible effects on the environment from fossil fuel plants in power generation, researchers are working hard to find solutions to decrease Green House Gas (GHG) emissions. One such step is to encourage the technology of Renewable Energy Sources (RES) and Microgrids.

As more and more RES with intermittent nature are integrated into the grid, significant efforts are required to make the grid stable and reliable. Stability gets effected as the output of the renewable resources keeps on fluctuating therefore, it is difficult to build proper balance between generation and load [1]. With a 100% share of RES in the generation portfolio, the situation deteriorates more. Therefore, as more conventional energy resources being replaced by RES, demand for additional ancillary services escalates.

Static renewable sources being electronically coupled with the grid, are not able to provide inertia naturally. Thus, it results in reduced system inertia, causing large fluctuations in the frequency at a larger rate, i.e., the high rate of change of frequency (ROCOF) [2, 3]. This makes the system more volatile and can cause instability which ultimately leads it to blackouts [4]. Further, when such remote microgrids having low or no rotational energy, interacts with the main grid, it threatens the overall system stability. Another problem with less share of conventional sources is the reduction in primary and secondary control reserves. Therefore, making system further unreliable [5]. Therefore, an appropriate controlling strategy is needed for the proper functioning of these small grid clusters [6, 7]. Several studies have been made in the recent past addressing this issue.

Wind turbines have some capability to provide inertia as they consist of rotating part with stored kinetic energy. Proper controlling with optimized strategies has been proposed to extract this rotating energy to emulate inertia. Literatures discussed the droop control techniques for improving frequency response [8, 9]. With these controls, wind turbines can contribute to emulate synthetic inertia but it may also enforce the electrical and mechanical stress on wind turbines. Besides wind power, solar photovoltaics have also a significant share in the generation portfolio. In Ref. [10], a power reserve is maintained by limiting the active power setpoint below Maximum Power Point. This methodology forces the solar panels to operate under its full capacity. Therefore, financially not suitable for all the geographical conditions. After briefly reviewing all the above literatures, the author concludes that a separate group of sources or dump units are required which can provide ancillary services to microgrids. Accordingly, researchers suggest the need of Virtual Synchronous Machines (VSM) [11, 12]. The Virtual Synchronous machines impersonate the features of conventional synchronous machines. VSM consists of three essential parts, i.e., converters, controllers and energy storage devices (static DC sources). These all together can provide support to weaker grids to maintain voltage and frequency. Several controlling strategies can be employed to provide frequency and inertia support [13, 14]. These methods are briefly described in Table 9.1.

As discussed above that it will be more suitable to use separate dump units to provide ancillary services. Supercapacitors, ultracapacitors, battery banks, electrical vehicle (EV) batteries, flywheels and fuel cells can be used as dump loads for providing different ancillary services.

Considering electric vehicles as simple battery storage units which therefore can be controlled to provide services such as handling power system emergencies, blackouts, voltage and reactive power control; hence improving reliability and efficiency of the grid. EV batteries used through droop control techniques for providing frequency response for grid having a high penetration of wind generation are discussed in Refs. [15, 16]. Apart from EV batteries, separate battery banks are also be used to provide frequency response and is discussed in Ref. [17]. With the evolving technology of supercapacitors and their fast dynamics draws the attention of researchers to exercise them in power grids. The fast dynamics and high storage capacity with long life make them suitable to provide ancillary services in week microgrids. References [18, 19] explored the use of supercapacitors for emulating inertia of the system. To enhance the generation portfolio of the

Table 9.1 Tabular briefing of different methods for frequency support.

Methods	Description
Inertia Emulation [13]	Provides power in proportion to rate of change of frequency
Fast Power Reserve [14]	A fixed amount of power released for a certain period at the time of disturbance
Droop Control [13]	Provides power in proportion to the frequency deviation
Deloading method [14]	Ensures a fixed or variable reserve to support frequency and other services.

power grid, fuel cells are very attractive options. Being non-intermittent, they can provide continuous supply as long as they have input fuel [20]. Reference [21] discussed voltage control strategies to integrate fuel cells with the grid.

After reviewing the aforementioned literatures, the author found that using one type of static source for providing several ancillary services is incongruous. Exploiting one of between, i.e., batteries or supercapacitors for providing both primary frequency response and inertia control can increase the electrical stress on devices. Battery systems and supercapacitors have different reaction times, i.e., have different charging and discharging rates. So, operating either one for providing both services is not a wise strategy. In addition to this, the contribution of fuel cells in providing ancillary services, especially in supporting frequency is not explored much. Apart from this, there is no defined methodology for mathematical and numerical estimation of emulated digital inertia in the system by static ancillary service providers. Utilities could estimate numerically, the inertia needed to maintain frequency under limits and calculates how much inertia is emulated through the DC sources via controllers, which could be also scheduled along with ancillary services.

In this work, a mathematical formulation is proposed to quantify the emulated digital inertia in the system after deploying primary frequency response (PFR) and virtual inertia control (VIC). Further, the characteristics of the battery are utilized to provide PFR. To stipulate VIC here, supercapacitors are deployed due to their faster dynamic response. In the later section, fuel cell attributes are also analyzed to provide primary frequency response to support frequency. For this study, a green microgrid (all sources are powered from renewable energy) is modeled. The generating section comprises of Bio-fuel generator (conventional synchronous machines, acting as swing generator), Solar PV, Fuel cells with Battery systems and Supercapacitors acting as dump units. Battery and supercapacitors only get activated when a disturbance occurs, producing a frequency error signal. To create a disturbance, two types of events are designed. First is the sudden change in a large section of the load. In the second, solar power is varied at different instances. The methodology will analyze both controllers i.e. PFR through batteries and VIC through supercapacitors for each disturbance. These events are analyzed for two scenarios, first is low penetration of RES and later computes results in presence of high penetration of RES. The effectiveness of controllers and supporting units to emulate inertia are discussed graphically and are then validated numerically through proposed mathematical formulation. Moreover, the MATLAB simulation environment used for analyzing microgrid with controllers.

9.2   Proposed Methodology

9.2.1   Response in Conventional Grids

Conventional generators have an inbuilt ability to provide inertial support due to their rotating parts. The reserve kinetic energy in the rotating parts of the synchronous generator can provide inertial support for few seconds during any disturbances. When a disturbance occurs causing a power imbalance, the frequency of the system starts fluctuating. System dynamics relationship with frequency and inertia depends on the swing equation. The swing equation for the system is defined in Equation (9.1).

$$J\frac{d\omega}{dt} = (T_m - T_e) = T_a \qquad (9.1)$$

Where,

J is the moment of inertia of generator and turbine in kg.m^2.

ω is the angular velocity of the rotor in mechanical rad/s.

T_m is the shaft torque produced by the prime mover in N-m.

T_e is the electromagnetic torque in N-m.

T_a is the net accelerating torque of generator in N-m.

The moment of inertia can be expressed in terms of inertia constant (H) in J/VA which is shown in Equation (9.2).

$$H = 0.5 J\frac{(\omega)^2}{S} \qquad (9.2)$$

Where,

S is the rated total power in VA.

Therefore, swing equation can be defined as.

$$\frac{d\omega}{dt} = \frac{\omega.(P_m - P_e)}{2HS} \text{ or } P_a = \frac{2H}{f}\frac{df}{dt} \qquad (9.3)$$

Equations describes about the overall inertial effect on system frequency which is directly linked to generator rotor speed.

9.2.2   Strategy for Digital Inertia Emulation in Hybrid Renewable Energy Microgrids

As the penetration of RES is increased in system, the amount of power reserve for the inertial response with primary and secondary control is reduced. To meet this scarcity, a strategy must be implanted in renewable energy systems so that active power reserve can be restored in the system. Equation (9.4) shows the change in active power reference due to the addition of RES.

$$P_{in,ref,new} = K_{in,conv} \, P_{ref,conv} K_{in,renw} + P_{ref,renw} \qquad (9.4)$$

Where,

$P_{in,ref,new}$ is the new reference inertial power set point of microgrid after integration of R.E.S.

$K_{in,conv}$ is the percentage share of conventional synchronous generator for inertial power set point in microgrid.

$P_{ref,conv}$ is the reference active power set point of conventional synchronous generator in microgrid.

$K_{in,renw}$ is the percentage share of RES for inertial power set point in microgrid through frequency support controllers.

$P_{ref,renw}$ is the reference active power set point of RES in microgrid.

The basic idea of stating Equation (9.4) is that, when a microgrid consists of only conventional synchronous generator then $P_{in,ref,new} = P_{ref,conv}$ i.e. $K_{in,conv}$ is 1 or 100% and $P_{ref,renw} = 0$. This means that all the inertial support is given by synchronous generators which have inbuilt ability to provide inertial support.

Now, as share of RES increases i.e. $P_{ref,renw} > 0$, need of $P_{ref,conv}$ will decrease and therefore the share of conventional generators in inertial support will decrease i.e. $K_{in,conv}$ will decrease. Also, without any control $K_{in,renw} = 0$. Thus, the new inertial active power set point i.e. $P_{in,ref,new}$ will decrease. Therefore, to maintain the value of $P_{in,ref,new}$ in presence of RES, value of $K_{in,renw}$ should be increase through primary frequency and inertia emulation control.

The sources contributing to frequency response, should be able to provide energy until frequency reaches its stable state. Therefore, the required amount of digital energy to emulate inertia and frequency support will govern through Equations (9.5) and (9.6).

$$E_{freq,ref} = \int_{t_{dist}}^{t_{stab}} P_{freq,ref} \, dt = \int_{t_{dist}}^{t_{stab}} (P_{PFC,ref} + P_{IN,ref}) \, dt \qquad (9.5)$$

$$E_{freq,ref} = \int_{t_{dist}}^{t_{stab}} \left(K_{PFC}\, df\, dt + K_{IN}\, \frac{df}{dt}\, dt \right) \qquad (9.6)$$

Now, linearizing the equations for small time interval just after the time of disturbance gives the computing formula of digital energy required for frequency response through power inverters, shown in Equation (9.7).

$$E_{freq,ref} = K_{PFC}\, \Delta f (t_{stab} - t_{dist}) + K_{IN}\, \frac{\Delta f}{\Delta t}(t_{stab} - t_{dist}) \qquad (9.7)$$

with digital frequency response power for emulating inertia and primary frequency response, represented in Equation (9.8).

$$P_{freq,ref} = K_{P.F.C}\, \Delta f + K_{IN}\, \frac{\Delta f}{\Delta t} \qquad (9.8)$$

Where,

$E_{freq,ref}$ is the digital energy required for maintaining frequency response.
$P_{freq,ref}$ is the digital energy required for maintaining frequency response.
K_{PFC} is the droop control constant for PFC.
K_{IN} is the droop control constant for inertia control.
Δf is the change in frequency error signal after disturbance.
$\frac{\Delta f}{\Delta t}$ is the rate of change frequency error i.e. ROCOF signal after disturbance.

To implement the controlling scheme, frequency deviation should be first detected locally and through droop control mechanism, active and reactive power reference set points of DC sources will be set for inverters.

From Equation (9.8), the definition of Primary Frequency Control can be modeled as shown in Equation (9.9).

$$P_{PFC,ref} = K_p\, \Delta f \qquad (9.9)$$

Similarly, definition for digital inertia emulation can be defined through Equation (9.10).

$$P_{IN,ref} = K_{IN}\, \frac{\Delta f}{\Delta t} \qquad (9.10)$$

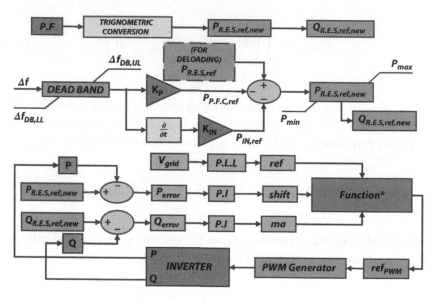

Figure 9.1 Block diagram of control strategy.

Figure 9.1 shows the block diagram of the control scheme which is to be employed in the ancillary service providers to ensure the stability of system. Function* shown in figure is developed to generate reference three phase sinusoidal pulse for pulse width modulation generator.

The major advantage of applying inertia control through Equation (9.10) is that it makes the overall control fast. The controller responds faster to a disturbance as it senses the rate of change of frequency, unlike PFC which only reacts to change in frequency. The importance of inertial controller will be more prominent in the case of large disturbances, as it creates a fast drift between generation and load. Therefore, the inertia emulation control activates in the early moment of disturbance, thus stabilizing the frequency at a faster rate.

A dead band should be introduced in controller with $f_{DB,UL}$ as the upper limit and $f_{DB,LL}$ being the lower limit of frequency error signal respectively. This avoids the controllers to react for very small mismatches. This also ensures the state of health of batteries and supercapacitors. Maximum and Minimum power limits are the specific limits for the upper and lower range should be fixed. This will ensure the optimal use of ancillary service providers.

9.2.3 Proposed Mathematical Formulation for Estimation of Digital Inertia Constant for Static Renewable Energy Sources

In the present work, the battery system with supercapacitors is introduced in the microgrid to improve the overall system inertia. Quantifying the amount of power produced by DC sources for inertia emulation is a typical task. Here, a general methodology will be introduced to find the amount of energy emulated through DC sources to increase the system inertia.

Sources like battery, supercapacitor, fuel cells fall under the category of DC voltage sources. So, typically a state of charge (SOC) can be defined for all these types of sources which finally depends on their internal configuration. To investigate the electrical characteristics of these sources, the general equation of SOC ($Z_{s.o.c,t}$) of DC source at any time, 't' can be defined by Equation (9.11).

$$Z_{s.o.c,t} = \frac{Power\ delivered\ from\ source\ at\ time\ t\ (P_t)}{Nominal\ power\ of\ source\ (P_n)} \qquad (9.11)$$

With (P_t) can be defined as.

$$P_t = V_t C_{eq} \frac{dV_t}{dt} \qquad (9.12)$$

Where,

$P_{D.C,in}$ is the active power from DC sources for inertia emulation.

V_t is the equivalent voltage at time t.

C_{eq} is the electrical equivalent capacitance of source.

$\frac{dV_t}{dt}$ is the rate of change of voltage due to charging or discharging of equivalent capacitance.

This equation can be treated as analogous to swing equation of conventional synchronous generator as stated in Equation (9.3).

From Equation (9.11), equivalent DC energy for inertia emulation ($E_{DC,in}$) can be defined as,

$$E_{D.C,in} = \int P_t\ dt = \int P_n\ Z_{s.o.c,t}\ dt \qquad (9.13)$$

In Equation (9.13), SOC of DC source will be allowed to be varied under the certain limit to generate required inertial power. So, change of SOC for certain small time frame (just after the time of disturbance) can be rewritten as $\Delta Z_{soc,t}$. Also, considering certain losses in power inverters to convert E_{DC} into equivalent AC power, a factor $K_{inv,in}$ should also be included in Equation (9.13).

This factor will ensure that power from DC source for inertia emulation should be equivalent to inertial power from synchronous generator i.e. $E_{Syn,acc}$. Therefore, the final equivalent DC power $E_{DC,in,equiv}$ is shown in Equation (9.14).

$$E_{D.C,in,equiv} = (P_n \Delta Z_{s.o.c,t}). K_{inv,in} \tag{9.14}$$

Similarly, for conventional generators inertial power $E_{Syn,acc}$ is expressed as,

$$E_{Syn,acc} = \int P_a \, dt = \int \frac{2J\omega_e}{p} d\omega \approx \frac{2J\omega_e}{p} \Delta\omega \tag{9.15}$$

Now, comparing Equations (9.14) and (9.15), equivalent moment of inertia factor ($J_{eqv,DC,in}$) for the DC source can be defined as a factor (Equation 9.16), responsible for emulating the static energy equivalent to rotating kinetic energy of synchronous generator having the same capacity as of static DC source.

$$J_{eqv,DC,in} = \frac{P_n . K_{inv,in} \cdot p_{DC}}{2\,\omega_{e,DC}} \frac{\Delta Z_{s.o.c,t}}{\Delta\omega_{e,DC}} = \frac{K_{in,eqv} . P_n \cdot p_{DC}}{2\omega_{e,DC}} \tag{9.16}$$

Where,

$K_{in,eqv}$ is the factor which represents overall inertia factor of DC source which is needed to be adjusted at certain value for proper frequency response.

P_n is the nominal power of DC source.

$K_{inv,in}$ is the factor responsible to compensate inverter losses.

p_{DC} is the number of poles of the equivalent synchronous generator.

$\omega_{e,DC}$ is the angular synchronous speed of the equivalent synchronous generator.

Further, to compute a simple mathematical expression for estimation of digital inertia in a microgrid, previous equations can be reformed with some assumptions. The sampling period for measurement is less in comparison to any physical changes in the system due to the relatively slow dynamics of the system [22]. Therefore, a change in mechanical power can be neglected for fast sampling time. This assumption is considered to estimate emulated digital inertia.

Considering a small sampling time Δt, $P_n \Delta Z_{soc,t}$ will represent the change in dc power according to load change or power imbalance ΔP in system. Therefore,

$$E_{DC,in,equiv} = (P_n \Delta Z_{s.o.c,t}). K_{inv,in} \approx \Delta P \, \Delta t \qquad (9.17)$$

Similarly, considering the assumption, electrical speed (ω_e) and nominal speed (ω) is not differed much, the conventional swing equation with synchronous speed (ω) can be rewritten as,

$$E_{Syn,acc} \approx \frac{2J\omega_e}{p} \Delta\omega \approx 2\pi\,\omega\Delta f \, J \qquad (9.18)$$

Where,

$$\omega = \frac{2\pi f}{p/2} \qquad (9.19)$$

Therefore, by comparing Equations (9.17) and (9.18), the expression for moment of inertia of equivalent generator $(J_{eqv,gen})$ in kg. m^2 is expressed in Equation (9.20).

$$J_{eqv,\,gen} = \frac{\Delta P \, \Delta t}{2\,\pi\,\omega\,\Delta f} \qquad (9.20)$$

Therefore, equivalent inertia constant for system $(H_{eqv,system})$ in seconds can be defined as

$$H_{eqv,\,system} = \frac{\Delta P.\Delta t.\omega_s}{2\,\pi\,\Delta f \, S} \qquad (9.21)$$

Table 9.2 Equivalent synchronous generator design parameters.

Size (S)	Number of poles (p)	Synchronous speed (ω_s)
100 kVA	4	157.07 ad/s

Where,

ΔP is the amount power imbalance occurring due to sudden change in generation or load.

Δt is the time just after the disturbance. For this research, this is the time taken by frequency to reach its first nadir point, here normally, it is around 100 ms.

The basic methodology for deriving Equation (9.21) is that, all the sources of the system is considered as a single equivalent synchronous generator having equivalent ω_s and number of poles. The effect of frequency controllers in RES will be seen in values of Δf and Δt which are the main variables on which $H_{eqv,system}$ will depend. Thus, calculating the $H_{eqv,system}$ through the discussed methodology for a small microgrid system, can provide the contribution of controllers in improving the overall system inertia. In this work, an equivalent synchronous generator with a base rating (S) equal to 100 kVA, number of poles = 4. Therefore, ω can be calculated through Equation (9.19) and its value comes out to be approximately 157 rad/s, for this research. The values of the equivalent synchronous generator are summarized in Table 9.2 and will be used in the next section to analyze the results.

9.3   Results and Discussions

9.3.1   Test System

The authenticity of the proposed methodology and controller design is tested by modeling an islanded microgrid with Solar PV, Bio-fuel generator, Fuel Cells, Battery System and Supercapacitors are designed and simulated in MATLAB Simulink environment as shown in Figure 9.2(a). The proposed controller (Figure 9.1) is implemented on different distributed generators (battery, supercapacitors and fuel cells) which are connected to a diesel synchronous generator. Figure 9.2(b) shows the overall architecture of single distributed generator (DG) connected to diesel generator. Here, P and Q is the active power and reactive power output of DG. Reference signals $P_{R.E.S,ref,new}$ and $Q_{R.E.S,ref,new}$ are compared with P and Q. The compared values are further given to controllers (Figure 9.1) and are then fed to SPWM generator to generate reference pulses for inverter.

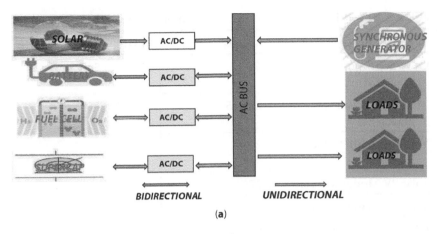

(a)

Figure 9.2(a) Overview of simulated Microgrid.

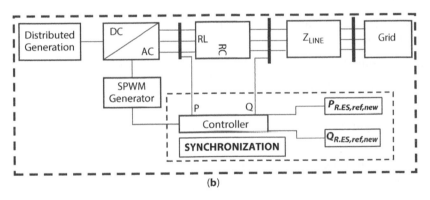

(b)

Figure 9.2(b) Architecture of single DG unit connected to a synchronous generator.

For studying different cases with lower and higher penetration of RES, two types of the synchronous generator are modeled with ratings 85 and 60 kVA, respectively. To integrate R.E.S with AC system, 50 kW (as its maximum limit) AC/DC inverters are modeled with active and reactive power controls. In the case of solar PV and fuel cells, the inverter will dispatch the power according to the prespecified values.

Further, for batteries and supercapacitors, the inverter will react according to the frequency error signal and rate of change of frequency error signal, respectively. Moreover, microgrid consists of a 0.4 Km distribution line and is modeled at 400 V line to line with 50 Hz frequency.

Table 9.3 Network parameters considered for modeling system.

Type of sources	Values	Total maximum capacity
Governor droop constant value (Kd)	6	85 kVA; 65 kVA
Maximum Power (MP) of 1 module (W)	213.15	45 kW
Voltage at MPP (V) for 1 module	29	
Solar PV Modules in series	27	
Solar PV strings in parallel	8	
E.V Battery nominal capacity (Ah)	65	30 kW
E.V Battery nominal DC voltage	500	
E.V Battery permissible SOC range	20–100	
Fuel Cells in series	500	50 kW
Fuel Cell nominal DC voltage (V)	610	
Ratio of Hydrogen to Oxygen	1.415	
Supercapacitor nominal DC voltage (V)	300	30 kW
Supercapacitor rated capacitance (F)	1,200	
K_P	75% of ΔP_L	
K_{IN}	ΔP_L	
Proportional/Integral Controller factor (K_p/K_I)	0.02/2	
Interconnect PV Filter (R/C)	1 mΩ/959.6 µF	
Series Filter Design (R_s/L_s) for Inverter	4.8 mΩ/1.5 mH	
Shunt Filter Design (R_{sh}/C_{sh}) for Inverter	1,500 Ω/0.638 µF	

Controllers are designed to limit the frequency deviation under ±1 Hz to make system reliable and stable. The values of K_p in Table 9.3 is adjusted in a way that battery can provide power 75% of total power imbalance (ΔP_L) in system caused due to a disturbance. Similarly, K_{IN} can be designed to provide power equals to the total imbalance power (ΔP_L) cause due to a disturbance.

To investigate the performance of frequency with inertia emulation, the following are the cases to be evaluated.

Case 1: Sudden change in load and generation (Solar PV) conditions with lower penetration of R.E.S.

Case 2: Sudden change in load and generation (Solar PV) conditions with higher penetration of R.E.S.

Case 3: Extended case for exploring the attributes of the fuel cells to support frequency.

Above mentioned cases case will be analyzed by firstly, without any control. Secondly, with only Primary Frequency Response (PFR) control. In the third scenario, both Virtual Inertia Control (VIC) as well PFR control will be applied. For every case, a graphical representation of frequency response with the numeric value of increased inertia will be displayed as results.

9.3.2   Simulation and Study of Case 1

To analyze the dynamics of PFC and VIC for case 1 i.e. for lower penetration of RES, two scenarios will be discussed. In scenario A, 30% of the total dynamic load (90 kW) will be altered to create a disturbance at different instances. For scenario B, solar PV generation will be changed. The scenarios are discussed in the following subsections.

9.3.2.1   Investigation of Scenario A

To investigate scenario A, microgrid consists of 85 kVA synchronous generator, Solar P.V generation is 15 kW and power generation from the fuel cell is 15 kW. This makes overall 33.33% penetration of RES. This case is analyzed through three sub scenarios. In the first sub scenario, no control is given, i.e., battery and supercapacitors are ideal. For the second, droop control for primary frequency control is given through battery. Lastly, for the third sub scenario, in addition to batteries with PFC, supercapacitors are introduced to emulate inertia through virtual inertia control.

To simulate a disturbance, at t = 2 s, 30% of total load i.e., 27 kW out of 90 kW is removed. This results in frequency deviation and is recorded in Figure 9.3. Similarly, at t = 4 s, again 27 kW is added to the system. In this case, frequency starts decreasing. With PFC and VIC, frequency is improved. Absorption of excessive power and delivering the required power at the time of disturbances from battery and supercapacitor are shown in Figure 9.4. Supercapacitors being fast in charging and discharging, are the ideal choice to implement inertia control. This can be seen through Figure 9.5 which shows the normalized values of SOC. When the load is suddenly increased, battery and supercapacitors, discharge to provide active power support to stabilize frequency, therefore, their SOC decreases. At t = 4 s in Figure 9.6, SOC of battery changes from 0.7 to 0 in nearly 1 s while SOC of supercapacitor changes from 0.7 to 0 in nearly 0.5 s. This clearly shows the effectiveness of supercapacitors for fast-acting inertia controller.

Conventionally, governors of the synchronous generators have a responsibility to stabilize frequency by controlling the mechanical power of the turbine. In the presence of external frequency controllers, Figure 9.6, shows

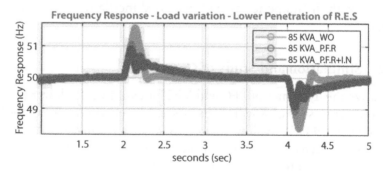

Figure 9.3 Frequency response for sudden load variation with less low penetration of Res.

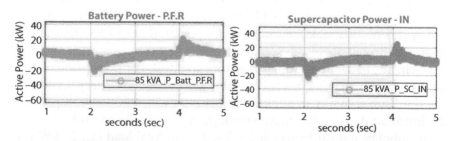

Figure 9.4 Battery and supercapacitor power for sudden load change with less RES share.

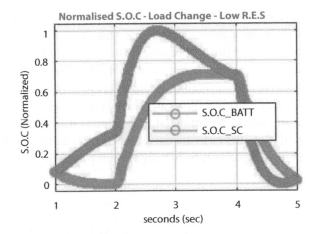

Figure 9.5 Normalized S.O.C. graphs.

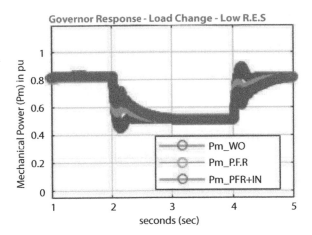

Figure 9.6 Governor response.

the governor's response (Pm). Controllers relegate the sharp changes in mechanical power and smoothens the curve. Thus, reduces stress on governors and mount the stability and reliability of the grid.

9.3.2.2   Investigation of Scenario B

Solar PV being intermittent in nature will affect the frequency of the system. To investigate, PV active power will be changed at different time intervals. At time, t = 1.5 s, irradiance vary such that, solar power changes from 15 to 5 kW and then at t = 3 s, power changes from 5 to 25 kW. Further, at t = 4 s, changes from 25 to 15 kW. These variations are shown in Figure 9.7. Further, this will create a power imbalance, thus, triggering the frequency oscillations. To stabilize the frequency, controllers are added, and corresponding results are shown in Figure 9.8. Here, results are represented, first, without control and in second, improved result with inertia controller together with PFC. Figure 9.9 illustrates the governor response in presence of frequency controllers. Normalized graphs of SOC, recorded in Figure 9.10, shows similar results as in scenario A. Supercapacitor rapidly charges and discharges in comparison to battery system to provide inertia control.

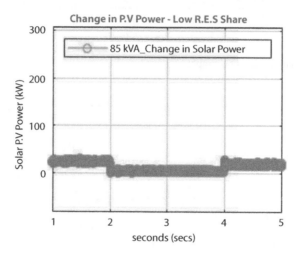

Figure 9.7 Change in solar power.

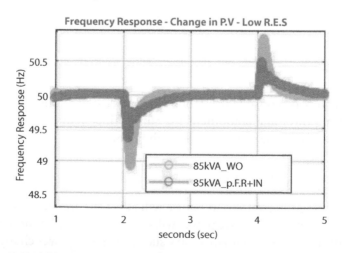

Figure 9.8 Frequency response for P.V. change.

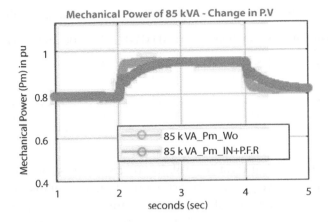

Figure 9.9 Governor response for P.V change.

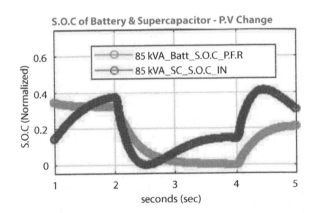

Figure 9.10 Normalized S.O.C graphs.

9.3.2.3   Discussion for Case 1

This section will discuss the important aspects of scenario A from case 1. To validate the results and the contribution of controllers in increasing the system inertia mathematically, Equations (9.19) and (9.20) are used. As discussed in Section 9.2.3, the numerical estimation of the emulated system inertia is summarized in Table 9.4 with frequency values. The table clearly shows the increase in the numeric value of system inertia according to different controllers. Inertia controller together with PFC increases the system inertia by 24.2% from the 'no controller' scenario. While PFC increases inertia by merely 5% from 'no controller' scenario. This is because maximum frequency deviation decreases due to the additions of

Table 9.4 System inertia calculation for 30% change in loading condition.

Type of control	Frequency error (Δf) (Hz)	$J_{eqv,gen}$ (kg. m^2)	$H_{eqv,system}$ (s)
No control	1.60	5.319	1.312
PFC	1.08	5.629	1.388
VIC	0.92	6.607	1.630

supercapacitors with inertia control. Inertia control of supercapacitor provides the rapid active power support in initial seconds of disturbance.

Thus, it can be concluded that batteries and supercapacitors with PFC and inertia controller, efficiently reacts to frequency change and successfully stabilize the frequency under the recommended limits to increase the reliability and robustness of microgrid.

9.3.3 Simulation and Study of Case 2

This case is designed to study the effects of higher penetration of R.E.S. on system frequency. To simulate this case, solar PV generation is increased to 30 kW. Further, the generation from the fuel cells is also increased to 25 kW. Thus, RES contributes to 61% in the generation portfolio. Accordingly, to maintain power balance, the need of conventional generator is decreased and therefore, its size reduced to 60 kVA. To, analyze the dynamics of PFC and VIC, two scenarios will be considered. In scenario A, 30% of total load will be changed to create disturbance. For scenario B, solar PV generation will be changed. The scenarios are discussed in following sub sections.

9.3.3.1 Investigation of Scenario A

At t = 2 s, 30% of total load i.e., 27 kW out of 90 kW is removed. Frequency controllers are introduced to improve response and are shown in Figure 9.11. Similarly, at t = 4 s, again 30% of total load added to system. In this case frequency starts decreasing. With PFC and VIC, frequency is improved. The active power of battery system and supercapacitor are shown in Figure 9.12.

Figure 9.13 shows the normalized values of SOC of battery and supercapacitors. At, t = 4 s, SOC of supercapacitor rapidly discharge from 0.7 to 0 in around 0.6 s whereas battery changes from 1 to 0.2 in nearly 1 s. This clearly shows the effectiveness of supercapacitors to be used with fast-acting inertia controller. One important observation from Figure 9.13 is

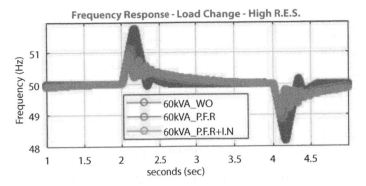

Figure 9.11 Frequency response for sudden load variation with high penetration of R.E.S.

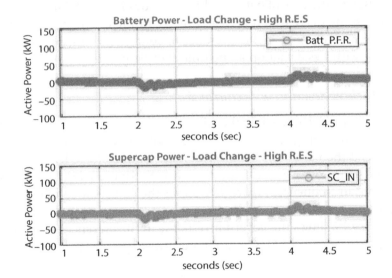

Figure 9.12 Battery and supercapacitor power for sudden load change with high RES share.

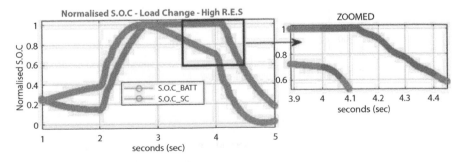

Figure 9.13 Normalized SOC of battery and supercapacitor.

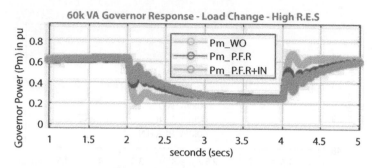

Figure 9.14 Governor response for sudden load change with high RES share.

that, the supercapacitor starts discharging at 4th second, just after disturbance. But, in the case of battery which provides PFR, SOC starts decreasing after some delay which is clearly marked in figure. Figure 9.14 shows
the governor response in the presence of controllers, ensuring smoother
response with less deviation at the time of disturbance.

9.3.3.2 Investigation of Scenario B

This case is modeled to study the effects of solar power variation with high
RES share in microgrid. At time t = 1.5 s, solar power changes from 35 to
20 kW and then at t = 2.5 s, power deviates from 20 to 30 kW. Further, at
t = 3.5 s, solar power varied from 30 to 40 kW (Figure 9.15). Thus, causing
deviations in frequency. Figure 9.16 shows the contribution of controllers
in restoring frequency under limits.

Figure 9.17 shows the governor response in the presence of controllers.
Normalized graphs of SOC are recorded in Figure 9.18. Supercapacitor

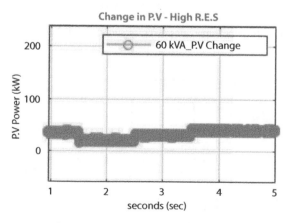

Figure 9.15 Solar power variation.

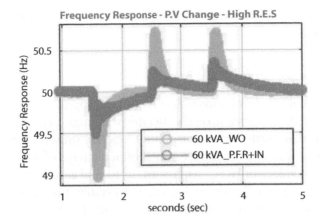

Figure 9.16 Frequency response for PV.

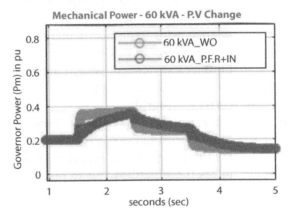

Figure 9.17 Governor response.

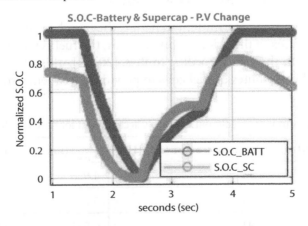

Figure 9.18 Normalized S.O.C graphs.

rapidly charges and discharges in comparison to battery system to provide inertia control.

9.3.3.3   Discussion for Case 2

Case 2 deals with the problems of low inertia microgrid system. Due to the reduction in size of conventional generator with high penetration of RES, physical inertia of system reduces. Table 9.5 clearly shows the increment of system inertia numerically. Effect of higher percentage of RES can be seen by comparing values of $H_{eqv,system}$ between case 1 and case 2 under 'NO control' scenario. There is 7.36 % of decrement in system inertia in case 2 from case 1. This is because of frequency nadir points. In case 1 of 'No control' scenario, maximum frequency deviation is 51.60 Hz while in case 2 with 'No control' maximum frequency deviation is 51.84 Hz. When comparing within case 2, Inertia controller together with PFC increases the system inertia value by 30% whereas with PFC, inertia increases by 13.4% only. When comparing $H_{eqv,system}$ in presence of VIC scenario for cases 1 and 2, it can be reckoned that numerical values of system inertia are comparable and therefore, inertia controller together with PFC is able to maintain the system inertia in low inertia microgrids.

Another noticeable observation is the response time of the controller. Inertia controller activates by sensing the rate of change of frequency. This property makes the units to respond faster. Figure 9.14 clearly shows that the inertia controller makes the supercapacitor to respond faster than the battery.

9.3.4   Simulation and Study for Case 3

As fuel cells are non-intermittent in nature, they can be used for providing ancillary services to the grid. In this research, the fuel cell is modeled and connected with the grid according to Refs. [20, 23]. This case is simulated to explore the attributes of fuel cells in providing frequency support, thus

Table 9.5 System inertia calculation for 30% change in loading condition.

Type of control	Frequency error (Δf) (Hz)	$J_{eqv,gen}$ (kg. m^2)	$H_{eqv,system}$ (s)
No control	1.84	4.956	1.222
P.F.C	1.19	5.619	1.386
V.I.C	0.93	6.537	1.612

Table 9.6 Dynamics of fuel cell active power set points.

Conditions	Frequency	Fuel cell active power set point
Sudden Load Addition	$f < f_{DB,LL} < 50$	$P_{F.C,set\ point,new} = P_{F.C,set\ point,old} + K_{P.F.R}\ \Delta f$
Sudden Load Removal	$f > f_{DB,UL} > 50$	$P_{F.C,set\ point,new} = P_{F.C,set\ point,old} - K_{P.F.R}\ \Delta f$
Normal Operation	$f_{DB,LL} < f < f_{DB,UL}$	$P_{F.C,set\ point,new} = P_{F.C,set\ point,old}$

creating a more decentralized system. Here, fuel cell is performing two functions. Firstly, it is acting as a static generator, providing 20 kW support to microgrid. Secondly, active power of fuel cell is controlled via inverter to provide primary frequency support through de-loading technique. The dynamics of fuel cell controller are governed through Table 9.6.

Apart from fuel cell control, battery and supercapacitor are also deployed with P.F.R and inertia control. For this case, 60 kVA synchronous generator with 30 kW solar P.V is designed to simulate low inertia microgrid. A disturbance is created by adding and removing 30% of load i.e. 27 kW out of 90 kW (same as previous cases).

9.3.4.1   Discussion for Case 3

Controlling fuel cells can reduce the electrical stress on batteries and supercapacitor while providing the ancillary services. Figure 9.19 shows the change in active power of fuel cell. Fuel cells have slow chemical dynamics but relatively fast electrical response. It can be noticed from figure that fuel cell is able to capture the new reference set point quickly, in nearly 0.1 s.

This observation deduces that fuel cells are competent enough to provide primary frequency support.

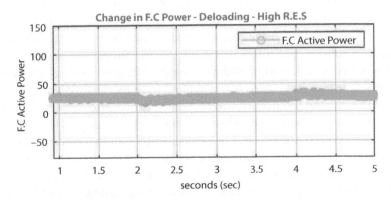

Figure 9.19 Fuel cell active power variation for deloading technique.

Table 9.7 Modified active power requirements due to decentralize control.

Cases	Battery (kW)	Supercapacitor (kW)	Fuel cell (kW)
Case 2	22	25.6	25
Case 3	12	16	20 ± 9

Further, this case validates that by controlling fuel cells as ancillary service providers, system become more decentralized. Moreover, the active power requirement from battery and supercapacitors is reduced, therefore, moderating electrical stress on them. Modified active power requirement from different units are shown in Table 9.7.

So, chapter used a modular decentralized controlling strategy in which all the static energy sources can dispatch power at the time of sudden disturbance. This ensures the state of better stability, reliability and flexibility with less electrical stress over different units.

9.4 Conclusion

The application of renewable energy systems as distributed power generation sources has proved to be astounding in achieving the goals of sustainable development. The application of the same as ancillary services, striving to improve the dynamic stability of standalone microgrids, is investigated in this article. The study is conducted for both low and high levels of RES penetration. Low inertia, the most important issue especially in standalone microgrids with high RES share, is effectively countered using the operational strategy, proposed here. This chapter deduces that, in comparison with batteries and fuel cells, supercapacitors with fast charging and discharging properties are found to be a better option in providing inertia control. This research also proposes the use of exclusive method to estimate system inertia, in presence of multiple sources and infers that a microgrid, comprising of multiple AC and DC sources, can be modelled as an equivalent synchronous generator of proportionate size. This inference is applied to numerically estimate the system inertia, during the occurrence of a disturbance. The chapter also investigates the application of fuel cells as an ancillary service provider using the de-loading control strategy and is found to successfully stabilize deviations in frequency. Further, the coordinated operation of the fuel cell incorporated system is found to reduce the electrical stress on individual supporting units. The proposed strategy shall assist the utilities in increasing their RES share, as a tool for estimating the emulated inertia, ensuring better stability.

References

1. Lara-Jimenez, J.D., Ramirez, J.M., *et al.*, Inertial frequency response estimation in a power system with high wind energy penetration, in *IEEE Power Tech*, 2015.
2. Akhtar, Z., *et al.*, Primary frequency control contribution from smart loads using reactive compensation, *IEEE Transactions on Smart Grid*, pp. 6(5), 2356–2365, 2015.
3. Shafiullah, Md. *et al.*, The study of dependency of power system stability on system inertia constant for various contingencies, in *1st International Conference on Electrical Engineering and Information and Communication Technology*, 2014.
4. Rezkalla, M., Pertl, M. and Marinelli, M., Electric power system inertia: requirements, challenges and solutions, *Electrical Engineering*, vol. 100, no. 4, p. 2677–2693, December 2018.
5. Ulbig, A., Borsche, T. and Andersson, G., Impact of low rotational inertia on power system stability and operation, *IFAC Proceedings Volumes*, vol. 47, no. 3, pp. 7290–7297, 2014.
6. Olivares, E.D., Mehrizi-Sani, A., Etemadi, H.A., Cañizares, A.C., Iravani, R., Kazerani, M., Hajimiragha, H.A., Gomis-Bellmunt, O., Saeedifard, M., Palma-Behnke, R., Jiménez-Estévez, A. G. and Hatziargyriou, D.N., Trends in Microgrid Control, *IEEE Transactions on Smart Grid*, pp. 1905–1919, July 2014.
7. Alsharafi, A.S., Besheer, A.H. and Emara, H.M., Primary Frequency Response Enhancement for Future Low Inertia Power Systems Using Hybrid Control Technique, *Energies*, vol. 11, no. 4, p. 699, 2018.
8. Ruttledge, L. and Flynn, D., Emulated Inertial Response From Wind Turbines: Gain Scheduling and Resource Coordination, *IEEE Transactions on Power Systems*, vol. 31, no. 5, pp. 3747–3755, 2016.
9. Gonzalez-Longatt, F., Impact of synthetic inertia from wind power on the protection/control schemes of future power systems: Simulation study, in *11th IET International Conference on Developments in Power Systems Protection (DPSP 2012)*, 2012.
10. Liu, Y., Zhu, L., Zhan, L., Gracia, R., King, J.T. and Liu, Y., Active power control of solar PV generation for large interconnection frequency regulation and oscillation damping, *International Journal of Energy Research*, pp. 353–361, 2015.
11. Thomas, V., Kumaravel, S. and Ashok, S., Virtual synchronous generator and its comparison to droop control in microgrids, in *2018 International Conference on Power, Instrumentation, Control and Computing (PICC)*, 2018.
12. Rahmani, A.M., Herriot, Y., Sanjuan, L.S., and Dorbais, L., Virtual synchronous generators for microgrid stabilization : Modeling, implementation and experimental validation on a microgrid laboratory, in *2017 Asian Conference*

on Energy, Power and Transportation Electrification (ACEPT), Singapore, 2017.

13. Zhao, H., Wu, Q., Hu, S., Xu, H. and Rasmussen, N.C., Review of energy storage system for wind power integration support, *Applied Energy*, vol. 137, pp. 545–553, 2015.

14. Mohammad, D., Mokhlis, H. and Mekhilef, S., Inertia response and frequency control techniques for renewable energy sources: A review, *Renewable and Sustainable Energy Reviews*, vol. 69, no. 2017, pp. 144–155, 17 11 2016.

15. Almeida, P.R., Soares, F. and Lopes, J.P., Electric vehicles contribution for frequency control with inertial emulation, *Electric Power Systems Research*, vol. 127, no. 2015, p. 141–150, 2015.

16. Marinelli, M., Martinenas, S., Knezovic, K. and Andersen, P.B., Validating a centralized approach to primary frequency control with series-produced electric vehicles, *Journal of Energy Storage*, vol. 7, no. 2016, pp. 63–73, 7 2016.

17. Knap, V., Sinha, R., Swierczynski, M.J., Stroe, D.I. and Chaudhary, S., Grid Inertial Response with Lithium-ion Battery Energy Storage Systems, in *23rd IEEE International Symposium on Industrial Electronics, ISIE, 2014*, 2014.

18. Zhu, J., Hu, J., Hung, W., Wang, C., Zhang, X., Bu, S., Li, Q., Urdal, H. and Booth, D.C., Synthetic Inertia Control Strategy for Doubly Fed Induction Generator Wind Turbine Generators Using Lithium-Ion Supercapacitors, *IEEE Transactions on Energy Conversion*, vol. 33, no. 2, pp. 773–783, 2018.

19. Yang, L., Hu, Z., Xie, S., Kong, S. and Lin, W., Adjustable virtual inertia control of supercapacitors in PV-based AC, *Electric Power Systems Research*, pp. 71–85, 2019.

20. Zhu, Y.T.K., Development of models for analyzing the load-following performance of microturbines and fuel cells, *Electric Power Systems Research*, pp. 1–11, 2002.

21. Fernando, S.Y.T., Chau, K.T. and Lu, H.-C.H., Voltage Control Strategies for Solid Oxide Fuel Cell Energy System Connected to Complex Power Grids Using Dynamic State Estimation and STATCOM, *IEEE Transactions on Power Systems*, pp. 3136–3145, 2017.

22. EL-Shimmy, M., *Dynamic Security of Interconnected Electric Power Systems—Volume 2*, LAP Lambert Academic Publishing, 2015.

23. Alshehri, F., Suárez, G.V., Torres, R.L.J., Perilla, A., and Meijden, v.d.M., Modelling and evaluation of PEM hydrogen technologies for frequency ancillary services in future multi-energy sustainable power systems, *Heliyon*, vol. 5, no. 4, 2019.

10

Power Quality Issues in Microgrid and its Solutions

R. Zahira[1*], D. Lakshmi[2] and C.N. Ravi[3]

[1]*Department of Electrical and Electronics Engineering, BSA Crescent Institute of Science and Technology, Chennai, India*
[2]*Department of Electrical and Electronics Engineering, Academy of Maritime Education and Training (AMET), Chennai, India*
[3]*Engineering, Vidya Jyothi Institute of Technology, Hyderabad, India*

Abstract

Grid is the electrical node connecting electric power sources to the consumer loads. Grid distributes the various generated power to the demanded consumers. Transmission lines are connected to National power grid to power the various state loads. Microgrid is the small grid commonly used in distribution system. As the name indicates, this is the small grid as compared to transmission line grid. Power handling capacity of this grid is limited to kilo watts (KW) to few mega watts (MW). Microgrids may operate independently without taking power from the bulk power provider or National grid is called stand-alone microgrid. Most of the case microgrid is connected to National grid or bulk power provider. For both stand alone or National grid connected microgrid power quality is the major issue. Research is continued for many decades to solve this and to improve the quality of power in microgrid. As renewable energy sources (RES) commonly connected to microgrid to satisfy the demands of the local consumers and to reduce the operating cost. RES such as solar, wind, fuel cell will supply real power and not reactive power into the microgrid and hence create the reactive and its associated voltage problem in the microgrid. This connection of RES creates additional power quality issues. This chapter gives overview of different type of microgrid, inclusion of RES in the microgrid and the analysis of power quality improvement.

Keywords: Microgrid, wind power, solar power, RES, power quality, total harmonic distortion

---

Corresponding author: zahirajaved@gmail.com

C. Sharmeela, P. Sivaraman, P. Sanjeevikumar, and Jens Bo Holm-Nielsen (eds.) Microgrid Technologies, (255–286) © 2021 Scrivener Publishing LLC

10.1   Introduction

Each day almost half a billion people worldwide lack electricity. A major part of India is comprised by villages and majority of people in rural areas live without the access of electricity, where connection of grid system (macro grid) is restricted. Microgrids provide a solution for supply of electrical energy with ecological awareness. With basic requirements a microgrid has to utilize the distributed generation such as RES and keep the electrification for the local load.

To electrify the villages of local loads all the available form of energies such as RES should be utilized as distributed generators. Remote places where the electrification is difficult can be electrified using this microgrid. Recent advancements in microgrid provide avenue for the integration of RES and also to provide quality power supply for the local consumer loads.

Global warming is a threat to mankind and depletion of the fossil fuel is another threat for the ever increasing electrical power demand. Toxic emission from the conventional power generation gives degraded biodiversity. In the name of development the natural recourses are depleted and the environment is polluted causing social unfairness. On the contrary green energy such as RES gives the required power for mankind and does not harm the environment. Non-conventional RES are of less power generating capacity and not suitable for long distance transmission and hence it is best suitable for distributed generation in the small sized grid called microgrid. The development and deployment of RES distributed generators gives two benefits: one is clear emission free power generation and second one is satisfying the local load demands and avoids transmission line losses (Mahela and Shaik, 2016).

The role of power electronic devices has become vital in distributed generation and integrating the PES with grid. Power electronic devices act as interface between RES and power grid. Because these devices harmonics are introduced in the system, these cause distortion of source voltage and increase in losses and may lead to malfunctioning of protective relays, mains and other control units. Hence, it is necessary to reduce the THD of the system within standard limit (Huang *et al.*, 2011).

The Microgrid is a bundle of the several DGs (resource such as photovoltaic, wind, solid oxide fuel cells (SOFC), gas turbines, and biomass and diesel power). The microgrid has received substantial attention in the electric power system due to its environmentally friendly features (Huang *et al.*, 2011).

When the loads are switched to islanded mode from the grid, there exists more power quality issues (Moghaddam *et al.*, 2014). Introduction of extra harmonic takes place into the grid because of rise in the usage of sensitive equipment and non-linear loads in the domestic as well as industrial area (Xiaozhi *et al.*, 2011). The use of renewable energy has been increasing due to degradation of fossil fuels. Hence, more research has been done with RES to reduce the cost and utilize the natural sources of energy. Arturo Soriano *et al.* (2013) modeled a wind turbine by considering the aerodynamic power and control with the non-linear, fuzzy, and predictive techniques.

Wind energy conversion system has become popular because of the green energy concept. Wind turbine based on the doubly fed induction generator (DFIG) has been used, due to its advantage of variable speed operation with the excitation converter rated at the slip power of the generator rating. Wind energy is reliable and suitable for the Indian weather condition and provides electrical energy at free fuel cost. Installation and maintenance cost are the cost for the electrical power generation and can be reclaimed in due course of service period. The most common generator is DFIG (doubly fed induction generator) used in the wind mill, which converts the mechanical energy of wind turbine into electrical energy. As the wind velocity is nature-dependent DFIG is best suitable in the wind mill power generation (Nian *et al.*, 2012). Another major advantage of wind mill is that it generates AC power which is best suitable for the AC microgrid.

10.1.1   Benefits of Microgrid

- Improves reliability
- Enhancement resilience/recovery
- Low energy cost for consumers and businesses
- Improvement in the environment and promotion of clean energy
- Strengthening the central grid and enables grid modernization
- Bolsters cyber security
- Brings economic value to society
- Improves community well-being
- Meets the end user needs
- Provides way for inclusion of RES.

10.1.2   Microgrid Architecture

The Architecture comprises of Micro generation, Energy storage system, Load and control system and power electronic interfacing converter as

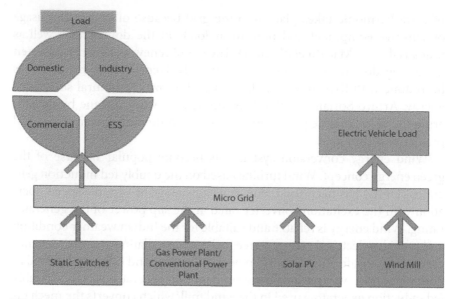

Figure 10.1 Schematic arrangement of Microgrid.

shown in Figure 10.1. Microgrid is the collection of distributed power sources, local loads and energy storage arrangements.

The distributed generators are used along with power electronics converters to match the voltage and frequency of the microgrid. As the power electronics industry developed leaps and bounds it is simple task to integrate the distributed generators with microgrid. Such needs include greater reliability and safety at the local level.

10.1.3   Main Components of Microgrid

- Distribution system
- DG sources
- Energy storage (ES)
- Controllers and Loads.

10.2   Classification of Microgrids

Microgrids are broadly classified into two categories: Off-grid System—mostly found in rural areas, which operate in isolation and Grid tied system—in which a single common coupling with main grid but will operate independently. Further classification is based on

- Capacity
- Location
- Type of distribution resource which suits the circumstance.

The Table 10.1 gives the types of Microgrid based on the power handling capacity. When the power rating of the grid increases the service to the consumers and generators participation is more and brings more complex in the power system.

10.2.1   Other Classifications

Microgrids can also be classified

- By load demand
- By rating
- AC/DC type.

10.2.2   Based on Function Demand

- Simple microgrid
- Multi DG microgrid
- Utility microgrid.

10.2.3   By AC/DC Type

- DC microgrid
- AC microgrid
- AC/DC hybrid microgrid.

Table 10.1 Types of Microgrid based on the power handling capacity.

Type	Capacity (MW)
Simple Microgrid	Lesser than 2
Corporate Microgrid	Between 2 and 5
Feeder area Microgrid	Between 5 and 20
Substation area Microgrid	Greater than 20
Independent Microgrid	Depending on loads on an island, a mountainous area or a village

10.3   DC Microgrid

DC microgrid with solar resource for generation and storage battery is the simplest, cost effective, reliable and very efficient solution for the rural areas which is isolated from grid. Figure 10.2 shows the framework of DC microgrid which consists of DG, ES, and DC load connected to a DC bus via a converter and the DC bus is connected to AC loads via an inverter to supply both DC and AC loads.

10.3.1   Purpose of the DC Microgrid System

(1) Increasing distributed PV units.
(2) Energy consumption reduced
(3) Supply power to loads through regular distribution even under blackout condition of commercial grid.

System efficiency and system size are reduced in DC microgrid when compared to AC microgrid. Less number of power electronic converters is required, the overall efficiency of the system gets improved. No need of transformer for voltage conversion, thereby the size of DC microgrid gets

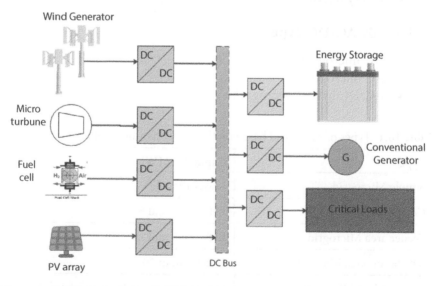

Figure 10.2 Structure of a DC microgrid.

reduced significantly. However, there is only need of voltage stabilization. Compared to AC microgrid, a support for frequency stabilization is not required in case of DC microgrid.

Sweden and Japan has established 5MW DC microgrid structure. Both of these microgrids feed DC power to data centres in their respective countries. DC microgrid at Sweden operates at 380 V, whereas the microgrid at Japan works at 400 V.

10.4   AC Microgrid

All DERs and loads are connected to a common AC bus. DC generating units and energy storage will be connected to the AC bus by DC-to-AC inverters, and further, AC-to-DC rectifiers are used for supplying DC loads. Structure of AC microgrid is as shown in Figure 10.3.

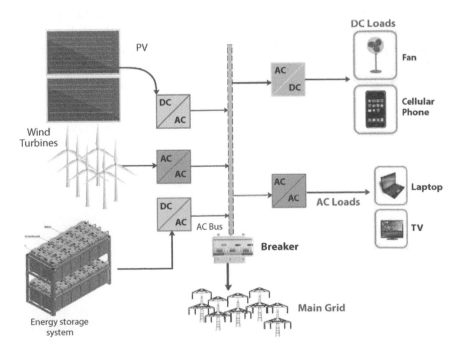

Figure 10.3 Structure of AC microgrid.

10.5   AC/DC Microgrid

The combination of AC and DC bus is called as AC/DC hybrid microgrid. Structure of AC/DC Microgrid is shown in Figure 10.4 in which the AC bus and DC bus allow for direct supply to AC loads and DC loads.

The AC and DC links are linked together through two transformers and two four quadrant operating three phase converters. The AC bus of the hybrid grid is tied to the utility grid. The AC and DC grids have their corresponding sources, loads and energy storage elements, and are interconnected by a three phase converter. The AC bus is connected to the utility grid through a transformer and circuit breaker. In the proposed system, PV arrays are connected to the DC bus through boost converter to simulate DC sources. A DFIG wind generation system is connected to AC bus to simulate AC sources. A battery with bidirectional DC/DC converter is connected to DC bus as energy storage. A variable DC and AC loads are connected to their DC and AC buses to simulate various loads.

PV modules are connected in series and parallel. As solar radiation level and ambient temperature changes, the output power of the solar panel alters. A capacitor is added to the PV terminal in order to suppress high frequency ripples of the PV output voltage. The bidirectional DC/DC converter is designed to maintain the stable DC bus voltage through charging or discharging the battery when the system operates in the autonomous operation mode. The three converters (boost converter, main converter,

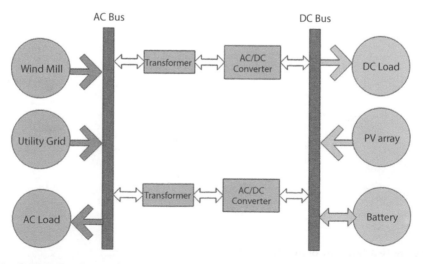

Figure 10.4 Structure of hybrid microgrid.

and bidirectional converter) share a common DC bus. A wind generation system consists of doubly fed induction.

10.6   Enhancement of Voltage Profile by the Inclusion of RES

Voltage is important power quality parameter. Under voltage cause the degraded performance of electrical equipments and over voltage reduces the life of the electrical equipments. Hence the electrical power supplied to the consumers should be rated value and regulation must be within the allowable tolerance. During peak hours voltage in the micro-grid become under voltage and during lean hours become over voltage. This voltage problem can be reduced by the inclusion of RES. The power generated in the local distributed generators such as RES will satisfy the local power demand and avoid large power taken from the National grid. As the power generated in the near location voltage and power drop in the distribution line is reduced and improves the voltage profile. In this section solar and wind power inclusion in the microgrid is discussed in detail.

Distributed generator (DG) of photo voltaic panel is the semi conductor material which converts solar irradiation into electrical energy. It is the green energy produce electrical energy without generating pollution and renewable in nature. It is not affect the eco system of the earth. Wind turbine is another machine which converts free wind energy into mechanical energy. Wind turbine is coupled to induction generator which converts mechanical energy into electrical energy. Wind turbine generating cost very less can be neglected but the initial cost for the commissioning is huge. These solar PV and wind power generation are green and renewable in nature. For the demonstration standard microgrid 33 bus system is considered. Two solar photo voltaic (PV) and two wind power generators are considered to include in the microgrid. The voltage is improved and hence the losses and operating cost of the microgrid is reduced.

10.6.1   Sample Microgrid

For the demonstration of voltage improvement standard 33 bus microgrid is considered. Figure 10.5 shows the single line diagram. It has 33 buses and 32 branches; each bus has its own real and reactive power demand. First bus is considered as the bulk power supplier terminal or substation. All other buses are load buses connected to its local load. This radial line

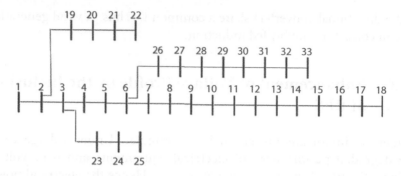

Figure 10.5 33 bus microgrid.

microgrid has one radial line and 3 branch radials. The voltage in all the buses is calculated using load flow analysis.

In radial line resistance dominates the reactance and hence classical Newton or Gauss Seidel may not be helpful and KCL based forward and backward sweep load flow are normally used to finding bus voltages and power losses in the microgrid. Consider the radial distribution network as given in Figure 10.6, with branch 'k' connected between two nodes 'm' and 'm + 1'. The real and reactive power in sending bus or node-m is P_m, Q_m the branch resistance and reactance is R_k and jX_k.

Voltage of the mth bus is calculated using Equation (10.1). During backward sweep the end node voltage are considered as 1 PU. In the forward sweep first node voltage of backward sweep is retained and other node voltages are calculated using KVL.

$$V_m = |V_{m+1}| - \left\{ \left(\frac{|P_{m+1} + jQ_{m+1}|}{|V_{m+1}|} \right)^* * Z_k \right\} \qquad (10.1)$$

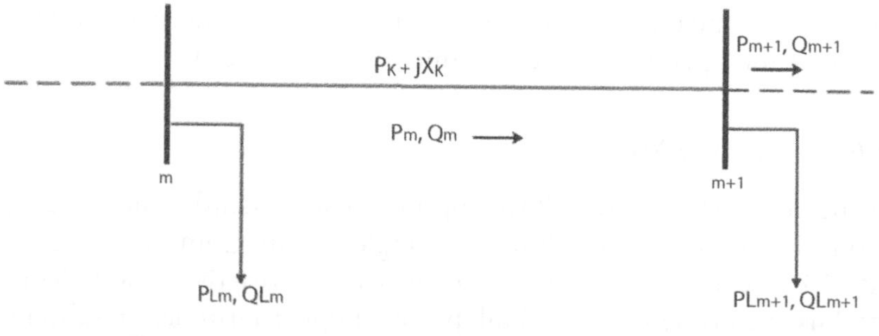

Figure 10.6 Radial line power flow.

Table 10.2 MG Demand and impedance value.

Line No.	P (in KW)	Q (in Kvar)	R (in ohms)	X (in ohms)	Bus	
					From	To
1	100	60	0.0922	0.047	1	2
2	90	40	0.493	0.2511	2	3
3	120	80	0.366	0.1864	3	4
4	60	30	0.3811	0.1941	4	5
5	60	20	0.819	0.707	5	6
6	100	50	0.1872	0.6188	6	7
7	100	50	0.7114	0.2351	7	8
8	60	20	1.03	0.74	8	9
9	60	20	1.044	0.74	9	10
10	45	30	0.1966	0.065	10	11
11	60	35	0.374	0.1238	11	12
12	60	35	1.468	1.155	12	13
13	120	80	0.541	0.7129	13	14
14	60	10	0.591	0.526	14	15
15	60	20	0.746	0.545	15	16
16	60	20	1.289	1.721	16	17
17	90	40	0.732	0.574	17	18
18	90	40	0.164	0.1565	2	19
19	90	40	1.504	1.3554	19	20
20	90	40	0.409	0.4784	20	21
21	90	40	0.708	0.9373	21	22
22	90	50	0.451	0.3083	3	23
23	240	100	0.898	0.7091	23	24
24	420	100	0.896	0.7011	24	25

(*Continued*)

Table 10.2 MG Demand and impedance value. (*Continued*)

Line No.	P (in KW)	Q (in Kvar)	R (in ohms)	X (in ohms)	Bus From	To
25	60	25	0.203	0.1034	6	26
26	60	25	0.284	0.1447	26	27
27	60	20	1.059	0.9337	27	28
28	120	70	0.804	0.7006	28	29
29	200	600	0.507	0.2585	29	30
30	150	70	0.974	0.963	30	31
31	115	90	0.31	0.3619	31	32
32	60	40	0.341	0.5302	32	33

Real and reactive power load and line resistance and reactance are given in Table 10.2. First column gives the line number of branch, column 6 specifies the starting bus of the branch and column 7 specifies the end bus of the branch. Columns 5 and 4 give reactance and resistance of the distribution line. Columns 3 and 2 give the reactive and real power demand of the microgrid

Voltage magnitude before inclusion of solar PV power and wind power generation is shown in Figure 10.7. In this figure it is clear that the minimum voltage occurs at bus 18 as it is last bus, the magnitude of voltage is 0.68 PU. This is poor voltage and hence two PV generators and two wind power generators are connected to this system to improve the voltage profile in all buses.

To improve the voltage profile solar PV of maximum rating 800 KW is connected to the buses 31 and 29. Based on the irradiation of sun the PV power generation varies and the pattern of generation is given in Figure 10.8. Wind mill for the electric power generation is connected in buses 3 and 28.

Minimum and maximum power generation in the wind mill is 55 and 650 KW respectively. Figure 10.9 gives the electric power generating pattern of the wind mill for the different time of the day.

After inclusion of solar PV and wind mill in the microgrid the voltage profile in all the buses are improved and given in Figure 10.10. After inclusion of the RES the minimum voltage occurs at bus 18 and the voltage magnitude is 0.74 PU. This voltage is better than the microgrid without RES. The voltage profile comparison is given in Figure 10.11.

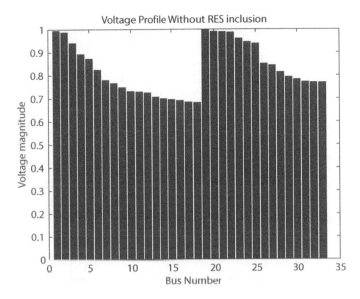

Figure 10.7 Voltage Profile before RES inclusion.

As the local load is supplied by the distributed generator (DG) such as solar PV and wind mill, the current taken from the bulk power network connected at bus-1 is reduced and hence the voltage drop in the distribution lines are reduced and voltage in all the buses are improved. Increase in the KW size of the DG will further improves the voltage level or multiple number of DG will further improves the voltage profile as required. The constraint in the DG inclusion is the capital investment. The geographical suitability of the particular DG is important for the full efficient power generation and inclusion in the microgrid. From the study result the inclusion of RES will improves the voltage profile of the microgrid.

10.7 Power Quality in Microgrid

Demand of electrical power is increasing day by day and the requirement of power quality is also very much concerned in this modern era. Olden power system consists of power inefficient and linear loads which will not cause the power quality issues in much. In the modern era most of the loads are energy efficient and uses power electronics components for its functionality. One such example is SMPS (Switched Mode Power Supply) is the advanced power supply having high efficiency as compared to normal power supply. Apart from these non-linear loads usages is increased

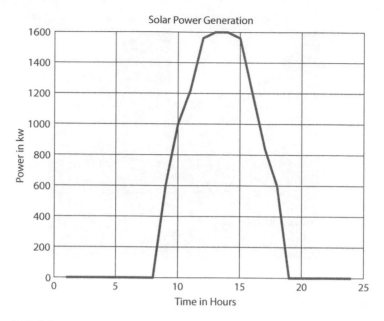

Figure 10.8 Solar power generation.

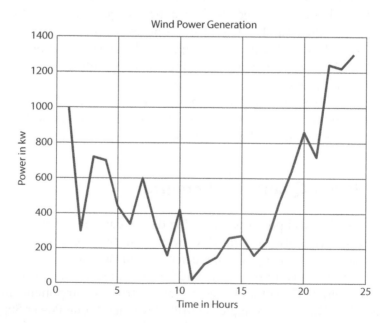

Figure 10.9 Wind power generation.

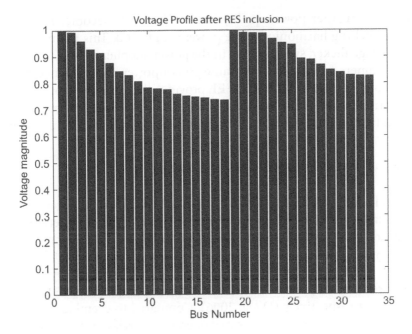

Figure 10.10 Voltage Profile after RES inclusion.

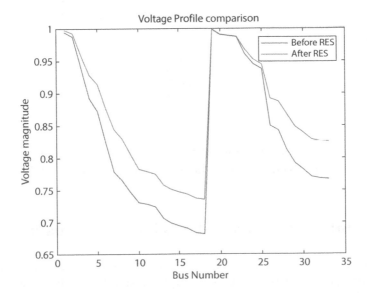

Figure 10.11 Voltage Profile comparison.

and causes further power quality issues. The loads become smarter and cause switching harmonics in the power supply end. This harmonics produce voltage flicker, swell and sag in the power supplier, this will disturb all the consumers connected in the same grid or power supply. Hence the statutory body such as SEMI, IEC, IEEE provides the guidelines for the allowable harmonics level and voltage deviation. The power supply provider has to maintain these guidelines for the quality power supply to his consumers.

10.8 Power Quality Disturbances

Voltage flicker, voltages swell, voltage sag, switching and fault transients are the common power quality issues. Harmonics during stable operating condition and abnormal state are important impurity in the quality power supply in microgrid. Harmonics are the multiples of fundamental frequency, in India as 50 Hz is used for the fundamental power frequency, the dominant 3rd, 5th, 7th, and 9th harmonics having frequencies 150, 250, 350 and 450 Hz respectively (De la, 2006). Compared to even harmonics odd harmonics are important for the mal operation of relay and circuit breaker, overheating and vibration of rotating and stationary machines, improper operation of medical equipment (Afonso *et al.*, 2000). From these unfavored functions the odd harmonics need to eliminate from the microgrid.

To measure the cumulative effect of all harmonics, it is common to use THD (total harmonic distortion). It gives the overall harmonic measure and given in the Equation (10.2):

$$THD_i = \frac{\sqrt{\sum_{n=2}^{N} I_n^2}}{I_1} \tag{10.2}$$

Where, N is highest number of harmonic, n is harmonic number, I_n is nth harmonic RMS current, I_1 is the RMS value of fundamental frequency current.

10.9 International Standards for Power Quality

The quality of power is identified by different standards like CBEMA curve, ITIC curve, IEC 61000, EN 50160:2001, IEEE standards. The general international standards for harmonic disturbances are the IEC (International Electro technical Commission) and IEEE. The IEEE framed the Standard

519-1981, in the year 1981, which created recommended practices and guidelines for setting the borderline for the disturbances created by several power electronics devices. Then in 1992 the IEEE 519 standard is revised, in which there were restrictions for consumers. The main focus concerning at the connection point with the power utility which would not create a hazard for excessive voltage distortion (De la, 2006). IEEE 1159-1992, IEEE 1250-1995 and IEEE 1100-1992 are the standards framed for monitoring power quality, sensitive equipment services and grounding and powering sensitive equipment.

10.10 Power Quality Disturbances in Microgrid

The Microgrid is a collection of more than one DG, with integrated source like PV cells, wind turbine, solid oxide fuel cells (SOFC), and diesel generator (Huang *et al.*, 2011). Owing to its ecological features, microgrid has received extensive notice in the electric power system. It turns up as a nonconventional source, and in addition, it acts as a green energy scenario for supporting utility grid (Tidjani *et al.*, 2017). Harmonics introduced into the utility grid increases with increase in non-linear load and usage of sensitive power electronics equipment in the domestic and industrialized area. (Xiaozhi *et al.*, 2011). Further power quality disturbances are created when the loads are transmitted to the islanded mode from the grid-connected mode (Moghaddam *et al.*, 2014).

10.10.1 Modeling of Microgrid

The nonlinear loads connected with DG system through bus creates distorted voltage and current waveform whose THD is measured as 16.19 and 24.64%. To mitigate the distortion based on power quality standards, passive filters are used (Al-Zamil and Torrey, 2001). While using the passive filter, there are certain drawbacks such as it has predefined filter component rating which is calculated based on system rating. If the grid is extended based on load then filter component ratings are recalculated based on new system rating. As the system expands the passive filters becomes bulky and in turn increase the cost. Hence, Active filters are preferred for varying load system. The DG's with SOFC, wind turbines and solar energy system in addition with battery source is designed as shown in Figure 10.12. For compensating the distortions, a six-pulse inverter connected with controller to the three-phase AC voltage system.

The phase voltage of inverter output is stepped waveform, which contains harmonics, so to reduce harmonics content in the system an LC filter

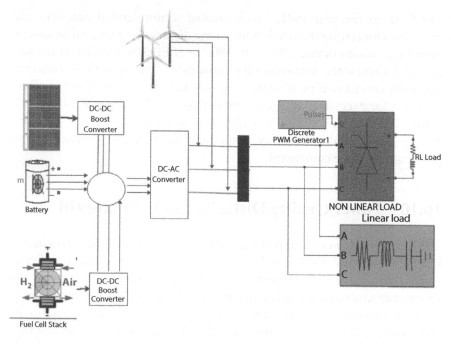

Figure 10.12 Non-linear loads connected to DG's.

is incorporated. From Figures 10.13 (a) and (b) it is clear that distortion created by linear load is only 5.35%. Distortion of 5% is allowed based on the harmonic standard.

As the microgrid is coupled to non-linear load, distortion level of voltage raises 16.19% and current distortion raises to 24.64% as shown in Figures 10.14(a) & (b) and Figures 10.15(a) & (b) which do not satisfy the IEEE 519-1992 harmonic standards.

10.11   Shunt Active Power Filter (SAPF) Design

SAPF is one of the well-liked solutions for mitigating the power quality disturbance in an Electric power grid. SAPF reduces the harmonics distortion, retains power factor and stabilizes the reactive power. By installing SAPF in a low voltage (LV) power grid it avoids the propagation of current harmonics and compensates one or more loads (Zahira, 2018). For compensating the distorted waveform, it extracts the distorted voltage and the current values from the Point of common coupling (PCC). The voltage and current extracted from PCC are in abc coordinate, which is converted

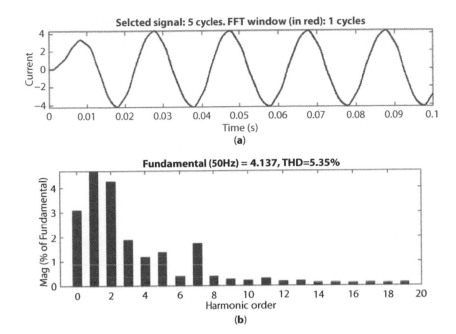

Figure 10.13 (a) Current waveform distortion level with linear load. (b) Distortion level of current with linear load.

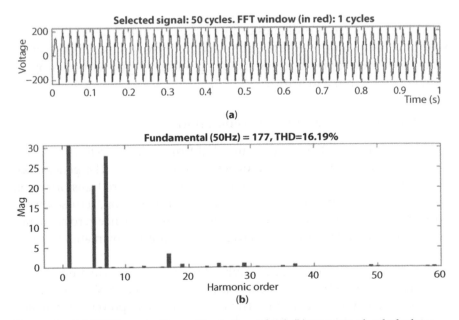

Figure 10.14 (a) Voltage waveform with non-linear load. (b) Distortion level of voltage with non-linear load.

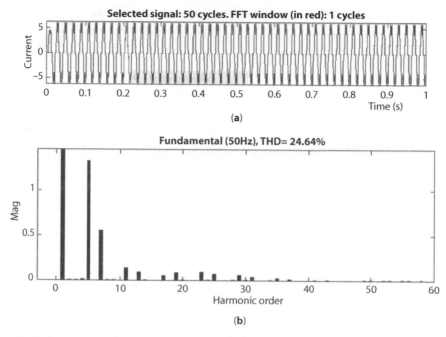

Figure 10.15 (a) Current waveform with non-linear load. (b) Distortion level of current with non-linear load.

to Alpha-Beta-Zero coordinates using Clarke transformation in controller block. By comparing with reference value compensation signal are generated. Generated signal is fed as switching pulses in gate terminals of the voltage source (Bin and Minyong, 2012).

10.11.1   Reference Current Generation

With Synchronous Reference Frame (SRF) method, 3Φ reference frame is transformed into the 2Φ stationary reference frame. The generalized instantaneous reactive power is based on Alpha-Beta-Zero transformation or Clarke Transformation. By using Clarke transformation, zero-sequence components are separated from its sequence axis and hence zero sequence components v_0 and i_0 are removed from the transformation matrix (Zahira, 2018).

Equation (10.3) shows abc to Alpha-Beta-Zero transformation of voltage and Equation (10.4) gives current transformation. V_a, V_b, V_c and i_a, i_b, i_c are phase voltages and currents. The real and reactive power is calculated from Equations (10.5) and (10.6), where p_0 is instantaneous zero-sequence power, p is the instantaneous real power and q is the instantaneous reactive power (Geethalakshmi and Kavitha, 2011). Equation (10.7) gives the zero sequence current, Equation (10.8) gives compensation current values in Alpha-Beta coordinate and in Equation (10.9) Alpha-Beta current coordinates are converted as abc coordinates (Afonso *et al.*, November 2000).

$$
\begin{bmatrix} V_\alpha \\ V_\beta \\ V_o \end{bmatrix} = \sqrt{2/3} \begin{bmatrix} 1/\sqrt{2} & 1/\sqrt{2} & 1/\sqrt{2} \\ 1 & 1/2 & -1/2 \\ 0 & \sqrt{3}/2 & -\sqrt{3}/2 \end{bmatrix} * \begin{bmatrix} V_a \\ V_b \\ V_c \end{bmatrix} \tag{10.3}
$$

$$
\begin{bmatrix} i_\alpha \\ i_\beta \\ i_o \end{bmatrix} = \sqrt{2/3} \begin{bmatrix} 1/\sqrt{2} & 1/\sqrt{2} & 1/\sqrt{2} \\ 1 & 1/2 & -1/2 \\ 0 & \sqrt{3}/2 & -\sqrt{3}/2 \end{bmatrix} * \begin{bmatrix} i_a \\ i_b \\ i_c \end{bmatrix} \tag{10.4}
$$

$$
\begin{bmatrix} p \\ q \end{bmatrix} = \begin{bmatrix} V_\alpha & V_\beta \\ -V_\beta & -V_\alpha \end{bmatrix} * \begin{bmatrix} i_\alpha \\ i_\beta \end{bmatrix} \tag{10.5}
$$

$$
P_o = v_{o*}\, i_o \tag{10.6}
$$

$$
i_o = i_{co}^* \tag{10.7}
$$

$$
\begin{bmatrix} i_{c\alpha}^* \\ i_{c\beta}^* \end{bmatrix} = \frac{1}{v_\alpha^2 + v_\beta^2} \begin{bmatrix} V_\alpha & V_\beta \\ V_\beta & -V_\alpha \end{bmatrix} * \begin{bmatrix} p \\ q \end{bmatrix} \tag{10.8}
$$

$$
\begin{bmatrix} i_{ca}^* \\ i_{cb}^* \\ i_{cc}^* \end{bmatrix} = \sqrt{\frac{2}{3}} \begin{bmatrix} \frac{1}{\sqrt{2}} & 1 & \frac{1}{\sqrt{2}} \\ \frac{1}{\sqrt{2}} & -\frac{1}{2} & -\frac{\sqrt{3}}{2} \\ \frac{1}{\sqrt{2}} & -\frac{1}{2} & -\frac{\sqrt{3}}{2} \end{bmatrix} * \begin{bmatrix} i_{co}^* \\ i_{c\alpha}^* \\ i_{c\beta}^* \end{bmatrix} \qquad (10.9)
$$

10.12 Control Techniques of SAPF

The DC voltage control (outer loop) and current control (inner loop) are the two control loops used to evaluate the filter performance of standard SAPF control model. Output voltage of the inverter, (V_{pwm}), is adjusted with respect to the voltage at the PCC (V_{pcc}), to make the output current (i_F) to match harmonic reference values obtained from harmonic current extraction methods (Kale and Ozdemir, 2005).

Figure 10.16 shows the microgrid connected with SAPF. The SAPF is controlled by the different controllers for improving the quality of power in distributed generations. There are different types of controllers available for reducing distortions. In this section, SPWM, SMC, Fuzzy controller and optimization based controllers are discussed.

To achieve the optimum current tracking by fixed frequency driving signal we have to focus on current control. The performance of the SAPF

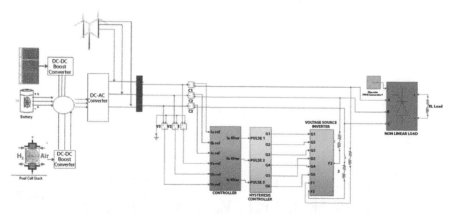

Figure 10.16 Microgrid connected with SAPF.

is affected by the selection of control techniques (Aredes and Monteiro, 2002). Hence, it is very important to choose the control technique and implementation of the same (Zhang *et al.*, 2010). Different control techniques are discussed and the output is compared in the following sections with the measured THD values.

10.13   SPWM Controller

Harmonic reduction and switching losses are the efficiency parameters of an inverter which depends on the modulation strategies (control) used. The inverter output voltage and output frequency can be directly controller by SPWM technique according to the sine functions (Islam *et al.*, 2013).

SPWM is mostly used to digitalize the control, so a sequence of voltage pulses are produced by switching the power switches. The width of these pulses is modulated to attain the controlled inverter output and minimize the harmonic content. In the SPWM technique, the PWM signals are generated by comparing a high frequency triangular carrier wave and the sinusoidal waves (Hussin *et al.*, 2010). In general, three sinusoidal waves can be used for the three-phase inverter. The sinusoidal waves (reference signals) have 120° phase difference with each other. Selection of frequency of these sinusoidal waves is based on on the required inverter output frequency. The carrier triangular wave is usually a high frequency (in several KHz) wave.

10.14   Sliding Mode Controller

The Sliding Mode (SM) Controller (SMC) is a kind of non-linear controller, which was introduced for controlling variable structure systems (VSSs). In this approach, an active control makes the input current follow the line voltage, using an analog multiplier to generate the reference signal (Miret *et al.*, 2004). It is a non-linear control method that alters the dynamics of a non-linear system by application of a discontinuous control signal that forces the system to "slide" along a cross-section of the system's normal behavior. The state-feedback control law is not a continuous function of time. Instead, it can switch from one continuous structure to another based on the present position in the state space. Hence, the sliding mode control is a variable structure control method. The basic idea behind the sliding control is the specification of the sliding surface. There are three basic steps in designing the SMC: 1) Proposal of a sliding surface, 2) Testing for the sliding mode surface existence and 3) Stability analysis inside the surface (Cardenas *et al.*, 1998).

10.15   Fuzzy-PI Controller

Fuzzy logic technique involves fuzzification, defuzzification, knowledge base, inference mechanisms. The knowledge base is intended to give a best dynamic response under contingency in process parameters and exteriorinstability. In recent years, fuzzy logic controllers (FLC) have generated a great deal of interest in certain applications. The advantages of FLCs are robustness, no need to accurate mathematical model, can work with imprecise inputs, and can handle non-linearity (Ross, 2004). The compensation process is based on sensing line currents (Herrera *et al.*, 2008).

Figure 10.17 shows generation of gating pulse with Fuzzy-PI controller. In which error signal 'e' is generated by comparing the predefined DC voltage (V_{dcref}) and the voltage across DC capacitor of SAPF (V_{dc}) generates. This error signal is fed, asinput to the fuzzy PI controller. The output variable of the fuzzy logic controller is considered as the peak value of the line-current (I_{smax}).

First, instantaneous reference line currents (i_{saref}, i_{sbref} and i_{scref}) are generated with I_{smax}, active power demand and losses. Secondly, the difference of instantaneous reference line currents and load currents generates reference current (i_{faref}, i_{fbref}, i_{fcref}). Finally, pulses are generated by comparing reference current and compensating current.

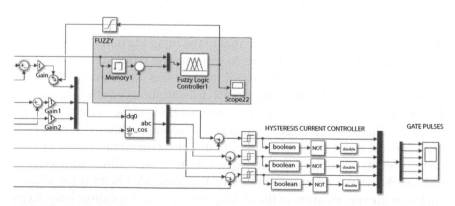

Figure 10.17 Generation of gating pulse with Fuzzy-PI controller.

10.16   GWO-PI Controller

Gray Wolf Optimizer (GWO) is a population based meta-heuristics algorithm that simulates the leadership hierarchy and hunting mechanism of gray wolves (Mirjalili *et al.*, 2014). The GWO algorithm mimics the leadership hierarchy and hunting mechanism of gray wolves in nature.

Four categories of gray wolves such as alpha (α), beta (β), delta (δ), and omega (ω) are used for simulating the managing hierarchy. The proposed algorithm is applicable for challenging problems with unknown search spaces. The foremost phase of gray wolf hounding are tracking, chasing, and approaching the prey pursuing, encircling, and harassing the prey until it stops moving.

Gray wolves are well thought-out as apex predators, which are at the peak of the food chain. Gray wolves prefer to live in a group; each group contains 5–12 members on average. All the associates in the group have a very authoritarian communityladder as shown in Figure 10.18.

The social hierarchy consists of four levels as follows.

The first level is the alpha (*α*) wolves that are the leaders of the pack and they are a male and a female. They are responsible for making decisions about hunting, time to walk, and sleeping place. The pack members have to dictate the alpha decisions and they acknowledge the alpha by holding their tails down. The alpha wolf is considered the dominant wolf in the pack and the pack members should follow all his/her orders.

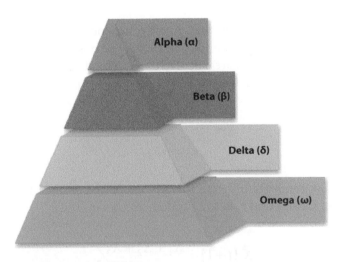

Figure 10.18 GWO community ladder.

The second level is called Beta (β), which are subordinate wolves, which help the alpha in decision-making. The beta wolf can be either male or female and it considers the best candidate to be the alpha when the alpha passes away or becomes very old. The beta reinforces the alpha's commands throughout the pack and gives the feedback to alpha.

The third level is delta (δ) wolves that are not alpha or beta wolves and they are called subordinates. Delta wolves have to submit to the alpha and beta but they dominate the omega (the lowest level in wolves' social hierarchy). There are different categories of delta such as Scouts, Sentinels Elders, Hunters, and Caretakers.

The fourth (lowest) level is called Omega (ω) wolves. They are considered as the scapegoat in the pack; they have to submit to all the other dominant wolves. In the GWO, we consider the fittest solution as the alpha, and the second and the third fittest solutions are named beta and delta, respectively. The rest of the solutions are considered as omega. In GWO algorithm, the hunting is guided by α, β, and δ. The ω solutions follow these three wolves. During the hunting, the gray wolves encircle the prey. Figure 10.19 shows the search agent updating algorithm with GWO.

The mathematical model of the encircling behavior is presented in the following Equations (10.10) and (10.11).

$$D = |C \cdot Xp\,(t) - A \cdot X(t)| \tag{10.10}$$

$$X(t+1) = Xp\,(t) - A \cdot D \tag{10.11}$$

Where t is the current iteration, A and C are coefficient vectors, X_p is the position vector of the prey, and X indicates the position vector of a gray wolf. The vectors A and C are calculated as in Equations (10.12), (10.13) & (10.14) (Mirjalili *et al.*, 2014)

$$A = 2a \cdot r1 \cdot a \tag{10.12}$$

$$C = 2 \cdot r_2 \tag{10.13}$$

Where components of a are linearly decreased from 2 to 0 over the course of iterations and r_1, r_2 are random vectors in [0, 1].

$$\vec{X}\,(t+1) = \frac{\overrightarrow{X_1} + \overrightarrow{X_2} + \overrightarrow{X_3}}{3} \tag{10.14}$$

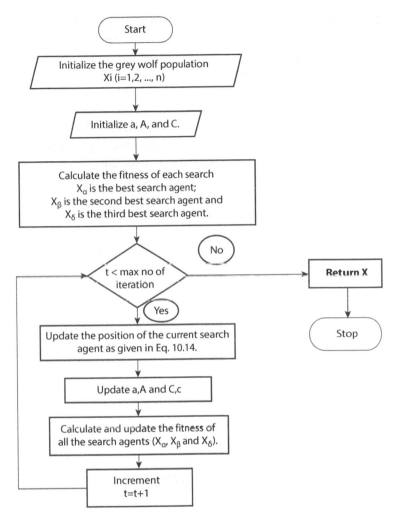

Figure 10.19 Flowchart for updating search agent in GWO.

10.17   Metaphysical Description of Optimization Problems With GWO

The prospective social pyramid assists GWO to save the preeminent solutions attained so far over the course of iteration. The following are the point to be noted for solving optimization problem.

1. The anticipated surrounding system defines a circle-shaped zone in the region of the solution, which can be elongated to higher dimensions as a hyper-sphere.

2. The arbitrary parameters A and C support candidate solutions to have hyper-spheres with diverse arbitrary radii.

3. The proposed hunting method allows candidate solutions to locate the probable position of the prey.

4. Exploration and exploitation are secured by the malleable values of 'a' and 'A'.

5. The adaptive values of parameters 'a' and 'A' allow GWO to smooth transition between exploration and exploitation.

6. As the 'A' component decreases, half of the iterations are committed to travelling around ($|A| \geq 1$) and the other half are committed to exploitation ($|A| < 1$).

7. The important parameters to be adjusted in GWO is 'a' and 'C'.

In Figures 10.20(a) & 10.20(b), the waveform attains near sinusoidal, with mitigated harmonics level. Table 10.3 gives the details of harmonic

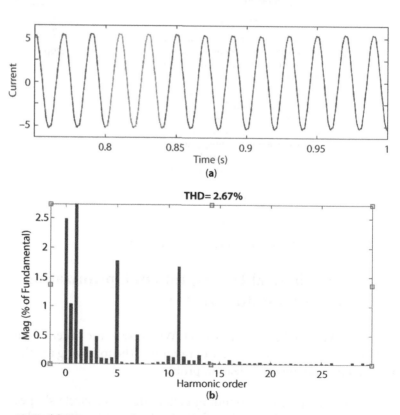

Figure 10.20 (a) Current waveform with compensation. (b) Distortion level of current after compensation.

Table 10.3 Harmonic orders and THD levels.

Harmonic order	Line 1		Line 2		Line 3	
	Without APF	With APF	Without APF	With APF	Without APF	With APF
3	0.03%	0.13%	1.43%	0.28%	0.59%	0.12%
5	22.33%	1.88%	22.49%	1.85%	22.09%	1.91%
7	9.32%	1.07%	7.87%	1.09%	7.87%	1.06%
11	6.96%	0.13%	6.06%	0.11%	5.6%	0.13%
13	4.02%	0.17%	3%	0.18%	2.91%	0.17%
17	2.74%	0.17%	2.08%	0.16%	1.79%	0.17%

Table 10.4 THD and measured power factor.

Parameter	THD	Power factor
Linear load	5.30%	1
Non-linear load	24.64%	0.821
Non-linear load with SAPF	2.66%	0.9925

Table 10.5 Individual phase percentage THD.

Phases	Without filter	Without filter
A	25.78 %	2.67%
B	25.22 %	2.62%
C	24.64 %	2.57%

order from fifth to seventeenth. Majority of disturbances are created with this level of harmonic order. The highest distortion level varies from 22.33 to 2.74% for all the phases. So the compensator is incorporated and it is examined that the distortion level is minimized in the range of 1.88 to 1.06%. Table 10.4 shows the overall THD value and power factor for linear load, non-linear load and compensated non-linear load. Table 10.5 gives the THD value of uncompensated and compensated system for each phase.

10.18   Conclusion

Need of the society is to satisfy the electrical energy demand without harming nature. Conventional power generation produces the electrical energy along with pollution and depletes the resources. This disturbs the biosystem and nature. The conventional power generation is at remote location and needs the very long transmission line. This transmission line further makes energy loss. Whereas microgrid uses the advantages of RES. RES produce the electrical power without pollution. But the problem in RES is power quality mainly the voltage and harmonics. In this book chapter improvement of voltage profile using RES and improvement in harmonics disturbance is explored. THD is the standard measure for power quality used in this analysis.

References

Kathiravan, R., & Kumudini Devi, R.P., Optimal power flow model incorporating wind, solar, and bundled solar–thermal power in the restructured Indian power system, *International Journal of Green Energy*, 14(11), 934–950, 2017.

Shuaib, Y.M., Kalavathi, M.S., & Rajan, C.C.A., Optimal capacitor placement in radial distribution system using gravitational search algorithm, *International Journal of Electrical Power & Energy Systems*, 64, 384–397, 2015.

Su, W., Wang, J., & Roh, J., Stochastic energy scheduling in microgrids with intermittent renewable energy resources, *IEEE Transactions on Smart Grid*, 5(4), 1876–1883, 2013.

Chauhan, R.K., *Challenges and Opportunities for DC Micro Grid.*

Che, L., *Microgrids and distributed generation systems: Control, operation, coordination and planning*, Illinois Institute of Technology, 2015.

Zeng, Z., Yang, H., Zhao, R., & Cheng, C., Topologies and control strategies of multi-functional grid-connected inverters for power quality enhancement: A comprehensive review, *Renewable and Sustainable Energy Reviews*, 24, 223–270, 2013.

Zahira, R., *Design and performance analysis of a shunt active filter for power quality improvement.*

Singh, B., Al-Haddad, K., & Chandra, A., A review of active filters for power quality improvement, *IEEE transactions on industrial electronics*, 46(5), 960–971, 1999.

Zahira, R., & Lakshmi, D., Control Techniques for Improving Quality of Power—A Review, *International Journal of Research in Arts and Science*, 5(Special Issue Holistic Research Perspectives [Volume 4]), 107–123, 2019.

Li, Y., Vilathgamuwa, D.M., & Loh, P.C., Microgrid power quality enhancement using a three-phase four-wire grid-interfacing compensator, *IEEE Transactions on Industry Applications*, 41(6), 1707–1719, 2005.

Xiaozhi, G., Linchuan, L., & Wenyan, C., Power quality improvement for mircrogrid in islanded mode, *Procedia Engineering*, 23, 174–179, 2011.

Serban, I.O.A.N., & Marinescu, C., Power quality issues in a stand-alone microgrid based on renewable energy, *Rev. Roum. Sci. Techn.–Électrotechn. Et Énerg*, 53(3), 285–293, 2008.

Pepermans, G., Driesen, J., Haeseldonckx, D., Belmans, R., & D'haeseleer, W., Distributed generation: definition, benefits and issues, *Energy Policy*, 33(6), 787–798, 2005.

Zahira, R., Fathima, A.P., & Muthu, R., Hardware and Simulation Modelling of Shunt Active Filter Controlled by Sliding Mode, *International Journal of Applied Engineering Research*, 9(24), 8229–8235, 2014.

Melício, R., Mendes, V.M.F., & Catalão, J.P.D.S., Comparative study of power converter topologies and control strategies for the harmonic performance of variable-speed wind turbine generator systems, *Energy*, 36(1), 520–529, 2011.

Marei, M.I., El-Saadany, E.F., &Salama, M.M., A novel control algorithm for the DG interface to mitigate power quality problems, *IEEE Transactions on Power Delivery*, *19*(3), 1384–1392, 2004.

Kale, M., & Özdemir, E., A new hysteresis band current control technique for a shunt active filter, *Turkish Journal of Electrical Engineering & Computer Sciences*, *23*(3), 654–665, 2015.

Li, X., Song, Y.J., & Han, S.B., Study on power quality control in multiple renewable energy hybrid microgrid system, In *2007 IEEE Lausanne Power Tech*, IEEE, pp. 2000–2005, 2007, July.

Temma, K., Kono, Y., Shimomura, M., Kataoka, M., Goda, T., & Uesaka, S., Proposal and development of power quality improvement method under islanding operation in a micro-grid, *IEEJ Transactions on Power and Energy*, *126*, 1032–1038, 2006.

Das, S., Das, D., & Patra, A., Operation of solid oxide fuel cell based distributed generation. *Energy Procedia*, *54*, 439–447, 2014.

Hoseinpour, A., Barakati, S. M., & Ghazi, R., Harmonic reduction in wind turbine generators using a Shunt Active Filter based on the proposed modulation technique, *International Journal of Electrical Power & Energy Systems*, *43*(1), 1401–1412, 2012.

Hassan, A.A., Fahmy, F.H., Nafeh, A.E.S.A., & El-Sayed, M.A., Modeling and simulation of a single phase grid connected photovoltaic system, *WSEAS Transactions on Systems and Control*, *5*(1), 16–25, 2010.

Cobben, J.F.G., Kling, W.L., &Myrzik, J.M.A., Power quality aspects of a future micro grid, In *2005 International Conference on Future Power Systems*, IEEE, pp. 5, 2005, November.

Barote, L., & Marinescu, C., Software method for harmonic content evaluation of grid connected converters from distributed power generation systems, *Energy*, *66*, 401–412, 2014.

Kathiravan, R., & Kumudini Devi, R.P., Optimal power flow model incorporating wind, solar, and bundled solar-thermal power in the restructured Indian power system, *International Journal of Green Energy*, *14*(11), 934–950, 2017.

11

Power Quality Improvement in Microgrid System Using PSO-Based UPQC Controller

T. Eswara Rao[1], Krishna Mohan Tatikonda[2]*, S. Elango[3] and J. Charan Kumar[4]

[1]*Dept. of Electrical and Electronics Engineering,Coimbatore Institute of Technology, Coimbatore, Tamilnadu, India*
[2]*Dept. of Electrical and Electronics Engineering, Andhra Loyola Institute of Engineering and Technology, Vijayawada, A.P., India*
[3]*Dept. of Electrical and Electronics Engineering, Coimbatore Institute of Technology, Coimbatore, Tamilnadu, India*
[4]*Dept. of Electrical and Electronics Engineering, Sri Vani Educational Society Group of Institutions, Chevuturu, A.P., India*

Abstract

This chapter proposes a concept of new control techniques for unified power quality conditioner to improve the power quality in microgrid system. Here, wind energy system is considered for designing of microgrid system. In this chapter a SCIG based wind energy system is considered as one of the DG source. To get maximum reliability from wind energy system an MPPT based DC–DC converter is implemented. For improving power quality of the proposed microgrid system, this chapter is implemented with unified power quality conditioner. Suitable control techniques are designed for both series and shunt converters of UPQC. To achieve better power quality improvement under different load conditions a PSO optimization technique is implemented in this chapter. This proposed microgrid system with UPQC controller under different controllers are implemented and tested in MATLAB.

Keywords: Grid-connected system, optimization technique, power quality, custom power device, MPPT and wind energy system

*Corresponding author: t.krishnamohan02@gmail.com

C. Sharmeela, P. Sivaraman, P. Sanjeevikumar, and Jens Bo Holm-Nielsen (eds.) Microgrid Technologies, (287–308) © 2021 Scrivener Publishing LLC

11.1 Introduction

In the present scenario, the increasing demand for electrical energy is increasing rapidly. The utilization of general conventional power generation systems like gas, coal and nuclear power plants causes pollution and greenhouse effects. To overcome these environmental problems and meet the electrical demands, the non-conventional sources play a key role in the present energy generation systems. The main advantage of these renewable sources are pollution free, low maintenance cost and economical [1, 29]. There is more number of renewable systems available in market, but compared to all the wind and solar energy systems play a key role due to their simplicity in structure, available sources in environment and high efficient conditions.

Also based on the available natural conditions, the wind energy system is also one of the major renewable sources after PV system. The ratio of electrical energy generation is based on the availability of wind in nature. The changes of weather conditions effect the generated output from the wind system. Therefore, to achieve maximum output and for increasing the efficiency from the Wind System, an MPPT technique is implemented. Also, the system needs to maintain synchronization with the grid. For this, to match the frequency levels and system rating the solar system is connected to voltage source inverter [2]. The control diagram for the inverter is designed with general PWM technique and the reference signals are chosen from the grid parameters.

Power Quality also one of the major concern in present power system scenario. The main causes of power quality issues are mainly due to failure in synchronization, voltage unbalances, changes in load appliances, harmonic effects [3, 30–32]. There are lot of compensating devices available in market, but out of all these, interline unified power quality conditioner plays a key role to improve power quality in multi feeder microgrid based power system. UPQC is a combination of two converters connected in back–back namely, series and shunt converters.

Basically, the harmonics and reactive power are major concerns in power system which is associated with grid [33]. Flexible AC transmission systems are proposed in this chapter for improving the reliability of transmission system, quality of electrical power by reducing the problems (i.e. harmonics, power factor effects). UPQC controller compensates the voltage and current problems in microgrid system effected by different non-linearities. This chapter also implements conventional and PSO controllers for better controlling DC link capacitor voltage and reactive powers of the system [5].

11.2   Microgrid System

The main theme of microgrid system improves the reliability of small DG systems and also it reduces the system cost. Microgrid is a set of energy sources and loads and operates and is connected to and synchronous with macrogrid; sometimes it can also operate like island mode [6]. Microgrid effectively integrates with other energy DG sources likely renewable energy sources and can operate in emergency condition as well as also changes between island mode to grid mode.

In the present situation, the coordination of grid sustainable power sources, for example, wind energy system is the most significant application. These points of interest incorporate the ideal motivators in numerous nations that effect clearly on the business acknowledgment of grid associated wind [7, 8]. This condition forces the need of having great quality planning apparatuses and an approach to precisely foresee the dynamic execution of three-stage grid-associated Wind under various working conditions so as to settle on a cool-headed choice on whether to consolidate this innovation into the electric utility grid.

Figure 11.1 shows the basic structure of micro grid system. In this chapter for designing micro grid, wind energy system is chosen as distributed generation system [9]. SCIG used in wind system converts mechanical energy to electrical energy. To extract maximum output from the DG system an MPPT-based DC–DC converter is proposed. A PO-based MPPT technique is proposed to improve the reliability system. Power quality is the second concern in this chapter. AC–DC converters are proposed in AC grid system to operate DC loads and for controlling the motor load applications a DC–AC converters are proposed [10].

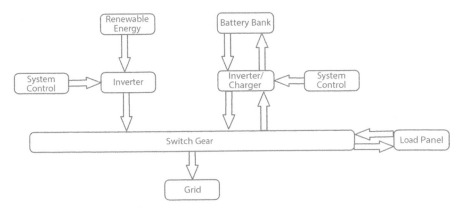

Figure 11.1 Structure of general Microgrid.

Figure 11.1 shows the basic structure of microgrid system. In this chapter for designing microgrid, wind energy system is chosen as distributed generation system [9]. SCIG used in wind system converts mechanical energy to electrical energy. To extract maximum output from the DG system an MPPT-based DC–DC converter is proposed. A PO-based MPPT technique is proposed to improve the reliability system. Power quality is the second concern in this chapter. AC–DC converters are proposed in AC grid system to operate DC loads and for controlling the motor load applications which DC–AC converters are proposed [10].

11.2.1   Wind Energy System

Wind turbines also play a key role in present disturbed energy systems because of wind availability in nature. In these, the energy conversion is done in two stages i.e one is turbine blades converts wind speed to mechanical energy and later it converts to electrical energy with the help of electrical generator [11]. In addition with these components, the wind turbine also consists of gear box mechanism to convert low speed shaft to high speed shaft. Also pitch angle controller is applied to rotate the wind blades as per the direction of wind to improve the reliability. The speed of wind reached to wind turbine is measured with help of wind vane. The structure of general wind turbine system with conventional generator is shown in Figure 11.2 [12, 13].

11.2.1.1   Modeling of Wind Turbine System

Wind power is proportional to wind speed cubed. Wind energy is the kinetic energy of the moving air. The kinetic energy of a mass m with the velocity v as shown in Equation (11.1) [14]

$$E_{kin} = 0.5mv^2 \tag{11.1}$$

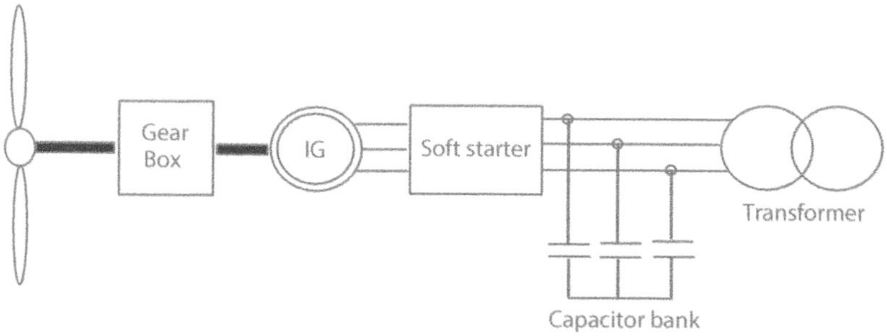

Figure 11.2 Basic diagram of wind turbine.

The air mass m can be determined from the air density ρ and the air volume V according to equation

$$m = \rho V \tag{11.2}$$

Then, the mechanical power for wind turbine as in Equation (11.3)

$$E_{kin} = 0.5 \rho v^3 \tag{11.3}$$

$$V = A * V * \ t \tag{11.4}$$

Then the wind power given in Equation (11.5)

$$P_{wind} = 0.5 \rho A v^3 * C_p \tag{11.5}$$

Where C_p is the coefficient of power, generally the value of C_p is 0.54.

11.2.2 Perturb and Observe MPPT Algorithm

In perturb and observe method, the system tracks the changes in array voltage and subsequently measure the change in output power. The flowchart for P&O algorithm is shown in Figure 11.3. In this flowchart, the voltage and current of Wind is measured used to calculate the power [16]. The obtained power is measured with instantaneous powers. From these results the required reference current signal is measured. This loop is repeated continuously.

The main disadvantage of this P&O technique is that it is not applicable for continuous changes in environmental conditions [17].

11.2.3 MPPT Converter

To extract maximum output from the wind energy system a MPPT based dc-dc converter is proposed. The output AC from the wind system is converted to DC with the help of rectifier and applied to DC–DC boost converter [18]. The duty cycle required for this boost converter is obtained with the help of MPPT controller. The control circuit for boost converter is shown in Figure 11.4. In Figure 11.4, the power from wind turbine is calculated and compared with time to time instantaneous power values.

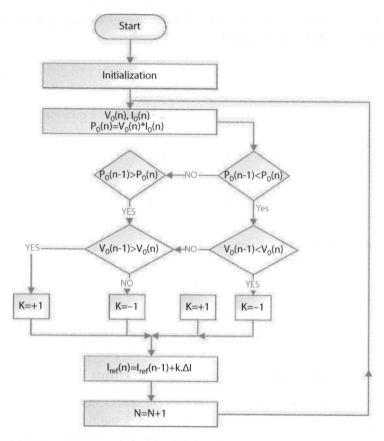

Figure 11.3 Flow chart representation of P&O technique.

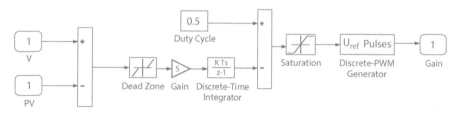

Figure 11.4 DC–DC converter MPPT controller.

PWM controller is used to generate duty cycle based on this comparison reference signal [18]. Here, perturb and observe maximum power tracking controller is implemented and the operation of this control algorithm is explained in previous section.

11.3   Unified Power Quality Conditioner

The proposed microgrid system is designed for multi feeders to operate loads. In this structure, the loads considered as linear and non-linear loads. The problems caused by these different loads are compensated with one of the custom power device called as Unified power quality conditioner connected between feeders [19]. The structure of Interline unified power quality conditioner is shown in Figure 11.5. It consists of two converters are separated by a common DC-link capacitor.

11.3.1   UPQC Series Converter

The series converter is used to control the fluctuations in system voltages such as sag, swell and disturbances. The control signals required for series converter is generate with the help of DC-link voltage of the UPQC and grid voltages. These voltages are transformed to two-phase coordinates i.e. dq-axis frame, after making comparison of these applied to PWM converter to generate gate signals [20].

Figure 11.6, Control Strategy of Series Active Filter, the instantaneous reactive power algorithm (IRPT) is based on Clarke's transformation. The voltage and current vectors in phase is transferred to αβ coordinates. The instantaneous reactive power algorithm (IRPT) is based on Clarke's transformation. The voltage and current vectors in phase is transferred to αβ coordinates. I_{la}, I_{lb} and I_{lc} represents the load current in a, b and c phases

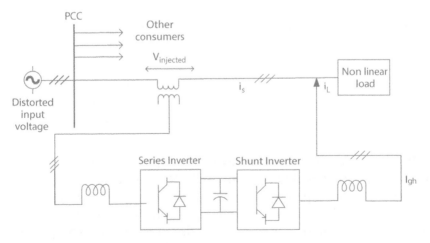

Figure 11.5 Single line diagram of UPQC.

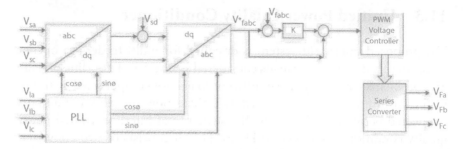

Figure 11.6 Structure of proposed PSO based UPQC Series control diagram.

respectively [21]. I_{alpha} and I_{beta} represent the load current in α and β axis as shown in Equations (11.6) and (11.7).

$$\begin{pmatrix} V_\alpha \\ V_\beta \end{pmatrix} = \sqrt{\frac{2}{3}} \begin{pmatrix} 1 & -\frac{1}{2} & -\frac{1}{2} \\ 0 & \frac{\sqrt{3}}{2} & -\frac{\sqrt{3}}{2} \end{pmatrix} \begin{pmatrix} Va \\ Vb \\ Vc \end{pmatrix} \quad (11.6)$$

$$\begin{pmatrix} i_\alpha \\ i_\beta \end{pmatrix} = \sqrt{\frac{2}{3}} \begin{pmatrix} 1 & -\frac{1}{2} & -\frac{1}{2} \\ 0 & \frac{\sqrt{3}}{2} & -\frac{\sqrt{3}}{2} \end{pmatrix} \begin{pmatrix} i_{La} \\ i_{Lb} \\ i_{Lc} \end{pmatrix} \quad (11.7)$$

The real and reactive power for the load can be calculated by the voltage and current in α-β coordinates as shown in Equations (11.8).

$$\begin{pmatrix} p_L \\ q_L \end{pmatrix} = \begin{pmatrix} i_{L\alpha} & i_{L\beta} \\ i_{L\beta} & -i_{L\alpha} \end{pmatrix} \begin{pmatrix} V_\alpha \\ V_\beta \end{pmatrix} \quad (11.8)$$

P_L and Q_L are the instantaneous real and imaginary power consumed by the load. The P_L and Q_L, contain both DC and AC terms [22]. But for voltage harmonic suppression and reactive power compensation, the AC term of P_L, and AC and DC terms of Q_L, should be provided by the active power filter. So the reference signal of the compensation voltage can be represented in Equation (11.9)

$$
\begin{pmatrix} V_{ca^*} \\ V_{cb^*} \\ V_{cc^*} \end{pmatrix} = \sqrt{\frac{2}{3}} \begin{pmatrix} 1 & 0 \\ -\frac{1}{2} & -\frac{\sqrt{3}}{2} \\ -\frac{1}{2} & -\frac{\sqrt{3}}{2} \end{pmatrix} \begin{pmatrix} V_{c\alpha^*} \\ V_{c\beta^*} \end{pmatrix} \tag{11.9}
$$

11.3.2 UPQC Shunt APF Controller

The shunt converter control diagram is designed by using the concept of instantaneous PQ-theory. The purpose of PQ theory is to generate the reference current signals which are required for compensating current harmonics. These reference powers are in comparison with rated electricity and then transformed to reference currents with the assistance of conventional PI controllers. After making comparison of these applied to PWM converter, it generates gate signals [23].

The source voltage and load currents are transformed to synchronous frame like abc/dqo frame to analyze the disturbances caused by load parameters. The reference current signals required for shunt converter are obtained by using the αβ-coordinates of voltage and currents [24]. The role of DC-voltage controller is to generate magnitude required for reference current signals and then converted to three phase components using dqo–abc transformation technique as shown in Figure 11.7.

$$
\begin{pmatrix} V_d \\ V_q \\ V_0 \end{pmatrix} = T \begin{pmatrix} V_a \\ V_b \\ V_c \end{pmatrix} \tag{11.10}
$$

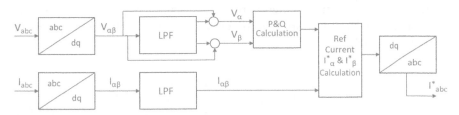

Figure 11.7 Control structure of the shunt inverter.

Where,

$$T = \sqrt{\frac{2}{3}} \begin{pmatrix} \cos\theta & \cos(\theta - \frac{2\pi}{3}) & \cos(\theta + \frac{2\pi}{3}) \\ \sin\theta & \sin(\theta - \frac{2\pi}{3}) & \sin(\theta + \frac{2\pi}{3}) \\ \frac{1}{\sqrt{2}} & \frac{1}{\sqrt{2}} & \frac{1}{\sqrt{2}} \end{pmatrix}$$

Instantaneous three-phase currents and voltages are transformed to α–ß co-ordinates as shown in Equations (11.11), (11.12), (11.13) and (11.14).

$$I_\alpha = \frac{2}{3} I_a - \frac{1}{3}(I_b - I_c) \tag{11.11}$$

$$I_\beta = \frac{2}{\sqrt{3}}(I_b - I_c) \tag{11.12}$$

$$V_\alpha = \frac{2}{3} V_a - \frac{1}{3}(V_b - V_c) \tag{11.13}$$

$$V_\beta = \frac{2}{\sqrt{3}}(V_b - V_c) \tag{11.14}$$

The source side instantaneous real and imaginary power components are calculated by using source currents and phase voltages as given in Equation (11.15):

$$\begin{pmatrix} P \\ Q \end{pmatrix} = \begin{pmatrix} V_\alpha & V_\beta \\ -V_\beta & V_\alpha \end{pmatrix} \begin{pmatrix} i_\alpha \\ i_\beta \end{pmatrix} \tag{11.15}$$

I^*_{salpha} and I^*_{sbeta} are the reference currents of shunt APF in α–β co-ordinates given in Equation (11.16):

$$\begin{pmatrix} I*_{s\alpha} \\ I*_{s\beta} \end{pmatrix} = \frac{1}{V_\alpha^2 + V_\beta^2} \begin{pmatrix} V_\alpha & V_\beta \\ -V_\beta & V_\alpha \end{pmatrix} \begin{pmatrix} \overline{p} + P_0 + P_{loss} \\ 0 \end{pmatrix} \qquad (11.16)$$

$$I^*_a = I^*_{sa} \qquad (11.17)$$

$$I^*_b = \frac{-I^*_{sa} + \sqrt{3}I^*_\beta}{2} \qquad (11.18)$$

$$I^*_c = \frac{-I^*_{sa} + \sqrt{3}I^*_\beta}{2} \qquad (11.19)$$

These reference source current signals are then compared with sensed three-phase source currents, and the errors are processed by hysteresis band PWM controller [25] to generate the required switching signals for the shunt APF switches.

11.4   Particle Swarm Optimization

It is a bio prodding preparing mechanical assembly. It is made reliant on the activities of winged animals, point, and various animals. Who are pro and electrical planner? It is an energetic stochastic displaying framework reliant on the improvement and information on swarms [26]. PSO applies the possibility of social dialog for basic reasoning.

11.4.1   Velocity Function

$$V_{r(k+1)} = V_{r(k)} + t_{1r}(P_r - X_{r(k)}) + t_{2r}(G - X_{i(k)}) \qquad (11.20)$$

PSO is initialized with a group of random particles and then searches for optimal by updating generations. The procedure to obtain the Partical is shown in flowchart Figure 11.8. In every iteration, each particle is updated by following two "best" values [27]. The best solution obtained by fitness is called Pbest and next best signal is obtained by using PSO by any particle in the population [28].

11.4.2   Analysis of PSO Technique

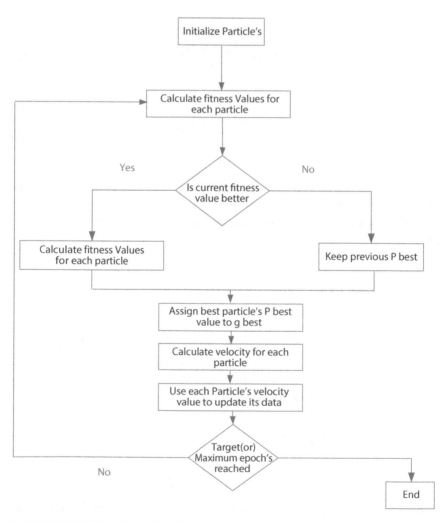

Figure 11.8 Algorithm for PSO technique.

11.5   Simulation and Results

The proposed system is implemented using a) PI and b) PSO based UPQC controller to control the active and reactive powers. In MATLAB analysis, the proposed system is tested under two different conditions, i.e under sag implementation in the system conditions and during fault condition. The experimental MATLAB diagram is shown in the following Figure 11.9. The parameters of wind turbine system and grid system are shown in Table 11.1 and Table 11.2.

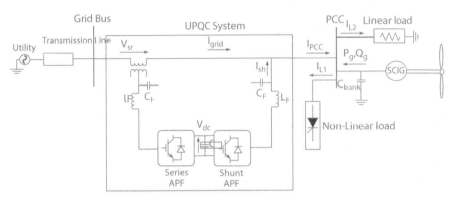

Figure 11.9 Structure of Proposed Microgrid System with UPQC.

Table 11.1 System parameters for wind turbine system.

Parameter variable	Value
Nominal Wind Speed	10 m/s
Wind System Power	8 kW
Wind Turbine Bus Voltage	690 V
Generator (SCIG) specifications	
Generator Rating	10 kW
Stator Resistance	0.435 Ω
Stator Leakage Inductance	0.446 Ω
Mutual Inductance	0.43 Ω
No. of Pole Pairs	2
Inertia Constant	0.08 kg.m²

Table 11.2 System parameters.

Parameter variable	Value
Grid Voltage	415 V, 50 Hz
Line Series Inductance	0.05 mH
DC-Link Capacitance	100 μF
DC-Link Voltage	800 V
Switching Frequency	2 kHz
Non-Linear Load	10 kW
IGBT Collector Voltage	1,200 V
Forward Current	50 A

11.5.1   Case 1: With PI Controller

Here, the simulation is done for grid interfaced wind energy system using P&O MPPT technique. An UPQC controller is implemented with PI controller to improve the Power Quality. The simulation results are shown below.

Figure 11.9 shows the simulation result for active and reactive powers of the proposed system under fault condition. Here, the fault condition is applied to the system during the period 0.3 to 0.45 s. Also a step change condition is applied to the system and the corresponding changes in the measured powers are shown in Figure 11.9. The changes in grid current

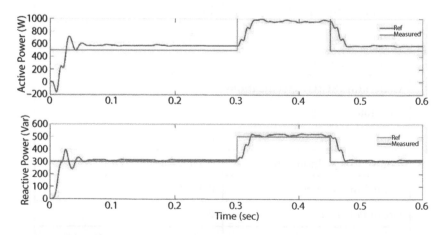

Figure 11.9 Simulation result for active and reactive powers with PI based UPQC.

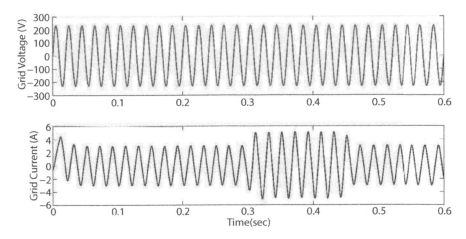

Figure 11.10 Simulation result for Grid Voltage and Grid Current.

caused by sudden load changes are compensated by using UPQC controller and also it compensate the active and reactive power. The grid voltage
and currents during this condition is shown in Figure 11.10.

The swell is initiated in the system use of the non-linear load, unbalanced
load or critical load in the load side. The voltage swell signal is shown in Figure
11.11. The mitigation is achieved through the use of proposed controller.

The normal voltage of the system is 230 V. Figure 11.11(a) illustrates
the disturbance voltage in swell condition. Initially, 230 V is maintained
in the constant level to at 0–0.05 s, then it is increased the voltage to 30 V
(i.e. 260 V) at 0.05–0.1 s due to the sudden load variation. During Swell
Condition, the excess 30 V voltage is compensated using series converter
of UPQC and stored in DC-link capacitor. The simulation result for UPQC
injected voltage is shown in Figure 11.11(b) and the compensated load
voltage is illustrated in the Figure 11.11(c).

11.5.2   Case 2: With PSO Technique

Here, the simulation is done for grid interfaced wind energy system using
P&O MPPT technique. An UPQC controller is implemented with PSO
technique to improve the Power Quality.

Figure 11.12 shows the simulation result for active and reactive powers of the proposed system with PSO controller. A step change condition
is applied to the system and the corresponding changes in the measured
powers are shown. The grid voltage and currents during this condition is
shown in Figure 11.13.

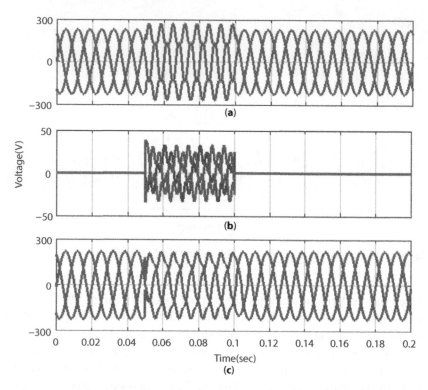

Figure 11.11 Analysis of the (a) Voltage swell, (b) Injected voltage and (c) Output voltage.

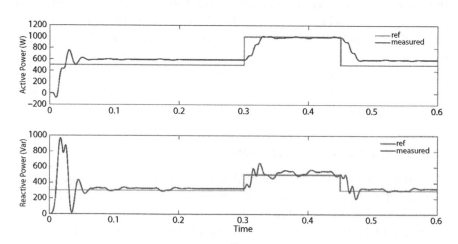

Figure 11.12 Simulation result for active and reactive powers with PSO technique.

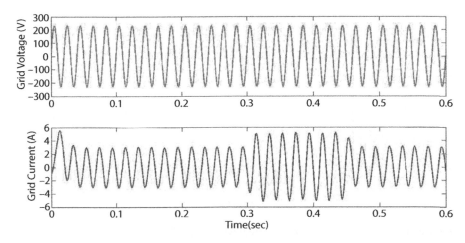

Figure 11.13 Simulation result for Grid Voltage and Current due to change in load.

The THD ratio is analyzed for the performance testing of the proposed controller. Before connected UPQC, the THD ratio is 8.93% and it reduced from 12.85%, 4.75% after connected with UPQC device. The UPQC with PSO device also decreases the harmonics in the signal to 3.34% as shown in Figures 11.14, 11.15 and 11.16.

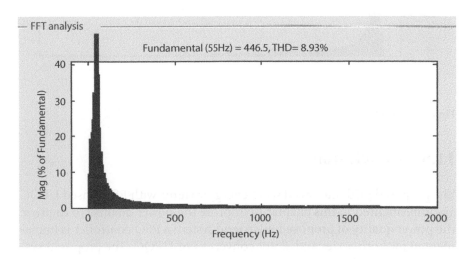

Figure 11.14 THD for Non-Linear Current without UPQC.

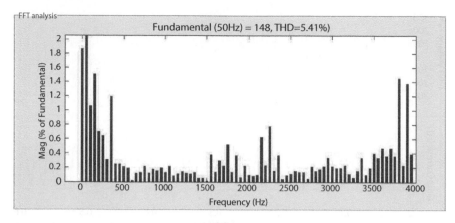

Figure 11.15 THD for Non-Linear Current with UPQC PI controller.

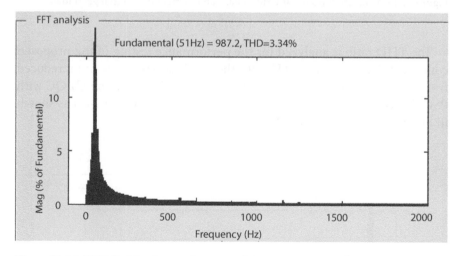

Figure 11.16 THD for Non-Linear Current with UPQC PSO controller.

11.6 Conclusion

The proposed grid interfaced wind energy systems with PSO-based UPQC are implemented in this chapter to improve the power quality. To improve the power quality of proposed microgrid system a PSO controller is implemented for both series and shunt converters of UPQC. The proposed system is tested under two cases such as improving the efficiency to improve reliability of proposed system and improvement of quality of the system. To achieve reliability of microgrid system, the DG system is implemented with MPPT technique and to get better power quality a PSO technique is implemented for UPQC. The experimental results in MATLAB/Simulink are verified. The harmonic distortion effected by non-linear current is 3.34% with PSO-UPQC controller, 5.41% with UPQC controller. So that, the PSO technique provides better result in power quality improvement as compared with conventional controllers.

References

1. Wang, F., Duarte, J.L. and Hendrix, M.A.M., *Grid-Interfacing Converter Systems with Enhanced Voltage Quality for Microgrid Application Concept and Implementation*, IEEE, 2011.
2. Wang, F., Duarte, J.L. and Hendrix, M.A.M., Pliant active and reactive power control for grid-interactive converters under unbalanced voltage dips, *IEEE Transactions on Power Electronics*, in press, 2010.
3. Heydt, G.T., *Electric Power Quality*, (2nd edition), Stars in a Circle Publications, 1994.
4. Han, B., Bae, B., Kim, H. and Baek, S., Combined operation of upqc with distributed generation, *IEEE Trans. Power Delivery*, vol. 21, no. 1, pp. 330–338, Jan. 2006.
5. Wang, F., Duarte, J.L. and Hendrix, M.A.M., Reconfiguring grid interfacing converters for power quality improvement, in *Proc. IEEE Benelux Young Researchers Symposium\in Electrical Power Engineering*, pp. 1–6, 2008.
6. Farhangi, H., The path of the smart grid, *IEEE Power Energy Mag.*, vol. 8, no. 1, pp. 18–28, Jan./Feb. 2010
7. Bae, S., Kwasinski, A., Dynamic Modeling and Operation Strategy for a Microgrid with Wind and PV Resources *IEEE 2012 Transactions on Smart Grid.*
8. Tao, H., *Integration of sustainable energy sources through PEC in small DG Systems*, PhD dissertation, Eindhoven University of technology, 2008.
9. Liu, X., Wang, P. and Loh, P.C., A Hybrid AC/DC Microgrid and Its Coordination Control, *IEEE Trans. Smart Grid*, vol. 2, no. 2, pp. 278–286, June. 2011.
10. Ito, Y., Yang, Z. and Akagi, H., DC Microgrid Based Distribution Power Generation System, in *Proc. IEEE Int. Power Electron. Motion Control Conf.*, vol. 3, pp. 1740–1745, Aug. 2004.
11. Arulampalam, A., Mithulananthan, N., Bansal, R.C. and Saba, T.K., Microgrid Control of PV -Wind-Diesel Hybrid System with Islanded and Grid Connected Operations, in *Proc. IEEE Int. Conf. Sustainable Energy Technologies*, pp. 1–5, 2010.
12. Hook, K.S., Liu, Y. and Atcitty, S., Mitigation of the wind generation integration related power quality issues by energy storage, *EPQU J.*, vol. XII, no. 2, 2006.
13. Bhadra, S.N., Kastha, D., Banerjee, S., *Wind Electrical Systems*, Oxford University Press, New Delhi, 2009.

14. Shuhui, Optimal and Direct-Current Vector Control of Direct-Driven PMSG Wind Turbines, *IEEE Transactions on Power Electronics*, Vol. 27, No. 5, May 2012.

15. Wang, Yundong, *Modeling and Real-Time Simulation of Non-Grid-Connected WECS*, 978-1-4244-4702-2/09/$25.00 ©2009 IEEE.

16. Hohm, Ropp, Comparative Study of MPPT Algorithms Using an Experimental, Programmable, MPPT Test Bed, in *IEEE*, pp. 1699–1702, 2000.

17. Sera, Teodorescu, Hantschel, and Knoll, M., Optimized maximum power point tracker for fast-changing environmental conditions, *IEEE Trans. Ind. Electron.*, vol.55, no. 7, pp. 2629–2637, Jul. 2008.

18. Li, Y.W. and Kao, C.-N., An accurate power control strategies for PEIDG units operating in a LV multi bus micro grid, *IEEE Trans. Power Electron.*, vol. 24, no. 12, pp. 2977–2988, Dec. 2009.

19. Han, B., Bae, B., Kim, H. and Baek, S., Combined operation of unified power-quality conditioner with distributed generation, *IEEE Trans. Power Delivery*, vol. 21, no. 1, pp. 330–338, Jan. 2006.

20. Wang, F., Duarte, J.L. and Hendrix, M.A.M., Reconfiguring grid interfacing converters for power quality improvement, in *Proc. IEEE Benelux Young Researchers Symposium\in Electrical Power Engineering*, pp. 1–6, 2008.

21. Zobaa, A.F., Abdel Aleem, S.H.E. and Balci, M.E., *Introductory Chapter: Power System Harmonics—Analysis, Effects, and Mitigation Solutions for Power Quality Improvement*, March 20th 2018 Published: May 30th 2018.

22. Bollen, M.H., *Understanding Power Quality Problems: Voltage Sags and Interruptions, Power, Energy and Industry Applications*, Wiley-IEEE Press, 2000.

23. Tey, L.H. Member, IEEE, So, P.L., Senior Member, IEEE, and Chu, Y.C., Member, IEEE, Improvement of Power Quality Using Adaptive Shunt Active Filter, *IEEE Transactions on Power Delivery*, Vol. 20, No. 2, April 2005.

24. Peng, F.Z. and Lai, J.S., Generalized instantaneous reactive power theory for three-phase power systems, *IEEE Trans. Instrum. Meas.*, vol. 45, no. 1, pp. 293–297, Feb. 1996.

25. Bhonsle, D.C. and Kelkar, R.B., Design and simulation of single phase shunt active power filter using MATLAB, *2011 International Conference on Recent Advancements in Electrical, Electronics and Control Engineering*, Sivakasi, pp. 237–241, 2011.

26. Felice Browni, I., Selvamalar Beaulah Ponrani, U., Comparison of PSO and DE Algorithm Based MPPT Algorithm for Solar Energy System, In *International Journal of Electrical and Electronics Engineers* ISSN-2321-2055 (E) http://www.arresearchpublication.com IJEEE, Volume 07, Issue 01, Jan–June 2015.

27. Renuka, and Sreedharan, S., An enhanced PSO algorithm for improving the RES penetration and small signal stability in power system, Renuka *et al. Renewables 5:6*, https://doi.org/10.1186/s40807-018-0053-4, 2018.

28. Reyna, A.A.C., *Applications of the differential evolution optimization algorithm in power systems planning, operation and control*, Citeseer, 2006.

29. C. Sharmeela, Sivaraman, P., and S. Balaji (2020). Design of Hybrid DC Mini Grid for Educational Institution: Case Study, Lecture Notes in Electrical Engineering, 580, pp. 125–134.

30. Sivaraman, P., and Sharmeela, C. (2020). Existing issues associated with electric distribution system. In Baseem Kahn, Hassan Haes Alhelou & Ghassan (Eds.), *Handbook of Research on New Solutions and Technologies in Electrical Distribution Networks*, (pp. 1–31), Hershey, PA: IGI Global.

31. Sivaraman, P., and Sharmeela, C. (2020). Power Quality and its Characteristics. In Sanjeevikumar Padmanaban, C. Sharmeela, Jens Bo Holm-Nielsen, Power *Quality in Modern Power Systems*, Elsevier.

32. Sivaraman, P., and Sharmeela, C. (2020). Power System Harmonics. In Sanjeevikumar Padmanaban, C. Sharmeela, Jens Bo Holm-Nielsen, Power *Quality in Modern Power Systems*, Elsevier.

33. R. Mahendran, P. Sivaraman and C. Sharmeela, "Three Phase Grid Interfaced Renewable Energy Source using Active Power Filter" 5th International Exhibition & Conference, GRIDTECH 2015, April, 2015, pp. 77–85, New Delhi, India.

12

Power Quality Enhancement and Grid Support Using Solar Energy Conversion System

CH. S. Balasubrahmanyam[1], Om Hari Gupta[1*] and Vijay K. Sood[2]

[1]National Institute of Technology Jamshedpur, Jamshedpur, India
[2]Ontario Tech University, Oshawa, Canada

Abstract

Converter-based loads are increasing due to their numerous advantages such as easy control, modularity and reduced cost. Converters suffer from reactive power consumption and generate harmonics that are injected into the system. Conventionally, passive power filters and capacitor banks take care of harmonics and reactive power respectively. However, they are bulky and possess challenges like series and parallel resonance. The shunt active power filters (APFs) could be considered the resolution for the same. If the shunt APF is operated in distribution-static compensator (D-STATCOM) mode, both i.e. load harmonics and reactive power could be compensated. A solar energy conversion system has been used in this study for the compensation of both load harmonics and load reactive power along with injection of the power generated. MATLAB-based simulations are carried out for the implementation of the same. Results depict the successful operation of the solar energy conversion system with grid support and enhancement of power quality.

Keywords: Solar energy, distribution network, D-STATCOM, shunt filter, converter

12.1 Introduction

The introduction of distributed generators (DGs) into the future distribution grid will provide benefits like a reduction in power transmission

---

*Corresponding author: omhari.ee@nitjsr.ac.in

C. Sharmeela, P. Sivaraman, P. Sanjeevikumar, and Jens Bo Holm-Nielsen (eds.) Microgrid Technologies, (309–328) © 2021 Scrivener Publishing LLC

losses and added flexibility to the grid since the generation will be close to the consumer [1]. However, energy generated from the sustainable and renewable assets (like solar, wind, small hydro, biogas and biomass) cannot be directly integrated into the grid, as the energy form is both intermittent and variable. It is noteworthy that the generated power is likely to be at a variable voltage and variable frequency whereas the grid uses power at a (relatively or largely) constant voltage and constant frequency only. Hence, the use of interfacing power-electronics-based conversion technology is essential to match the DG with the grid power [2]. Basically, the converters are of two types: current source and/or voltage source types and the choice will be made subject to various requirements such as power quality and impact on the grid particularly when the interfacing point is at a weak AC system. With the use of these converters, the power can be suitably converted to be injected into the existing power network keeping in mind the degradation of power quality such as overvoltage, swell, flicker, frequency deviations and production of DC components, harmonics, sub-harmonics, inter-harmonics, etc. [3]. Power quality issues are of vital concern for customers since modern loads are more sensitive to electrical parameters and power disturbances. The use of current source converters is accompanied by increased reactive power needs which are of concern. However, the use of voltage source converters (VSCs) provides an added feature of autonomous regulation of active as well as reactive power which is immensely desirable. The advances in control theory and multilevel conversion topologies coupled with the reduction in the cost of semiconductors and computational resources have provided an added impetus to the conversion technology. This will permit the resolution of major issues like reactive power management as well as mitigation of harmonics in the distribution network by local compensation techniques i.e., near load centres for reasons of higher efficiency and power quality.

The devices for mitigation of harmonics can be either passive or active power devices (or custom power devices, CPDs). The CPDs can be used for various tasks such as reactive power compensation, harmonic compensation, or compensation of both harmonics as well as reactive power. When compensating the reactive power alone, CPD is considered working in a static compensator (STATCOM) mode; if compensating harmonics alone, it is assumed to be working in active power filter (APF) mode, and if compensating both reactive power and harmonics, it is assumed to be working in distribution-STATCOM (D-STATCOM) mode [4]. Since, ideally, no active component is required for harmonics and reactive compensation, the CPDs can be designed by using a VSC connected to either an active voltage source or a DC link capacitor. Moreover, to protect the sensitive loads from sag, swell, overvoltage, under voltage and other power quality variations, voltage or compensation should also be provided by a series compensator. There are separate devices for improvement in voltage and current qualities. Based on this classification, the devices are classified into three categories. First is a shunt APF—compensates current harmonics. Series APF is the second one which compensates for voltage harmonics. Third device is a package combining both shunt as well as series APFs which can compensate both voltage as well as current harmonics. There are some devices like D-STATCOM for load current harmonic and reactive compensation. Dynamic voltage restorer (DVR) takes care of voltage harmonics as well as sag and swell [5]. The combination of D-STATCOM and DVR is called a unified power quality conditioner (UPQC).

Apart from injecting renewable-based power, the solar energy conversion system (SECS) can also be utilized for other superior services like supply of load reactive power requirement as well as enhancement of power quality at the point of load connection. This lowers the capacities of centralized active power filters (APFs) located at different sub-stations [6]. The duties of the shunt APFs stated in the literature are performed using different control techniques for generation of reference currents such as instantaneous reactive power theory [7, 8], enhanced phase locked loop (EPLL) [9], synchronous reference frame theory [10], and instantaneous p–q theory, [11] etc. Also, adaptive robust soft computing control strategies like least mean square [12] are frequently employed for Gaussian assumption to eliminate the noise/harmonics. For non-Gaussian and non-stationary situations, least mean fourth [13] algorithm is used. Further, to improve the steady state misalignments and convergence rate, a new robust normalised mixed norm adaptive algorithm [14] is used. A renewable-based unified power quality conditioner is proposed in Ref. [15], which can improve quality of current using shunt VSC and protects sensitive loads by improving voltage quality using series VSC.

A solar-based dynamic active compensation using unified power flow controller (UPFC) which is the combination of STATCOM and SSSC is implemented in Ref. [16]. In this, the reactive power compensation and unbalanced three phase sag and swell compensation is implemented. During sunshine hours, solar output is connected to the inverter so that both active and reactive powers are supplied to the load and utility while for non-sunshine hours, the solar is disconnected so only reactive power compensation can be done.

A photovoltaic interactive shunt APF is implemented in Ref. [17] using fuzzy-based algorithm to eliminate harmonics in order to enhance voltage quality of the grid. The SAF theory is used to control the voltage across DC capacitor and to control the power flow into the grid through VSC. Fuzzy logic has been used to generate the crest of the reference current which is multiplied with unit vector sine of phase angle generated by PLL and fuzzy logic does not need any transfer function modelling and it can deal with non-linear functions also.

A solar-based single phase grid-tied converter using modified pack U-cell (PUC) multi-level inverter (MLI) implemented to eliminate current harmonics is proposed in Ref. [18]. The PUC is one of the good MLI topologies with 6 switches and 2 DC link capacitors for 5-level MLI. In this, finite control set-model predictive control (FCS-MPC) is used for high grid current quality, good capacitor voltage stabilization across capacitors (as capacitor voltage stabilization is one of the major tasks to be achieved in controlling MLI's) and for minimum switching frequency. It also reduces the number of controllers—causing lower losses in the inverter side.

A UPQC-DG is proposed in Ref. [19] using SRF based power angle control (PAC) with an improved performance for the unbalanced load compensation. The PAC is used to improve the utilization of VA rating of the shunt and series APFs of considered UPQC-DG and it is proved that with the proposed technique, the VA loading is reduced by 21.1%.

The above control strategies for the generation of reference currents incorporate a heavy computational burden which can be expensive to implement. Therefore, this chapter presents a solar energy system with power quality enhancement (SEPQ) based on instantaneous active power averaging theory which involves less computations and has a quick response. For performance investigation, MATLAB-based simulations are used to verify the successful operation of the presented scheme.

The remainder of the chapter has been organised as follows. Section 12.2 briefly discusses the renewable energy and its conversion. The power system harmonics and their causes are discussed in Section 12.3. Section 12.4 presents the effects of the load power factor on the system. Then Section 12.5 introduces the solar energy system with power quality enhancement (SEPQ). Section 12.6 includes the results and Section 12.7 concludes the chapter.

12.2   Renewable Energy and its Conversion Into Useful Form

There are several renewable energy resources available. *Wind* energy is one of the major renewable energy assets that is accessible almost all over the world. As the wind speed is variable, the electric generation acquired from wind energy cannot be injected directly into the grid. So, for grid integration, two schemes are in common practice, namely: doubly fed induction generator (DFIG) based wind energy conversion and synchronous generator-based wind energy conversion. In both of these schemes, PE based converters are used to synchronize the output of wind energy conversion system (WECS) with that of the grid. *Biomass* energy is generated by burning organic wastes to produce heat and then it is converted into electricity. *Geothermal* energy is produced from the underground layers of the earth which is used to convert water into steam and this steam is used to rotate the turbine of a generator to produce electricity. *Tidal* energy is a form of hydropower obtained from the tides and then converted into electricity.

Solar energy has also been among the popular renewable energy capitals because of its abundant availability, static generation and low maintenance. The block drawing of a solar energy conversion system (SECS) is given in Figure 12.1. The output from the solar panels depends on irradiance and temperature. Maximum power-point tracking (MPPT) method has been utilized for the extraction of maximum power at a particular irradiance and temperature. PE converters are used to synchronize SECS with the grid.

12.3   Power System Harmonics and Their Cause

A non-linear load injects harmonics into the system and acts as a current source. Due to this injection, the bus voltage quality becomes poor. Consider a typical 3-phase system with a sinusoidal voltage source V_s and feeder impedance Z_s supplying linear and non-linear (or harmonic current source) loads, as given in Figure 12.2—complete system data is given in Table 12.1. A switch S_1 is used for the connection as well as disconnection of non-linear load (or harmonic current source) which is simply a 3-phase

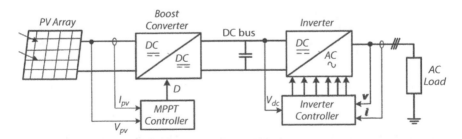

Figure 12.1 Block diagram of SECS.

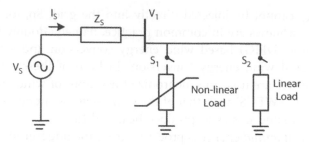

Figure 12.2 Equivalent diagram of supply system having different loads.

Table 12.1 System details for harmonics analysis.

S. N.	Parameter	Value
1	Voltage (V_s)	415 V (L-L)
2	Source impedance (Z_s)	0.501 Ω
3	System Frequency, f	50 Hz
4	3-phase Linear load	90 kW, u.p.f.
5	3-phase non-linear load	90 kW

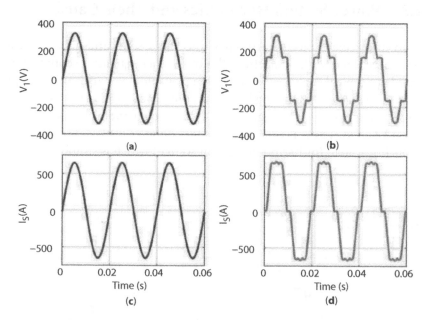

Figure 12.3 Phase-A (a) bus voltage with linear load, (b) bus voltage with non-linear load, (c) source current with linear load, and (d) source current with non-linear load.

full wave uncontrolled rectifier with resistive load. Similarly, S_2 is used for the making and braking of linear load circuit. The higher loads are intentionally connected in order to show visible impact of the non-linear load. At a time, either linear or non-linear load is connected to the system.

In Figures 12.3(a) and (b), phase-A bus voltages are depicted for linear and non-linear loads, respectively. Similarly, in Figures 12.3(c) and (d), phase-A source currents are depicted for linear and non-linear loads, respectively. When the non-linear load is attached to the system through switch S_1 after disconnecting the linear load using S_2, the source current I_S is distorted and due to that the bus voltage V_I also gets non-sinusoidal. Figures 12.4(a) and (b) present the voltage spectrums with linear and non-linear loads, respectively. Figures 12.4(c) and (d) present the current spectrums with linear and non-linear loads, respectively. It is clear that the voltage THD is increased from 0 to 18.85% while current THD is changed

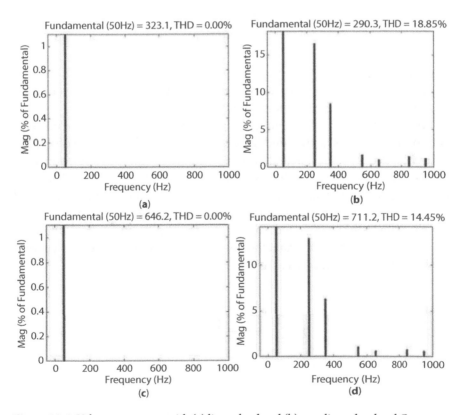

Figure 12.4 Voltage spectrums with (a) linear load and (b) non-linear load and Current spectrums with (c) linear load and (d) non-linear load.

from 0 to 12.45%. Therefore, if the current distortions are not compensated, the voltage profile will deteriorate.

12.4 Power Factor (p.f.) and its Effects

Most common loads have a lagging p.f. and consume reactive power from the system. It is well known that due to non-unity p.f., the current drained from the system is larger than that at unity p.f. Also, the poor power factor increases the voltage regulation—which is not desirable. For the improvement of the p.f., the conventional way is to connect a capacitor at a bus where the load has been connected. This is clarified in Figure 12.5—switch S_3 is used to connect/disconnect the capacitor to the system. The capacitance (for star configuration) can be obtained by using Equation (12.1) as given below:

$$C = \frac{Q_C}{3\omega V_1^2} \tag{12.1}$$

where, $Q_c = P_L (\tan \theta_1 - \tan \theta_2)$, V_1 = phase voltage of bus, $\omega = 2\pi f$, $f =$ system frequency, P_L = load active demand, θ_1 and θ_2 are the power factor angles before and after compensation, respectively.

For a 3-phase system, a lagging load is connected to the bus—complete system data for this is provided in Table 12.2. The p.f. is improved to unity with a capacitor, value calculated using Equation (12.1), can be connected or disconnected by controlling switch S_3. Figures 12.6(a) and (b) present the voltages and currents, respectively when capacitor is not connected and when it is connected. It can be witnessed from Figure 12.6 that when the capacitor is not connected, the current ($I_{S,lag}$) is lagging behind the voltage ($V_{1,lag}$) and when the capacitor is connected, the voltage and current ($V_{1,upf}$ and $I_{S,upf}$) are in phase.

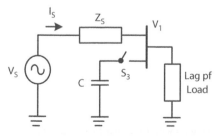

Figure 12.5 Equivalent diagram of capacitor bank attached in parallel with lagging load.

Table 12.2 System details for p.f. analysis.

S. N.	Parameter	Value
1	Voltage (V_s)	415 V (L-L)
2	Grid frequency, f	50 Hz
3	Load power	50 kW
4	Load pf.	0.8 lag
5	Capacitor bank rating	37.5 kVAR
6	Type of connection	Star grounded
7	Capacitance per phase	0.693 mF

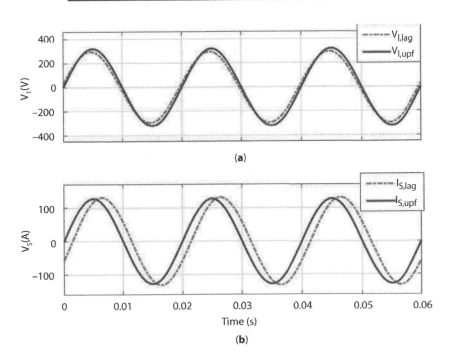

Figure 12.6 (a) Voltages and (b) currents with and without capacitor bank.

12.5 Solar Energy System With Power Quality Enhancement (SEPQ)

The SECS is one of the most promising energy sources. Therefore, in this chapter, a grid connected SECS is simulated for obtaining both the tasks, i.e. injection of the active power generated from the photo-voltaic system and enhancement of power quality. It is assumed that linear and non-linear loads are attached to the system which causes both distortions and reactive power requirement demand, as presented in Figure 12.7.

The diode bridge rectifier is connected as a non-linear load which draws a distorted current. A linear load, with lagging p.f., is also connected to develop some reactive power demand. So, the load current can, now, be described by the formula as given in Equation (12.2) below:

$$i_l = i_{lp} + i_{lh} + i_{lq} \tag{12.2}$$

where i_{lp} is the active component, i_{lh} is the harmonic component, and i_{lq} is the reactive element of the load current. Among these three components, i_{lh} and i_{lq} are to be taken care of by the compensator. The relation can be written as given below in Equation (12.3):

$$i_{pv} = i_{lh} + i_{lq} = i_l - i_{lp} \tag{12.3}$$

The current of Equation (12.3) should be injected by the compensator. The SECS is functioned in D-STATCOM mode i.e. apart from supplying power generated, it also provides harmonic and reactive compensations.

The steps followed are included in the flow diagram shown in Figure 12.8. The reference current for VSC is estimated by instantaneous averaging theory in which the component analogous to active power is extracted by averaging the instantaneous power. Using this active power 'P' and measured rms voltage 'V_{pcc}', the active element of load current is obtained i.e.,

$$I_{lp} = \sqrt{2}P/3V_{pcc} \tag{12.4}$$

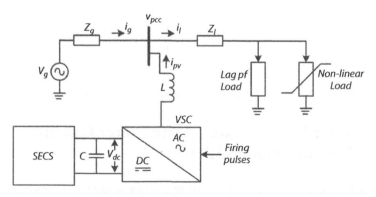

Figure 12.7 Equivalent diagram of SEPQ.

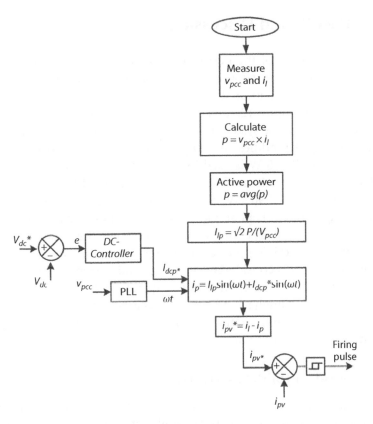

Figure 12.8 Flow chart for control of SECS in D-STATCOM mode.

This component i.e. the current of Equation (12.4) is to be drawn from the utility. Moreover, to balance the DC bus voltage (v_{dc}), another active current component is to be drawn from the grid i.e. I_{dcp}—to be obtained from the DC controller illustrated in Figure 12.8. If SECS is generating sufficient power, then I_{dcp} will be negative i.e. power being injected to the system else SECS is not generating sufficient power. Now, the reference current for VSC i.e., $i_{pv}*$ can be obtained using i_l (obtained from measurement), I_{lp}, $I_{dcp}*$, and ωt (obtained from phase locked loop, PLL) as given below in Equation (12.5):

$$i_{pv}^* = i_l - I_{lp}\sin(\omega t) - I_{dcp}^*\sin(\omega t) \qquad (12.5)$$

where $I_{lp}\sin(\omega t) = i_{lp}$. The hysteresis controller is used to produce the firing pulses corresponding to the reference current $i_{pv}*$ and measured compensator current i_{pv}, as depicted in Figure 12.8.

12.6   Results and Discussions

For the investigation of the performance of the presented power quality enhancement and grid support using solar energy conversion system, MATLAB-based simulation study has been performed. The typical system, as shown in Figure 12.7, has been used in the simulation study. The rated voltage of 3-phase system is 415 V, rated v_{dc} is 1,400 V. An array consisting of 10 series modules and 40 parallel strings of photovoltaic model TDB156x156-60-P 225 W is used in this study. The ratings of the considered PV array are 10 × 40 modules of each 225 W, total PV array voltage of 370 V, a peak power of 90 kW at 1 kW/m² irradiance. The boost converter switching frequency is kept at 5 kHz, converter inductor is of 50 mH and capacitor is of 18 mF. The DC to AC converter is then used in hysteresis current control (HCC) mode. For better illustration, one phase of the three-phase system is considered for voltage and current waveforms.

The solar energy system with power quality enhancement (SEPQ) is used in 3 modes, namely: 1. STATCOM (reactive power compensation); 2. Shunt APF (harmonic compensation); 3. D-STATCOM (reactive power and harmonic compensation).

12.6.1   Mode-1 (SEPQ as STATCOM)

In this mode of operation, SEPQ is used to supply the reactive power demand of the load (Q_L). Therefore, load extracts only active power from the grid. This reduces voltage drop which leads to better voltage regulation and reduction in I²R losses which results in high efficiency of transmission lines. Figures 12.9(a), (b), and (c) illustrate the grid voltage (V_g), current (I_g) and SEPQ current (i_{pv}), respectively. Moreover, Figures 12.10(a), (b), and (c) depict v_{dc}, active powers (of SEPQ, load and grid), and reactive powers (of SEPQ, load and grid), respectively—where, P_{pv} = SEPQ active power, P_L = load active power, P_g = grid active power, Q_{pv} = SEPQ reactive power, and Q_g = utility reactive power. It can be seen that Q_L is supplied by the SEPQ when it is connected at t = 0.04 s. Moreover, since P_L is less than P_{pv}, the excess amount of power is being supplied to the grid—that can be witnessed from Figure 12.10(b) as P_g becomes negative. In this case, the connected load is 27 kW at 0.8 pf lag., P_{pv} is 36 kW and Q_{pv} is 20 kVAR.

12.6.2   Mode-2 (SEPQ as Shunt APF)

In this mode of operation, SEPQ is used to compensate load harmonics. Shunt APF eliminates harmonics in the current and only fundamental

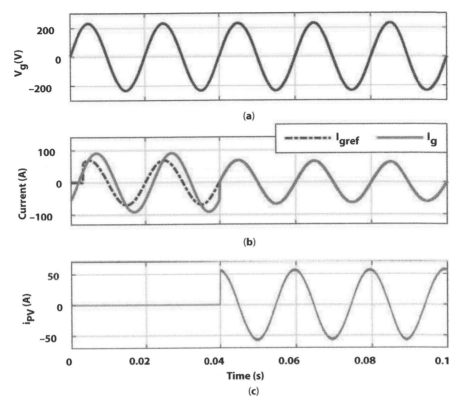

Figure 12.9 (a) V_g, (b) i_g with i_{ref}, and (c) SEPQ current for mode-1.

component is drained from the utility which reduces magnitude of current drawn from grid and reduces distortions at bus voltages. For the harmonic compensation, Figures 12.11(a), (b), and (c) illustrate V_g and I_g and i_{pv}, respectively. Figures 12.12(a) and (b) present the grid current spectrum without SEPQ and with SEPQ, respectively. Moreover, Figure 12.13(a) illustrates v_{dc}, Figure 12.13(b) illustrates P_{pv}, P_L and P_g, and Figure 12.13(c) depicts Q_{pv}, Q_L and Q_g for mode-2 i.e., harmonic compensation. It is noticed that the harmonics are eliminated from the grid current when SEPQ is connected at $t = 0.04$ s. The current total harmonic distortion (THD) reduces to 1.73 from 28.77% after the connection of SEPQ. Initially, at $t = 0.0$ s three-phase full wave uncontrolled rectifier is connected to the system and at $t = 0.6$ s another load of same type is connected to the system making a total load of 50 kW + j4 kVAR on the system. When the load is increased, the excess active power for load is supplied by the grid—refer Figure 12.13(b). The active power supplied by SEPQ is 36 kW and reactive power supplied by SEPQ is 4.2 kVAR.

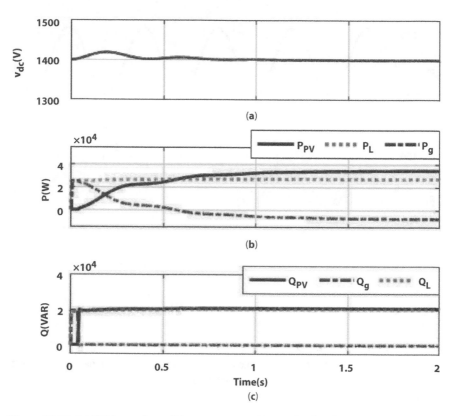

Figure 12.10 (a) DC bus voltage, (b) active power of SEPQ, load and grid, and (c) reactive power of SEPQ, load and grid.

12.6.3   Mode-3 (SEPQ as D-STATCOM)

Figures 12.14(a), (b), and (c) show V_g, i_g, and i_{pv}, respectively. From time 0 to 0.04 s (i.e. two power frequency cycles), SEPQ remains disconnected and at time 0.04 s, it was connected. It is clear that the grid current was distorted when the SEPQ was not connected. After the connection of SEPQ, the grid current distortions are eliminated. For better comparison, Figures 12.15(a) and (b) depict the current spectrums before and after the connection of SEPQ, respectively. The dominant harmonics are 5, 7, 11, 13 and 17 before connection of SEPQ and afterwards, these lower order harmonics are nearly eliminated. Overall, the current THD reduced from 13.83 to 1.89%.

Figure 12.16(a) illustrates v_{dc}, Figure 12.16(b) illustrates P_{pv}, P_L and P_g, and Figure 12.16(c) depicts Q_{pv}, Q_L and Q_g for mode-3. The load connected

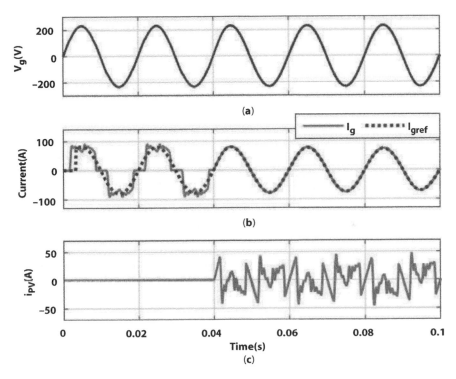

Figure 12.11 (a) V_g, (b) i_g with i_{ref}, and (c) SEPQ current for mode-2.

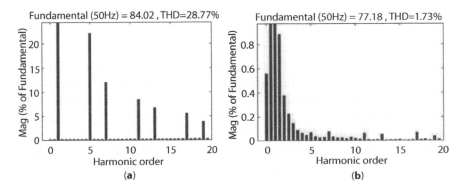

Figure 12.12 Grid current spectrum (a) without SEPQ and (b) with SEPQ.

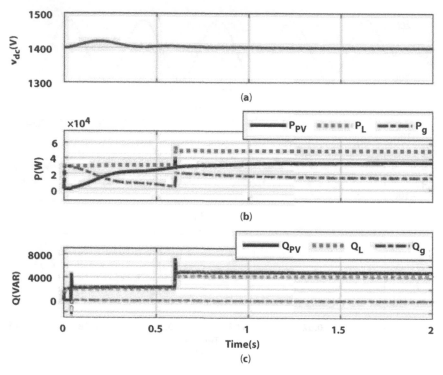

Figure 12.13 (a) DC bus voltage, (b) active power of SEPQ, load and grid, and (c) reactive power of SEPQ, load and grid.

to the system was three-phase full wave uncontrolled rectifier as a harmonic load of 12 kW and a linear load of 22 kW + j16 kVAR. Initially, up to 0.04s the SEPQ was not connected, so P_L and Q_L are supplied by the utility and can be noticed in Figure 12.16. At 0.04 s the SEPQ is connected, from thereon the load active power demand is nearly equal to that of generated using SEPQ, the grid active power becomes nearly zero—that can be witnessed from Figure 12.16(b). Further, since the SEPQ is being operated in D-STATCOM mode the load reactive power demand has been fully fulfilled by the SEPQ and therefore, the grid is not supplying any reactive power—refer Figure 12.16(c). It can also be realized in Figure 12.16(a) that v_{dc} deviates only during the transient conditions and once the transient period is over, it also becomes steady.

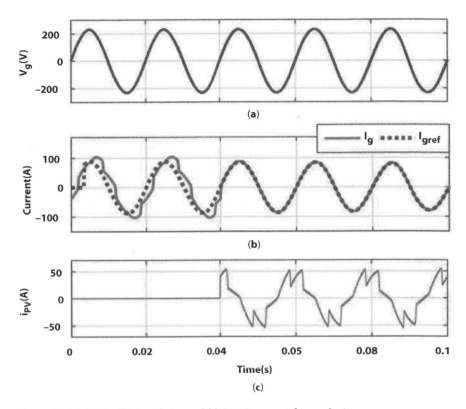

Figure 12.14 (a) V_g, (b) i_g with i_{ref}, and (c) SEPQ current for mode-3.

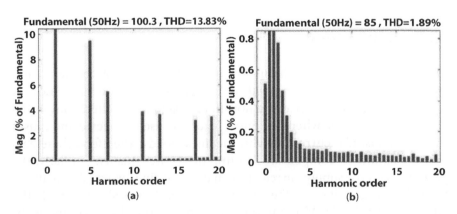

Figure 12.15 Grid current spectrum (a) without SEPQ and (b) with SEPQ.

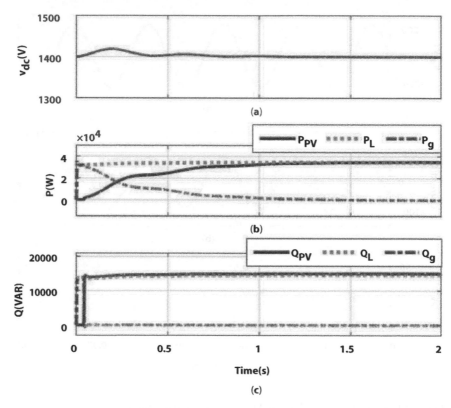

Figure 12.16 (a) DC bus voltage, (b) active power of SEPQ, load and grid, and (c) reactive power of SEPQ, load and grid.

12.7 Conclusion

This chapter presented a discussion on the possibility of harmonic and reactive compensation along with power generation by using a SECS. It is evident that the presence of a non-linear load creates alterations in the common bus voltage where the linear loads are also connected and causes the non-sinusoidal current flow in the linear loads. Therefore, these harmonics should be compensated to improve power quality. Similarly, the poor p.f. rises the supply current and, in turn, the line losses. Also, it affects the voltage regulation. So, the reactive compensation is also required. The APF in a D-STATCOM mode can take care of both these requirements. This was powered by a solar energy conversion system. The simulation results proved the feasibility of the same. Not only reactive power but harmonics were also compensated apart from power generation by the solar energy conversion system.

References

1. Chiradeja, P. and Ramakumar, R., An approach to quantify the technical benefits of distributed generation, *IEEE Trans. Energy Convers.*, vol. 19, no. 4, pp. 764–773, Dec. 2004.
2. Singh, M., Khadkikar, V., Chandra, A. and Varma, R.K., Grid interconnection of renewable energy sources at the distribution level with power-quality improvement features, *IEEE Trans. Power Deliv.*, vol. 26, no. 1, pp. 307–315, Jan. 2011.
3. Dugan, R.C. and McDermott, T.E., Operating conflicts for distributed generation on distribution systems," in *2001 Rural Electric Power Conference. Papers Presented at the 45th Annual Conference (Cat. No.01CH37214)*, p. A3/1–A3/6, 2001.
4. Dinesh, L., Sesham, H. and Manoj, V., Simulation of D-Statcom with hysteresis current controller for harmonic reduction, in *Proceedings—ICETEEEM 2012, International Conference on Emerging Trends in Electrical Engineering and Energy Management*, pp. 104–108, 2012.
5. Shakir and Sharma, M., IRPT Based DVR Application for Voltage Enhancement, in *2019 6th International Conference on Signal Processing and Integrated Networks, SPIN 2019*, pp. 34–38, 2019.
6. Agarwal, R.K., Hussain, I. and Singh, B., Dual-function PV-ECS integrated to 3P4W distribution grid using 3M-PLL control for active power transfer and power quality improvement, *IET Renew. Power Gener.*, vol. 12, no. 8, pp. 920–927, Jun. 2018.
7. Singh, B. and Solanki, J., A comparison of control algorithms for DSTATCOM, *IEEE Trans. Ind. Electron.*, vol. 56, no. 7, pp. 2738–2745, 2009.
8. Herrera, R.S., Salmerón, P. and Kim, H., Instantaneous reactive power theory applied to active power filter compensation: Different approaches, assessment, and experimental results, *IEEE Trans. Ind. Electron.*, vol. 55, no. 1, pp. 184–196, Jan. 2008.
9. Naidu, T.A., Arya, S.R. and Maurya, R., Multiobjective Dynamic Voltage Restorer with Modified EPLL Control and Optimized PI-Controller Gains, *IEEE Trans. Power Electron.*, vol. 34, no. 3, pp. 2181–2192, Mar. 2019.
10. Labeeb, M. and Lathika, B.S., Design and analysis of DSTATCOM using SRFT and ANN-fuzzy based control for power quality improvement, in *2011 IEEE Recent Advances in Intelligent Computational Systems, RAICS 2011*, pp. 274–279, 2011.
11. Watanabe, E.H., Aredes, M., Afonso, J.L., Pinto, J.G., Monteiro, L.F.C. and Akagi, H., Instantaneous p-q power theory for control of compensators in micro-grids, in *Proceedings of the 2010 10th Conference-Seminar International School on Nonsinusoidal Currents and Compensation, ISNCC 2010*, pp. 17–26, 2010.
12. Widrow, B., McCool, J. and Ball, M., The Complex LMS Algorithm, *Proc. IEEE*, vol. 63, no. 4, pp. 719–720, 1975.

13. Walach, E. and Widrow, B., The Least Mean Fourth (LMF) Adaptive Algorithm and Its Family, *IEEE Trans. Inf. Theory*, vol. 30, no. 2, pp. 275–283, 1984.

14. Chishti, F., Murshid, S. and Singh, B., Robust Normalized Mixed-Norm Adaptive Control Scheme for PQ Improvement at PCC of a Remotely Located Wind-Solar PV-BES Microgrid, *IEEE Trans. Ind. Informatics*, vol. 16, no. 3, pp. 1708–1721, Mar. 2020.

15. Devassy, S. and Singh, B., Modified p-q theory based control of solar PV integrated UPQC-S, in *IEEE Industry Application Society, 52nd Annual Meeting: IAS 2016*, 2016.

16. Dash, R. and Swain, S.C., Effective Power quality improvement using Dynamic Activate compensation system with Renewable grid interfaced sources, *Ain Shams Eng. J.*, vol. 9, no. 4, pp. 2897–2905, Dec. 2018.

17. Thangaraj, K. and Gopalasamy, S., Power Quality Analysis and Enhancement of Grid Connected Solar Energy System, *Circuits Syst.*, vol. 07, no. 08, pp. 1954–1961, Jun. 2016.

18. Sahli, A., Krim, F., Laib, A. and Talbi, B., Energy management and power quality enhancement in grid-tied single-phase PV system using modified PUC converter, *IET Renew. Power Gener.*, vol. 13, no. 14, pp. 2512–2521, 2019.

19. Patel, A., Mathur, H.D. and Bhanot, S., Improving Performance of UPQC-DG for Compensation of Unbalanced Loads, in *India International Conference on Power Electronics, IICPE*, vol. 2018-December, 2018.

13

Power Quality Improvement of a 3-Phase-3-Wire Grid-Tied PV-Fuel Cell System by 3-Phase Active Filter Employing Sinusoidal Current Control Strategy

**Rudranarayan Senapati[1]*, Sthita Prajna Mishra[2],
Rajendra Narayan Senapati[3] and Priyansha Sharma[4]**

[1]*School of Electrical Engineering, KIIT University, Bhubaneswar, Odisha, India*
[2]*Department of Electrical and Electronics Engineering in GMRIT,
Andhra Pradesh, India*
[3]*Department of Finance, Government of Odisha, Bhubaneswar, India*
[4]*School of Electronics and Telecommunication Engineering, KIIT University,
Bhubaneswar, Odisha, India*

Abstract

The aim of the modern power sector is to produce power as when required at the suitable sites, then transmitting and distributing the same to various load centers, maintaining the quality (frequency and voltage at a specified value) and reliability at an economical price. The objective of this chapter is to resolve various power quality issues with a cost effective solution and harmonic mitigation by Active power filter (series and shunt active filters), in a Grid connected PV-Fuel Cell system with a focus on time domain control strategy (sinusoidal current control strategy) based on instantaneous *pq*-theory. Shunt power filter is to mitigate the harmonic current component and recompense the reactive power owing to their exact and reckless operation, whereas Series active filter takes care of voltage sags and swells due to source or load side disturbance. The strategy is implemented using MATLAB 2016A, to extricate sinusoidal current from the source.

Keywords: Power quality, Series Active Filter (SAF), Shunt Active Power Filter (ShPF), sinusoidal current control strategy, Solid Oxide Fuel Cell (SOFC)

*Corresponding author: rsenapatifel@kiit.ac.in

C. Sharmeela, P. Sivaraman, P. Sanjeevikumar, and Jens Bo Holm-Nielsen (eds.) Microgrid Technologies, (329–376) © 2021 Scrivener Publishing LLC

13.1   Introduction

As the world looks forward to sustainable development, there has been increasing demand for clean energy sources with greater quality. In the past few years, the growth of energy is tremendous due to rapid progress in technology and heavy competition to reach out the soaring demands and economic developments. Energy consumption determines the development of a region. From the statistics of the last 2–3 years, the world energy consumption has been increasing at 5.2% annually, particularly emphasizing India, the annual per capita consumption is at 5%. Moreover, the percentage contribution of energy from the Renewable Energy Sources (RESs like wind, solar, tidal, geothermal, biomass, etc.) out of the total has also been increasing. By 2014, it is expected that contribution from RESs may reach to 22.8% globally [1, 2]. Present study indicates consistent advancement in drawing energy from RESs rather depending mostly on unreliable widespread sources, exhaustible with inimical impression over the environment. Power generation through RESs is prospering to promote sustainable energy world. Although substantial quantity of energy is generated, it has become very difficult as well as challenging for power engineers to reconcile the rising expectations of getting high quality of power which is only possible by the mitigation of harmonics in power system specifically caused by nonlinear loads. A usual assumption for most utilities is that the central generation utility produces sinusoidal voltage. In the transmission system, voltage variation is less and may possibly be kept within the specified limit. But in distribution systems due to unbalanced loading, at a large number of locations, the voltage distortions is significant. At several load points, the current waveform rarely seems to be a sine wave. This anomaly gives rise to the concept of *harmonics,* for the description of distortion in waveform leading to the deterioration of the quality of electrical power with a decrease in the efficiency of the system. In general good quality of power must have low interruption frequency, limited amplitude fluctuation along with less harmonic distortion, low flicker in the voltage at supply end, as well as less percentage of phase unbalancing and supply frequency fluctuation, etc. The lack of quality power result in loss of production, damage to appliances, increase in power losses, interference with communication lines and many more.

The primary causes of voltage or current related issues are as follows.

1. Microprocessor and Microcontroller-based faster islanding and isolation.
2. High efficiency, adjustable-speed motor drives raising the level of harmonic over power systems.

3. Deregulation of utilities with reduced awareness of harmonic control and lower reliability.
4. Highly interconnected network, where the failure of any component jeopardize the system stability.
5. Introduction of Distributed Generation (DGs) into the power with enhanced harmonic levels.

The menace that runs through all the above reasons for rising stress over the power quality (PQ) is due to the continuous drive from the manufacturer side for the increase in productivity through faster, more productive and efficient machinery for all utility customers who encourage the effort to make their customers more profitable. The installed machineries and equipment suffer the most from common power disruptions as well as they are the source of additional PQ issues. During the entire processes of automation, the competent operation of machineries and their control moreover depends on the quality of power. With the advent of renewable, the modern grid is integrated with numbers of DG sources and various power electronic controllers to control the power flow changing the power market scenario beneath the horde of custom power.

Power quality puts the boundaries in the deviation levels of voltage, frequency and waveform shape of power supply for proper functioning of the equipment. Without these limitations according to the IEEE standard, equipment may mal-operate and may not produce desired output. Various causes and terms related to power quality issues are addressed by power engineers day by day. Few important terms related to PQ have been described in Ref. [3] such as reactive power compensation, harmonic compensation, voltage regulation, harmonic pollution, etc.

Power quality issues are inevitable when numbers of DGs are connected. There is a close relation between DG and power quality. Considering both supply side and load side, there are several DGs involved so as several loads and the power has to be transferred through a common distribution line. Therefore, proper coordination is required to be maintained from each source to satisfy the load pattern. Implementation of DGs will either enhance the PQ or deteriorate the service for end users which is a major concern now-a-days. As PQ is the combination of voltage and current, the quality of voltage can be considerably improved even with a slightest level of backup storage capacity implemented in the Series Connected Photo-Voltaic Distributed Generator (SPVG) [3, 4]. Nonetheless, in a productive and reliable way their mix with the utility grid still remains as a challenge.

Nowadays irrespective of the supply voltage, vast application of nonlinear power electronic loads results into serious PQ issues, like poor power factor, voltage sags/swells and harmonics. Meanwhile, advancements in the digital electronics, communication and process control have raised numerous sensitive loads for requirement of ideal power supply. Thus, PQ enhancement devices in the purpose of performance improvement at the distribution end, results in the introduction of Custom Power Device (CPD) like APFs, as installed for ensuring the high-quality power supply. In case of stiff sources, PQ problems are observed as less severe whereas non-stiff sources, i.e., high input impedance sources introduce harmonic voltage into the system resulting severe PQ issues. Beside use of power electronics converters at large scales is also viable for the introduction of harmonics into the system which is the major reason for poor PQ. Therefore, now it is very much essential for taking rectification of the PQ problems into consideration to maintain the Total Harmonic Distortion (THD) within prescribed limits as per the IEEE standards. Hence for elimination of harmonics, filters are an essential requirement.

On the basis of switching operation of filter elements, filters are classified as passive filters, which include manual switching of passive elements such as capacitor and inductors and active filters that include power electronic switching.

As the filtering characteristics of the shunt passive filter are determined by the impedance ratio of the source and the shunt passive filter, therefore shunt passive filter has the following issues:

- As passive filters are installed rigidly in place and the passive elements in the filters have very less therefore neither the tuned frequency not the size of the filter can be easily changed which makes the filter unsuitable for changing system conditions, i.e., not dynamic in nature (operation is independent of varying load and utility source impedance).
- The parallel resonance between the system and filter results in amplification of current at harmonics restricting a designer to select tuned frequencies to ensure adequate bandwidth between shifted frequencies and harmonics (even and odd).
- The grounded neutrals of star connected banks provide a low impedance path for 3rd harmonics resulting amplification in few cases.
- Special protective and monitoring devices are required.
- Passive filters are unsuitable for loads like cycloconverters or power system with inter harmonics.
- Passive filters having negligible control on reactive power limits the increase of load demand.

- Size of the filter becomes bulky for THD control resulting over voltage with the banks are switched in and under voltage with switched out.
- It posses resonance problems, system impedance dependency performance, harmonic current absorption of nonlinear load, etc., further leading to harmonic propagation through the power system.

Apart from that it is only helpful for the part of electrical system upstream of the filter connection point, i.e., harmonics continues to flow between the downstream loads and the filter's point of connection limits its use to a few harmonics with a huge chance of introducing resonance further into the power system.

Focusing on the various active power filters (APFs) are conceivable substitute for minimizing effects arising due to non-linear loads on the power network which passages to recompense harmonics produced by nonlinear loads. To attain compensation aims, generation of reference signal is significant meant for the design purpose as well as in control purpose of active filters. Many control strategies has been realized, out of which the most effective is sinusoidal current control strategy for mitigation of the harmonics and also others PQ issues as generated due to unbalanced or unstable system owed to the non-linear loading condition [5].

13.2   Active Power Filter (APF)

The control aspect of APFs has drawn lots of attention. Based on both simulations and experiments have also been carried to prove the effectiveness of APFs to be able to produce required amount of lead or lag in phase around the resonant frequency for the stability of the system. In Refs. [4, 5] selective filters such as harmonic selective filters have been used to separate low frequency harmonic component from fundamental component. A comparison between another set of filters has been done in Ref. [6] i.e. Adaptive, Weiner and Kalman filters in which Kalman Filter is best among all to reduce THD by more than 50% and an extended Kalman filtering approach has been used in Ref. [7] for the frequency estimation due to the presence of noise, notch and harmonics in the system [8–10].

APFs are advantageous in removing all types of harmonic currents from the sensitized non-linear loads, e.g., with lagging loads, it can compensate reactive power factor and behaves as a damping resistor to be protected from harmonic resonance along with low capital cost as required for reduced ampere rating.

13.2.1 Shunt Active Power Filter (ShPF)

Shunt active filter (ShPF) is connected in parallel comprising of non-linear load whose harmonic currents are required to be compensated. The principle of operation of ShPF is based on production of current harmonics equal in magnitude but in phase opposition i.e. 180° to the harmonics present in the grid. ShPF along with compensating reactive power also mitigates harmonics and distortion [11, 12].

Coming over the applied control techniques, in Ref. [13] the control technique of the ShPF has been developed consisting of two current inside loops and a DC-bus voltage outside loop. Since, Lyapunov function is used to solve any problem due non-linearity so, in Ref. [14], the control strategy based on Lyapunov function has been used along with the ShPF. The experimental validation of the ShPF system has been done using a DS1104 DSP of d-SPACE and tested for different condition of operation. Again in Refs. [15, 16] another experimental verification has been done for ShPF consisting of dual parallel topology based APF where 110-V, 50-Hz mains providing power to a 3 kW load has been considered.

The ShPF is connected across comprising of non-linear load whose harmonic currents are required to be compensated. The principle of operation of ShPF is based on production of current harmonics equal in magnitude but in phase opposition i.e. 180° to the harmonics present in the grid. ShPF along with compensating reactive power also mitigates harmonics and distortion [17, 18].

13.2.1.1 Configuration of ShPF

The schematic diagram of ShPF has shown in Figure 13.1.

Figure 13.1 consists of two components, i.e., PWM converter and active filter controller (AFC). A PWM converter, mainly accountable to process power and synthesize the compensating values of current which has to be drained from the network. AFC is accountable for processing signal and to define the real time instantaneous compensating current values, which is passed continuously to PWM converter section. In general ShPF works in a closed loop method. It sense current that flows through load, and computes the instant values of the compensating/

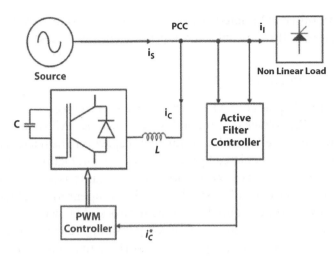

Figure 13.1 Schematic diagram of ShPF.

shunt current reference value i_c^* for the PWM converter section. Either voltage source converter (VSC) or current source converter (CSC) can be used in ShPF. CSC can be used for its robustness but in today's scenario ShPF is used in commercial purpose almost uses VSC owing to its higher efficiency with low initial cost as compared to CSC and reduced physical dimensions [37].

13.2.2   Series Active Power Filter (SAF)

The filtering characteristics of ShPF depend on the source impedance (inductive in nature). However, the source impedance should be insignificant at the fundamental frequency to reduce the fundamental voltage drop appreciably which can be fascinated by the insertion of active impedance in series with the ac source which can be realized by the series active filter (SAF) through the voltage source PWM inverter. The SAF acts as controllable voltage source whereas ShPF acts as a controllable current source. Both of these designs are executed desirable with VSI, with a capacitor acting as a dc bus.

The SAF is connected in series with the power supply and is used as a voltage booster. It compensates for voltage as a constant voltage source (CVS) [19]. A single-phase SAF has been has been designed in such a manner that it can operate bidirectional without any use of dc capacitor with a simpler hardware implementation [20] used to solve any deviation in voltage and other PQ related issues. They are more competent than shunt compensators as they are able to compensate current issues.

13.2.2.1 Configuration of SAF

The schematic diagram of SAF shown in Figure 13.2 consists of two components, i.e., PWM voltage control and AFC. The basic SAF voltages are synthesized by the converter with a common dc capacitor. The reference voltage for this converter is calculated by the AFC as shown in Figure 13.2 which has the input signal as load voltage and load current (same as source current).

A PWM voltage controller synthesizes the compensating values of voltage from power to be drained from the network. AFC will be processing signal to define the real time instant compensating voltage values continuously to PWM converter [38]. The SAF working in a closed loop method senses the voltage and computes the instant values of the compensating/series voltage reference value v_c^* for the PWM controller.

SAF uses voltage source inverter (VSI) due to its higher efficiency, low initial cost and compact size. It is acclaimed without any supply rather associated with a capacitor as an energy storing component linked at dc end of the converters for SAF to perform like a compensator. In supplement, the exchange of average energy should remain zero among the power filter and the power system.

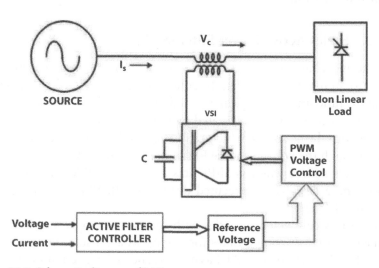

Figure 13.2 Schematic diagram of SAF.

13.3   Sinusoidal Current Control Strategy (SCCS) for APFs

The aspects of compensation for the APFs are determined by the control algorithm as enforced in the AFC. There are several reasons for considering 3-φ 3-wire system. One of the major advantages is the easiness of controlling the line current harmonic values in pq– reference frame. Sinusoidal current control strategy (SCCS) is based on Instantaneous power theory, which is based upon the transformation from abc– frame to $\alpha\beta0$– frame. But the reason for not adopting control in abc– reference frame is that in 3-φ system the 3-phases are mutually dependent on each other, so independent control of the quantities is difficult. To make the control simple, 3-φ quantities are converted into 2-φ mutually independent quantities, so that easier control is possible in pq– domain [38], which is a stationery reference frame as proposed by H. Akagi. The purpose for choosing this control strategy is its simplicity in implementation. So far several applications on this strategy have been seen in different literatures. For a system with multiple renewable energy systems integrated, implementing a robust control becomes cumbersome, as the control of renewable itself requires a lot of complexities.

The control involves 3-φ quantities first converted into 2-φ quantities. Then these 3-phase quantities are used to evaluate the instantaneous powers in time domain, both instantaneous active as well as reactive power can be estimated. By using low pass filter, the harmonic power can be extracted, used to generate the compensating current with the zero sequence power is known. The neutral point clamped capacitor voltage can be used to evaluate the zero sequence power. Hence the above mentioned method is termed as sinusoidal current control (SCC) strategy as the compensating current is sinusoidal in nature [39].

Advantages of pq– Theory over all other compensating theory are it can be valid for both steady state as well as transient state. Instantaneous power can be defined on $\alpha\beta0$– frame i.e. in three phase form. So, three phase system can be considered as a single unit but not the addition of three individual 1-φ circuits. abc– frame to $\alpha\beta0$– frame transformation is also known as Clarke transformation.

The zero sequence power, p_0 is expressed in terms of $\alpha\beta0$– frame of reference, as the instantaneous Watt power, p and instantaneous VAR power, q are calculated from the instantaneous power theory.

Mathematically:

$$
\begin{bmatrix} p_0 \\ p \\ q \end{bmatrix} = \begin{bmatrix} v_0 & 0 & 0 \\ 0 & v_\alpha & v_\beta \\ 0 & v_\beta & -v_\alpha \end{bmatrix} \begin{bmatrix} i_0 \\ i_\alpha \\ i_\beta \end{bmatrix}
\tag{13.1}
$$

The 3-φ instantaneous active power is defined by both instantaneous active power with the instantaneous zero sequence power. In case of 3-φ 3-wire (3P3W) system, instantaneous zero sequence power does not exist so for this type of system, $P_{3-\phi}$ can be treated as p only. Hence,

$$
P_{3-\phi} = v_\alpha i_\alpha + v_\beta i_\beta
\tag{13.2}
$$

Whereas,

$$
p = \underbrace{\bar{p}}_{\substack{\text{Average Value} \\ \text{of the Active Power}}} + \underbrace{\tilde{p}}_{\substack{\text{Oscillating Component} \\ \text{of the Active Power}}}
\tag{13.3}
$$

From Equation (13.3), it can be observed that instantaneous active power can be divided into two parts i.e., $\bar{p}$ and $\tilde{p}$, where $\bar{p}$ is referred to the average value or dc value of active power which implies total energy transfer in the system and $\tilde{p}$ defines the oscillating component of active sequence power and the instantaneous imaginary power can be defined as:

$$
q = v_\beta i_\alpha - v_\alpha i_\beta = \frac{1}{\sqrt{3}} (v_{ab}i_c + v_{bc}i_a + v_{ca}i_b)
\tag{13.4}
$$

Where, i_a, i_b, i_a and v_a, v_b, v_c are the instantaneous current and voltage in abc – frame, whereas i_α, i_β, i_0 and v_α, v_β, v_0 are the instantaneous current and voltage in $\alpha\beta 0$– frame.

As the converters used now a days are basically acts a non-linear load, the energy flow between the systems has a boundary condition. Comparing to the response of the converter and the generation of harmonic components and reactive power with the conventional approaches the analysis of different type of power is not sufficient using average or rms value as variables. So in a nonlinear circuit, time domain analysis has to be carried out for analysis of energy flow [21].

A 3-φ sinusoidal voltage which consists of only positive and zero sequence voltages are considered for the realization of zero sequence power. Symmetrical component in frequency domain only is applicable for steady state operation. Hence it can be converted into time domain for analysis of both steady state and transient state. For voltage, Equation (13.5) is used as follows:

$$
\left.\begin{aligned}
v_a &= \sqrt{2}V_+ \sin(\omega t + \theta_{v_+}) + \sqrt{2}V_0 \sin(\omega t + \theta_{v_0}) \\
v_b &= \sqrt{2}V_+ \sin\left(\omega t - \frac{2\pi}{3} + \theta_{v_+}\right) + \sqrt{2}V_0 \sin(\omega t + \theta_{v_0}) \\
v_c &= \sqrt{2}V_+ \sin\left(\omega t + \frac{2\pi}{3} + \theta_{v_+}\right) + \sqrt{2}V_0 \sin(\omega t + \theta_{v_0})
\end{aligned}\right\} \quad (13.5)
$$

Whereas Equation (13.6) used for current is as follows:

$$
\left.\begin{aligned}
i_a &= \sqrt{2}I_+ \sin(\omega t + \theta_{i_+}) + \sqrt{2}I_0 \sin(\omega t + \theta_{i_0}) \\
i_b &= \sqrt{2}I_+ \sin\left(\omega t - \frac{2\pi}{3} + \theta_{i_+}\right) + \sqrt{2}I_0 \sin(\omega t + \theta_{i_0}) \\
i_c &= \sqrt{2}I_+ \sin\left(\omega t + \frac{2\pi}{3} + \theta_{i_+}\right) + \sqrt{2}I_0 \sin(\omega t + \theta_{i_0})
\end{aligned}\right\} \quad (13.6)
$$

In order to obtain zero sequence components, the above equation is required to be converted into αβ0-frame by using Clarke transformation. For voltage, Equation (13.7) is used as follows:

$$
\left.\begin{aligned}
v_\alpha &= +\sqrt{3}V_+ \sin(\omega t + \theta_{v_+}) \\
v_\beta &= -\sqrt{3}V_+ \sin(\omega t + \theta_{v_-}) \\
v_0 &= +\sqrt{6}V_0 \sin(\omega t + \theta_{v_0})
\end{aligned}\right\} \quad (13.7)
$$

Whereas Equation (13.8) used for current is as follows:

$$\left. \begin{array}{l} i_\alpha = +\sqrt{3}I_+ \sin(\omega t + \theta_{i_+}) \\ i_\beta = -\sqrt{3}I_+ \sin(\omega t + \theta_{i_-}) \\ i_0 = +\sqrt{6}I_0 \sin(\omega t + \theta_{i_0}) \end{array} \right\} \tag{13.8}$$

From Equations (13.7) and (13.8), the instantaneous zero sequence power can be obtained as:

$$p_0 = 3V_0I_0 \cos(\theta_{v_0} - \theta_{i_0}) - 3V_0I_0 \cos(2\omega t + \theta_{v_0} + \theta_{i_0}) = \bar{p}_0 + \tilde{p}_0 \quad (13.9)$$

So the instantaneous zero sequence power can be divided into two parts which consists of average power and oscillating component of power which is at double the line frequency. Here $\bar{p}_0$ is unidirectional energy flow as conventional active power and $\tilde{p}_0$ represents the oscillating component whose average value is zero. Interesting fact about zero sequence power is $\bar{p}_0$ cannot be obtained alone without the oscillating component $\tilde{p}_0$. Hence the total zero sequence components always associated with both average as well as oscillating component [40].

The physical significance of instantaneous power in $\alpha\beta0$-frame has been illustrated in Figure 13.3 which reveals that the total instantaneous active power flow and instantaneous reactive power flow in between the two systems, i.e., source and load for a power distribution system.

$p + p_0 \rightarrow$ Total Instantaneous power flow in unit-time.
$q \rightarrow$ Power exchange between three phases without any transfer of energy

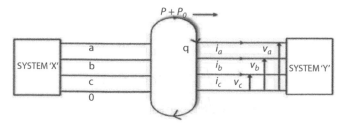

Figure 13.3 Physical significance of instantaneous power in $\alpha\beta0-$ frame.

The active and reactive current components are derived from the instantaneous *abc* voltages and currents are represented as:

$$
\begin{bmatrix} i_\alpha \\ i_\beta \end{bmatrix} = \underbrace{\frac{1}{v_\alpha^2 + v_\beta^2} \begin{bmatrix} v_\alpha & v_\beta \\ v_\beta & -v_\alpha \end{bmatrix} \begin{bmatrix} p \\ 0 \end{bmatrix}}_{Active\,Part} + \underbrace{\frac{1}{v_\alpha^2 + v_\beta^2} \begin{bmatrix} v_\alpha & v_\beta \\ v_\beta & -v_\alpha \end{bmatrix} \begin{bmatrix} 0 \\ q \end{bmatrix}}_{Reactive\,Part}
$$

$$(13.10)$$

With the use of Inverse Clarke Transformation *abc* real and imaginary current can be obtained as:

$$
\begin{bmatrix} i_{a(p)} \\ i_{b(p)} \\ i_{c(p)} \end{bmatrix} = \sqrt{\frac{2}{3}} \begin{bmatrix} 1 & 0 \\ -\dfrac{1}{2} & \dfrac{\sqrt{3}}{2} \\ -\dfrac{1}{2} & -\dfrac{\sqrt{3}}{2} \end{bmatrix} \frac{\left(v_\alpha i_\alpha + v_\beta i_\beta \right)}{v_\alpha^2 + v_\beta^2} \begin{bmatrix} v_\alpha \\ v_\beta \end{bmatrix} \tag{13.11}
$$

And

$$
\begin{bmatrix} i_{a(q)} \\ i_{b(q)} \\ i_{c(q)} \end{bmatrix} = \left(\frac{v_{ab} i_c + v_{bc} i_a + v_{ca} i_b}{v_{ab}^2 + v_{bc}^2 + v_{ca}^2} \right) \begin{bmatrix} v_{bc} \\ v_{ca} \\ v_{ab} \end{bmatrix} \tag{13.12}
$$

Whereas v_{ab}, v_{bc}, v_{ca} are the line voltages. Also $i_{a(p)}, i_{b(p)}, i_{c(p)}$ and $i_{a(q)}, i_{b(q)}, i_{c(q)}$ are the real and imaginary current components which generate real and imaginary power respectively. The line voltage does not contain any zero sequence component: $v_{ab} + v_{bc} + v_{ca} = 0$.

As the line voltage is free from zero sequence components, hence Equations (13.11) and (13.12) can be re-written as:

$$
\begin{bmatrix} i_a \\ i_b \\ i_c \end{bmatrix} = \begin{bmatrix} i_0 \\ i_0 \\ i_0 \end{bmatrix} + \begin{bmatrix} i_{a(p)} \\ i_{b(p)} \\ i_{c(p)} \end{bmatrix} + \begin{bmatrix} i_{a(q)} \\ i_{b(q)} \\ i_{c(q)} \end{bmatrix} \tag{13.13}
$$

Among the two classifications of instantaneous power theory, one of them has already been described, i.e., instantaneous pq–theory. The other one is instantaneous abc–theory where use of Clarke transformation (abc–to $\alpha\beta0$–transformation) is avoided. In this process instead of calculating real and imaginary power, active and non-active current may be calculated from abc phase voltage and currents.

13.4   Sinusoidal Current Control Strategy for ShPF

There is an obvious question raised for selection of the ShPF. The reasons cited are:

- Complexity of control in case of other compensators which require additional components.
- Cost effective control for low and lab-scale applications.

Again the complexity in tuning of filter components is reduced by ShPF as applied to 3-φ 3-Wire system performing harmonic current suppression, reactive power compensation and power factor improvement.

"Based on various studies on different control approach for ShPF and after observing their drawbacks, the proposed work has been carried out with a simple and old control strategy based on Instantaneous pq-theory on ShPF as shown in Figure 13.4 representing the basic control strategy for a 3P3W system towards current compensation.

The instantaneous power calculation block calculates the instantaneous power and the instantaneous active power are passed through high-pass filter to get the harmonic power. The compensating power selection block adds the line losses to the harmonic active power to obtain the active power to be compensated. The reactive power is obtained from the instantaneous power calculation block. These two are used for current reference calculation, which in turn is fed to PWM generator to generate firing pulses for shunt inverter. Input for the control block meant for calculation of the instantaneous power is the phase voltages at the PCC and the line currents of the nonlinear load to be compensated, i.e., a discriminated compensation characteristic for ShPF, that performs as an open circuit for harmonic currents produced by the other nearby non linear loads. The current references are calculated using Equations (13.10)–(13.13).

As quoted earlier, the ShPF may support harmonic damping along the power line to evade the *harmonic propagation* as ensued due to harmonic

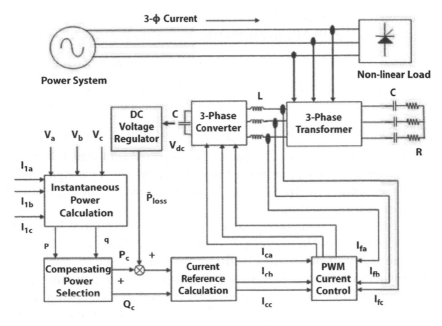

Figure 13.4 Basic control strategy of 3-Phase 3-Wire ShPF.

resonance of the series inductors and shunt capacitors in power factor correction.

There four functional control blocks in the AFC are: Calculation of instantaneous power, Selection of power compensation, DC Voltage regulator, Calculation of current reference.

The instantaneous power of the non-linear load is measured by the instantaneous power calculation block. As per the pq–Theory, the real and imaginary powers exist, due to non existence of the zero-sequence power. The performance of the ShPF is evaluated by the compensating power selection block, i.e., part of the real and imaginary power of the nonlinear load is selected which to be compensated by the ShPF.

Furthermore, an extra amount of *real power* (p) is measured by the DC voltage regulator ensuing additional energy flow to or from the DC capacitor for maintenance of voltage about a constant reference. This real power ($\bar{p}_{loss}$) is supplemented with the compensating real power (p_c), all together along with the compensating imaginary power (q_c) make its way to the block for the calculation of the reference current for evaluation of the instantaneous compensating reference current from the compensating powers and voltages.

The power circuit of ShPF is a 3-φ VSC constructed with IGBTs and series diodes. The PWM current control pressurizes the VSC to operate as a controlled *current* source. To prevent high $\dfrac{di}{dt}$, interconnection of VSC with the power system is fashioned with an inductor (*commutation inductor* or *coupling inductor*) in series. The leakage inductance of a usual power transformer is sufficient to afford $\dfrac{di}{dt}$ limitation which removes the series inductor. In that case, a small passive filter, depicted with R and C, for filtration of the current ripples about the switching frequency is equipped at the primary end of the transformer. A 3P3W control has been explained for system without neutral.

The constant instantaneous power control strategy assures the supply delivers one part of the power ($\tilde{p}$). As per the *pq*–Theory, the constant instantaneous watt power may be drawn from the supply so as the ShPF will compensate the oscillating volt-amp power ($\tilde{p}$). Furthermore, the compensated RMS current is diminished through the compensation of the total reactive power, $q = \bar{q} + \tilde{q}$ of the load. There is no zero-sequence power for the concerned 3-φ 3-Wire system. Due to harmonics as well as irregularity in supply, the compensated current is non-sinusoidal assuring constant real power (p) to be drawn from the source which will be more interesting with no real-power swinging among the source and the desired load.

The SCCS for ShPF, was the first ever strategy established with the *pq*–Theory introduced by Akagi *et al.* in 1983. It is set up with much near to the nonlinear load to draw a fixed instantaneous power from the supply and compensate the oscillating real power ($\tilde{p}$). It is supplied with a part of oscillating instantaneous active load current in a 3-φ system without neutral results a zero powered zero-sequence component. The optimal power flow provided by shunt current compensation has been illustrated in Figure 13.5.

The illustration of the control block of AFC for SCCS can be seen in Figure 13.6.

- *Positive sequence voltage detector:*

At load terminal the value of three phase voltage mainly consists of Positive Sequence Component. If there will be either negative sequence or Zero Sequence component then three phase voltage can be unbalanced and may also comprise harmonics from other components. Thus it is necessary to determine fundamental positives sequence voltage for this SCCS and it is possible through positive voltage detector.

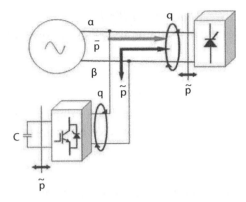

Figure 13.5 Optimal Power Flow Provided by Shunt Current Compensation.

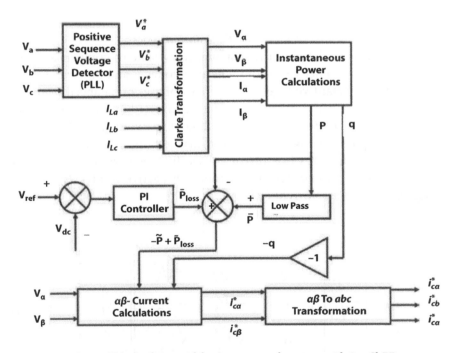

Figure 13.6 Control block of sinusoidal current control strategy with 3-φ ShPF.

- *Phase-Locked-loop (PLL) circuit:*

The power network deliberately records the elemental components of frequency of the system voltages under consideration. This synchronizing circuit automatically defines the system frequency with the phase angle of positive sequence component of input signal.

- *Instantaneous Power Calculation Block:*

This block computes the instantaneous values of power of the passive load/nonlinear load.

- *Compensating Power Selection Block:*

This block selects some portion of real and imaginary power of the given nonlinear load which is to be compensated by the power filter.

- *DC Voltage Regulator:*

DC Voltage Controller defines a supplementary quantity of active power for which an extra energy flows into the capacitor for keeping its value of voltage around a static reference value.

- *Compensating Current Reference Calculation Block:*

This block helps in defining the instantaneous value of compensating or shunts current reference from compensating voltages and powers.

Three phase instant voltages and currents phases of balanced or unbalanced source in the *abc*–reference frame is converted into instant voltages and currents on the *αβ*0–axis [28]. The three phase voltage can be converted into two phase voltage by means of Clarke transformation as shown in matrix form and this two phase voltage further participate in power ccalculation module in order to determine both active and reactive power along with two phase current i_α, i_β.

$$\begin{bmatrix} v_0 \\ v_\alpha \\ v_\beta \end{bmatrix} = \sqrt{\frac{2}{3}} \begin{bmatrix} \dfrac{1}{\sqrt{2}} & \dfrac{1}{\sqrt{2}} & \dfrac{1}{\sqrt{2}} \\ 1 & -\dfrac{1}{2} & -\dfrac{1}{2} \\ 0 & \dfrac{\sqrt{3}}{2} & \dfrac{\sqrt{3}}{2} \end{bmatrix} \begin{bmatrix} v_a' \\ v_b' \\ v_c' \end{bmatrix} \qquad (13.14)$$

Similarly, 3-φ line current scan be converted into two phase by using Clarke Tranformation it also help in determining real and imaginary power along with two phase voltage (v_α', v_β').

$$
\begin{bmatrix} i_0 \\ i_\alpha \\ i_\beta \end{bmatrix} = \sqrt{\frac{2}{3}} \begin{bmatrix} \frac{1}{\sqrt{2}} & \frac{1}{\sqrt{2}} & \frac{1}{\sqrt{2}} \\ 1 & -\frac{1}{2} & -\frac{1}{2} \\ 0 & \frac{\sqrt{3}}{2} & \frac{\sqrt{3}}{2} \end{bmatrix} \begin{bmatrix} i_a \\ i_b \\ i_c \end{bmatrix}
\tag{13.15}
$$

Three instant powers that is zero-sequence component, the active component p, reactive component q the instant phase voltages and line currents can be represented in matrix format as shown below:

$$
\begin{bmatrix} p_0 \\ p \\ q \end{bmatrix} = \begin{bmatrix} v_0 & 0 & 0 \\ 0 & v_\alpha' & v_\beta \\ 0 & v_\beta & -v_\alpha' \end{bmatrix} \begin{bmatrix} i_0 \\ i_\alpha \\ i_\beta \end{bmatrix}
\tag{13.16}
$$

From matrix active and reactive power is given as follow:

$$
p = v_\alpha'.i_\alpha + v_\beta'.i_\beta
\tag{13.17}
$$

$$
q = v_\beta'.i_\alpha + v_\alpha'.i_\beta
\tag{13.18}
$$

The block diagram of SCCS epitomizes the entire algorithm of the controller for 3P3W ShPF which compensates the oscillating real power and the imaginary power of the load (constant instantaneous power control strategy). Later the effect of the low-pass filter dynamic and the PI-Controller in the dc voltage regulator can be addressed transients. According to the shunt current compensation, the real power of the nonlinear load must constantly be measured and is separated into average ($\bar{p}$) and oscillating ($\tilde{p}$) parts instantaneously leads to Equation (13.19).

$$
p_c = \tilde{p} = p - \bar{p}
\tag{13.19}
$$

In a true exercise, the separation of $\tilde{p}$ from p can be realized through a block called *selection of the powers to be compensated* by a low pass filter with careful selection of cutoff frequency due to implicit dynamics lead to compensate errors during transients. The total imaginary power to be compensated is:

$$-q = -\bar{q} + \tilde{q} \qquad (13.20)$$

The cause of appending a minus sign is same as explained earlier for compensation of the real oscillating power. Contrarily to compensate $-\tilde{p}$, for the compensation in the above equation does not need any energy storage elements. For the load and the current for active filter, the usual load current convention is followed. To compensate the oscillating flow of energy $(-\tilde{p})$, the dc capacitor of the PWM converter must be sufficiently large to store energy, for less voltage variations, but the PWM converter (a boost type) may lose its controllability with the lower peak dc voltage than that of the ac voltage. A Part of oscillating instantaneous active current on α-axis and β-axis are:

$$i_{\alpha\tilde{p}} = \frac{v_\alpha}{v_\alpha^2 + v_\beta^2}(-\tilde{p}) \qquad (13.21)$$

$$\text{And } i_{\beta\tilde{p}} = \frac{v_\alpha}{v_\alpha^2 + v_\beta^2}(-\tilde{p}) \qquad (13.22)$$

Similarly, Part of instantaneous reactive current on α-axis and β-axis will be:

$$i_{\alpha q} = \frac{v_\beta}{v_\alpha^2 + v_\beta^2}(-q) \qquad (13.23)$$

$$i_{\beta q} = \frac{-v_\alpha}{v_\alpha^2 + v_\beta^2}(-q) \qquad (13.24)$$

The ShPF assures about the drawing of average real power, $\bar{p}$ of the load compensating the oscillating real and imaginary power from the power system. Hence, the *constant instantaneous power control strategy* contributes optimum compensation from power flow end, even under improper and irregular supply. The compensating currents of the ShPF and the supply current come as sinusoidal due to the compensation for $\tilde{p}$ and $\tilde{q}$

which will be in phase with the voltage due to the compensation for $\bar{q}$. For supply irregularities, the compensated current will be non-sinusoidal and constant real power is drawn.

In real time operation, the separation of active and reactive power is analysed by a low-pass filter. Reference currents $i_{ca}^*, i_{cb}^*, i_{cc}^*$ for switching of PWM inverter is set up from Inverse Clarke Transformation. The switching scheme of IGBT's is set up by relating the reference currents and continuously sensing the currents from lines. The $\alpha\beta$–current may be calculated as follow:

$$
\begin{bmatrix} i_{c\alpha}^* \\ i_{c\beta}^* \end{bmatrix} = \frac{1}{v_\alpha^{'2} + v_\beta^{'2}} \begin{bmatrix} v_\alpha^{'} & v_\beta^{'} \\ v_\beta^{'} & -v_\alpha^{'} \end{bmatrix} \begin{bmatrix} -p + \bar{P}_{loss} \\ q \end{bmatrix}
\tag{13.25}
$$

These two phase compensating currents are two phase currents which are then converted into three phase currents by means of inverse Clarke transformation.

$$
\begin{bmatrix} i_{c_a}^* \\ i_{c_b}^* \\ i_{c_c}^* \end{bmatrix} = \sqrt{\frac{2}{3}} \begin{bmatrix} \frac{1}{\sqrt{2}} & 1 & 0 \\ \frac{1}{\sqrt{2}} & -\frac{1}{2} & \frac{\sqrt{3}}{2} \\ \frac{1}{\sqrt{2}} & -\frac{1}{2} & -\frac{\sqrt{3}}{2} \end{bmatrix} \begin{bmatrix} i_{c0}^* \\ i_{c\alpha}^* \\ i_{c\beta}^* \end{bmatrix}
\tag{13.26}
$$

The current references may be used to generate firing pulses for the PWM inverter [29].

13.5   Sinusoidal Current Control Strategy for SAF

The justification over the selection of SAF, can be broadly listed as:

- It is hard to comprehend a large-rating PWM converter with swift current respond and low loss in compensating the harmonic components with high efficiency as in the main circuit of ShPF.
- Injected currents by ShPF may flow into the capacitors connected on the power system.

Again SAF compensates the current distortions resulted due to non-linear loads with an appointment of high impedance path enforcing the high frequency current to pass through the passive filter in parallel. Hence the proposed work is once again carried out with instantaneous pq–theory on SAF, applied on a 3P3W system. The basic block diagram of a 3P3W SAF for compensation of voltage is illustrated in Figure 13.7. The input for the control block is for calculation of the instantaneous power (phase voltages at the PCC) and the line currents of the nonlinear load to be compensated, that performs as an open circuit for harmonic currents produced by the other nearby non linear loads. With no zero-sequence current, the relation among the source voltage, load voltage and active filter voltage is given by,

$$
\begin{bmatrix} v_{sa} \\ v_{sb} \\ v_{sc} \end{bmatrix} = \begin{bmatrix} v_a \\ v_b \\ v_c \end{bmatrix} - \begin{bmatrix} v_{Ca} \\ v_{Cb} \\ v_{Cc} \end{bmatrix} \tag{13.27}
$$

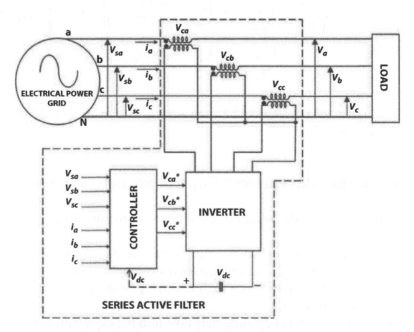

Figure 13.7 Basic block diagram of 3-P-3-W Series Active Filter.

Here the voltages are calculated by the dual pq–theory (assumed as the currents, and the real and imaginary powers are known and the voltage components should be calculated in case of presence of series voltage compensation which is the dual of shunt current compensation) as given in Equation (13.28):

$$
\begin{bmatrix} p_0 \\ p \\ q \end{bmatrix} = \begin{bmatrix} i_0 & 0 & 0 \\ 0 & i_\alpha & i_\beta \\ 0 & -i_\beta & i_\alpha \end{bmatrix} \begin{bmatrix} v_0 \\ v_\alpha \\ v_\beta \end{bmatrix}
\tag{13.28}
$$

Here the oscillating real power $\tilde{p}$ and the oscillating imaginary power $\tilde{q}$, where the zero sequence powers $\tilde{p}_0$ and $\tilde{p}_0$ are assumed to be zero due to zero-sequence current. With these oscillating powers, the instantaneous voltages to be injected by the SAF for load harmonic voltage compensation by using:

$$
\begin{bmatrix} v^*_{C\alpha} \\ v^*_{C\beta} \end{bmatrix} = \frac{1}{i_\alpha^2 + i_\beta^2} \begin{bmatrix} i_\alpha & -i_\beta \\ i_\beta & i_\alpha \end{bmatrix} \begin{bmatrix} \tilde{p} \\ \tilde{q} \end{bmatrix}
\tag{13.29}
$$

The basic SAF voltages are synthesized by three single-phase converters with a common dc capacitor. The reference voltage for these converters is calculated by the AFC (Figure 13.7) which has as input signals the load voltages and currents (equal to the source currents).

A certain amount of $\bar{p}$ should be added to $\tilde{p}$ with an objective to compensate the losses like ShPF. The reference voltages v^*_{Ca} and v^*_{Cb} can be converted to the abc– reference by:

$$
\begin{bmatrix} v^*_{Ca} \\ v^*_{Cb} \\ v^*_{Cc} \end{bmatrix} = \sqrt{\frac{2}{3}} \begin{bmatrix} 1 & 0 \\ -\dfrac{1}{2} & \dfrac{\sqrt{3}}{2} \\ -\dfrac{1}{2} & -\dfrac{\sqrt{3}}{2} \end{bmatrix} \begin{bmatrix} v^*_{C\alpha} \\ v^*_{C\beta} \end{bmatrix}
\tag{13.30}
$$

The SAF generates the voltage for the harmonic voltage compensation in the load producing oscillating active and reactive power at the load end confirming the voltage from the source side have purely sinusoidal waveforms.

The control block diagram of SAF has been illustrated in Figure 13.8. The voltage v^*_{Cabc} needs to be obtained for compensating the harmonic

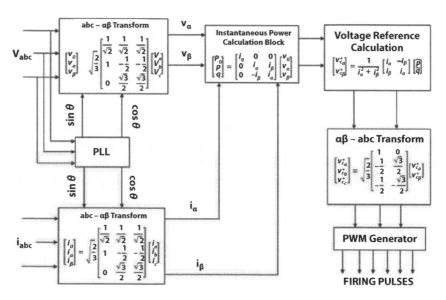

Figure 13.8 Control circuitry of series active filter.

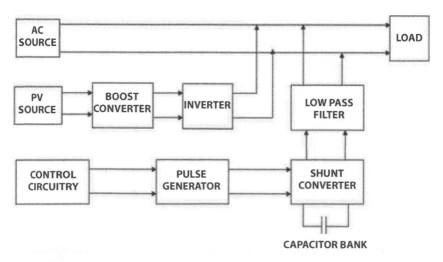

Figure 13.9 System block diagram for shunt active filter.

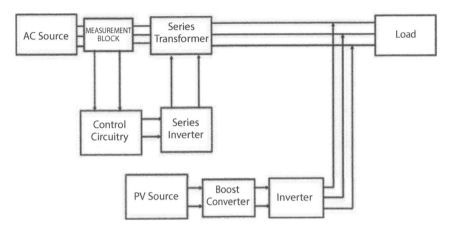

Figure 13.10 System block diagram for series active filter.

component of load, producing the oscillating real and reactive power. Thus the source and load voltages so obtained are purely sinusoidal.

The detailed modelling of grid connected renewable system are discussed as follows.

In Figure 13.9, a ShPF is integrated with grid connected PV-system to inject desired power to grid and load. It consists of a PV system whose voltage is stepped up by a boost converter. This voltage is fed to the inverter then it feeds the load and the grid. Figure 13.10 illustrates the SAF based detailed modeling of grid connected renewable system.

The SAF is integrated to a PV connected system to inject desired power to grid and load. It consists of a PV system whose voltage is stepped up by a boost converter.

13.6   Solid Oxide Fuel Cell (SOFC)

The Solid Oxide Fuel Cell (SOFC) are advanced power production systems producing electricity from fuel oxidation without deviation and demonstrate the changeover of chemical energy to electrical energy and vice versa at high temperatures (>700 °C) with high performance, fuel mobility and massive greenhouse gas deterioration. The FCs are characterized basically by their electrolyte content; the SOFC has a ceramic electrolyte or solid oxide material. Acknowledging the feasibility of long-term stable activity of SOFCs on hydrocarbon fuels (natural gas, methanol, ethanol, and other renewable bio-fuels) provides valuable gains in

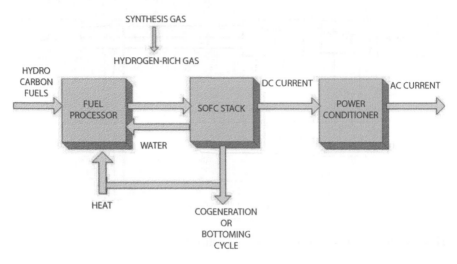

SYNTHESIS GAS

HYDROGEN-RICH GAS

HYDRO
CARBON
FUELS

FUEL
PROCESSOR

SOFC STACK

DC CURRENT

POWER
CONDITIONER

AC CURRENT

WATER

HEAT

COGENERATION
OR
BOTTOMING
CYCLE

Figure 13.11 Schematic diagram of a typical SOFC system.

terms of technological infrastructure, extending from distributed generation to combined power and heat to emergency power systems in automotive [34, 35].

SOFC system's high optimal temperature embraces the abrupt reaction kinetics and steam rebuilding. Utilizing the SOFC over other FC was the fundamental perks of its enormous combined heat and power efficiency, fuel versatility, long-durability, relatively affordable and minimal radiation. The standard SOFC block diagram is referenced in Figure 13.11.

13.6.1   Operation

The constitution of the four-layer stack of few millimeters thick together makes up SOFC under which three of them are made up of ceramic layers as the name suggested. The basic structure of SOFC has been presented in Figure 13.12. SOFC stack is created by aligning the number of cells in cascade. The attenuation of high temperature by stack allows the ceramic to shift ionically and electrically active [36]. Near the cathode, oxygen is reduced to oxygen ions. Electrochemical oxidization of fuel takes place through the diffusion of ions by solid oxide electrolyte to the anode giving water and two electrons as the by product. Now the by-product includes a pair of electrons moves through the outer circuit, providing DC to the connected load. With the entering back of pair of electrons to anti-anode material, the cycle keeps on repeating until the requirements meet.

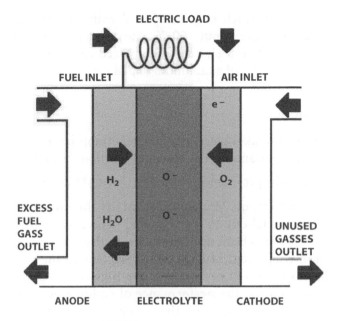

Figure 13.12 Basic structure of SOFC.

13.6.2 Anode

To achieve the smooth flow of fuel approaching the electrolyte the ceramic layer of anode must be fabricated with permeable and coarse-grained in nature. It is the strongest and thickest of all layers of FC due to its work to provide mechanical support and least polarization losses. A cermets consisting of nickel mixed with the ceramic material is used for electrolytes. Usually, the YSZ (Ytria-Stabilized Zirconia), a nano-material-based catalyst, helps in stopping the grains of nickel from increasing. The disadvantage towards the efficiency of FC can be majorly notice due to the large particles of nickel which may minimize the contact surface of ion conduction. The fundamental work of anode is to use the diffuse ions of oxygen for oxidization of hydrogen fuels. Chemical reaction related to this is: $H_2 + O_2 \rightarrow H_2O + 2e^-$.

13.6.3 Electrolyte

An impenetrable layer of ceramic is introduced, which conducts the oxygen, called the electrolyte. For the prevention of losses from the leakage current, the electronic conductivity of the electrolyte is kept at minimum. The high temperature of SOFC maintains the dynamics of oxygen ions to achieve a good performance which may be affected with an approaching lower limit of the temperature about 700 °C. Most recommended Electrolyte comprises of YSZ) (often 8%), scandia stabilized zirconia (ScSZ) (usually 9 mol% Sc2O3–9ScSZ) and gadolinium doped ceria (GDC).

13.6.4   Cathode

Reduction of oxygen takes place in a thin penetrable layer over electrolyte called cathode or anti-anode. The chemical reaction dealing with the process according to Kroger–Vink Notation is: $\frac{1}{2}O_2(g)+2e\ '+V_o^{\bullet\bullet}\rightarrow O_o^{\times}.$

Lanthanum Strontium Manganite (LSM) is the most commercially used cathode material due to its congenial nature with zirconia doped electrolytes. The stress built up is limited with the matching of the thermal expansion coefficient of LSM with YSZ. Due to the poor conduction of LSM, it works well as a cathode at a high temperature. With the fall in the temperature, the performance of cathode decreases. Due to its poor feature of conductivity, the active reaction is restricted to a boundary limit called triple-phase boundary (TPB). At TPB the conjunction of air, electrode and electrolyte is observed. To overcome this boundary limit, the cathode needs to conduct ions of oxygen and electrons. Structural development in the cathode with the mixture of LSM and YSZ is used.

13.6.5   Comparative Analysis of Various Fuel Cells

The maximum efficiency so obtained till date is 60% as achieved by PEM, AFC including SOFC. But a high stack range is shown by SOFC of 1 kW to 2 MW. The list of application and advantage by SOFC is also marked high with limited drawbacks, which includes high temperature operation as a major disadvantage.

13.7   Simulation Analysis

Effectiveness of the proposed SCCS through ShPF and SAF, the simulation was carried out on a 3P3W system for non-linear load. The proposed strategy was simulated using MATLAB/SIMULINK 2016a with a system having Intel Core i5 processor with clock frequency 2.4 GHz, 8 GB RAM. The analysis of both ShPF and SAF was carried in different environments.

Table 13.1 Brief analysis of various FCs.

Fuel cell	Operating temp.	Common electrolyte	Stack size	Efficiency	Applications	Advantages	Disadvantages
Polymer Electrolyte Membrane (PEM)	50–100 °C 122–212 °F	Perfluoro sulfonic acid	<1 kW–100 kW	60% transport 35% stationary	• Backup power • Portable power • Distributed generation • Transportation Specialty vehicles	• Solid electrolyte reduces corrosion & electrolyte management problems • Low temperature • Quick start-up	• Expensive catalysts • Sensitive to fuel impurities • Low temperature waste heat
Alkaline (AFC)	90–100 °C 194–212 °F	Aqueous solution of potassium hydroxide soaked in a matrix	10–100 kW	60%	• Military • Space	• Cathode reaction faster in alkaline electrolyte, leads to high performance • Low cost components	• Sensitive to CO2 in fuel and air • Electrolyte management
Phosphoric Acid (PAFC)	150–200 °C 302–392 °F	Phosphoric acid soaked in a matrix	100 kW, 400 kW	40%	• Distributed generation	• Higher temperature enables CHP • Increased tolerance to fuel impurities	• Pt catalyst • Long start up time • Low current and power
Molten Carbonate (MCFC)	600–700 °C 1,112–1,292 °F	Solution of lithium, sodium, and/ or potassium carbonates, soaked in a matrix	300 kW–3 MW	45–50%	• Electric utility • Distributed generation	• High efficiency • Fuel flexibility • Can use a variety of catalysts • Suitable for CHP	• High temperature corrosion and breakdown of cell components • Long start up time • Low power density
Solid Oxide (SOFC)	700–1,000 °C 1202–1832 °F	Yttria stabilized zirconia	1kW–2 MW	60%	• Auxiliary power • Electric utility • Distributed generation	• High efficiency • Fuel flexibility • Can use a variety of catalysts • Solid electrolyte • Suitable for CHP & CHHP • Hybrid/GT cycle	• High temperature corrosion and breakdown of cell components • High temperature operation requires long start up time and limits

13.7.1   Shunt Active Power Filter

The analysis of ShPF is performed in two different environments as follows:

1. Study of Operation of ShPF for a 3-φ 3-wire (3P3W) System with passive non-linear load condition.
2. Study of Operation of ShPF for a hybrid system of PV-grid with constant irradiance condition.
3. Study of Operation of ShPF for PV-SOFC grid integrated system.

The non-linear load parameters for ShPF can be seen in Table 13.2.

13.7.1.1   ShPF for a 3-φ 3-Wire (3P3W) System With Non-Linear Loading

The simulation was carried out for the system model illustrated in Figure 13.9. Figure 13.13 represents performance of source voltage and current of a 3φ3W system considering ShPF.

The system was tested with a voltage source of 2,000 V Peak. With the introduction of ShPF, the source current waveform is obtained with peak amplitude 600 A. These waveforms disclose about the compensation of ShPF for the disturbances at source end. Figure 13.14 illustrates load end parameters.

Due to nonlinear load (rectifier circuit using RL) the load voltage and load current were distorted and unbalanced in absence of compensation, but with SCCS, both the load voltage and load current become balanced and smooth as shown in Figure 13.14 represents the performance of load

Table 13.2 Load parameters (ShPF).

Item	Value	
	Case—A	Case—B
Resistance	60 Ω	10 Ω
Inductance	0.15 mH	–
Grid Voltage	2 kV	230 V (RMS)
DC Link Capacitance	10,000 μF	200 μF
PV Voltage	–	V

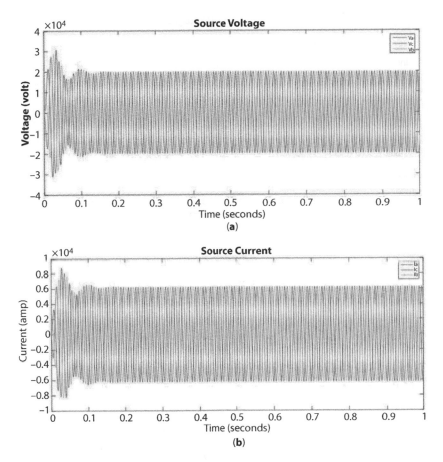

Figure 13.13 (a) Source Voltage, (b) Source Current.

voltage and load current of 3-φ 3-wire system. Figure 13.15 represents compensating waveforms of ShPF.

The load is found to have sinusoidal terminal voltage. It draws a non sinusoidal current which causes the source current to distort. The harmonic in source current has been eliminated using ShPF.

The potential of the DC-link capacitor as connected across the converter is noticed to be constant over the entire course of action shown in Figure 13.16.

A theoretical analysis of ShPF is accomplished for 3-φ 3-W system under passive loading condition using non linear load. The SCCS drives the ShPF ensuring the supply to draw constant sinusoidal current under steady state condition. The FFT analysis of the source current has been shown in Figure 13.17. It is observed that besides fundamental, 5th, 7th,

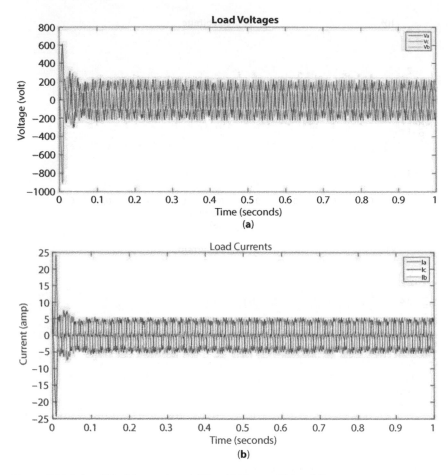

Figure 13.14 Load End Parameters: (a) Load Voltage, (b) Load Current.

9th harmonics exist, but these harmonics are quite suppressed. The 5th harmonic percentage is little higher than 0.02% while that of the 7th harmonic is less than 0.01%. The resultant THD of source current is 0.03% because of the ShPF compensation process.

13.7.1.2   For a PV-Grid System (Constant Irradiance Condition)

Several simulations have been performed considering the parameters as given in Table 13.3.

Figure 13.18 illustrates the Injected current by the ShPF. The waveforms so associated disclose about the compensation of the abnormalities by the ShPF at the supply end.

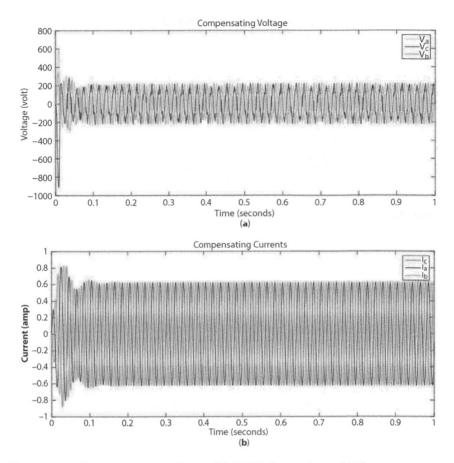

Figure 13.15 Compensating waveforms of ShPF: (a) Shunt voltage, (b) Shunt current.

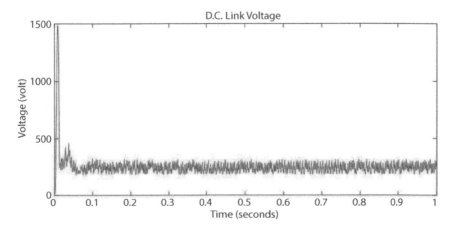

Figure 13.16 DC link voltage.

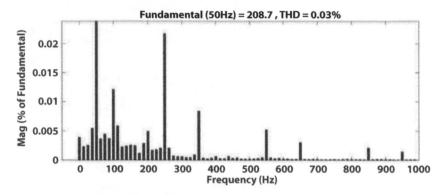

Figure 13.17 FFT analysis of source current.

Table 13.3 Simulation parameter.

Load Parameter	Value
Load Resistance	10 Ω
Grid Voltage (RMS)	230 V
DC Link Capacitance	200 μF

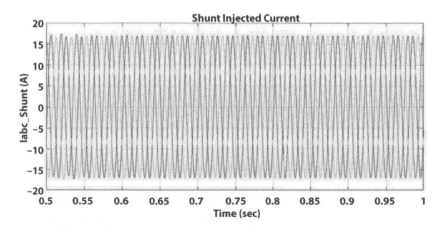

Figure 13.18 Injected current by shunt compensator of a PV-grid system.

Figure 13.19 illustrates the grid injected voltage and current.

The FFT analysis result of the system has been illustrated in Figure 13.20.

Moreover, the current THD of grid injected voltage side is found as 1.40% due to the compensation. The grid injected voltage as well as current are almost sinusoids and does not have significant content of dominant harmonics. It is observed that more of the current is diverted through the filter. So it can be inferred that the shunt component must have high current carrying capacity.

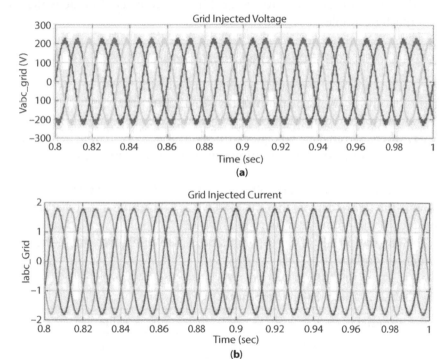

Figure 13.19 PV-grid network: (a) Grid injected voltage (b) Grid injected current.

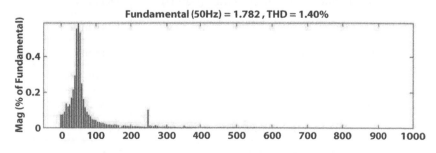

Figure 13.20 Harmonic analysis of grid injected current waveform.

The DC Link voltage does not fluctuate much. Its fluctuation is around 1.25 V, which is within limit of 5%. There exists only one dominant harmonics, i.e. 5th harmonics, which has been suppressed significantly. Its value is of the order of 0.1%. Some of the inter harmonics of very low magnitude seen to exist. Although these inter harmonics are not of concern but these are still can be eliminated by passive filter." The above results show that, the injected current waveform of the ShPF is sinusoidal which indicates the achievement of the basis of SCCS. Apart from that it also provides an effective injection of power to the grid in interconnected mode which is very much desirable.

13.7.1.3   For a PV-SOFC Integrated System

The grid connected PV system is incorporated with SOFC in this section. Table 13.4 shows the basic parameters of SOFC.

The standalone condition of SOFC voltage can be analyzed in Figure 13.21, where a transient voltage can be seen due to switching action and the voltage profile for the remaining time period is obtained as smooth for the value of 230 V.

In Figure 13.22, the load voltage by ShPF linked with SOFC has been shown. The figure depicts that the load voltage has some initial fluctuation but lately it maintains its peak to peak value.

The current profile of the system is described in Figure 13.23. After 0.6 s it gets smoother.

Table 13.4 Simulation parameter of SOFC.

Parameter	Value
Absolute Temperature	1,273 K
Nos. of Cells in Series	450
Response time for hydrogen (kmol/(s-atm))	0.834 ms,
Response time for water (kmol/(s-atm))	0.281 ms
Response time for oxygen (kmol/(s-atm))	0.025 ms
Ohmic loss per cell	0.0328 mW
Electrical response time(s)	0.8 s
Fuel processor response time(s)	5 s
Ratio of hydrogen to oxygen	1.145

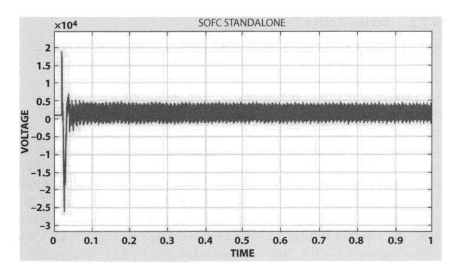

Figure 13.21 SOFC voltage.

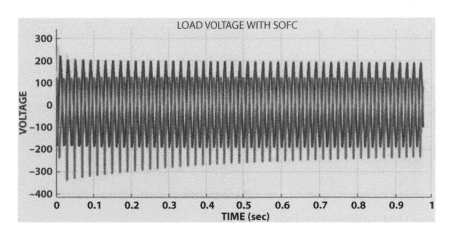

Figure 13.22 Load voltage with SOFC.

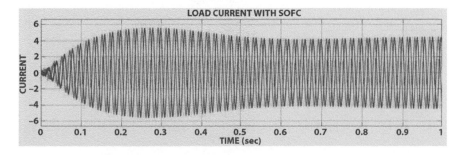

Figure 13.23 Load current with SOFC.

13.7.2   Series Active Power Filter

13.7.2.1   SAF for a 3-φ 3-Wire (3P3W) System With Non-Linear Load Condition

SCCS was applied to grid connected PV system to see for tolerance to voltage disturbances. Figure 13.24 shows the grid voltage at different instances.

In Figure 13.24 it can be observed that there is voltage sag between 0.5 and 1 s and voltage swell in between 1.5 and 2.0 s. But series active filter maintains the voltage level fixed at 311 V RMS. The load voltage is found to be fixed due to the voltage injected by the SAF as seen in Figure 13.25.

The injected voltage by the series inverter has been presented in Figure 13.26. The injected voltage adds up to grid voltage during 0.5–1.0 s and nullifies during 1.5–2.0 s. This has been taken care by SAF by injection of voltage during the same period.

The harmonic analysis of load voltage is obtained has been shown in Figure 13.27.

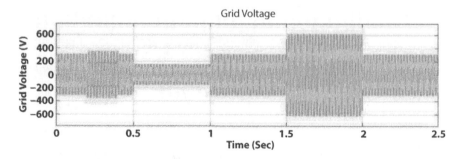

Figure 13.24 Grid injected voltage.

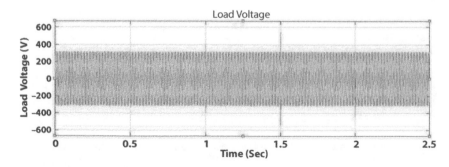

Figure 13.25 Load voltage waveform.

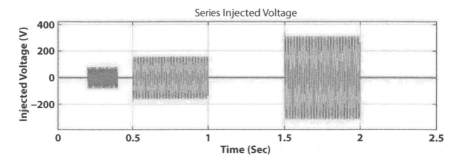

Figure 13.26 Series inverter injected voltage.

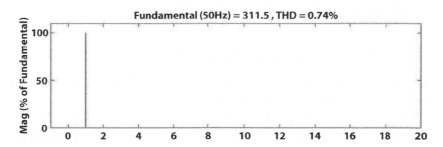

Figure 13.27 Harmonic analysis of load voltage.

The THD in load voltage is found to be 0.74%. The RMS value of load voltage is 311.5 V. Presence of higher order harmonics are suppressed by SAF which can be seen from the THD analysis. The Grid current is shown in Figure 13.28.

The harmonic analysis of the grid current has been shown in Figure 13.29. The THD in grid current was found to be 22.35%. The RMS value of grid current was 8.623 A. Presence of 5th order harmonics has been

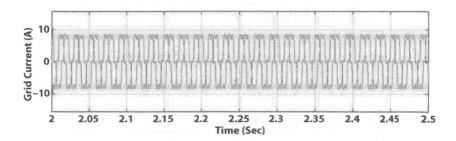

Figure 13.28 Grid current waveform.

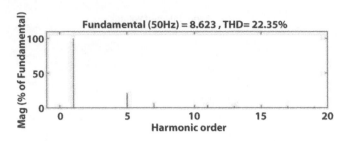

Figure 13.29 THD of Grid current.

suppressed by SAF significantly. Its magnitude in respect of fundamental is found to be below 20%.

13.7.2.2   For a PV-Grid System (Constant Irradiance Condition)

Followings are the simulation parameters that have been maintained consistently throughout all the simulations.

The simulation is carried out to observe the performance of SAF under constant irradiance of PV and SOFC. The simulation and circuit parameters are provided in Tables 13.5 and 13.6 respectively. Continuous irradiance is assumed in grid-tied mode with load demand less than the generation has been considered.

Here the performance of grid-connected PV-SOFC system without SAF has been illustrated. Figure 13.30 shows the characteristics of grid Injected

Table 13.5 Simulation parameters.

Terminal parameters	Magnitude
Non-Linear Load Parameters	
Non-Linear Resistance (R)	100 Ω
Non-Linear Inductance (L)	0.15 mH
Linear Load Parameters	
Linear Nominal line voltage	1,000 V
Linear Active Power (P)	10 kW
Linear Reactive Power (Q)	100 Var
Capacitance of DC Link	1,000 μF

Table 13.6 Circuit parameters.

Parameter	Value
Boost Converter Operating Frequency	5,000 Hz
Dc Link Capacitance	1,000 μF
Nominal Voltage	415 V
Linear Active Power Load	10 kW
Linear Reactive Power Load	100 VAR
Rectifier Load of Resistance	60 Ω
Rectifier Load of Inductance	0.15 mH

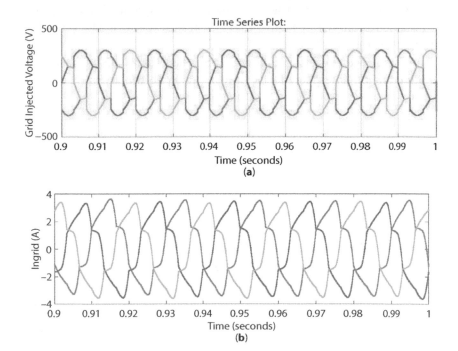

Figure 13.30 Grid injected: (a) Source voltage, (b) Source current.

voltage (phase voltages of each phase) and behavior of grid injected current for 3P3W grid integrated PV system.

The voltage and current waveform show that without SAF the source parameters are non-sinusoidal owing to non-linear nature of the load.

The load voltage and the current by load are observed as balanced and smoother. Figure 13.31 presents the PV output voltage and current.

Figure 13.32 shows load phase voltage and load phase current. The load voltage has a peak value of 230 V and that of load current has a peak value of 2.341 A. The shape of load current wave signifies the presence of an inductive load. Figure 13.32 illustrates the Load voltage and load current waveforms.

The PV inverter output voltage has a peak of 230 V and the current has 2.3 Amp peak. The voltage and current waveform bear the harmonics which needs to be mitigated using SAF.

13.7.2.3 For a PV-SOFC Integrated System

With the same simulation parameter of SOFC as given in Table 13.4, SAF is incorporated along with the PV integrated grid system. The voltage profile obtained is shown in Figure 13.33. A peak to peak of 340 V has been obtained without any fluctuation.

The initial fluctuation in Figure 13.33 is less than 0.05 s indicates the introduction of time delay for SAF to react. With the action of SAF, the

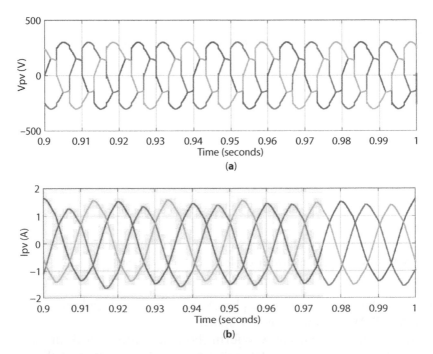

Figure 13.31 PV inverter output: (a) Voltage (b) Current.

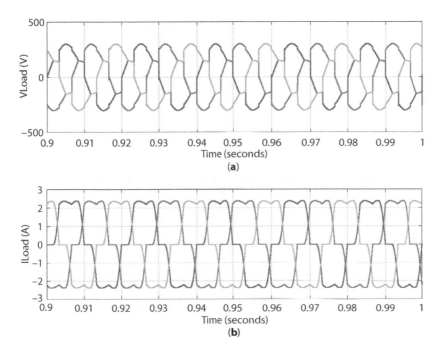

Figure 13.32 (a) Load voltage (b) Load current.

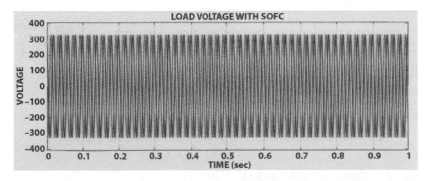

Figure 13.33 Inverter voltage output with SOFC and SAF.

load voltage profile improved and the voltage is steady after 0.05 s with a peak to peak value of 300 V. Figure 13.34 shows the current profile of SAF with SOFC.

With the inclusion of SAF with SOFC in Grid Integrated PV-system, the load current is noted to be smoother after the initial fluctuations.

The ShPF based on SCCS offers assurance against current harmonics as well as improves the power factor. The performance of both ShPF

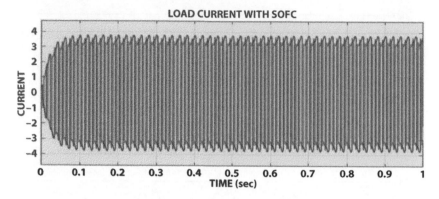

Figure 13.34 Inverter current output with SOFC and SAF.

and SAF are studied. The grid injected current in case of ShPF under the PV-integrated condition is found to be 1.4%. The efficacy of the proposed methodology for ShPF can be validated by comparing the performance of some other techniques proposed by other authors, can be seen in Table 13.7. Similarly, The SAF based on SCCS offers assurance against voltage sag and swell. Besides this, it offers harmonic isolation to load voltage, as

Table 13.7 Validation table for ShPF.

Author	Proposed methodology	Grid current THD
Jain *et al.* [30]	Fuzzy Logic Controller	1.42%
Tang *et al.* [31]	Shunt Active filter with LCL Filter	3.49%
Proposed SCCS	SCCS applied to Three Phase Three Wire Strategy	1.40%

Table 13.8 Validation table for SAF.

Author	Proposed methodology	Grid voltage THD
Wang *et al.* [32]	Hybrid control approach based on reference generation	5.7%
Kim *et al.* [33]	Shunt Active filter with LCL Filter	1.37%
Proposed SCCS	SCCS applied to Three Phase Three Wire Strategy	0.74%

evident from the results. The THD in load voltage is found to be 0.74% which is quite satisfactory. The performance of SAF can be validated by comparing the performance of some other techniques proposed by other authors, which is can be seen in Table 13.8.

13.8   Conclusion

A concept oriented study of APF using SCCS has been carried out for 3P3W system using passive and non-linear load, with fluctuating voltage condition. Even though the voltage and current in three phases are subjected to disturbance in transient state, the control strategy leads to drawing of constant current by the load during steady state condition. Moreover, from the in second fold of simulation study, the THD value in source current is found to be as low as 1.40% and THD in load voltage is observed to be 0.74% which is quite satisfactory and found below the values observed, given in various literatures so far. Due to its efficacy SOFC is integrated and evaluated in the same platform as in Modern Power System Fuel Cell is almost mandatory for smoother operation.

References

1. Aredes, M., Hafner, J. and Heumann, K., Three-Phase Four Wire Shunt Active Filter Control Strategies, *IEEE Transactions on Power Electronics*, Vol. 12, No. 2, pp. 311–318, March 1997.
2. Jia, H.J., Yu, Y.X. and Wang, C.S., Chaotic phenomenon in power system and its studies, *Proceedings of the CSEE*, vol. 7, no. 21, pp. 26–30, 2001.
3. Anwer, N., Siddiqui, A.S. and Anees, A.S., Electrical Power and Energy Systems: A lossless switching technique for smart grid applications, *Int. J. Electr. Power Energy Syst.*, vol. 49, pp. 213–220, 2013.
4. Shahid, A. and Azhar, H., A modular control design for optimum harmonic compensation in micro-grids considering active and reactive power sharing, *Proc. Int. Conf. Harmon. Qual. Power, ICHQP*, pp. 601–605, 2014.
5. Camacho Santiago, A., Castilla Fernandez, M., Miret Tomas, J., Matas Alcala, J., Guzman Sola, R., Control strategies based on effective power factor for distributed generation power plants during unbalanced grid voltage, *Annu. Conf. IEEE Ind. Electron. Soc.*, pp. 7134–7139, 2013.
6. Dhar, S. and Dash, P.K., Performance analysis of a new fast negative sequence power injection oriented islanding detection technique for photovoltaic photo-voltaic based voltage source converter based micro grid operation, *IET Gener. Transm. Distrib.*, vol. 9, no. 15, pp. 2079–2090, 2015.

7. Effatnejad, R., Choopani, K. & Effatnejad, M., Designing the parallel active filter for improvement of the power quality in microgrids, in *Industrial Informatics and Computer Systems (CIICS), 2016 International Conference*, pp. 1–5, March, 2016.

8. Sankar, R.R., Prasad, S.D. & Kumar, K.S., Power quality improving using a voltage source converter, in *2015 International Conference on Electrical, Electronics, Signals, Communication and Optimization (EESCO)*, January 2015.

9. Franklin, A., Yan, R. & Saha, T.K., Investigation of a micro-grid operation: A case study of Heron Island network, Australia, in *Power Engineering Conference (AUPEC), 2013 Australasian Universities*, pp. 1–6, September 2013.

10. Gabbar, H.A., Bower, L., Pandya, D., Agarwal, A., Tomal, M.U. and Islam, F.R., Resilient micro energy grids with gas-power and renewable technologies, *Proc.—ICPERE 2014 2nd IEEE Conf. Power Eng. Renew. Energy 2014*, pp. 1–6, 2014.

11. Joshua, S.S. and Ravishankar, A.N., Development of utility interactive inverters for controlling renewable energy penetration into grid, *Proc. IEEE Int. Conf. Technol. Adv. Power Energy, TAP Energy 2015*, pp. 472–478, 2015.

12. Kumar, D. and Zare, F., Analysis of harmonic mitigations using hybrid passive filters, *16th Int. Power Electron. Motion Control Conf. Expo. PEMC 2014*, pp. 945–951, 2014.

13. Kanakasabapathy, P. and Rao, V.V., *Control Startegy for Inverter based Micro-Grid, Power And Energy Systems: Towards Sustainable Energy (PESTSE 2014)*, pp. 5–10.

14. Mohiti, M., Mahmoodzadeh, Z. and Vakilian, M., A hybrid micro grid islanding detection method, *2013 13th Int. Conf. Environ. Electr. Eng.*, pp. 342–347, 2013.

15. Mosobi, R.W., Chichi, T., & Gao, S., Modeling and power quality analysis of integrated renewable energy system, in *Power Systems Conference (NPSC), 2014 Eighteenth National*, pp. 1–6, December, 2014.

16. Zhang, M. and Chen, J., Islanding and Scheduling of Power Distribution Systems With Distributed Generation, *IEEE Trans. Power Syst.*, vol. 30, no. 6, pp. 3120–3129, 2015.

17. Akagi, H., Watanabe, E.H. & Aredes, M., *Instantaneous power theory and applications to power conditioning*, John Wiley & Sons, February 2007.

18. Akagi, H., Kanazawa, Y., Fujita, K. & Nabae, A., Generalized theory of the instantaneous reactive power and its application, *The Transactions of the Institute of Electrical Engineers of Japan. B*, Vol. *103*, No. 7, pp. 483–490, 1983.

19. Aredes, M. and Watanabe, E.H., New control algorithms for series and shunt three-phase four-wire active power filters, *IEEE Transactions on Power Delivery*, Vol.10, No. 3, pp. 1649–1656, 1995.

20. Buticchi, G., Barater, D., Concari, C. & Franceschini, G., Single-phase series active power filter with transformer-coupled matrix converter, *IET Power Electronics*, Vol. *9*, No. 6, pp. 1279–1289, 2016.

21. Senapati, R., Sahoo, R.K., Pradhan, S., & Senapati, R.N., Sinusoidal current control strategy for 3-phase shunt active filter in grid-tied PV system, In *2017 International Conference on Energy, Communication, Data Analytics and Soft Computing (ICECDS)*, IEEE , pp. 1272–1277, August, 2017.

22. Aredes, M. and Watanabe, E.H., New control algorithms for series and shunt three-phase four-wire active power filters, *IEEE Transactions on Power Delivery*, Vol.10, No. 3, pp. 1649–1656, 1995.

23. Cavallini, A., Montanari, G. C., Compensation Strategies for Shunt Active-Filter Control, *IEEE Transactions on Power Electronics*, Vol. 9, issue.6, pp. 587–593, 1994.

24. Kulworawanichpong, T., Areerak, K., Areerak, K. & Sujitjorn, S., Harmonic identification for active power filters via adaptive TABU search method, in *Knowledge-Based Intelligent Information and Engineering Systems*, Springer Berlin/Heidelberg, pp. 687–694, 2004.

25. Khatri, M. and Kumar, A., Experimental Investigation of Harmonics in a Grid-Tied Solar Photovoltaic System, *International Journal of Renewable Energy Research*, vol. 7(2), pp.901–907, 2017.

26. Issaadi, W., An Improved MPPT Converter Using Current Compensation Method for PV-Applications, *International Journal of Renewable Energy Research*, vol. 6(3), pp. 894–913, Sep. 2016.

27. Aboudrar, I., and El Hani, S., Hybrid algorithm and active filtering dedicated to the optimization and the improvement of photovoltaic system connected to grid energy quality, *International Journal of Renewable Energy Research*, vol. 7(2), pp. 894–900, 2017.

28. Bhatt, P.K., and Kumar, S.Y., Comprehensive Assessment and Mitigation of Harmonic Resonance in Smart Distribution Grid with Solar Photovoltaic, *International Journal of Renewable Energy Research*, vol. 7(3), pp.1085–1096, Sep 2017.

29. Senapati, Rudranarayan, Senapati, R.N.and Moharana, M.K., Sinusoidal Current Control Strategy for UPQC in Grid Connected PV-Fuel Cell Microgrid. *International Journal of Engineering and Technology (IJET)*, vol. 9.4, 2800–2813, 2017.

30. Jain, S.K., Agrawal, P., & Gupta, H.O., Fuzzy logic controlled shunt active power filter for power quality improvement, *IEE Proceedings-Electric Power Applications*, 149(5), 317–328, 2002.

31. Tang, Y., Loh, P.C., Wang, P., Choo, F.H., Gao, F., & Blaabjerg, F., Generalized design of high performance shunt active power filter with output LCL filter, *IEEE Transactions on Industrial Electronics*, 59(3), 1443–1452, 2012.

32. Wang, Z., Wang, Q., Yao, W., & Liu, J., A series active power filter adopting hybrid control approach, *IEEE Transactions on Power Electronics*, 16(3), 301–310, 2001.

33. Kim, Y.S., Kim, J.S., & Ko, S.H., Three-phase three-wire series active power filter, which compensates for harmonics and reactive power, *IEE Proceedings-Electric Power Applications*, 151(3), 276–282, 2004.

34. Wandhare, R.G., Thale, S. and Agarwal, V., Reconfigurable hierarchical control of a microgrid developed with PV, wind, micro-hydro, fuel cell and ultra-capacitor. *2013 Twenty-Eighth Annual IEEE Applied Power Electronics Conference and Exposition (APEC)*, IEEE, 2013.
35. Kumar, S.S., *et al.*, Grid Tied Solid Oxide Fuel Cell Power Generation System for Peak Load Management, *2019 IEEE International Conference on Electrical, Computer and Communication Technologies (ICECCT)*, IEEE, 2019.
36. Zou, L., and Zhou, H.-C., Hydrogen storage in metal-organic frameworks, *Nanostructured Materials for Next-Generation Energy Storage and Conversion*, Springer, Berlin, Heidelberg, 143–170, 2017.
37. Senapati, R., Study and analysis of performance of 3-phase shunt active filter in grid-tied pv-fuel cell system employing sinusoidal current control strategy, *International Journal of Renewable Energy Research (IJRER)*, 8(1), 67–81, 2018.
38. Senapati, R., Sahoo, R.K., Senapati, R.N., & Panda, P.C. Performance evaluation of Sinusoidal current control strategy unified Power Quality Conditioner, In *2016 International Conference on Electrical, Electronics, and Optimization Techniques (ICEEOT)*, IEEE, pp. 1404–1408, March, 2016.
39. Senapati, R., Mishra, S.P., Illa, V., & Senapati, R.N., Improvement of the Current Profile in Grid-Tied Hybrid Energy System by Three-Phase Shunt Active Filter, In *Innovation in Electrical Power Engineering, Communication, and Computing Technology*, Springer, Singapore, pp. 45–60, 2020.
40. Senapati, R., & Senapati, R.N., Performance Evaluation of 3-Phase Active Filter in Grid integrated PV System Employing Sinusoidal Current Control Strategy, *International Journal of Power Systems*, 4, 2019.

14

Application of Fuzzy Logic in Power Quality Assessment of Modern Power Systems

V. Vignesh Kumar[1] and C.K. Babulal[2]*

[1]Department of Electrical and Electronics Engineering, National Institute of Technology Karnataka, Surathkal, Mangalore, India
[2]Department of Electrical and Electronics Engineering, Thiagarajar College of Engineering, Madurai, Tamil Nadu, India

Abstract

The modern power system network is subjected to several changes due to rapid technological advancements including penetration of renewable energy sources, distributed generation and microgrids. Along with this, the extensive use of power electronic converters had resulted the power quality assessment as an important task that is to be performed for improving the reliability of the system. In these circumstances, the prime concern is to have single index for evaluating power quality which is capable of accounting all the power quality disturbances. This chapter mainly focuses on the significant power quality indices such as power factors and harmonic distortion factors that are related to waveform distortion. The amalgamation of power quality indices namely total harmonic distortion (THD), total demand distortion (TDD), displacement power factor (DPF), transmission efficiency power factor (TEPF) and oscillation power factor (OSCPF) into a single fuzzy logic based power quality index is explained in this chapter. The newly developed power quality index is computed for different distortion conditions in Matlab environment to authenticate its effectiveness and the results obtained are presented in a lucid manner. Finally, this chapter concludes that the advantages of fuzzy logic approach in handling the imprecise data and uncertainties can be exploited for the evaluation of power quality in modern power systems. This helps in better understanding about the severity levels of power quality disturbances and ranking them.

*Corresponding author: ckbeee@tce.edu

C. Sharmeela, P. Sivaraman, P. Sanjeevikumar, and Jens Bo Holm-Nielsen (eds.) Microgrid Technologies, (377–404) © 2021 Scrivener Publishing LLC

Keywords: Fuzzy logic system, power quality, harmonics, power factor, total demand distortion (TDD), total harmonic distortion (THD)

14.1   Introduction

In recent years, penetration of renewable energy sources based power generation systems into the existing electric grid has been proliferating to alleviate the carbon foot prints from the atmosphere. The electrical energy harnessed from the renewable energy sources such as solar, wind, geothermal, tidal, etc. must be suitably tailored while integrating it to the grid for reliable operation. This has mandated the deployment of power converters for processing the renewable power output to be compatible with grid [1]. Power converters also play a vital role in the operation of distributed generation and microgrids environment in the modern day power system. Apart from these areas, power converters are widely utilized in industrial electric drives, domestic appliances and in emerging technologies like electric vehicles (EVs) [2–5]. The operation of power semiconductor devices which are the basic building blocks of power electronic converter circuits results in the highly distorted non-sinusoidal current and voltage waveforms [6].

In the modern power system that is subjected to above mentioned major changes and populated with power converter circuits, it is essential to keep the power quality according to the international standards such as IEEE, IEC, etc. Therefore, it is of paramount importance to evaluate the electric power quality for accurate measurement of the power quality disturbance level and choosing appropriate power quality mitigation technique [7–9]. For this purpose, different power quality indices (PQIs) like total harmonic distortion (THD), total demand distortion (TDD), displacement power factor (DPF), transmission efficiency power factor (TEPF) and oscillation power factor (OSCPF) were proposed in the literature [10–14] and are being used for power quality evaluation. But these PQIs will give different values in different operating conditions thereby resulting in an ambiguity in determining and ranking the power quality disturbance [15–18]. Hence, having a single power quality index that represents these PQIs would benefit the power system engineer in making decisions regarding power system quality.

The inherent capability of fuzzy logic to handle the uncertainties and ambiguities in real time problems can be utilized for assessing the power quality [19–23]. This chapter deals with the application of fuzzy logic principle to develop a single universal index by amalgamating the existing PQIs for the evaluation of electric power quality. In order to authenticate the effectiveness of new power quality index, it is tested under different sinusoidal and non-sinusoidal conditions and the results obtained were discussed in detail.

14.2   Power Quality Indices

The various power quality indices that are considered in this chapter for the evaluation of power quality disturbances are explained in this section.

14.2.1   Total Harmonic Distortion

In power system, harmonics are defined as the voltage or current waveforms having frequency components which are multiples of the fundamental frequency. The pictorial representation of fundamental sinusoidal wave and its harmonics are depicted in Figure 14.1 (a). The harmonics get added with the fundamental wave and resulting complex waveform is given in the Figure 14.1 (b). In an electrical network, harmonics are generated mainly due to the non-linear loads and are added with the fundamental source frequency. Total harmonic distortion (THD) is factor used to quantify the amount of harmonics added to the fundamental frequency component.

According to IEEE standard 519:2014 [10], Total Harmonic Distortion (THD) is mathematically expressed as the ratio of equivalent root mean

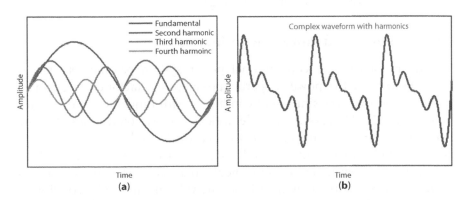

Figure 14.1 (a) Fundamental and other harmonics of a sinusoidal waveform, (b) Complex sinusoidal waveform with harmonics.

square value of all the harmonic voltages upto 50th harmonic order to the root mean square value of fundamental voltage and is given by Equation (14.1).

$$\text{THD} = \frac{\sqrt{\sum_{h=2}^{50} V_h^2}}{V_1} \qquad (14.1)$$

where h denotes the harmonic order and V_1 is the fundamental quantity of voltage. In the power quality assessment, often the THD is referred to the voltage harmonic distortion [10].

14.2.2   Total Demand Distortion

The distortion in current waveforms can be quantified using THD index but it can lead to misinterpretation if the fundamental load current value is low. In order to alleviate this intricacy, Total Demand Distortion (TDD) factor is used exclusively for measuring current distortion levels [10]. The TDD can be mathematically expressed as provided in the Equation (14.2).

$$\text{TDD} = \sqrt{\frac{\sum_{h=2}^{50} I_h^2}{I_L^2}} \qquad (14.2)$$

where h denotes the harmonic order and I_L is the maximum demand load current at the point of common coupling (PCC).

14.2.3   Power and Power Factor Indices

The definitions of the conventional power system parameters such as active power, reactive power, apparent power, power factor etc. are created by assuming the pure sinusoidal conditions with fundamental frequency alone [11, 12]. However, those definitions and simplifications that are used for the power quality analysis will become invalid when the system is subjected to harmonic distortion. Hence, it is necessary to redefine these quantities in relevant to nonsinusoidal situations and also care should be taken such that the new definitions are valid in sinusoidal conditions. Prior to introducing the new power factor indices, classical definitions for single phase system are presented in the following text in brief manner.

The instantaneous value of sinusoidal voltage and current can be given as in Equations (14.3) and (14.4) respectively.

$$v(t) = \sqrt{2} V_{rms} \sin(\omega t) \tag{14.3}$$

$$i(t) = \sqrt{2} I_{rms} \sin(\omega t + \varnothing) \tag{14.4}$$

where V_{rms} and I_{rms} are root mean square value of voltage and current respectively, ω is the angular frequency and $\varnothing$ is the phase angle difference between voltage and current. The active power is the power that is actually utilized by the load and is expressed as in Equation (14.5).

$$P = V_{rms} \cdot I_{rms} \cos(\varnothing) = \frac{1}{T} \int_0^T v(t) \cdot i(t) dt \tag{14.5}$$

where T is the time period of the sinusoidal wave. The apparent power is the maximum active power that can be transmitted from source to the load. It can be expressed as the product of root mean square value of voltage and current as provided in Equation (14.6).

$$S = V_{rms} \cdot I_{rms} \tag{14.6}$$

The power factor is then defined as the ratio of active power that is utilized by load to do the work to the maximum active power that can be supplied to the load and is given in Equation (14.7).

$$PF = \frac{P}{S} \tag{14.7}$$

The power factor conveys the efficiency of the equipment utilization and power transmission. It also helps in understanding about the oscillatory behavior of power transfer. In order to characterize these attributes of the power under nonsinusoidal situations, Willems [12] has proposed new definitions for power factor which is explained in the subsequent sections.

14.2.4   Transmission Efficiency Power Factor (TEPF)

This is almost similar to the classical power factor term that is used for representing the power utilization by load in the conventional power systems.

It is given the name transmission efficiency power factor so as to specifically indicate the percentage of the power transmitted from the source to the load with respect to the maximum power that can be transmitted. The transmission efficiency power factor is mathematically defined as in Equation (14.8).

$$TEPF = \frac{P}{S} \tag{14.8}$$

where P and S are the active and apparent power as defined in Equations (14.5) and (14.6) respectively.

14.2.5   Oscillation Power Factor (OSCPF)

In order to express the oscillatory behavior of the power transmitted from the source to the load, Willems, J.L. had introduced the oscillation power factor. It is defined as ratio of the active power transmitted by a source to the root mean square value of the instantaneous power by taking into account the oscillating components in the waveform. It is given mathematically in the Equation (14.9).

$$OSCPF = \frac{P}{S_{rms}} \tag{14.9}$$

where, P is the active power as defined in Equation (14.5) and S_{rms} is the root mean square value of the instantaneous power which is represented in Equation (14.10).

$$S_{rms} = \sqrt{P^2 + (S_{osc})^2} \tag{14.10}$$

where, S_{osc} is the root mean square value of the oscillating components in the power and is given in Equation (14.11).

$$S_{osc} = \left(\frac{1}{\sqrt{2}}\right) S \tag{14.11}$$

The oscillation power factor can also be expressed in terms of the transmission efficiency power factor [12] as in Equation (14.12).

$$OSCPF = \frac{TEPF}{\sqrt{\left(\frac{1}{2}\right) + TEPF^2}}$$ (14.12)

The value of oscillatory power factor will become zero when the power transmitted is purely oscillatory in nature. That is, when there will not be net energy transfer from source to load with active power, P value being zero in Equation (14.9). On the other hand, if the instantaneous power is a constant which means there is no oscillatory component as in DC excitation, then $S_{osc} = 0$ and $S_{rms} = P$, resulting the oscillating power factor value to become unity. Thus, larger value of OSCPF indicates the presence of lesser amount of oscillating components in the power. In the case of sinusoidal excitation for pure resistive load, the active power and apparent power will be equal, there by yielding the maximum value of OSCPF as 0.816. It is worth mentioning that OSCPF accounts the unavoidable oscillations even under sinusoidal conditions. The minimum value of OSCPF remains to be zero which happens with pure reactive load where the net active power is zero.

14.2.6   Displacement Power Factor (DPF)

The IEEE working committee had recommended the use of another important power factor called as displacement power factor [11]. The DPF is calculated by considering only the fundamental voltage and current waveforms and thereby it inherently excludes the effect of harmonics in the power factor calculation. It is computed by taking the cosine of phase angle difference between the fundamental sinusoidal voltage and current as given in Equation (14.13).

$$DPF = \cos \varphi_1$$ (14.13)

14.3   Fuzzy Logic Systems

Most of the real world engineering problems can be solved by exploiting the objective knowledge and the subjective knowledge of the system. Objective knowledge provides information about the mathematical model which is used in the problem formulation and subjective knowledge represents the linguistic information such as rules, expert suggestions and design requirements. Fuzzy logic can effectively coordinate these two forms of knowledge

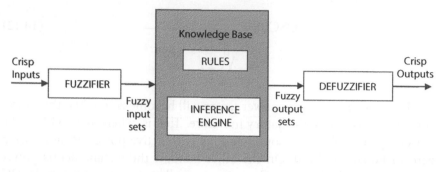

Figure 14.2 Block diagram of fuzzy logic system.

by handling the numerical data and linguistic information simultaneously [20–23]. The general block diagram representing the components of fuzzy logic system is shown in Figure 14.2. Generally fuzzy logic system can be conceived as a non-linear mapping tool which maps the input data vector into a scalar output data. The attributes of fuzzy logic are; it can handle imprecise input, it does not require accurate mathematical model and it can deal effectively nonlinearity in the system.

Fuzzy logic system has four components namely fuzzifier, rules, inference engine, and defuzzifier. The fuzzifier converts the real world numerical inputs into linguistic variables based on the membership function. It is required to activate rules to compute the output variable. Rules are collection of IF-THEN statements or lookup tables which is framed from the expert knowledge. Inference engine is the brain of fuzzy logic system which performs an important function of mapping the input variables into output fuzzy sets. It interprets the rule base similar to human thinking using different methods of inferential procedures for making decision. In many applications, crisp number is required at the output of a fuzzy logic system which is done by the defuzzifier based on the membership function.

14.4   Development of Fuzzy Based Power Quality Evaluation Modules

The concept of developing a single universal index for power quality evaluation of a power system network from the existing power quality indices is done in three stages. This section discusses in detail about this and in each stage the developed fuzzy module is tested under different conditions in a systematic way to authenticate the design rules.

14.4.1   Stage I: Fuzzy Logic Based Total Demand Distortion

In an electric power system network, TDD value reflects the amount of distortion in the current waveform. However, in certain situations it is difficult to quantify the distortion level accurately using TDD value alone. According to IEEE standard 519-2014 [10], TDD values have to be correlated with the short circuit level (SC level) in order to confirm whether the distortion is within limits or not. SC level as defined in [10], is the ratio of the short circuit current, I_{SC} in amperes to the load current, I_L in amperes. The current distortion limits recommended by IEEE standard 519-2014 for the systems rated 120 V through 69 kV is given in Table 14.1.

It is evident from this table that though TDD can quantify the distortion in current waveform, it cannot represent directly whether distortion levels are violating the permissible limits. This can be explained with the help of a non-linear circuit shown in Figure 14.3. The circuit is energized with a sinusoidal voltage source having root mean square value equal to 230 V and fundamental frequency of 50 Hz. The value of load resistance, R_{load} = 130 Ω and Triac is triggered with firing angle of 25°. It can be noted that the distortion limits given in Table 14.1 is applicable only at the PCC of the system as mentioned in [10]. However, the circuit in Figure 14.3 is considered merely for the purpose of understanding the ambiguity in judging the distortion limits violation and for simplicity.

Two cases with different values for line resistance R_{line} are taken for the circuit in Figure 14.3. This circuit is simulated in the Matlab Simulink environment with the parameters mentioned above and the TDD values are computed as 12% in both the cases. In the first case, R_{line} = 3 Ω leads to the

Table 14.1 Harmonic current distortion limit as per IEEE-519:2014.

I_{SC}/I_L	$3 \le h < 11$	$11 \le h < 17$	$17 \le h$ < 23	$23 \le h$ < 35	$35 \le h$ ≤ 50	TDD
<20	4.0	2.0	1.5	0.6	0.3	5.0
20 < 50	7.0	3.5	2.5	1.0	0.5	8.0
50 < 1,000	10.0	4.5	4.0	1.5	0.7	12.0
100 < 1,000	12.0	5.5	5.0	2.0	1.0	15.0
>1000	15.0	7.0	6.0	2.5	1.4	20.0

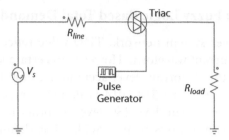

Figure 14.3 Single phase AC voltage controller circuit with resistive load.

SC level of 43. Referring to Table 14.1, it can be seen that for this SC level the TDD should be within 8%. When comparing this with computed TDD value, it clearly indicates that distortion in this case is outside the limit. In the second case, line resistance taken as R_{line} = 1 Ω, results in SC level of 130. As in the previous case, TDD distortion limit is identified from Table 14.1. It states that the TDD value should be within 15% for SC level of 130 from which it can be inferred that the distortion is within the limit for the second case. It is worth mentioning here that even though TDD values are same, in one case the distortion is within the limit and in other it is outside the limit.

In order to resolve this ambiguity in determining the distortion level limits violation, the fuzzy logic concept is used in developing a new index namely fuzzy total demand distortion factor (FTDDF). The block diagram of the fuzzy logic system for computing FTDDF is shown in Figure 14.4. The fuzzy system shown in this figure takes TDD and SC level as inputs and amalgamates them to produce FTDDF. In order to test its performance under different distortion conditions, the fuzzy system shown in Figure 14.4 is built using Fuzzy Tool Box in Matlab. The design procedure for rule base, development of membership functions and testing of fuzzy module in Figure 14.4 are explained in the succeeding texts.

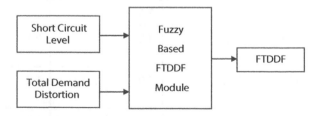

Figure 14.4 Block diagram of FTDDF module.

In the FTDDF module, the input variable SC level is expressed in terms of five linguistic variables namely low (L), somewhat low (SL), medium (M), somewhat high (SH), and high (H) whereas TDD is expressed by seven linguistic variables viz. very low (VL), low (L), somewhat low (SL), medium (M), somewhat high (SH), high (H), and very high (VH). Similarly, output variable is represented with seven linguistic variables such as low (L), moderately low (ML), somewhat low (SL), medium (M), somewhat high (SH), moderately high (MH), and high (H). All these linguistic variables are described by the mathematical membership functions as shown in Figure 14.5. The triangular and trapezoidal membership functions are selected such that it maps the actual behavior of the input and output variables.

Once the TDD and SC level for the given electrical system are computed and converted to linguistic variables based on the membership functions given in Figure 14.5, fuzzy system output which is typically FTDDF can be obtained from the rule base given in Table 14.2. This rule base can be implemented as IF-THEN rules in the fuzzy system and proper choice of inference while designing the rules is important to obtain the appropriate output [19]. Centroid method is used for defuzzification in this fuzzy system. At the defuzzification stage, the linguistic variable for the output obtained from the rule base is converted to the numerical value which then can be easily interpreted by the user.

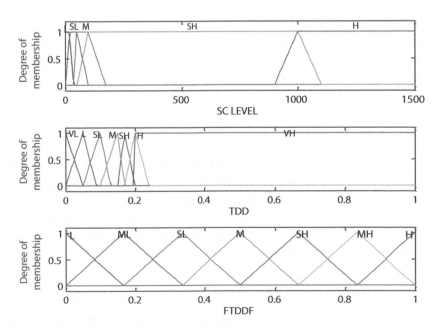

Figure 14.5 Representation of input and output variables for FTDDF module.

Table 14.2 Rule base for FTDDF module.

SC Level \ TDD	VL	L	SL	M	SH	H	VH
L	H	MH	SH	M	SL	ML	L
SL	H	H	MH	SH	M	SL	ML
M	H	H	H	MH	SH	M	SL
SH	H	H	H	H	MH	SH	M
H	H	H	H	H	H	MH	SH

Table 14.3 Rule viewer output of FTDDF module for two cases.

Case	Input		Output
	S.C Level	TDD	FTDDF
1	43	0.12	0.735
2	130	0.12	0.875

The FTDDF value will convey directly the extent of distortion in the current waveform. The high value of TDD for relatively low SC level will result in low value of FTDDF. Similar interpretations of Table 14.1 were made using the fuzzy system shown in Figure 14.4 and it is observed that FTDDF value above 0.85 represents the distortion is within the limits. Now, the FTDDF value for two cases of the circuit shown Figure 14.3 is computed and the output obtained from rule viewer window in Matlab Fuzzy Toolbox is shown in Table 14.3.

It is evident from Table 14.3 that FTDDF value for case 1 is below 0.85 which indicates that distortion is outside the permissible limits whereas in case 2 the distortion is within limits. Further, in order to prove the accuracy of the developed fuzzy based index, the fuzzy system in Figure 14.4 is tested with values of TDD and SC level obtained from different sinusoidal and nonsinusoidal conditions of an electrical system.

14.4.1.1 Performance of FTDDF Under Sinusoidal Situations

The circuit shown in Figure 14.3 is simulated in Matlab with 230 V, 50 Hz sinusoidal voltage source and load resistance of 50 Ω. Two different values

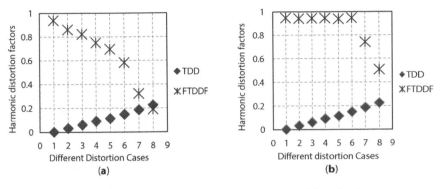

Figure 14.6 TDD and FTDDF values for sinusoidal condition (a) SC level 17.7, (b) SC level 51.1.

for line resistance $R_{line} = 3\ \Omega$ and $R_{line} = 1\ \Omega$ corresponding to SC level of 17.7 and 51.1 respectively are considered. At each SC level, the circuit in Figure 14.3 is operated at firing angle $\alpha = 0°, 10°, 15°, 20°, 25°, 30°, 35°, 40°$ and this operating conditions are named as distortion cases 1 to 8 accordingly. The TDD values are computed for all these cases. Then, these TDD and SC level values are given as input to the FTDDF module developed in Matlab Fuzzy Toolbox to determine their respective FTDDF value. The results obtained are illustrated in Figure 14.6.

It can be observed from this figure that the variation in TDD value is similar in both SC level. There is an increase TDD values for increase in firing angle. Also, in Figures 14.6 (a) and (b), it can be seen that the FTDDF values are low when the distortion in current waveform is higher. Further, in Figure 14.6 (a), FTDDF indicates that distortion is within the limit in case 1 and case 2. For other distortion cases, it is outside the limits, which is primarily due to the low SC level. In Figure 14.6 (b), the FTDDF values are within in the limits for cases 1 to 6 whereas for case 7 and case 8, it lies outside the limits. It can be inferred that, the developed FTDDF module is capable of accurately determining the distortion limits violations by considering the SC level as given in Ref. [10] and also quantifies the degree of distortion in the current waveform.

14.4.1.2 *Performance of FTDDF Under Nonsinusoidal Situations*

The developed FTDDF module is now tested for nonsinusoidal situations with the circuit shown in Figure 14.3. In the Matlab-Simulink environment the source voltage is now made as nonsinusoidal which contains 13% of third harmonic in addition to the fundamental components. All other parameters

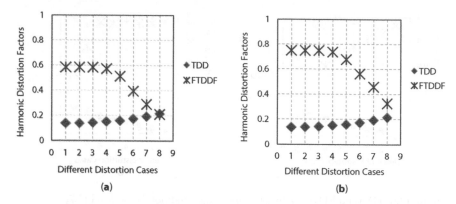

Figure 14.7 TDD and FTDDF values for nonsinusoidal condition (a) SC level 17.7, (b) SC level 51.1.

and circuit operating conditions are unchanged. The simulation is repeated with nonsinusoidal voltage source and the TDD values are calculated. As earlier, the FTDDF values are computed for all the cases with short circuit levels 17.7 and 51.1. The results obtained are depicted in Figure 14.7.

As expected, it can be seen in Figure 14.7 (a) that the FTDDF values are low compared to the ones in Figure 14.6 (a). This is because of the nonsinusoidal voltage source which results in increased distortion in the current waveform. Similarly, the same kind of response can be witnessed in Figure 14.7 (b) in comparison with Figure 14.6 (b). Moreover, the FTDDF values are higher in Figure 14.7 (b) than that of in Figure 14.7 (a) due to the fact that SC level is high. In both, Figures 14.7 (a) and (b) the FTDDF values indicate the distortion is outside the limits for all the cases. Hence, these results prove the veracity of the FTDDF in handling the nonsinusoidal situations.

Therefore, it is shown that the FTDDF developed using the concept of fuzzy logic greatly reduces the ambiguity in determining the distortion limit violations using TDD alone from IEEE standard 519-2014. The FTDDF also quantifies the amount of distortion in current waveform with significant accuracy and is capable of tracking changes in the TDD and SC level.

14.4.2 Stage II—Fuzzy Representative Quality Power Factor (FRQPF)

This section of the chapter explains the development of fuzzy logic based single index for power factor denoted as Fuzzy Representative Quality Power Factor (FRQPF). The block diagram of the developed fuzzy logic system to determine the FRQPF is shown in Figure 14.8.

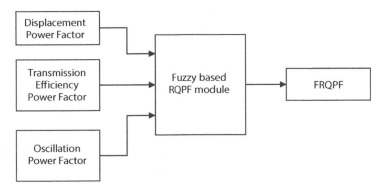

Figure 14.8 Block diagram of RQPF module.

The input variables to this fuzzy system are three power factors viz. displacement power factor, transmission efficiency power factor and oscillation power factor explained in Section 14.2. All the input variables are expressed by means of three linguistic variables namely low (L), medium (M) and high (H). In a similar manner the output variable of the fuzzy system in Figure 14.8 is represented by seven linguistic variable such as Low (L), Moderately Low (ML), Somewhat Low (SL), Medium (M), Somewhat High (SH), Moderately High (MH), and High (H). The choice of selecting the number of linguistic variable for the variable depends on the designer which is mostly based on the system knowledge. Triangular form of membership functions is used to represent input variables and output variables due to its simplicity and is shown in Figure 14.9.

In order to describe the knowledge of decision making twenty seven fuzzy rules or IF-THEN rules are framed in the fuzzy inference engine and few rules of which are stated below:

- If DPF is L and TEPF is L and OSCPF is M then FRQPF is ML
- If DPF is M and TEPF is M and OSCPF is H then FRQPF is MH
- If DPF is H and TEPF is H and OSCPF is H then FRQPF is H

The three input power factors can be determined for the system under evaluation using the electrical measuring instruments and Equations (14.5) to (14.13). The values of input variables are given to the RQPF module built in Matlab using Fuzzy Toolbox. Then, the fuzzy inference engine will produce the output variables based on the rules designed in the system. The defuzzification is done by center of gravity method and is required to

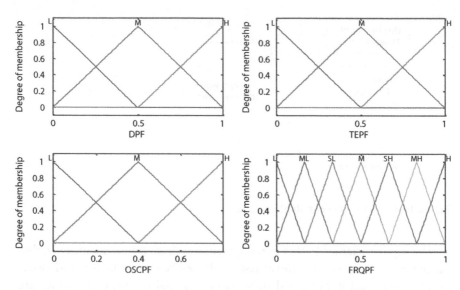

Figure 14.9 Representation of input and output variables for RQPF module.

obtain the output in numerical form for easier interpretation by the system operators.

The behavior of newly developed RPQF is tested for ideal and non-ideal values of input variables and is listed in Table 14.4. It is well known that the ideal value of displacement and transmission efficiency power factor is unity and for oscillation power factor it is 0.816 which is explained in Section 14.2. It can be seen from Table 14.4 that the ideal value of FRQPF is found to be 0.948 and its value decreases for any other values of input variables. It can be noted that the ideal case is the pure resistive circuit with no distortion whereas the non-ideal case corresponds to circuit having inductive and capacitive reactance with power factor less than unity. Thus higher the value of FRQPF, the better is the power quality and the low value of FRQPF is an indication of poor power quality.

Table 14.4 Rule viewer output for Ideal and Nonideal cases of RQPF module.

	Input			Output
Case	DPF	TEPF	OSCPF	FRQPF
Ideal	1.000	1.000	0.816	**0.948**
Non-ideal	0.633	0.741	0.585	**0.673**

14.4.2.1 Performance of FRQPF Under Sinusoidal and Nonsinusoidal Situations

In order to demonstrate the effectiveness of RQPF module over wide range of operating conditions, it is now tested for different loading conditions with sinusoidal and distorted nonsinusoidal voltage sources. The circuit shown in Figure 14.10, has a sinusoidal voltage source of 230 V, 50 Hz supplying a load through a line having an impedance of $5 + j5\Omega$.

Since the FRQPF index deals with power factor and to prove its performance under different operating conditions of the electrical network with varied reactive components the test cases are taken by considering different values for load impedance. These values of load impedance for corresponding to case 1 through case 7 are listed in Table 14.5. This circuit is simulated in the Matlab environment and values of displacement power factor, transmission efficiency power factor and oscillation power factor are computed. Now, these values are loaded in to the RQPF module developed in Matlab fuzzy tool box to determine the FRQPF value.

The results obtained are depicted in Figure 14.11 (a) for all the seven cases with sinusoidal excitation. It can be seen that for case 1 which represents a purely resistive load, the value of DPF and TEPF are unity, whereas OSCPF is 0.816 and the resulting output, FRQPF is 0.948. This

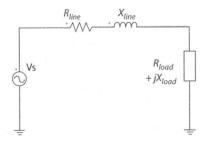

Figure 14.10 Circuit considered for demonstrating performance of FRQPF.

Table 14.5 Seven different loading cases considered for FRQPF evaluation.

Case Load values	1	2	3	4	5	6	7
R_{load} in ohms	1	Zero	Zero	20	20	20	20
X_{load} in ohms	Zero	20	5	20	113	5	−20

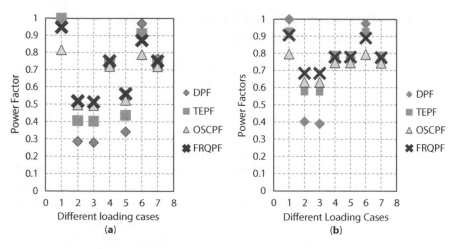

Figure 14.11 FRQPF values for different loading cases (a) Sinusoidal voltage source, (b) Nonsinusoidal voltage source.

again confirms the ideal case values shown in the Table 14.4. It can also be seen from Figure 14.11 (a) that for cases 2 and 3, which represents purely reactive loads the FRQPF value is reduced. Also from the FRQPF values of other cases, it can be said that the proposed FRQPF is sensitive to the variations in the loading conditions.

In a similar manner, the FRQPF is calculated for different loads applied to the circuit in Figure 14.10 with nonsinusoidal conditions. The voltage source now is made to possess a distorted sinusoidal waveform with the third, fifth, seventh, ninth, and eleventh harmonics in the simulation. The other parameters remain same as in the sinusoidal situation. As earlier, the new FRQPF is calculated for the entire seven cases in Table 14.5 and results are shown in Figure 14.11 (b). It can be observed from this Figure 14.11 (b) that for case 1 which represents the purely resistive load, the displacement power factor and transmission efficiency power factor values are different. It indicates the presence of oscillating components which is reflected in the oscillating power factor and hence in the output FRQPF. This is due to the presence of nonsinusoidal components in the source voltage waveform. Also, it can be seen that for all other cases the useful power transmitted to the load is less than the generated power which is evident from the FRQPF values. Thus, Figure 14.11 reveals the capability of FRQPF to successfully discriminate between the resistive and reactive loading conditions with pure sinusoidal and complex sinusoidal excitation voltage waveforms.

Hence, it can be stated that the developed RQPF module can significantly quantify the power factor including the oscillating components in the circuit through amalgamation of three power factors. This FRQPF index can further render its usefulness in deciding an appropriate power factor correction technique for the system under consideration.

14.4.3   Stage III—Fuzzy Power Quality Index (FPQI) Module

This section describes the third stage in the development of single universal index using fuzzy logic for the power quality assessment. The new index namely Fuzzy Power Quality Index (FPQI) evaluates the power quality by amalgamating the recommended power quality indices such as displacement power factor, transmission efficiency power factor, oscillation power factor, voltage total harmonic distortion and total demand distortion. The block diagram of the fuzzy logic system for computing FPQI is shown in the Figure 14.12. This module comprises of fuzzy total demand distortion module and fuzzy representative quality power factor module that are described in Section 14.4.1 and 14.4.2 respectively. These modules are built in Fuzzy Logic Toolbox available in Matlab software and the design procedure is explained in the subsequent texts.

The inputs to the newly developed FPQI module are output of RQPF module (FRQPF), output of FTDDF module (FTDDF) and Total harmonic distortion (THD). Three linguistic variables are used to represent the input variable THD; low (L), medium (M) and high (H). Triangular membership function is used to represent these three linguistic variables as shown in Figure 14.12. The other two input variables FRQPF and FTDDF are explained in the Sections 14.4.1 and 14.4.2 respectively. The new index FPQI that is the output of fuzzy FPQI module is represented by triangular

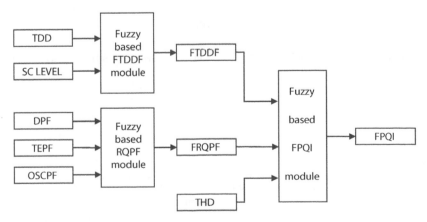

Figure 14.12 Block diagram of the fuzzy power quality index evaluation module.

membership function with nine linguistic variables: very low (VL), low (L), moderately low (ML), somewhat low (SL), medium (M), somewhat high (SH), moderately high (MH), high (H), and very high (VH) as depicted in Figure 14.13.

Fuzzy rule base is designed with one hundred and forty seven rules to compute the FPQI and the few of the rules are presented below:

- If FRQPF is L and FTDDF is L and THD is H then FPQI is VL.
- If FRQPF is ML and FTDDF is ML and THD is H then FPQI is L.
- If FRQPF is H and FTDDF is H and THD is L then FPQI is VH.

The developed FPQI module is tested with ideal case values for the inputs such that FTDDF = 1, FRQPF = 0.948 and THD = 0.05. Table 14.6 shows the output of the FPQI for the ideal case as '0.961'. This can be considered as the benchmark value for assessing the power quality. Hence, lower is the value of FPQI than this ideal value higher is the distortion and poorer is the quality of power. Next, consider a non-ideal case in which FRQPF = 0.751,

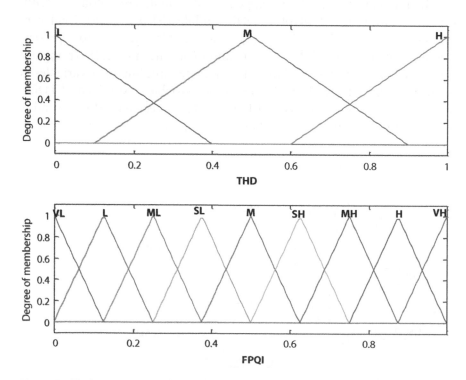

Figure 14.13 Representation of THD and FPQI variables for FPQI module.

Table 14.6 Rule viewer output of FPQI module.

	Input			Output
Case	FRPQF	FTDDF	THD	FPQI
Ideal	0.948	1.000	0.05	0.961
Non-ideal	0.751	0.645	0.45	0.652

FTDDF = 0.645 and THD = 0.45. As expected the value of FPQI is low and its value is 0.652 as shown in Table 14.6. This proves that the developed FPQI module could able to discriminate ideal and non-ideal case.

Extensive simulation studies and analysis is carried out in order to authenticate the performance of developed power quality index. FPQI is computed for different distortion cases under sinusoidal and nonsinusoidal situations and the values obtained are presented in the subsequent sections.

14.4.3.1 Performance of FPQI Under Sinusoidal and Nonsinusoidal Situations

The circuit shown in Figure 14.14 comprises of switching device and reactive component in order to have resemblance to the practical scenario. The source voltage is pure sinusoidal with root mean square value equal to 230 V and frequency of 50 Hz. The load impedance is set to $Z_{Load} = (50 + j30)\ \Omega$. Seven distortion cases are generated by varying the firing angle of the thyristor viz. $\alpha = 35°, 40°, 45°, 50°, 55°, 60°$ and $70°$. By setting the line resistance $R_{line} = 0.1\ \Omega$, the short circuit level obtained is 583. The TDD and THD values are measured for all distortion cases. The load voltage V_{bn} and

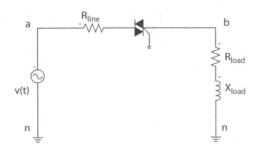

Figure 14.14 Single-phase nonlinear load supplied from sinusoidal source.

Table 14.7 Evaluation of FPQI from three stages under sinusoidal situations.

| | Fuzzy Logic based RQPF module | | | | Fuzzy Logic based FTDDF module | | | Fuzzy Logic Based FPQI module | |
| | Input | | | Output | Input | | Output | Input | Output |
Case	DPF	TEPF	OSCPF	FRQPF	SC level	TDD (in Percent of I_L)	FTDDF	THD (in percent of fundamental quantity)	FPQI
1	0.8856	0.8638	0.7737	0.827	583	3.09	0.941	4.12	0.904
2	0.8860	0.8563	0.7710	0.822	583	5.88	0.945	14.04	0.891
3	0.8871	0.8485	0.7682	0.816	583	9.84	0.947	24.63	0.826
4	0.8869	0.8397	0.7649	0.809	583	13.3	0.942	29.44	0.804
5	0.8866	0.8308	0.7615	0.803	583	16.3	0.845	34.22	0.777
6	0.8865	0.8215	0.7579	0.797	583	19.33	0.711	38.89	0.769
7	0.855	0.801	0.7496	0.785	583	25.14	0.5	48.79	0.709

the load current are used to calculate the displacement power factor, transmission efficiency power factor, and oscillation power factor. The entire circuit simulation is done in the Matlab Simulink environment. The FPQI values are calculated from the Fuzzy Toolbox are listed in Table 14.7 and illustrated in Figure 14.15 (a).

It can be observed from Figure 14.15 (a) that the values of FPQI for cases 1 and 2 indicate the system having significantly better power quality. Also, it is evidence from the FTDDF values that distortion is within the limits. Further, the power factor is also moderately good which can be shown by FRQPF values. In the remaining cases the value of power quality index is low which can be attributed to the increase in distortion level due to increase in the firing angle.

In the similar manner, the FPQI values are now calculated with nonsinusoidal voltage source having the fundamental plus third order harmonic component with root mean square value of 34.5 V. As in the previous case, the values of FPQI are computed for all the distortion cases with nonsinusoidal excitation. The results obtained are listed in Table 14.8 and also depicted in Figure 14.15 (b).

Inspection of Figure 14.15 (b) and Table 14.8, reveals that the power quality is diminished for all the cases which is apparent from the values of FPQI. This reason for poor power quality can be attributed to the nonsinusoidal nature of the voltage source. It can also be seen that, though the power factor values are moderately good, FPQI is decreased because of increase in total harmonic distortion. This proves the usefulness of the new index FPQI in rating and evaluating the power quality under different distortion conditions while considering the recommended PQIs.

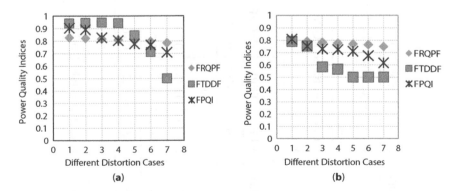

Figure 14.15 FPQI, FRQPF and FTDDF values (a) Sinusoidal case, (b) Nonsinusoidal case.

Table 14.8 Evaluation of FPQI from three stages under nonsinusoidal situations.

	Fuzzy Logic Based FPQI module III								
	Fuzzy Logic based RQPF module I				Fuzzy Logic based FTDDF module II				Output
	Input		Output		Input		Output	THD (in percent of fundamental quantity)	
Case	DPF	TEPF	OSCPF	FRQPF	SC Level	TDD (in Percent of I_L)	FTDDF		FPQI
1	0.8861	0.8584	0.7718	0.813	583	17.66	0.790	16.42	0.808
2	0.8866	0.8510	0.7691	0.791	583	18.45	0.752	24.62	0.752
3	0.8864	0.8433	0.7662	0.783	583	20.41	0.583	29.53	0.729
4	0.8877	0.8353	0.7632	0.776	583	22.29	0.564	33.91	0.724
5	0.8873	0.8271	0.7600	0.769	583	24.85	0.500	37.55	0.710
6	0.8870	0.8187	0.7568	0.763	583	27.5	0.500	41.93	0.675
7	0.8860	0.8000	0.7490	0.748	583	33.10	0.500	51.03	0.616

14.5   Conclusion

This chapter proposed a new fuzzy logic based power quality index namely FPQI for assessment of power quality in an electric power system. The advantages of fuzzy logic concepts such as ease of dealing with the ambiguities and uncertainties in real time scenario are largely exploited for the development of new power quality index. The idea of combining the existing power quality indices into a single universal index using fuzzy logic by means of three stages is introduced and explained in detail. The three modules viz. fuzzy based FTDDF module, fuzzy based RQPF module, and fuzzy based FPQI module are tested for sinusoidal and nonsinusoidal conditions individually and as a single system.

The effectiveness of FPQI to accurately quantify the power quality disturbances is authenticated by the results obtained from the tests carried out in Matlab environment. This work ultimately projects that having a single power quality index which represents the existing other power quality indices render a significant level of convenience for the power system engineers. The proposed method can provide assistance in establishing an appropriate power quality mitigation technique for the electrical system under study. In the deregulated environment, this approach will be useful in selecting the best supplier of power in the market. In the microgrid operation of power system, the proposed power quality assessment method will help in evaluating the impact of distributed generators in the power system.

References

1. Carrasco, J.M., Franquelo, L.G., Bialasiewicz, J.T., Galvan, E., PortilloGuisado, R.C., Prats, M.A.M., Leon, J.I., Moreno-Alfonso, N., Power-Electronic Systems for the Grid Integration of Renewable Energy Sources: A Survey, *IEEE Transactions on Industrial Electronics,* 53, 4, pp. 1002–1016, 2006.

2. Chakraborty, C., Iu, H.H.-C., Lu, D.D.-C., Power converters, control, and energy management for distributed generation, *IEEE Transactions on Industrial Electronics,* 62, 7, pp. 4466–4470, 2015.

3. Yadav, J., Vasudevan, K., Kumar, D., Shanmugam, P., Power Quality Assessment for an Industrial Plant, *In: Proceedings of the IEEE International Conference on Power Electronics, Drives and Energy Systems,* Chennai, India, Dec 18–21, 2018.

4. Purgat, P., Gerber-Popovic, J., Bauer, P., Modularity in power electronics: Conceptualization classification and outlook, *In: Proceedings of the 43rd Annual Conference of the IEEE Industrial Electronics Society,* Beijing, China, 1307–1312, Oct 29–Nov 1, 2017.

5. Kumar, L., Kumar Gupta, K., Jain, S., Power electronic interface for vehicular electrification, *In: Proceedings of the IEEE International Symposium on Industrial Electronics*, Taipei, Taiwan, pp. 1–6, May 28–31, 2013.

6. Debnath, S., Qin, J., Bahrani, B., Saeedifard, M., Barbosa, P., Operation, Control, and Applications of the Modular Multilevel Converter: A Review, *IEEE Transactions on Power Electronics*, 30, 1, pp. 37–53, 2015.

7. Milanovic, J.V., International Industry Practice on Power-Quality Monitoring, *IEEE Transactions on Power Delivery*, 29, 2, pp. 934–941, 2014.

8. Herath, H.M.S.C., Gosbell, V.J., Perera, S., Power quality (PQ) survey reporting: discrete disturbance limits, *IEEE Transactions on Power Delivery*, 20, 2, pp. 851–858, 2005.

9. Stanescu, C., Gal, S., Widmer, J., Pispiris, C., Power quality monitoring systems in Romanian electricity market, *In: Proceedings of International Symposium on Power Electronics, Electrical Drives, Automation and Motion*, pp.1394–1397, 2008.

10. *Recommended Practices and Requirements for Harmonic Control in Electric Power System*, IEEE Standard 519, 2014.

11. Practical definitions for power systems with nonsinusoidal waveforms and unbalanced loads: A discussion, *IEEE Transactions on Power Delivery*, 11, 1, pp. 79–87, 1996.

12. Willems, J.L., Reflections on apparent power and power factor in nonsinusoidal and polyphase situations, *IEEE Transactions on Power Delivery*, 19, 2, pp. 835–840, 2004.

13. McGranaghan, M.F., Dugan, R.C., Beaty, H.W., *Electrical Power Systems Quality*, New York, McGraw-Hill, 2004.

14. Arillaga, J., Watson, N.R., Chen, S., *Power System Quality Assessment*, John Willey & Sons, 2000.

15. Morsi, W.G., El-Hawary, M.E., A new fuzzy-based total demand distortion factor for non-sinusoidal situations, *IEEE Transactions on Power Delivery*, 23, 2, pp.1007–1014, 2008.

16. Rathina Prabha, N., Marimuthu, N.S., Babulal, C.K., Adaptive neuro-fuzzy inference system based total demand distortion factor for power quality evaluation, *Neurocomputing*, 73, 1, pp. 315–323, 2009.

17. Morsi, W.G., El-Hawary, M.E., A new fuzzy-based representative quality power factor for non-sinusoidal situations, *IEEE Transactions on Power Delivery*, 23, 2, pp.930–936, 2008.

18. Rathina Prabha, N., Marimuthu, N.S., Babulal, C.K., Adaptive neuro-fuzzy inference system based representative quality power factor for power quality assessment, *Neurocomputing*, 73, 13, pp. 2737–2743, 2010.

19. Mamdani, E.H., Assilian, S., An experiment in linguistic synthesis with a fuzzy logic controller, *International Journal of Man-Machine Studies*, 7, 1, pp. 1–13, 1975.

20. Ferreira, A.A., Pomilio, J.A., Spiazzi, G., de Araujo Silva, L., Energy Management Fuzzy Logic Supervisory for Electric Vehicle Power Supplies System, *IEEE Transaction Power Electronics*, 23, 1, pp. 107–115, 2008.
21. Gao, D., Jin, Z., Lu, Q., Energy management strategy based on fuzzy logic for a fuel cell hybrid bus, *Journal of Power Sources*, 185, 1, pp. 311–317, 2008.
22. Ishaque, K., Abdullah, S., Ayob, S., Salam, Z., Single input fuzzy logic controller for unmanned underwater vehicle, *Journal of Intelligent & Robotic Systems*, 59, pp. 87–100, 2010.
23. Kwan, T.H., Wu, X.F., Maximum power point tracking using a variable antecedent fuzzy logic controller, *Solar Energy*, 137, 1, pp. 189–200, 2016.

15

Applications of Internet of Things for Microgrid

Vikram Kulkarni[1]*, Sarat Kumar Sahoo[2] and Rejo Mathew[1]

[1]Dept. of Information Technology, MPSTME, NMIMS University, Mumbai, India
[2]Dept. of Electrical Engineering, Parala Maharaja College of Engineering (BPUT), Berhampur, India

Abstract

The deregulation of the electrical power system needs to address the monitoring and control aspects of systematic energy generation from different sources. The dynamic changes in the power demand make utilities to add/remove different Distributed Energy Resources (DER). The modern research in technology decreased the cost and featured the size of electronic devices enabling them to connect and become interactive known as Internet of Things (IoT). Smart monitoring and control aspects required for efficient energy management assures economic operations. This can be achieved using IoT. Microgrid is a combination of different distributed generators (DG) that includes the renewable/non-renewable energy sources. In microgrid IoT can help in integrating its physical components like sensors, actuators, converters, batteries, DG, protection and control equipment. The addition of data communication layer among the modules of microgrid drives the system towards Smart Grid. Energy management based on IoT can bridge needs of the utility companies operating microgrid and consumers.

Keywords: IoT, microgrid, energy management, sensors and renewable energy

15.1 Introduction

Microgrid is an interconnection of various distributed energy resources, this assures the continuous power supply for a group of interconnected loads. Microgrid operates within the defined power system boundaries

---

Corresponding author: Vikram.Kulkarni@nmims.edu

C. Sharmeela, P. Sivaraman, P. Sanjeevikumar, and Jens Bo Holm-Nielsen (eds.) Microgrid Technologies, (405–428) © 2021 Scrivener Publishing LLC

and will act as a single controllable system [1]. The power generation is done by enabling the small power generating sources. Microgrid assures flexibility and efficiency of power as it is connected to local generating resources as well as utility power grid [2]. The Microgrid is available at various sizes, it can range from individual home to a small city. If the power generation from Microgrid is excess than load then it can be supplied to Utility grid [3, 4].

Microgrid enables power generation from local resources and is distributed to local loads. Includes various minor power generating resources that makes Microgrid highly adaptable and efficient [5]. It is linked to both the local power generating units and the utilities power grid that increases the efficiency of by averting power outages [6]. After meeting the local needs, the extra power from the Microgrid can be sold to the utility. Microgrid capacity may be available at different ranges right from housing estate to municipal regions [7]. The simple block diagram of the Microgrid is as presented in Figure 15.1.

Microgrid is the solution for energy crisis in many developing and developed countries. The advantage from Microgrid is that the transmission losses are greatly reduced as it serves the local generation and local utilization concept. This substantially minimizes the cost of operation and also helps in decreasing the carbon emissions. Thus assures reliable energy with high quality [8]. The Microgrid operates in two modes, firstly Island mode and secondly Grid connected mode, the pictorial representation is as shown in Figure 15.2.

Smart Microgrid (SMG) is a distribution side electric Sub-network that is a combination of the information and data communication technology (ICT), monitoring and control technologies [9]. The block diagram of SMG is as shown in Figure 15.3. The SMG is a network built with the

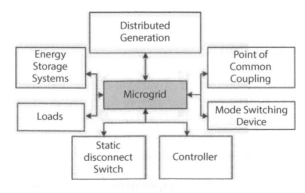

Figure 15.1 The microgrid operational diagram.

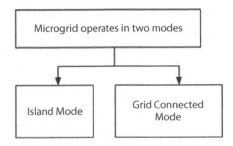

Figure 15.2 The operational modes of the microgrid.

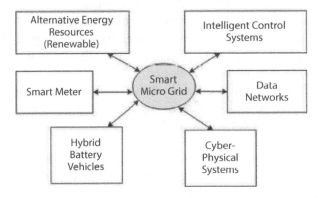

Figure 15.3 The block diagram of the smart micro grid.

combination of complex networking and Power systems. The working, maintenance and integration of technologies of SMG is considered as very complex and will face many technological challenges that must be addressed [10, 11].

SMG is introduced for improving the way of functioning Microgrid. SMG is an integration of the existing Microgrid technology with advanced data communication and controlling technologies [12]. Thus it improves the consumer integration and effective participation for systematic load utilization. With the introduction of SMG the manageability and efficiency of the power system improves [13]. The IoT is considered as resourceful for the efficient integration of the different technologies [14]. IoT is capable of addressing the different interaction issues among the diversified technologies and simplifies the interaction issues in SMGs. The IoT focuses much on the effective integration of physical systems and cyber systems. Thus IoT will make an end-consumer responsible and responsive [15].

SMG is very useful to balance the peak and average load of the power usage, this makes the Smartgrid more stabilized and reliable. SMG reduces the peak load, this accommodates the energy supply to the other loads, making less power generation and reduced transmission losses [16]. To make SMG efficient, the ICT plays key role. Along with the ICT, advanced technologies like smart meters, sensors, actuators, switching devices, telecommunications, and data processing also should work with respect to the load conditions and grid conditions [17].

Some important issues with the above technologies are listed below [18, 19],

1. The control mechanisms proposed should work with lower communication bandwidth requirements.
2. Load prediction at distribution should accurate,
3. The generation of the Renewable energy should be accurate,
4. Advanced energy storage mechanism with negligible switching losses should be developed,
5. With introduction of methods like load shedding, dynamic unit pricing and intelligent demand management helps in shaving the load on the grid.

All the above issues can be systematically resolved by integrating the IoT along with SMG. In the following sections the architecture of IoT and its applications to the SMG topics are elaborated.

15.2 Internet of Things

Internet of Things (IoT) is a multidisciplinary, complex, sensor initiated actuator based high level Embedded system connected with the software based control connected to the with internet and cloud systems [19]. The IoT is very useful in the industries like Smartgrid, Smart Cities, Healthcare and Industrial automation. The research on the IoT related topics has shown significant progress in the last decade [20]. The areas like Large-Scale devices integration, data proliferation and autonomy are very significant in case of IoT [21]. Figure 15.4 represents the block diagram of the IoT-based SMG.

The research in the areas of data analysis is much focused particularly in the streams of science and engineering [22]. The synthesis of the data from the sensing devices for modeling of control systems in real-time systems gives a scope for implementation of modern applications like smart grid, healthcare and smart cities [23]. Bridging of the above technologies in case of the IoT faces significant challenges as follows:

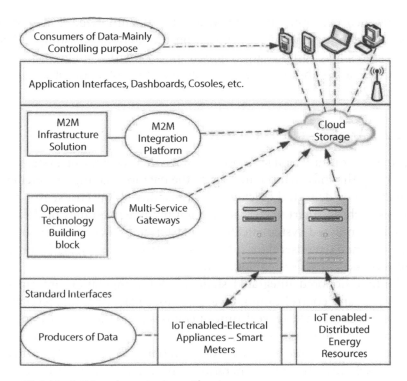

Figure 15.4 The IoT-based smart microgrid system.

15.2.1   Architecture and Design

To devise combination of control management, communication, and computation to fabricate the systematic deployment of IoT, Architecture and project scheme are essential features. We can consider the data communication interface between the power system network and the IoT as an example [24]. The above example includes the different devices permitting heterogeneous systems to be comprised in a plug-in and work manner, and this leads to massive propagation of technology and advancement of the larger cyber systems [25]. Standardized perceptions and architectures that authorize the integrated design and development of IoT are immediately needed. The methodology of the system and the tools required for supporting the system need to be specified [26]. Also for efficient inception of IoT we need to take care of the networking provisions, interoperability between multiple technologies, between hybrid and heterogeneous systems must be done [27].

The issue of cyber security is a very important issue in case of IoT, this will lead to the serious threat for ownership of the device. Hence proper security measures must be defined and the unauthorized access to the device must be restricted [28]. Based on the literature existing updated architectures and systems are required to safeguard confidentiality, reliability, and accessibility of data, in addition to protection of assets and humans [29].

15.2.2   Analysis of Data Science

The integration and collaboration between IoT devices or systems call for sensing the information, managing the data for making the intelligent decisions to be delivered quickly. The availability of low cost sensor based systems such as smart meters shall multiply large volumes of data that should be analyzed systematically in a faster and efficient order so as to make obtained data useful for intelligent controlling, particularly for transient processes in SG system [30, 31].

The time-honored integrated standards for computation, information attainment, and control cannot be applied for todays or future level applications that demand faster real-time operations [32]. The information sensing, communication, processing, accurate analysis, intelligence and control are the main important tasks of all the operations [33]. SG or SMGs involve many stakeholders from the generation to the utilization of power system.

The growing complication and connectivity among components such as smart meters, RES, and end-user components their numbers need reconsidering, this helps in the analysis of design criteria of IoT for SMG. The importance modifications between traditional grid and SMG are presented in Table 15.1.

15.3   Smart Micro Grid: An IoT Perspective

SMG is part of the advanced energy management of SG system which actively supplies the power resources to the part of distribution. SMG acts as IoT such as:

i.   Integrates the IoT-based devices and power generation resources and supplies the values to the simulation models to the make physical systems to work based on the future requirements.

ii. Actively monitors the dynamic connections between the control switches and IoT, ensure the timely responses are carried.

Table 15.1 The variations among traditional grid and smart micro grid.

Traditional grid	Smart micro grid
End user informs when the power is disconnected.	Utility recognizes if power is switched off and switches-on automatically.
Utility recompenses whatsoever it takes to meet peak demand.	Utility controls demand at peak. Reduces cost of utilization.
Wind and Solar based generation has high penetration, hence difficult to manage.	The penetrations occurred by wind energy and solar energy causes no problem for load supply.
Distributed generation cannot be managed firmly.	Can handle distributed generation securely.
Ten percent of power loss in transmission and distribution systems.	The power loss lessened by two percent with the significant decrease in CO_2 emissions & minimizing customer bills.

iii. Administers the parallel computing and distributed operations for analyzing the data and utilizing it to make the important operations.

iv. With the systematic analysis the SMG with IoT operates as a self-learning and self-organizing systems for making efficient future energy needs.

The important need is to calibrate the IoT devices according the needs of the power system requirements as directed by standard organizations and utility companies. Also advanced research focus is needed on the interoperability issues and making them to understand easily makes the system more efficient.

15.4   Literature Survey on the IoT for SMG

CoSSMic was based on the solar energy based SMG is an ICT European project. This project explores regulatory, executive and technical challenges that come across the multidisciplinary areas. This project also initiated the interaction between the end-user and the utility based consumer activity. Also this project has achieved an integration between the IoT and SMG [34].

A simulation based system is proposed based on the CERTS Micro-grid System. This system mainly analyzes the IoT data traffic and bandwidth utilization and proposed QoS based data traffic scheduling [35]. The authors in [36] have presented an introductory survey on different simulation tools, emulators and real-time test beds where the integrated IoT based SMG based can be implemented. The authors in Ref. [37] have implemented a smart micro grid project for the distribution side substation. This is an online monitoring system based on IoT that records pre-fault conditions and post-fault conditions. The authors in Ref. [38] have proposed the communication system protocol based on the wireless transmission system. The estimation of latency and scheduling of the IoT based data is transmitted as per requirements defined by IEEE and NIST. The algorithm proposed is based on Markov process and estimates the accurate dynamic traffic conditions and decreases the packet losses their by increases the reliability of the system.

The authors in Ref. [39] have proposed the two level cyber-attack detection scheme and assures the safety in the data operations. This algorithm will identify the data falsification done by hackers at the level of smart meter. The falsification of the data will lead to the negative effects to both the utilities and consumers. The authors in Ref. [40] have proposed and developed a micro-PMU for better understanding of the faults. The work proposed has developed the situational awareness in the distribution networks too. Based on the better classification techniques the authors have successfully categorized the data that increased the better understanding of the user behavior and has given a provision to utilities to estimate the better load conditions.

It is very interesting to develop a cost effective simulation based model for understanding the basic functioning of the Smart Grid based system. The authors [41] of this paper have developed a Co-Simulation model that was based on data-communication model and power systems. A CPSA based security assessment is developed to assess the vulnerable states. The IoT is now connected with the term IoT devices. The authors in the paper [42] have illustrated the effects of Cyber-attacks on the IoT based SG. According to the authors no single device should be compromised with the Cyber-attacks otherwise the entire system will have to face the adverse effects. The authors have presented an up-to-date knowledge on these aspects. The smartness of SMG lies in the integration of extensive range of physical power assets and information resources for advanced monitoring and control, making distribution infrastructure more intelligent by employing multiple technologies that are connected with energy management for scheduling generation and transmission systems enabling

SG operations for real-time information exchange with power markets allowing for power trade-off. The utilities must work together with different service providers for guaranteeing the systematic functioning of the smart grid. Data exchange with the end users is the significant for the utility to implement the DMS [43].

Most suitable regulatory policies must to be framed for smooth unification of the various technologies, including the energy storage and DER aggregators into the smart grid market. The per-unit cost information should be updated online for every shorter interval (hours or even minutes). The encouraging areas for the service in SG includes anticipating the renewable generation, planning tariff, end-user complaint management, HEMS, setting up and commissioning services, financial management, etc. [44]. The SMG is employing various kinds of advanced sensors, automatic controls and makes use of advanced software by utilizing the actual data to identify and segregate the faults and to rearrange the distribution network to the impact on the end-users and thus becoming itself as a "self-healing grid". The foremost objectives of self-healing grid is to improve the overall reliability and stability of the distribution network, and this can be carried out by the reconfiguration of the reclosers, switches and relays installed on the distribution feeder that instantly segregate the faulted section of the feeder and establishes service again to as many end-users as possible from alternative resources or feeders [45].

It is very important to take the decisions very quickly in order to implement the control actions that are to be implemented within the specified time defined by smart grid committee (generally ranges from few milliseconds to less than 5 min), hence it requires standard communication technology for reconfiguring the system. To achieve this it requires a standard communication with high bandwidth as defined by SGIP based on application, for example AMI requires a bandwidth of 10 to 100 kbps per node/device with an optimal latency between 2 and 15 s in home applications (generally uses Zigbee or PLC communication) and the delay more than this shall affect the DR. The data that is typically aggregated at AMI (aggregation point) is to be communicated to utility center, shall demand a bandwidth requirement of about 500 kbps. The latency requirements of DR can be estimated from as small as 500 ms up to 2 s to minutes. For actual monitoring and control, latency requirements are very low. According to Alcatel the maximum latency requirements for monitoring is 20 ms even though companies like UTC and Avista defines that it is below 200 ms. According to Avista and UTC, the data-rate necessary for DER will be 9.6 to 56 kbps same as AMI [46]. SMG is very important for government and end-users because it is improving the quality of power. But dependency of

SG on computer networks and internet resources is making it more viable to security attacks introducing the privacy problems like data protection of end user information. The cyber-attacks like Stuxnet, Night Dragon, and Duqu were discovered in the applications of SMG. Thus policies and regulations should be made for promoting the best practices and should plan that utility companies strictly adhere to security as important factor and should consider from a holistic point of view [47].

International Electro-technical Commission (IEC) is responsible for standardization of electrical and electronics related fields worldwide. The IEC TC57 commission is employed for defining standards for electric power system management and related data communication for the real-time operations and planning of generation, transmission and distribution and their respective information exchange so as to encourage power market. Table 15.2 gives information about different SMG technology areas and their respective hardware and software systems (IEC. 2010).

15.4.1   Advanced Metering Infrastructure Based on IoT for SMG

SMG is the combination of many intelligent sub-systems having their importance for strengthening the overall performance of grid. AMI is one of the most significant and an essential technology, holding the responsibility for the collection of data and information from different end-user loads and analyses it for utility centers. AMI has become most important tool for implementing the control and command signals for demand side management (DSM) aspects by end users and utility centers. This chapter explains the relationship between the SG and AMI, and enlightens all the important areas of the AMI [48].

AMI is based on two-way communication between end-users and utility companies. The important aspects of AMI are remote location smart meter reading without any errors, identification of problems in the communication network, reporting and analyzing the load usage, reviewing the energy usage and looking for alternative supply instead of completely load shedding.

15.4.2   Sub-Systems of AMI

AMI is a combination of software and hardware co-design that perform a vital role in transmission, distribution and measurement of energy consumption for utility centers. The various sub-systems of AMI include [49]:

Smart Home Based on IoT: Smart homes using the advanced smart sensors and actuators helps to save energy, helps in economic grid operations

Table 15.2 Advanced technologies for implementing SG.

Technology area	Hardware	System and software
Wide area monitoring, planning and control	PMU (Phasor measurement units)	SCADA, WAMS, WAAPCA
ICT (Information & communication technology)	Communication equipment (Broadband wired and wireless access)	CIS (Customer information system), ERP (Enterprise resources planning software).
Renewable energy and distribution generation integration	Battery storage, converter & inverter, Smart control systems, communication devices	SCADA, DMS, GIS.
Transmission Standardization	FACTS, PMU, connected with communication devices.	Automated recovery systems.
End-user side management	Remote controlled distribution generation and storage, Advance Sensors, actuators and transducers	OMS, GIS, DMS.
AMI	Smart meter, Sensors, Actuators, Smart displays, Home gate ways	MDMS
Electric vehicle charging infrastructure	Batteries Storage, Converters, Inverters, smart switches	Smart Power billing, G2V, and V2G methodologies.

and helps in enhancing the efficiency of SMG. With the help of computerized controls the interactive relationship between the consumer, utility and grid operator is established.

Smart Meters Based on IoT: The end-users energy information is collected at regular time intervals and is transmitted through communication networks to the utility and in return command signals and pricing information from utility is conveyed to the end-user. This avoids peak demand rates and helps to balance the energy load in different areas.

Communication Networks: The advanced data communication for AMI involves in the bidirectional flow of information from end-user to utility and vice versa. For this purpose networks like power line communications, broadband over power line, fiber optic communications, public networks or fixed radio frequency networks can used.

Meter Data Acquisition System: The smart meters from individual users in an area transmits the information, to data concentrator units that receives or sends data collected (or command signals) to and from smart meters to data concentrators to utility.

Smart-Meter Data Management System (SDMS): The utility center collects stores and evaluates the metering information.

Smart Devices: With the advent of the advanced electronic devices like modern sensors and smart actuators that are capable of measuring, communicating and controlling are deployed at the end-user premises according to the usage and functionality has instituted smart homes that deal with the energy management through the smart meters. Two important functions of smart meters are: metrology (hardware to measure and control the flow of energy to/from building) and secondly is communication [50].

15.4.3   Every Smart Meter Based on IoT has to Provide the Following Functionalities

Quantitative Measurement: The accurate measurement of data is very important for AMI, the HAN generally depends on Zigbee and PLC for communication of measured data from sensors to the smart meter and vice versa. Hence smart meter should precisely assess and quantify the different topologies, principles and methods.

Control and Calibration: A smart meter needs the standardization owing to dissimilarity in voltage values, sensor tolerances or other system errors, and recompenses the small variations in the system. Smart meters also deliver remote calibration and control ability through communication links.

Communications: The data collected by the smart meter can be communicated to utility via wired or wireless connection. It should also update the information to end-user or receive the commands from utility and can only be possible through standard communication.

Power Management: Generally the sensor based appliances communicate to the smart meter through the sensor networks, so the smart meter should manage the nonelectric metering appliances based on the priorities, whose power management is important for maximizing the service of battery and that to enhance the service of the network.

Display: The DSM starts from the customer response and participation. For enhance quality of AMI system the information supplied from utility should be easily acknowledged to the end user through smart meter display.

Synchronization: Timing synchronization is important for the reliable communication of information to utility to support functions such as evaluation of data and accurate billing. This is mostly desirable in a wireless network that has an asynchronous communication protocol.

15.4.4 Communication

The smart meter is a sensitive and complex device that handles large data between home appliances and utility center without any disruptions. The smart meter data is most trustworthy and the access is limited to few people. The communication standards and strategies are framed to safeguard the data transfer within the network and should be protected. Every smart meter is assigned with a unique identity and also all the appliances associated are also assigned with similar identity so as to secure the cryptographic encryption. The communication network should also support the smart meter even if power outage happens. Communication technologies employed should be economic, should have better transmission ranges, with standard security features, and should provide the required bandwidth [51].

The end user premises enabled by HAN mainly implements AMI and DR. For coordinating smart meter for its monitoring purposes HAN deploys various wireless technologies like Bluetooth, WiFi and Zigbee. Wired solutions may include the usage of Ethernet and PLC. Though wired communication support good data rates and security, Ethernet involves high cabling costs and less flexibility compared to wireless. The usage of PLC for HAN is still in preliminary stages [52].

Neighborhood area networks (NAN) are mainly employed between HAN and Wide area networks (WAN). There are two IEEE standards that are carefully related with NANs. The IEEE standard 802.15.4G mainly deals with out-of-doors environment with relatively low data rates (~less than 100 kbps) and associated with wireless smart metering utility network (SUN). Secondly, IEEE 802.11s is closely related to the network operations like node delivery and route selection of smart grid NANs. The privacy of data must be ensured from cyber-attacks for smart grid NANs [53].

WANs serves for smart grid between the NAN and utility center. WAN employs a high-bandwidth network for providing backhaul communication between different substations, distributed automation and data aggregation points covering for thousands of kilometers apart. Reliability and security are the most important aspects of the WANs. Most of the utility operators like AT &T, Verizon, and Sprint shall make use of private WANs for increased security instead of depending on public networks [54].

15.4.5 Cloud Computing Applications for SMG

Cloud computing (CC) is very important in the handling and managing the huge data. SMG has a great advantages by adapting CC and helps in managing different situations. CC is considered as very important in case of energy and information management. It helps in improving the security measures. Figure 15.5 shows difference functions carried by cloud computing for SMG.

Demand response based decisions is considered as very important for CC as it is based on large scale deployment. The integration of Artificial Intelligence (AI) along with the CC is very much beneficial to smart grid and SMG. AI and CC can make very important decision like integration of DERs, DR, and can able to schedule the prioritization of resources, can support efficient end user options and can strengthen the reliability of entire power systems operation.

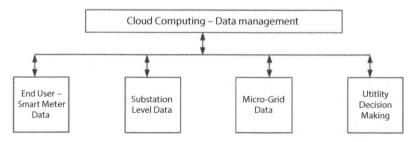

Figure 15.5 The Cloud computing application for IoT-based smart microgrid system.

15.5 Cyber Security Challenges for SMG

The SMG relies on superior computing and intelligent networking technologies for enhancing the reliability of power systems. For achieving this many intelligent devices are interconnected to the communication network, raising the issue for cyber security and should be treated as a high priority issue by SMG community [55]. Cyber Security is defined for specific applications and domains of SMG. Standards are defined for every level of operations by NIST and IEEE like communities for smooth functioning. Table 15.3 shows the cyber security standards for SMG [56].

The power blackout happened at Ukraine in DEC-2015 helps as a demonstrative sample of cyber-attacks append against the Electrical-grid. Hackers acquired control of the human-machine interfaces at three Ukrainian power plants and affected a blackout lasting for about 10 hours and upsetting over 2,25,000 citizens. The post operations conducted by expert teams determined that the corresponding attacks initially targeted susceptible software in the IT operations and detected BlackEnergy malware that routed through internal networks in minutes to affect the working of control systems. Electricity was re-established by detaching the computer systems and resuming the systems manually [57].

Table 15.3 Cyber security standards for SG.

Standard	Description
IEC 62351-1 to 6	Management of Power systems components that deals with information transfer to utility.
NERC CIP-002 and CIP-003 to CIP-009	A cyber-security agenda for the recognizing the cyber-attacks. Assets to support reliable operation of the Bulk Electric System.
IEEE 1686-2007	Standard for Substation level Cyber Security Capabilities.
ISO/IEC 27001:2005	Information security supervision systems—Constraints. Can handle distributed generation securely.
ANSI/ISA-99	Standard for Industrial Automation security.

NIST also recommends the cyber security as a most important factor because smart grid information is very important and it should be secured for efficient operation of SG. For SG applications there are three important cyber security objectives, confidentiality, availability, and integrity. The ideal trade-offs are necessary for balancing the most important aspects of SG information. The standards of communication efficiency and information security should not be compromised in the design of architectures and protocols as both are important considerations for the SG operations. The SG infrastructure incorporates millions of intelligent electronics devices across the network. For secure operations across SG network, the strict implementation for recognizing the device (authentication), its validation and access control becomes more important. For this, it is very important that every node in SG should have standard cryptography functions and should perform better data encryption. Utmost care should be taken to ensure that every node in SG is secure from cyber-attacks, for this, network operations should perform profiling testing regularly [58].

The cyber-attacks on SG communications and security challenges is one of priority research that strengthens the overall performance of SG operations. There are two types of security attacks, self-interested unruly users, and malicious unruly users. Self-interested unruly users try to find more network resources than authentic users by breaching communication protocols [59]. Secondly malicious misbehaving attacks shall persuade disastrous damage to the power supplies results in the power outage, which is prescribed in SG.

The malicious attacks are of three types that affect the accessibility, reliability and confidentiality of SG objectives. The attacks affecting the accessibility is also called as denial-of-service (DoS) attacks, that mainly interrupts, block or alter the SG communications. Attacks' targeting the reliability, aims for unlawful modifications or disrupting of the data communication in the SG. Attacks targeting confidentiality are intentional in obtaining the unauthenticated information from network components of SG [60].

The SG networking identified 'channel jamming' threat at PHY layer of networking protocol [61], this type of attack can cause the wide range of damages to the local area networks affecting the network performance particularly the substations and home areas by delaying the packet delivery time for critical messages to complete DoS. The threat 'Spoofing' is identified at the MAC layer where an attacker can take an advantage of the address fields in MAC frames and can mask that address to attacker node to communicate the fake information to other devices [62].

It is very significant to emphasize on the attacks in relation to the information and communication networks of SG. Signal based detection is carried at PHY layer or MAC layer where a DoS attacker can detect the presence of attack on the basis of received signal strength indicator (RSSI) information, if the RSSI of several data packets is greater than a threshold (that means the receiver node should properly receive them) but the packet decoder at receiver records errors in the received data, the attack detector can raise an alarm in the presence of an attacker [62, 63]. Some jamming resistant protocols include UFHSS, UDSSS and UFH-UDSS [64], DEEJAM [65] and Timing-channel (TC) [66], JADE [67], Packet-based detection solutions can be implemented at any of the layers of SG networking and can compare packet delivery ratio at regular time intervals if significant packet transmission failures are detected then it serves as an alarm for attacks [68].

Based on the above discussion, a secure SG will have to attain the security goals and Data confidentiality. The SG networking applications require the standard solutions designed specifically for this type of network applications that are making the cyber security a challenging research for the future in this area.

15.6 Conclusion

With the advent of modern technologies like ICT (information, communication technology) and IoT the traditional grid is getting transformed to the smart grid with increased advanced automation and becoming hope for future energy needs. The most important factor for considering the SG is efficient energy management with the initiation of distributed generation of energy with the association of renewable energy sources. The demand response is handled logically and peak loads can be shifted or postponed for other times. This way of managing the electricity shall not only increase the stability of the system but also decreases the carbon emissions and protects the environment.

The most important infrastructure for SMG is establishing AMI technology for introducing the bidirectional communication to learn about the electric usage between the end-user and utilities, thereby introducing dynamic tariff with active participation at end-user level. AMI includes the technologies like WAN, NAN, and HAN for communication purposes. Different communication technologies serve different purposes based on the types of applications and work with various data rates.

The interoperability issues among technologies like communication, information and data management need to be critically addressed and there is a lot of scope for future research.

Maintenance of power quality is one of the prime concerns addressed by SG. The smart meter at end-user premises and IoT at distribution systems shall manage the voltage levels and power factor. The smart meters shall record the voltage levels delivered at end user premises and informs the utility center about this information at regular time intervals. With this data utility centers shall optimize the voltage levels thereby increase the power quality of the system. With the better voltage, the appliances at the end-user premises work with higher efficiency.

The power systems situation based operation or event-based operations are not sufficient for controlling and cannot guarantee the system stability. The remote monitoring is the most prime advantage of SMG technology. The remote monitoring devices include distribution transformers, capacitor banks, phasor measurement units, smart meters, etc. The concepts of remote monitoring and wide area monitoring have generated technologies WAMS and WAMPAC in the support of SG for enhanced management of power losses, faults, and disturbances. These monitoring technologies will lower the power outages, increases the power delivery, decreases operational costs and increases the end-user satisfaction.

With the increased use of renewable energy resources like solar energy at end-user premises shall benefit the customer to tackle with real-time pricing for demand response billing, with reduced energy bills and better planning for load usage or peak shifting. Vehicle-to-grid and gird-to-vehicle charging becoming the prime concern with better utilization of energy resources because of their high impact on the power systems, hence high research is to be focused on this area by industry and academia.

The main concerns pertaining utilities like efficient data management, controlling, and communication of information needs to be concerned for efficient SMG operations. The privacy issues related to huge data integrity and confidentiality are the prime concern of SMG needs to be focused upon. The utilization of communication technologies increases the interconnections among various appliances of SMG that introduces the vulnerabilities because of cyber-security and related issues, which need to be addressed by fine-grained technical approaches based on smart grid issues.

Most attacks on IoT devices are external so there is a need to build security inside devices. So most countries have ruled that security should be built in first followed by hardware implementation. IoT Cyber security Alliance has been formed amongst industry leaders and experts in both domains. NIST has brought in new recommendations in line with policies drafted by many countries. As number of IoT devices are rising the number of access points are also increasing providing more access points to the attackers. As devices increase rate of upgrade needs to be increased as well. Need for IoT systems to automatically arm themselves in case of probable attack scenario has arrived. Onboarding of IoT devices—authentication, authorization and encryption have to be standardized.

References

1. Hussain, A., Bui, V.-H., Kim, H.-M., Microgrids as a resilience resource and strategies used by microgrids for enhancing resilience, *Applied Energy*, Volume 240, Pages 56–72, 2019, ISSN 0306-2619.
2. Hossain, A., Pota, H.R., Hossain, Md J., Blaabjerg, F., Evolution of microgrids with converter interfaced generations: Challenges and opportunities, *International Journal of Electrical Power & Energy Systems*, Volume 109, Pages 160–186, 2019, ISSN 0142-0615.
3. Kim, J.-S., So, S.M., Kim, J.-T., Cho, J.-W., Park, H.-J., Jufri, F.H., Jung, J., Microgrids platform: A design and implementation of common platform for seamless microgrids operation, *Electric Power Systems Research*, Volume 167, Pages 21–38, 2019, ISSN 0378-7796.
4. Vikram, K. and Sahoo, S.M., Energy Management System in Smart Grids, in *Smart Grid Systems: Modeling and Control*, AAP, CRC Press, June-2018, ISBN 9781771886253.
5. Michael Zachar, Prodromos Daoutidis, Scheduling and supervisory control for cost effective load shaping of microgrids with flexible demands, *Journal of Process Control*, Volume 74, Pages 202–214, 2019, ISSN 0959-1524.
6. Arboleya, P. *et al.*, Efficient Energy Management in Smart Micro-Grids: ZERO Grid Impact Buildings, in *IEEE Transactions on Smart Grid*, vol. 6, no. 2, pp. 1055–1063, March 2015.
7. Kohn, W., Zabinsky, Z.B. and Nerode, A., A Micro-Grid Distributed Intelligent Control and Management System, in *IEEE Transactions on Smart Grid*, vol. 6, no. 6, pp. 2964–2974, Nov. 2015.
8. Ouammi, A., Dagdougui, H., Dessaint, L. and Sacile, R., Coordinated Model Predictive-Based Power Flows Control in a Cooperative Network of Smart Microgrids, in *IEEE Transactions on Smart Grid*, vol. 6, no. 5, pp. 2233–2244, Sept. 2015.
9. Vikram, K., Sahoo, S.K., Load Aware Channel Estimation and Channel Scheduling for 2.4 GHz Frequency Band Wireless Networks for Smart Grid Applications, Volume 10, Number 4, Pg. No: 879-902, *International Journal on Smart Sensing and Intelligent Systems*. Massey University, New Zealand, Dec-2017.
10. Vikram, K., Sahoo, S.K., A Collaborative Frame Work for Avoiding the Interference in 2.4 GHz Frequency Band Smart Grid Applications Vol. No. 22,

No.1, Pg. No: 48–56, *Electronics Journal. Faculty of Electrical Engineering Banja Luka*, Bosnia and Herzegovina, Europe, June-2018.

11. Vikram, K., Venkata Lakshmi Narayana, K., A survey on Wireless Sensor Networks for Smart grid, *Sensors & Transducers Journal*, ISSN 1726-5479, U.K. vol. 186, Issue 3, pp.18–24, March 2015.

12. Lo, C. and Ansari, N., Decentralized Controls and Communications for Autonomous Distribution Networks in Smart Grid, in *IEEE Transactions on Smart Grid*, vol. 4, no. 1, pp. 66–77, March 2013.

13. Jiang, B. and Fei, Y., Smart Home in Smart Microgrid: A Cost-Effective Energy Ecosystem With Intelligent Hierarchical Agents, in *IEEE Transactions on Smart Grid*, vol. 6, no. 1, pp. 3–13, Jan. 2015.

14. Mohassel, R.R., Fung, A., Mohammadi, F., Raahemifar, K., A survey on Advanced Metering Infrastructure, *International Journal of Electrical Power & Energy Systems*, Volume 63, Pages 473–484, 2014, ISSN 0142-0615.

15. Depuru, S.S.S.R., Wang, L., Devabhaktuni, V., Electricity theft: Overview, issues, prevention and a smart meter based approach to control theft, *Energy Policy*, Volume 39, Issue 2, Pages 1007–1015, 2011, ISSN 0301-4215.

16. Rao, K.L.N., Vikram, K., Matrusri, K., Srikanth, D., Energy Conservation, Generation, Utilization, *International Journal of Advanced Trends in Computer Science and Engineering*, Vol. 3, No.1, Pages: 73–80, *Special Issue of ICETETS 2014*–Held on 24-25 February, 2014 in Malla Reddy Institute of Engineering and Technology, Secunderabad–14, AP, India, 2014, ISSN 2278-3091.

17. Yu, X. and Xue, Y., Smart Grids: A Cyber-Physical Systems Perspective, in *Proceedings of the IEEE*, vol. 104, no. 5, pp. 1058–1070, May 2016.

18. Cheng, L. Yu, T., Jiang, H., Shi, S., Tan, Z. and Zhang, Z., Energy Internet Access Equipment Integrating Cyber-Physical Systems: Concepts, Key Technologies, System Development, and Application Prospects, in *IEEE Access*, vol. 7, pp. 23127–23148, 2019.

19. Tu, H., Xia, Y., Wu, J., Zhou, X., Robustness assessment of cyber-physical systems with weak interdependency, *Physica A: Statistical Mechanics and its Applications*, Volume 522, Pages 9–17, 2019, ISSN 0378-4371.

20. Al-Rubaye, S., Kadhum, E., Ni, Q. and Anpalagan, A., Industrial Internet of Things Driven by SDN Platform for Smart Grid Resiliency, in *IEEE Internet of Things Journal*, vol. 6, no. 1, pp. 267–277, Feb. 2019.

21. Siryani, J., Tanju, B. and Eveleigh, T.J., A Machine Learning Decision-Support System Improves the Internet of Things' Smart Meter Operations, in *IEEE Internet of Things Journal*, vol. 4, no. 4, pp. 1056–1066, Aug. 2017.

22. Ciavarella, S., Joo, J. and Silvestri, S., Managing Contingencies in Smart Grids via the Internet of Things, in *IEEE Transactions on Smart Grid*, vol. 7, no. 4, pp. 2134–2141, July 2016.

23. Saleem, Y., Crespi, N., Rehmani, M.H. and Copeland, R., Internet of Things-Aided Smart Grid: Technologies, Architectures, Applications, Prototypes, and Future Research Directions, in *IEEE Access*, vol. 7, pp. 62962–63003, 2019.

24. Clerc, N., Beyl, I. and Hoeltzel, H., Internet of things services for a smart LV grid management, in *CIRED—Open Access Proceedings Journal*, vol. 2017, no. 1, pp. 1261–1263, 10 2017.
25. Lu, C. *et al.*, Real-Time Wireless Sensor-Actuator Networks for Industrial Cyber-Physical Systems, in *Proceedings of the IEEE*, vol. 104, no. 5, pp. 1013–1024, May 2016.
26. Rana, M.M. and Li, L., Microgrid state estimation and control for smart grid and Internet of Things communication network, in *Electronics Letters*, vol. 51, no. 2, pp. 149–151, 22 1 2015.
27. Chen, S. *et al.*, Internet of Things Based Smart Grids Supported by Intelligent Edge Computing, in *IEEE Access*, vol. 7, pp. 74089–74102, 2019.
28. Burg, Chattopadhyay, A. and Lam, K., Wireless Communication and Security Issues for Cyber–Physical Systems and the Internet-of-Things, in *Proceedings of the IEEE*, vol. 106, no. 1, pp. 38–60, Jan. 2018.
29. Humayed, A., Lin, J., Li, F. and Luo, B., Cyber-Physical Systems Security— A Survey, in *IEEE Internet of Things Journal*, vol. 4, no. 6, pp. 1802–1831, Dec. 2017.
30. Atat, R., Liu, L., Wu, J., Li, G., Ye, C. and Yang, Y., Big Data Meet Cyber-Physical Systems: A Panoramic Survey, in *IEEE Access*, vol. 6, pp. 73603–73636, 2018.
31. Wang, X., Wang, W., Yang, L.T., Liao, S., Yin, D. and Deen, M.J. A Distributed HOSVD Method With Its Incremental Computation for Big Data in Cyber-Physical–Social Systems, in *IEEE Transactions on Computational Social Systems*, vol. 5, no. 2, pp. 481–492, June 2018.
32. Tavčar, J. and Horváth, I., A Review of the Principles of Designing Smart Cyber-Physical Systems for Run-Time Adaptation: Learned Lessons and Open Issues, in *IEEE Transactions on Systems, Man, and Cybernetics: Systems*, vol. 49, no. 1, pp. 145–158, Jan. 2019.
33. Wang, Z., Qin, X., Liu, B. and Zhang, P., Joint Data Sampling and Link Scheduling for Age Minimization in Multihop Cyber-Physical Systems, in *IEEE Wireless Communications Letters*.
34. Amato, A., Aversa, R., Martino, B.D. and Venticinque, S., A Cyber Physical System of Smart Micro-Grids, *2016 19th International Conference on Network-Based Information Systems (NBiS)*, Ostrava, pp. 165–172, 2016.
35. Songxi, Liu *et al.*, Traffic scheduling with sustainable Cyber Physical Systems applying in smart grid, *2016 Seventh International Green and Sustainable Computing Conference (IGSC)*, Hangzhou, pp. 1–6, 2016.
36. Venkataramanan, V., Wang, P., Srivastava, A., Hahn, A. and Govindarasu, M., Interfacing techniques in testbed for cyber-physical security analysis of the electric power grid, *2017 Workshop on Modeling and Simulation of Cyber-Physical Energy Systems (MSCPES)*, Pittsburgh, PA, pp. 1–62017, doi: 10.1109/MSCPES.2017.8064543.
37. Khruslov, L., Rostovikov, M., Shishov, V. and Kireev, S., Cyber-Physical Power System of Micro Smart Grid on the base of transformer substation

7000kVA, *2018 20th International Symposium on Electrical Apparatus and Technologies (SIELA)*, Bourgas, pp. 1–4, 2018.

38. Chunxiao, Q., Wei, C. and Husheng, L., Distributed data traffic scheduling with awareness of dynamics state in cyber physical systems for distributed voltage control in smart micro-grid, *2015 International Conference on Transportation Information and Safety (ICTIS)*, Wuhan, pp. 75–81, 2015.

39. Bhattacharjee, S. and Das, S.K., Detection and Forensics against Stealthy Data Falsification in Smart Metering Infrastructure, in *IEEE Transactions on Dependable and Secure Computing*, Dec-2018.

40. Shahsavari, A., Farajollahi, M., Stewart, E., Cortez, E. and Mohsenian-Rad, H., Situational Awareness in Distribution Grid Using Micro-PMU Data: A Machine Learning Approach, in *IEEE Transactions on Smart Grid*, Feb-2019.

41. Neetesh Saxena, Victor Chukwuka, Leilei Xiong, and Santiago Grijalva. 2017. CPSA: A Cyber-Physical Security Assessment Tool for Situational Awareness in Smart Grid. *In Proceedings of the 2017 Workshop on Cyber-Physical Systems Security and PrivaCy (CPS '17). ACM*, New York, NY, USA, 69-79.

42. Kimani, K., Oduol, V., Langat, K., Cyber security challenges for IoT-based smart grid networks, *International Journal of Critical Infrastructure Protection*, Volume 25, Pages 36–49, 2019, ISSN 1874-5482.

43. Bayindir, Colak, I., Fulli, G., Demirtas, K., Smart grid technologies and applications, *Renewable and Sustainable Energy Reviews*, 66, 499–516, 2016.

44. Shomali, A., Pinkse, J., The consequences of smart grids for the business model of electricity firms, *Journal of Cleaner Production*, 112 (5), 3830–3841, 2016.

45. Emmanuel, M., Rayudu, R., Communication technologies for smart grid applications: A survey, *Journal of Network and Computer Applications*, 76, 133–148, 2016.

46. Mets, K., Ojea, J.A. and Develder, C., Combining Power and Communication Network Simulation for Cost-Effective Smart Grid Analysis, *IEEE Communications Surveys & Tutorials*, 16(3), 1771–1796, 2014.

47. Wang, W., Lu, Z., Cyber security in the Smart Grid: Survey and challenges, *Computer Networks*, 57(5), 1344–1371, 2013.

48. Anda, M., Temmen, J., Smart metering for residential energy efficiency: The use of community based social marketing for behavioural change and smart grid introduction, *Renewable Energy*, 67, 119–127, 2014.

49. Mohassel, R.R., Fung, A., Mohammadi, F., Raahemifar, K., A survey on Advanced Metering Infrastructure, *Electrical Power and Energy Systems*, 63, 473–484, 2014.

50. Uribe-Pérez, N., Hernández, L., de la Vega, D. and Angulo, I., State of the Art and Trends Review of Smart Metering in Electricity Grids, *Applied Sciences*, MDPI, 2016.

51. Ma, R., Chen, H.H., Huang, Y.R. and Meng, W., Smart Grid Communication: Its Challenges and Opportunities, *IEEE Transactions on Smart Grid*, 4(1), 36–46, 2013.

52. Han, D.m. and Lim, J.h., Smart home energy management system using IEEE 802.15.4 and Zigbee, *IEEE Transactions on Consumer Electronics*, 56(3), 1403–1410, 2010.

53. Meng, W., Ma, R. and Chen, H.H., Smart grid neighborhood area networks: a survey, *IEEE Network*, 28(1), 24–32, 2014.

54. Ho, Q.-D., Gao, Y., Rajalingham, G., Le-Ngoc, T., Smart Grid Communications Network (SGCN), *Wireless Communications Networks for the Smart Grid*, Springer, 2014.

55. Ericsson, G.N., Cyber security and power system communication—essential parts of a smart grid infrastructure, *IEEE Transactions on Power Delivery*, 25, 1501–1507, 2010.

56. Expert Group on the Security and Resilience of Communication Networks and Information Systems for Smart Grids, Cyber Security of the Smart Grids, SUMMARY REPORT, *European Commission*, 2012.

57. Cyber-Attack against Ukrainian Critical Infrastructure, Alert (IR-ALERT-H-16-056-01) https://ics-cert.us-cert.gov/alerts/IR-ALERT-H-16-056-01, Feb. 2016.

58. Wang, W., Lu, Z., Cyber security in the Smart Grid: Survey and challenges, *Computer Networks*, 57(5), 1344–1371, 2013.

59. Pelechrinis, K., Yan, G., Eidenbenz, S., Detecting selfish exploitation of carrier sensing in 802.11 networks, in: *Proc. of the IEEE Conference on Computer Communications (INFOCOM '09)*, 2009.

60. Lu, Z., Wang, W., Wang, C., From jammer to gambler: Modeling and detection of jamming attacks against time-critical traffic, in: *Proc. of IEEE INFOCOM 2011*, 2011.

61. Lu, Z., Wang, W. and Wang, C., Modeling, Evaluation and Detection of Jamming Attacks in Time-Critical Wireless Applications, *IEEE Transactions on Mobile Computing*, 3(8), 1746–1759, Aug. 2014.

62. Premaratne, U., Samarabandu, J., Sidhu, T., Beresh, R., Tan, An intrusion detection system for IEC61850 automated substations, *IEEE Transactions on Power Delivery*, 25, 2376–2383, 2010.

63. Lu, Z., Wang, W. and Wang, C., Modeling, Evaluation and Detection of Jamming Attacks in Time-Critical Wireless Applications, *IEEE Transactions on Mobile Computing*, 3(8), 1746–1759, Aug. 2014.

64. Popper, C., Strasser, M., Capkun, S., Anti-jamming broadcast communication using uncoordinated spread spectrum techniques, in: *IEEE Journal on Selected Areas in Communications*, 2010.

65. Wood, A.D., Stankovic, J.A., Zhou, G., DEEJAM: Defeating energy efficient jamming in IEEE 802.15.4-based wireless networks, in: *Proc. of IEEE SECON '07*, 60–69, 2007.

66. Xu, W., Trappe, W., Zhang, Y., Anti-jamming timing channels for wireless networks, in: *Proc. of ACM Conference on Wireless Security (WiSec)*, 203–213, 2008.

67. Richa, A., Scheideler, C., Schmid, S., Zhang, J., A Jamming-Resistant MAC Protocol for Multi-Hop Wireless Networks, *Proceedings 24th International Symposium, DISC 2010,* Cambridge, MA, USA, 179–193, September 13–15, 2010.
68. Toledo, A.L., Wang, X., Robust detection of MAC layer denial-of-service attacks in CSMA/CA wireless networks, *IEEE Transactions on Information Forensics and Security,* 3: 347–358, 2008.

16

Application of Artificial Intelligent Techniques in Microgrid

S. Anbarasi[1], S. Ramesh[2], S. Sivakumar[1] and S. Manimaran[3]*

[1]P.S.R. Engineering College, Sivakasi, Tamilnadu, India
[2]Vel Tech Rangarajan Dr. Sagunthala R&D Institute of Science and Technology, Chennai, Tamilnadu, India
[3]Tech Engineering Services, Chennai, Tamilnadu, India

Abstract

In this book chapter the application of artificial intelligent techniques in micro grid technology is presented. The installation of more renewable energy resources lead to the development of low voltage or medium voltage localized microgrid technologies. The loads in microgrid may operate either in stand-alone manner or integrated with grid. The microgrid system must satisfy the demand with an optimal installation, operation and costing. Hence, intelligent approaches are developed to provide optimal solutions in microgrid technologies.

The main objectives of intelligent approaches in microgrid technologies, for providing optimal control can be segregated into three arenas. The primary objective is to develop an optimal energy management system by proper scheduling of energy sources depends upon the availability of renewable energy resources. The second target is to introduce an intelligent energy storage system with optimal sizing, location and discharging rate of batteries. The third main objective is to provide optimal controlling in microgrid technologies by maintaining the quality of power in order to satisfy the demand without any frequency fluctuations, voltage deviations and harmonics. This book chapter describes all the three sectors where the intelligent approaches effectively utilized in microgrid technology for enhancing the reliability of the system in economic aspects.

Keywords: Artificial intelligence, distributed energy resources, economic power dispatch, energy management system, energy storage system, micro grid system, optimal sizing of batteries, power quality issues

Corresponding author: tsoundarapandiananbu@gmail.com

C. Sharmeela, P. Sivaraman, P. Sanjeevikumar, and Jens Bo Holm-Nielsen (eds.) Microgrid Technologies, (429–450) © 2021 Scrivener Publishing LLC

16.1 Introduction

The population increases every year and it was predicted that an extra population of 2 billion may be added up by 2040. Hence, the generated energy will not be adequate and it may create a huge repercussion on the energy requirement. Consequently, this leads to the existence of secondary energy resources like wind, solar, fuel cell, etc [23]. However, sufficient energy cannot be produced by a single renewable energy resource which turns towards the development of integrated energy resources by Distributed Generation (DG).

To enhance the generation capability a microgrid (MG) concept has been introduced in various research works, where a group of micro energy sources are located near to the load centers for supplying electrical power. The MG systems have proven as trust worthiness for delivering electrical power to the rural areas as well as islands which are unapproachable to the main power grid. Mostly, due to low power generation, the MG system can used as a supplementary for main grid and provides supply to the load during some of the natural disasters like thunderstorms, cyclones, and snow storm and it will be reconnected to the grid again.

In addition both AC and DC generating sources are available in microgrid which has major influence on the development of hybrid type AC/DC microgrid. In this hybrid type AC/DC microgrid need power electronic based devices such as inverters that produce harmonics. While considering these developments in microgrid the maintenance of power management and power quality for the load perturbations are really a challenging task. Hence, the intelligent approaches are developed to manage the effective control actions in micro grid so as to produce balanced generation and load with good quality of power by satisfying the economical constraints.

This book chapter is organized as follows. The introduction of microgrid in Section 16.1 is followed by the problems faced in micro grid in Section 16.2. The application of artificial intelligence (AI) techniques in microgrid technology is described in Section 16.3. This section is further segregated into three subsections in such a way to consolidate the major research works carried out in the AI approach in microgrid arena. The first subsection briefly describes the power quality issues occurred in microgrid and its enhancement with AI approach which is followed by the influence of AI in ESS. The next subsection deals with the contribution of AI in EMS issues. This chapter is ended with conclusion and highlighting the scope for future research works in this arena.

16.2 Main Problems Faced in Microgrid

Advancement needed in the patterns of power generation, transmission, and distribution sectors. The microgrid is a miniature model of main power grid which is an alternative source for appropriate period while interruptions or power failure occurred. The microgrid consists of integrated renewable energy sources of AC or DC type like wind turbine, solar PV module, fuel cell etc. The MG can be situated closer to the generating/distributed area and it can be operated in two modes either connected with power grid or in isolated operating mode.

Microgrid faces lots of real time challenges as mentioned below and it must be taken care for feasible operation of grid:

- The sizing of renewable energy resources should be suitably selected depends upon the load requirements.
- The sizing of energy storage system and the selection of type whether aggregated or distributed must be optimally chosen.
- The mode of operation of microgrid either interconnected with grid or isolated mode should be scheduled properly depends upon the requirements and availability of energy in storage system.
- Economical constraints must be considered.
- The fundamental requirement is to maintain the quality of power which can be achieved through mitigating the harmonics and enhancing the stability by reducing voltage and frequency fluctuations.

The abovementioned contentions should be considered in microgrid system for granting satisfied performances and aimed to reduce the cost of operation. This necessitates the EMS that consents proper control on grid, energy storage system, energy sources and load.

16.3 Application of AI Techniques in Microgrid

The intelligent approaches can be effectively applied in the control of energy management system as well as energy storage system to provide optimal solutions for microgrid problems. The application of intelligent approaches on microgrid system is discussed in detail in the subsequent sections.

16.3.1   Power Quality Issues and Control

16.3.1.1   Preamble of Power Quality Problem

Nowadays microgrids are uprising network model in the deregulated electricity market of electrical power systems. There is a great scope for incorporating renewable energy system (RES) based sources and energy storage systems in microgrids. However, concerns about reliability, power quality (PQ) and security make microgrids as complex systems especially for the period of the islanded operation that considers the impact of RES in to the picture.

So far discussed in Section 16.1 of this chapter, both AC and DC supply sources are incorporated with the distributed generation (DG) units associated with MG which necessitate integration of power electronic converters like rectifiers, choppers and inverters. The increased numbers of inverters interfacing with various DG units and nonlinear loads in microgrids make problems associated with PQ. The layout diagram of a simple microgrid with hybrid AC/DC power sources are depicted in Figure 16.1.

It is necessary for the microgrid to have essential features which would increase the overall performance and they are: emission free, higher energy intensity, higher expandability in terms of generation and transmission of power, easy to integrate RESs, cater to power quality level requirements with respect to non-linear load variations and able to provide consistent and robust systems.

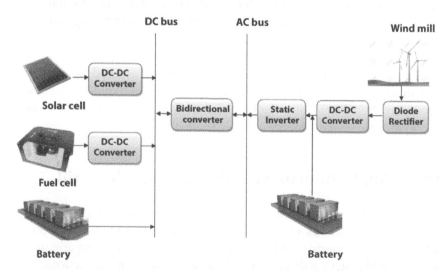

Figure 16.1 Microgrid with hybrid AC/DC power sources and power electronic converters.

16.3.1.2   Issues with Control and Operation of MicroGrid Systems

The important issues that may affect the control and operation of Microgrid are as follows:

1. Voltage fluctuation due to power variations in renewable sources i.e., due to wind and solar energy based sources.
2. Reliability issues with fuel cell as well as micro-turbines which never follow the variations in load level. This can be enhanced by using standby power applications battery or flywheel storage.
3. Non-uniform functioning of reciprocating engine may create unwanted flickering in the voltage and current magnitudes and even it gets amplified due to the response of the power system.

Due to the increased number of DGs in present scenario, the issues related to power quality become more phenomenal and it is highly unavoidable in microgrids. Many of the renewable energy systems need to have power electronic based interfacing with the main grid. In addition, the power electronic based interfaces are very much popular in home usages apparatus (use of power converters), industrial consumers and many other utilities.

In order to mitigate the problems associated with these interfaces, power quality improvement (PQI) equipments are employed. Some of the popular power electronic based PQI devices are active power filter (APF), dynamic voltage restorer (DVR), static synchronous compensator (STATCOM), uninterruptible power supply (UPS) systems, smart impedances, electrical springs (ESs), and multifunctional DGs (MFDGs).

Figure 16.2 represents the development of PQI devices for enhancing various power quality issues in MG systems.

Some of the major power quality issues are given below:

1. Sustained interruptions: Due to the presence of more DGs in microgrid architecture, the possible interruptions are more.
2. Voltage and frequency fluctuations: It represents the deviation of voltage and frequency with respect to the microgrid reference level.
3. Harmonics: Harmonics are the main disturbances that occur in rotating machines and inverters and this is much reduced with recent technologies.
4. Voltage sags: The voltage sag is also one of the power quality issues in which the decrease in voltage occurs for a short duration.

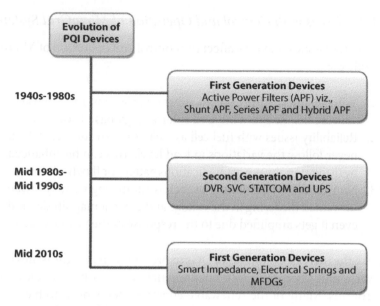

Figure 16.2 Evolution of PQI devices.

16.3.1.3 AI Techniques for Improving Power Quality Issues

Nowadays the microgrid technology is a uprising network model in the deregulated electricity market of electrical power systems. The assimilation of renewable energy resources increases the complexity of power system in terms of energy requirements and power quality issues, during the saved energy is dispatched to loads. This initiates the development of energy management techniques and optimization methodologies for assuring the quality of the electrical power system. The application of AI techniques for some of the power quality problems are described in the following subsections.

A. AI approach to reduce frequency fluctuations:

The frequency is a significant quantity that is having straight relation with the system stability of the system and it must be maintained at its nominal value to validate the dynamic of the energy equilibrium and the electric power generation. Recently, lots of investigations are executed to regulate the frequency by incorporating RESs and ESS. Accordingly, the integrated ESS can provide quick responses as well as improves real power compensation and system reliability particularly for the period of peak deviations in load in interconnected power system. In addition, the ESS provides some of the additional advancements such as load leveling, power factor correction, and black start capability [1]. The effect of ESS on LFC was conferred in many of the recent research works.

Optimal sizing method of vanadium redox flow battery to provide load frequency control in power systems with intermittent renewable generation was proposed by Martínez *et al.* [2]. Ogbonna *et al.* have suggested Neural network based LFC for restructuring power industry [3]. Figure 16.3 shows the two area LFC system with interconnected tie line.

A recent research article presented the improvement of fundamental power quality measures such as voltage and frequency with PSO based optimization methodology for effective tuning of secondary PI controller [4]. The optimal solution is obtained with the PSO algorithm depends upon the position of each particle and its velocity update as shown in Equations (16.1 & 16.2) below

$$V_i^{k+1} = wV_i^k + c_1 \cdot r_1 \left[X_{phest}^k - X_i^k \right] + c_2 \cdot r_2 \left[X_{gbest}^k - X_i^k \right] \quad (16.1)$$

$$X_i^{k+1} = X_i^k + V_i^{k+1} \quad (16.2)$$

Whereas, the first term wV_i^k (16.1) is called the inertia component, the second component $c_1 \cdot r_1 \left[X_{pbest}^k - X_i^k \right]$ is known as cognitive component and the third $c_2 \cdot r_2 \left[X_{gbest}^k - X_i^k \right]$ component is termed as social component.

The fitness function is the minimization of deviation in frequency in any form of conventional error values such as Integral Absolute Error (IAE), Integral Square Error (ISE), Integral Time Square Error (ITSE) or Integral Time Absolute Error (ITAE). The power control circuit of voltage source inverter (VSI) fed DG unit of microgrid is shown in Figure 16.4. The PSO

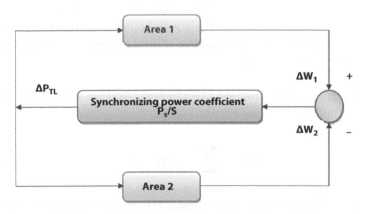

Figure 16.3 Two area LFC system with interconnected tie-line.

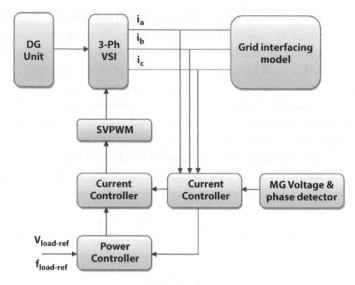

Figure 16.4 Power control circuit of VSI fed DG unit of microgrid.

algorithm was used for effective tuning of gain values of power controller by comparing with the voltage and frequency reference. Hence, the voltage & frequency errors can be controlled that enhances the power quality of system.

Recently, Siti *et al.* have proposed an ideal LFC approach in MG interconnected systems [5]. The main contributions of the LFC control in MG with interconnected RESs and battery systems are stated as follows:

- To manage balanced generation load demand in each area with a suitable optimization algorithm
- Analyzing the effect of ESS on frequency deviation
- The ESS contributes to the control operations that normally inject power at all time of the control prospect for balancing the power system.

The main objective function (16.3) considered for LFC approach is to minimize the Area Control Error

$$ACE_i = \sum_{j=1}^{i} \Delta P_{ij} + B_i \Delta w_i \tag{16.3}$$

Whereas, ACE is the area control error, P is real power transfer, B is synchronizing coefficient in interconnected system. The frequency limits and power transfer limits are taken as the constraints. In Ref. [5] the fmincon, a function included in MatLab's optimization toolbox, is used to optimize the objective function (16.3), taken for consideration. In this review article the optimization approach is used to minimize the frequency deviations between areas and optimize the battery to ensure a balance minimization between the generated power and the required demand of consumers. It was evidently proved that optimal battery control reduces frequency deviation, settling time as well as steady state error.

Another article [6] proposed a fuzzy based PI controller for controlling the frequency in MG power system associated with the fuel cell and electrolyzer hybrid system. In this review article, the stability oriented power quality issues are solved by controlling the frequency fluctuations in microgrid system. A self-organizing fuzzy based PI (FPI) controller was designed in the article so as to control the micro turbine and tie-line power flow more effectively. The frequency fluctuation, f, is directly related to the fluctuation in real power. Hence, threatening in power quality problems linked to the frequency stability constraint can be solved or avoided by satisfying the real power supply–demand balance. The objective function for this problem was formulated as Equation (16.4): Minimize:

$$\text{Change in Active power} =$$
$$(\text{Sum of power generation} - \text{Sum of real power demand}) \to 0$$

$$(16.4)$$

In Equation 16.4, the sum of power generations represents real power generations of wind, solar, fuel cell and micro-turbine power outputs and sum of real power demand represents the housing load as well as electrolyzer system demand for hydrogen energy storage which is subjected to bounded (inequality) constraints of wind, solar, fuel cell, micro-turbine and energy storage system real power outputs that varies between initial and maximum values.

The variation in input power of solar photovoltaic (PV) and wind power (WP) is evaluated through forecasted values. Different standard deviation values such as change in wind output power (dP_{WP}), change in solar output power (dP_{PV}) and change in housing load ($dP_{Housing}$) are considered and are multiplied by choosing an appropriate white noise model thereby the random output fluctuation between the generators and loads can derived for real-time simulation environment.

Fuzzy rule base is developed with 49 rules by considering triangular membership function for change in proportional and integral gain values (ΔK_p and ΔK_I). The changes in the output of fuel cell and electrolyzer are identified to be a first-order system. The tie-line power and the output change of the micro-turbine according to the frequency fluctuation are also represented. The variations due to tie-line power and frequency are observed during the islanding mode as well as interconnecting mode in order to validate the effectiveness of the fuzzy based PI control scheme. It is observed that the proposed control scheme helps to solve power quality issue resulting from frequency fluctuations.

B. AI approach to mitigate Harmonic Distortions:

In recent years, the increasing use of integrated AC and DC renewable resources leads to the usage of power electronic devices which create harmonics. This harmonics damage/degrade the performance of components in the power system network such as electrical machines, transformers and other electronic appliances. The presence of harmonics not only increases the amount of power losses but also affects the quality of power in the power system network.

Kuang-Hsiung et al. have proposed an intelligent control based shunt active power filter system for harmonic compensation in microgrid system. With the help of Elman neural network (ENN), shunt active power filter (APF) control is designed for microgrid system by considering master/slave control algorithm [7]. Here, the master unit in the storage system controls the flow of active and reactive power of microgrid during interconnection mode whereas the levels of voltage as well as frequency (V/f control) during islanded mode.

Due to the presence of number of rectifier and inverter units, non-linear loads, switched mode power supplies the generation of harmonics becoming more phenomenal in the power grid and hence power quality becomes poor in the power system network. Hence, the shunt APF is being suggested and depending on the current or voltage harmonic sources a smooth switching of harmonic compensation with respect to current and voltage is carried out. In addition, the shunt APF can perform switching operation through grid-connected as well as islanding modes to improve the steady-state and transient stability. The ENN based training strategy has been yielded with better shunt APF functioning during harmonics condition.

16.3.2   Energy Storage System With Economic Power Dispatch

16.3.2.1   Energy Storage System in Microgrid

Microgrid is a power system with small scale generation of electric power which incorporates distributed generating units (DG). The main purpose of microgrid is to locate the generation unit near to the utility area. Hence, most of the DG units are inhabited with renewable energy resources. The intermittency of renewable energy resources is the main problem faced during the development of microgrid. Due to this intermittency an inequality occurred between generation and demand.

Hence, to overcome this problem most of the research works were suggested to install energy storage system (ESS) in microgrid [8–10]. This ESS can provide balanced power dispatch by absorbing excessive as well as inadequate power generation in the period of peak generation and peak demand respectively. The ESS can provide uninterrupted and stable power supply by reducing frequency fluctuations during intermittent of renewable energy resources.

The microgrid with ESS and DG units is depicted in Figure 16.5, which consists of a viable building type load and DG units such as combustion diesel power system, PV system as well as wind power system. This DG and ESS are integrated with power grid bidirectional power transmitting capabilities. The uninterruptable power supply of the commercial building load demand is mainly dependent on the DG units, ESS and power grid.

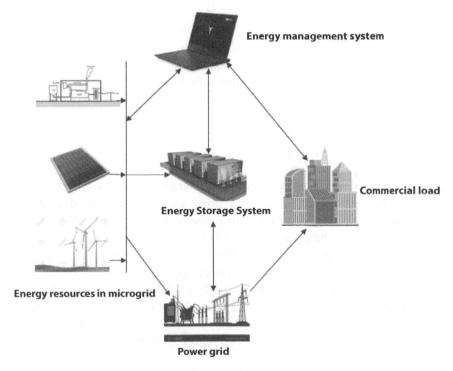

Figure 16.5 Energy storage system in microgrid.

The ESS plays a vital role in microgrid technology in order to provide stable power supply.

To enhance the power quality as well as to regulate the frequency measures, most of the research works are suggested to install Energy storage system with high power density and fast response. In the same way it is also suggested to install Energy storage system with adequate energy density with prolonged discharging time for long-term applications. It is clear from these technologies that the battery energy storage (BES) technology is considered to be very enticing option due to its professional experience and tendency to provide both adequate energy and power densities. The BES units are normally integrated to the microgrid in two ways [11]:

- Aggregated—where individual large BES unit is established near to the utility center
- Distributed—whereas numerous small size BES systems are established in various areas of microgrid.

Another factor to be considered in BES technology is choosing its size. The ratings of power and energy as well as cost of the BES system mainly rely upon its size. When sizing of battery is considered the desired benefits cannot be obtained with an undersized BES system meanwhile the oversized BES system turns to be economically unappealing. Hence, most of the research works are carried out now a day in the arena of optimal selection of sizing of batteries in order to provide economical operation of microgrid system.

16.3.2.2   Need for Intelligent Approaches in Energy Storage System

The integration of non-conventional energy resources in microgrid leads to the fluctuated power generation and it is suggested to install energy storage systems to maintain power system stability. This energy storage system can be charged and discharged for smooth as well as balanced generation of renewable sources. Hence it is essential to manage the energy storage systems with proper approach for maintaining the supply–demand balance during unpredicted load changes. This leads to the development of optimization approach for energy storage systems. Hence, recent research works are now focusing on development of intelligent approaches for microgrids extension problems with ESS systems.

Commonly, the optimization methodologies in microgrid techniques related to energy storage system were proposed mainly for the following aspects:

- Optimal storage capability of BES system to increase the resilience of the commercial structured microgrid and also focusing to reduce its cost of operation.
- Optimal sizing of BES technology with feasible numbers as well as ultimate depth of discharge with good accuracy
- Optimal management of local microgrid resources like dispatchable distributed generating sources, non-conventional distributed generating sources, analyzing optimal energy storage, as well as minimization of operating cost of microgrid
- Optimizing the usage of SMES in such a way to enhance the efficiency than a battery system with less distortions
- Optimal sizing of renewable energy resources and the battery storage system
- Optimal battery energy storage system (BESS) capacity

16.3.2.3 Intelligent Methodologies for ESS Integrated in Microgrid

As per the discussions on Section 16.3.2.2 of this chapter so many intelligent approaches were developed for effective utilization of ESS on microgrid technologies. In this section, a literature review of major research works carried out in microgrid system particularly in the field of developing intelligent approaches to find optimal operating strategies for ESS is described shortly in the following sub sections.

A. Mixed Iterative Adaptive Dynamic Programming (ADP) for Battery Energy Management And Control:
Accordingly, one of such iterative algorithm named mixed iterative Adaptive Dynamic Programming (ADP) algorithm was mainly suggested to find out the optimal battery energy management and control problem in smart residential microgrid systems [12]. The microgrid system proposed in this review article comprises power grid, the load, and the battery system. In this article, the charging/discharging power of battery was designed so as to optimize the EMS of microgrid technology.

The optimization methodology targeted to achieve three operational modes of batteries such as charging mode, idle mode and discharging mode have been considered in this article. In charging mode it was designed such as the power grid will supply power to load as well as battery while the load is low with the constraint of less electricity rate. In idle mode the grid supplies only to load and not to battery. In discharging mode the battery was considered to be act as a grid and supplies to load while the cost of electricity was assumed as high.

The main objective function (16.5) considered in this review article is

$$x_{t+1} = F(x_t, u_t, t) \qquad (16.5)$$

Whereas, t is the time, u is the control sequence and x_t is defined as the system state and it is termed as Equation (16.6)

$$x_t = [x_{1T}, x_{2T}]^T \qquad (16.6)$$

Whereas, $x_{1T} = P_{gt}$ (Power from main grid), $x_{2T} = E_{bt} - E_{bt}^0$ (Storage limit of batteries).

The proposed mixed iterative ADP method gave optimal solution and satisfied all the three modes of operation.

B. CVaR-Based Linear Optimization Programming for Energy Management Scheme in Microgrids:

The main objective focused in this research work is to find the optimal operating sector between the operating cost and grid resilience [13]. This article focused towards optimizing the battery energy management system for improving the resilience of the proposed microgrid with minimum cost of operation. The linear optimization programming problem which incorporates Conditional Value at Risk (CVaR) in the objective function was suggested in this research work. Generally, the microgrid comprises non-conventional energy resources such as PV or wind as fundamental energy resources.

However, these renewable energy resources suffer from uncertainty and unpredictability. Hence, a real-time optimal energy management needed and so an attempt was made in review article and tested for a low voltage microgrid that produces 1MW under its peak demand equipped with PV panel and battery storage system. The research work was carried in such a way to manage the battery storage for increasing the resilience of the commercial building microgrid with minimal operation costs under uncertainty in PV power generation. Hence an objective function was designed which incorporates CVaR as well as the constraints of operation. The constraints of battery energy storage system are elected in such a way that the storage level should be maintained within the limits as well as improving the charging and discharging rates. The main objective function formulated in this problem with linear programming approach is as follows (16.7)

$$J = \left[\sum\nolimits_{T=1}^{N} (Cost_t(P_t, C_t) + (w.CVaR_\beta)) \right] \qquad (16.7)$$

Whereas CVaR also known as average value at risk or mean shortfall for a given confidence level β, P is the power transfer.

In this research problem the energy is optimally managed with CVaR approach. The main constraints are minimizing the cost of operation cost as well as reducing the ambiguity occurs in PV power generation. This will undoubtedly reduce the electricity price. There by, the battery will give supply to the load for a stimulated period of time during the isolation of microgrid system.

B. Optimal Sizing of Batteries in Microgrids:

Recent research works in microgrid are mainly focused on energy storage system and it must be optimally sized to ensure reliable, resilient, and cost effective operation. Commonly, in energy storage system lots of research works were mainly focused to find optimal solutions on battery sizing, optimal locations of batteries, optimal scheduling of batteries and optimal depth of discharge of batteries in order to produce economic power dispatch.

Figure 16.6 clearly illustrates the intelligent approaches carried out in energy storage system. These intelligent approaches receives BES information such as capacity, charging and discharging rate of batteries as well as the data of renewable energy resources in microgrid as input source and produces optimal outputs as depicted in Figure 16.6 depends on the objective function selected for the problem.

Alsaidan et al. have discussed mixed-integer linear programming based intelligent approach to find optimal sizing of batteries in microgrid in order to reduce its operation cost and improve its supply reliability [14]. In this article the two types of battery connecting technology i.e., aggregated or distributed are highlighted. These two connections are discussed in Section 16.3.2.1 of this chapter. The optimal number of batteries connected in microgrid while the distributed type of battery technology was also discussed in this review article.

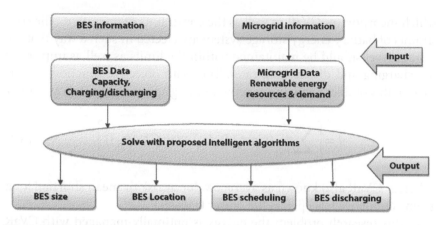

Figure 16.6 Intelligent approaches in energy storage system in microgrid.

The optimal capacity of battery and the sizing of renewable energy resources were also predicted by battery sizing algorithm and source sizing algorithm in recent research article [15]. This review article mainly targeted to maximize the reliability and minimizing the system operational cost. Accordingly, for thousand different combinations of solar PV and wind turbine power rating the battery energy storage system were calculated using battery sizing algorithm and the economical combinations were chosen.

Another approach named mix-mode' energy management strategy was also proposed to find the optimal sizing of battery [16]. In this approach the optimal battery sizing in kWh was evaluated using the particle swarm optimization (PSO) technique. This article evidently proved that the size of the BES has great influence on the operating cost of the microgrid.

16.3.3 Energy Management System

16.3.3.1 Description of Energy Management System

The effective distribution of energy within the microgrid system is another important issue to be addressed. Energy management is a process of organizing, supervising and controlling the flow of electrical energy between generation, transmission and distribution areas. The energy management can performed at various control centers called 'System Control Centers' by means of a computational control module known as Energy Management System (EMS). The main aim of this EMS is to provide generation-load balance in an economical way. If more numbers of renewable energy sources are connected in microgrid, it requires proper control

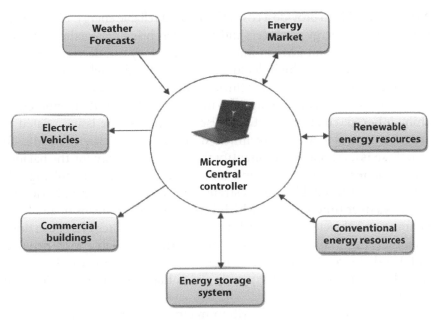

Figure 16.7 Energy management with microgrid central controller.

strategies to meet the energy between the renewable sources and microgrid which necessitates the development of EMS. The energy management with microgrid central controller is depicted in Figure 16.7. In microgrid, the energy management are often done by two methods namely,

- Generation Side management
- Demand side management.

Due to the complexity involved in relaxing consumer demands, the generation side management is always preferred [17]. However, the demand side management also motivates the consumers to decrease their electricity consumption.

16.3.3.2   EMS and Distributed Energy Resources

In microgrid, there are small Distributed Energy Resources (DERs) that consist of Small turbo-alternators, solar PV systems, wind generators, energy storage systems such as Fuel cells, batteries and hydrogen based energy storage system. The penetration of DERs in microgrid and the opening of energy markets nowadays create enormous challenges in design and planning aspects of grid connected system [18]. This leads to the development of

EMS that can able to provide a cost-effective and reliable energy. EMS creates the platform for energy producers and consumers bringing together [19]. The existence of DERs and EMS in microgrid technology can decrease the consumption of fossil fuels, high fluctuating Demand and Rescheduling investment for erection of transmission lines and distribution feeders.

In spite of various advantages of microgrids, the DERs in microgrid exhibit inherent challenges. DERs presence can raise the issues related to cost-effectiveness as well as technical difficulties in microgrid's EMS. To solve these issues, one has to identify the suitable strategy for the balance between generation of power and load demand. In general, solving this problem requires suitable control strategy between generator and load that minimizes over time schedule which is represented by means of an objective function subjected to constraints [17]. The load strategy has been done by considering available status (on/off) of the curtailable load demand (CLD) and the reschedule load management (RLM). This can be implemented for controlling the frequency and voltage variations in microgrid during actual scenario.

The major performance of EMS in microgrid technology is scheduled as follows:

- Integrating the energy storage system with the batteries charged with maximum level when electricity prices are high.
- Disconnecting the battery when it is not sufficiently charged when low electricity prices.
- Implementing effective control on DERs when the production cost of electricity decreases.
- Applying CLD based load strategy during unbalance between generation and load during higher electricity costs.
- To ensure high reliability, power quality, efficiency as well as secured operation of power system.
- Ability to perform switching operation in sources, batteries, converters, controllers, load with respect to the microgrid.

16.3.3.3   Intelligent Energy Management for a Microgrid

This section addresses a case study related to the development of intelligent approaches for EMS. With the help of AI techniques associated by conventional multi-objective optimization, the generalized problem formulation for an intelligent energy management of a microgrid is developed. By using artificial neural network, the solar generation, wind generation and load demand can be predicted well in advance. The solar generation is predicted ahead of 24 h whereas the wind and load demand are predicted 1 h ahead. The efficiency of microgrid be influenced by the battery on/off status which seems to be difficult in applied mathematics based optimization design [20].

The problem of energy management in microgrid is formulated with the generation scheduling as the fixed objective function whereas the battery/energy storage device functioning are not considered since the battery has the opportunity to charge from the grid/generation source. In general, microgrid functions in grid connecting mode of operation during normal condition so that the power can be either imported or exported from or to the grid. Whenever there is a disturbance due to power quality events, open circuits, short circuit faults, line outage and generator outage, the microgrid isolates load and will try to operate in islanding mode of operation till the disturbances doesn't create any harmful to the existing part of grid otherwise the location can be sectionalized using sectionalizing circuit breaker (SCB) [21].

In microgrid model, inverters play a key role in interconnecting DC based DERs with the AC power side. The PQ inverter and voltage source inverter are the two important inverter control schemes available to operate an inverter within the microgrid. Basically, PQ based inverter control scheme contributes necessary real and reactive powers as set values whereas the voltage source inverter (VSI) control scheme interfaces the battery and microgrid during islanding mode [22]. The objective functions for EMS in microgrid for any kind of intelligent approaches are mainly formulated by considering the operational cost which incorporates fuel consumption cost, actual electricity cost, purchasing cost and electricity selling price as well as output power with emission factor (16.8 & 16.9).

$$(X) = \sum_{i=1}^{N} F\,C_i(X_i) + X_b.X_B - X_s.X_S + M_i(P_i) \qquad (16.8)$$

$$f_2(X) = \sum_{i=1}^{n}\sum_{j=1}^{n} (EF_{ij}X_i) + GEF.X_B - (GEF - MGEF).X_s \qquad (16.9)$$

Where,

  X_i = Output power of unit i in kWH

FC_i = Fuel Consumption Cost of unit i in dollars per kWH
X_b = Actual electricity in dollars per kWH
X_B = Purchased electricity
X_s = Actual hour electricity selling price in dollars per kWH
X_S = Sold electricity in kWH
M_i = Maintenance cost of ith unit dollars per kWH
EF_{ij} = Emission factor of ith unit pounds per kWH, Where j is
     the emission type
MGEF = Microgrid average emission factor in pounds per kWH
GEF = main grid average emission factor in pounds per kW.

The fuel consumption FC_i for the controllable DG is expressed in Equation (16.10)

$$FC_i(X_i) = C_i \frac{P_i}{\eta_i} \qquad (16.10)$$

Whereas, C_i is the fuel price and η_i is the efficiency rate of ith unit. The intelligent approaches are simulated with the objective functions to get the optimal result. In similar way, various objective functions can be framed depends upon the requirements of EMS unit and optimal performance could be obtained in microgrid.

16.4   Conclusion

This book chapter mainly focused on the artificial intelligent approaches in microgrid technologies. The fundamental needs of microgrid system is to ensure the security of electricity supply, enhance the flexibility in operation and control, minimize installation and operating cost, mitigate power quality issues and proper scheduling and sizing of renewable sources integration. The purpose of this chapter is to give a research platform for the researchers in recent microgrid arena. The description of microgrid system and the problems faced while integrating the renewable energy sources and the need for developing intelligent algorithms are justified in this article.

In most of the recent research articles the AI approach is mainly used in three essential sectors of microgrid technologies as enhancing power quality, optimal maintenance of energy storage system and optimal control of energy management system. Hence the major consideration in this book chapter is given to these three sectors. Each one of them is construed with case studies in literature which will persuade more research developments in microgrid technology.

In recent scenario, more number of artificial intelligent algorithms is developed. However, very few of them are reported in microgrid research sector. The optimal scheduling of generating sources have been documented more in literature survey, in the same way optimal scheduling of loads can also be developed. Hence, there is a wide opening for the researchers for their commencement in microgrid technology.

References

1. Tungadio, D.H., Bansal, R.C. and Siti, M.W., Optimal control of active power of two micro-grids interconnected with two AC tie-lines, *Electric Power Components and Systems*, **45**(19): p. 2188–2199, 2017.
2. Martínez, M., Molina, M.G. and Mercado, P.E., Optimal sizing method of vanadium redox flow battery to provide load frequency control in power systems with intermittent renewable generation, *IET Renewable Power Generation*, **11**(14): p. 1804–1811, 2017.
3. Ogbonna, B. and Ndubisi, S., Neural network based load frequency control for restructuring power industry, *Nigerian Journal of Technology*, **31**(1): p. 40–47, 2012.
4. Al-Saedi, W., *et al.*, PSO algorithm for an optimal power controller in a microgrid, in *IOP Conference Series: Earth and Environmental Science*, IOP Publishing, 2017.
5. Siti, M.W., *et al.*, Optimal frequency deviations control in microgrid interconnected systems, *IET Renewable Power Generation*, **13**(13): p. 2376–2382, 2019.
6. Li, X., Song, Y.-J. and Han, S.-B., Frequency control in micro-grid power system combined with electrolyzer system and fuzzy PI controller, *Journal of Power Sources*, **180**(1): p. 468–475, 2008.
7. Tan, K.-H., *et al.*, Intelligent controlled shunt active power filter for voltage and current harmonic compensation in microgrid system, *Journal of the Chinese Institute of Engineers*, **41**(4): p. 269–285, 2018.
8. Aditya, S. and Das, D., Application of battery energy storage system to load frequency control of an isolated power system, *International Journal of Energy Research*, **23**(3): p. 247–258, 1999.
9. He, G., *et al.*, Cooperation of wind power and battery storage to provide frequency regulation in power markets, *IEEE Transactions on Power Systems*, **32**(5): p. 3559–3568, 2016.
10. Li, X., Hui, D. and Lai, X., Battery energy storage station (BESS)-based smoothing control of photovoltaic (PV) and wind power generation

fluctuations, *IEEE Transactions on Sustainable Energy*, **4**(2): p. 464–473, 2013.

11. Tan, X., Li, Q. and Wang, H., Advances and trends of energy storage technology in microgrid, *International Journal of Electrical Power & Energy Systems*, **44**(1): p. 179–191, 2013.

12. Wei, Q., *et al.*, Mixed iterative adaptive dynamic programming for optimal battery energy control in smart residential microgrids, *IEEE Transactions on Industrial Electronics*, **64**(5): p. 4110–4120, 2017.

13. Tavakoli, M., *et al.*, CVaR-based energy management scheme for optimal resilience and operational cost in commercial building microgrids, *International Journal of Electrical Power & Energy Systems*, **100**: p. 1–9, 2018.

14. Alsaidan, I., Khodaei, A. and Gao, W., A comprehensive battery energy storage optimal sizing model for microgrid applications, *IEEE Transactions on Power Systems*, **33**(4): p. 3968–3980, 2017.

15. Akram, U., Khalid, M. and Shafiq, S., Optimal sizing of a wind/solar/battery hybrid grid-connected microgrid system, *IET Renewable Power Generation*, **12**(1): p. 72–80, 2017.

16. Sukumar, S., *et al.*, Mix-mode energy management strategy and battery sizing for economic operation of grid-tied microgrid, *Energy*, **118**: p. 1322–1333, 2017.

17. Marzband, M., *et al.*, Experimental evaluation of a real time energy management system for stand-alone microgrids in day-ahead markets, *Applied Energy*, **106**: p. 365–376, 2013.

18. Chaouachi, A., *et al.*, Multiobjective intelligent energy management for a microgrid, *IEEE Transactions on Industrial Electronics*, **60**(4): p. 1688–1699, 2012.

19. Tabar, V.S., Jirdehi, M.A. and Hemmati, R., Energy management in microgrid based on the multi objective stochastic programming incorporating portable renewable energy resource as demand response option, *Energy*, **118**: p. 827–839, 2017.

20. Safamehr, H. and Rahimi-Kian, A., A cost-efficient and reliable energy management of a micro-grid using intelligent demand-response program, *Energy*, **91**: p. 283–293, 2015.

21. Kyriakarakos, G., *et al.*, A fuzzy logic energy management system for polygeneration microgrids, *Renewable Energy*, **41**: p. 315–327, 2012.

22. Eseye, A.T., *et al.*, Optimal energy management strategy for an isolated industrial microgrid using a modified particle swarm optimization, in *2016 IEEE international conference on power and renewable energy (ICPRE)*, IEEE, 2016.

23. Sharmeela, C., Sivaraman, P. and Balaji, S., *Design of Hybrid DC Mini Grid for Educational Institution: Case Study*, Lecture Notes in Electrical Engineering, 580: p. 125–134, 2020.

17

Mathematical Modeling for Green Energy Smart Meter for Microgrids

Moloko Joseph Sebake[1*] and Meera K. Joseph[2]

[1]Armscor, South Africa
[2]IEEE Computer Society, South Africa

Abstract

Although most smart meters around the world, are designed to measure electrical energy from a power utility provider or national grid, smart meters can also be designed to measure electrical energy from renewable energy sources such as solar power generation in microgrids. This paper represents a mathematical model that can be used when designing and building a smart meter, based on a microcontroller, for solar energy management (monitoring and control). These types of smart meters can be called Green Energy microgrid smart meters because they are designed to measure and report energy from energy sources that do not emit greenhouse gases. The smart meter design is based on a PIC16F877A microcontroller, and the design includes a MPPT solar charger controller, energy storage capacity, LCD display and mobile phone to manage the smart meter via Wi-Fi and Global System for Mobile communication (GSM) technology. To test the functionality of the model, a microcontroller C program was written, the circuit was designed and simulated with Proteus ISIS 7 software where a 120 Watt DC motor was used as a load and the results proved that the developed mathematical model is valid.

Keywords: Green energy, MPPT solar charge controller, mathematical model, smart meter for microgrids

17.1 Introduction

Few papers have been written around the design of a microgrid and smart metering system of a microgrid such as the paper titled: "Smart

---

Corresponding author: logosjm@gmail.com

C. Sharmeela, P. Sivaraman, P. Sanjeevikumar, and Jens Bo Holm-Nielsen (eds.) Microgrid Technologies, (451–470) © 2021 Scrivener Publishing LLC

Metering System for Microgrids" [10] but literature survey indicated that a simple integrated mathematical model that can be used, without going through multiple mathematical formulas, to compute energy consumed by the load when designing a microcontroller based smart meter was never proposed. This proposed mathematical model, to compute energy can be applied when developing a source code that runs inside the microcontroller. The modules that are used in the microcontroller are analogue to digital converter (ADC) module, which is used to convert current and voltages to digital values, and timer module, which is used to provide time. Before the proposed mathematical model can be presented, a theoretical background of the concepts such as smart meter, green energy, microgrid, MPPT charge controller are provided. The smart meter for the proposed model must be developed to fulfil the following functions:

- Measure DC voltage and DC current from the solar panel and make the readings available to a mobile phone.
- To control the electrical charge to prevent the solar panels from overcharging the battery.
- To display the solar panel voltage, current and load voltage on the LCD display, and make the readings available to a mobile phone.
- To enable the user via a mobile phone, to switch the load on and off.
- To be controlled via Wi-Fi when the user is within Wi-Fi proximity.
- To be controlled via GSM when the user is outside Wi-Fi proximity.
- Store the electrical energy from the solar locally in the battery banks.

17.1.1   Smart Meter

A smart meter is electricity meter like traditional electricity meter that has a communication module using technologies like GSM, 3G, PLC, ZigBee, LTE, optical fibre, Wi-Fi, etc. to communicate the energy consumption to the user. It is smart in the sense that it can be managed from anywhere at any time. It can monitor and notify the user of the energy usage anywhere and anytime in real time.

17.1.2 Green Energy

Green energy is energy that is produced from sources that do not emit greenhouse gases such as solar energy, hydro-power, wind power, biomass, landfill gas, geothermal, etc. Green energy is sometimes called renewable or sustainable energy because it is produced from natural sources such as wind, water and sunlight. It is far more environmentally friendly than other sources of energy such as coal combustion that emits greenhouse gases. In this report, our design is based on the solar type of energy.

17.1.3 Microgrid

Microgrids are localized energy grids that can operate independently from the national energy grid. Microgrids have the ability to strengthen grids resilience and mitigate grid disturbances as well as function as a grid resource for faster system response and recovery [2]. They can be powered from renewable energy sources like solar, wind, hydro, etc. Figure 17.1 below illustrates a microgrid power system powered from 60 kW Micro Gas Turbine solar

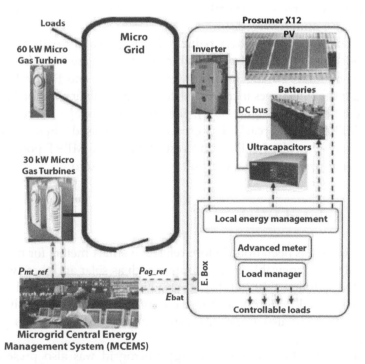

Figure 17.1 Example of microgrid system [6].

energy and 30 kW Micro Gas Turbine solar energy. This microgrid can also be managed centrally using a Microgrid Central Energy Management (MCEMS).

17.1.4   MPPT Solar Charge Controller

MPPT stands for, Maximum Power Point Tracking, which is based on maximum power transfer theorem. The theorem states, for a maximum power to be transferred to the load, the source impedance must be equal to the load impedance. By changing the duty cycle the load impedance is matched with the source impedance to extract maximum power from the solar panel [7].

It might result in the wasted power if a solar panel or an array of solar panels without a solar charge controller that can perform Maximum Power Point Tracking (MPPT) is used [1]. The solar charge controller can be designed based on MPPT algorithm in order to attain higher energy conversion efficiency from the solar panel.

MPPT is a type of solar charge controller that is based on MPPT control technique. Solar charge controller is designed to control the amount of charge transferred to the battery to prevent the battery from being overcharged and undercharged.

Overcharging of the battery reduces the lifespan of the battery. There are two MPPT algorithms that are available today, which are Perturb & Observe and Incremental Conductance [1], are mostly used and Figure 17.2 is the flowchart that illustrates incremental conductance algorithm for MPPT.

In the flowchart (Figure 17.2), the operating voltage is kept constant when MPPT point is reached, decreased and increased when the power is above and below the MPPT point respectively. The MPPT point is when change in power over change in voltage is equal to zero.

17.2   Related Work

Similar work has been done before related to smart meters for microgrids powered from renewable energy sources such as solar and these works are presented as follows. In Ref. [8] other author's paper, presented a microcontroller based design of a charge controller for PV (Photovoltaic) systems. A paper was also proposed on an example of a smart metering system for microgrid [9].

Smart meter for renewable energy microgrid was also presented by researchers from Cape Peninsula University of Technology [10]. Vikas and Bhardwaj also presented a work done on the implementation of

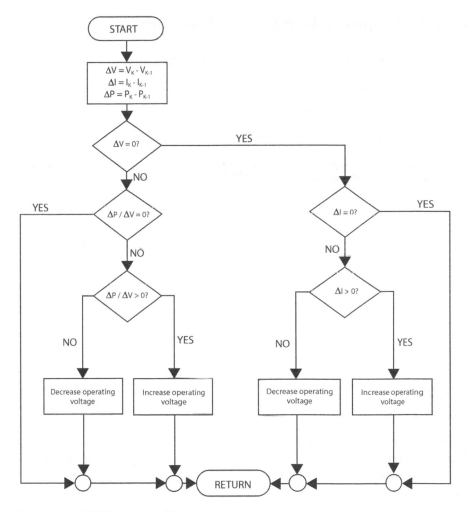

Figure 17.2 MPPT algorithm [1].

advanced energy meter using PIC microcontroller [11]. "A Single Phase Microcontroller Based Energy Meter" [12] is also a work done around the development of the energy meter.

In summary, an integrated microcontroller based mathematical model that can be used to calculate electrical energy consumed by the load in a microgrid environment was never proposed by any of the papers presented above. A novel approach was for developing and testing a new generation smart meter for domestic use is illustrated in [13]. As in Ref. [19] other authors have provided measures to control meter bypassing and tampering.

17.3   Proposed Technical Architecture

17.3.1   Green Energy Smart Meter Architecture

Figure 17.3 shows the technical architecture for a green energy smart meter for solar powered microgrids.

A. Green Energy smart meter architecture

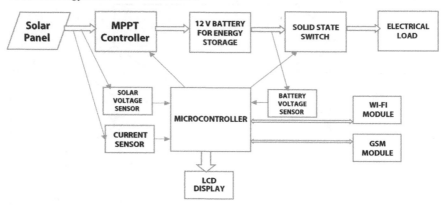

Figure 17.3 Technical architecture for a green energy smart meter for solar powered microgrids.

17.3.2   Solar Panel

Solar panels are used to collect solar energy from the sun, and convert it to electrical energy. For demonstration purposes, a solar panel with following characteristics and specifications can be used:

- Open circuit voltage (V_{OC})   21.1 V
- Short circuit current (I_{sc})   0.73 A
- Optimum operating voltage   18 V
- Optimum operating current   0.56 A

From the electrical characteristics of the solar panel stated above, the power output of the grounded solar power supply system can be increased by adding and connecting more solar panels either in series or parallel.

17.3.3   MPPT Controller

The MPPT solar charge controller is designed using BUCK converter and PIC (Peripheral Interface Controller) microcontroller. The PIC microcontroller is used to generate PWM (Pulse Width Modulation) signal that is used to control the output voltage of the buck converter. The control of the buck converter output voltage is achieved by varying the duty cycle of the PWM signal.

17.3.4   Battery

A 12 V battery of charge of 1,200 Ah can be used in this design for storing electrical energy from the solar panel. The battery is regarded fully charged if the DC voltage across it is between 12 and 13.8 V.

17.3.5   Solid-State Switch

The solid-state switch can be designed using the NPN MOSFET (Metal-Oxide-Semiconductor Field Effect Transistor) and be controlled from a digital pin of the microcontroller. The switch will be used to cuff the load when then energy units have run out.

17.3.6   Electrical Load

The electrical load can be a DC load like an inverter (12 Vdc to 230 Vac), DC (Direct Current) to AC (Alternating Current) converter, 5–9 V voltage regulator or dc load between 0 and 12 V.

17.3.7   Solar Voltage Sensor

Since the solar panel's maximum operating voltage is above 5 V DC and most microcontrollers take the maximum DC voltage of about 5 V on their analogue pins, then the voltage divider is used to stepdown solar voltage to maximum of 5 V. Below is the formula that is used to calculate the voltage to be fed into the microcontroller.

$$V\mu c = Vsolar * \frac{R1}{R1 + R2}$$

$V_{\mu c}$ is the maximum voltage to be fed to the analogue of the microcontroller and it is equal to 5 V

V_{solar} is maximum voltage from the solar panel, R1 is the resistor between the pin of the microcontroller and ground and R2 is the resistor between the pin of the microcontroller and the Vcc of the solar panel.

17.3.8 Batter Voltage Sensor

Since 12 V battery reaches the peak at 13.8 V and the microcontrollers normally take the maximum DC voltage of about 5 V on the analogue pin, the voltage divider is then required to stepdown battery voltage to a maximum of 5 V. Below is the formula that is used to calculate the voltage to be fed into the microcontroller.

$$V\mu c = Vbattery * \frac{R3}{R4 + R3}$$

$V_{\mu c}$ is the maximum voltage to be fed to the analogue of the microcontroller $V_{battery}$ is maximum voltage from the battery, R3 is the resistor between the pin of the microcontroller and ground and R4 is the resistor between the pin of the microcontroller and the Vcc of the battery.

17.3.9 Current Sensor

The current sensor that can be used to sense the amount of current from the solar panel is ACS712 current sensor. ACS712 is 5A, 20 A or 30A current sensor with a typical sensitivity of 100, 185, 166 mV/A [5].

17.3.10 Microcontroller

Microcontroller is the brain of the green energy smart meter. It reads and computes the voltage from the solar panel, current from the solar panel, voltage from the battery. It controls the solar charge controller by generating PWM signal, it displays the measurements on the LCD display, and it sends data and receives data to and from the GSM module and Wi-Fi through USART (Universal Synchronous Asynchronous Receiver Transmitter) protocol. The microcontroller used must have at least PMW module, ADC module, GPIO ports for LCD interfacing and solid-state switch control.

17.3.11 Wi-Fi Module

Wi-Fi module interfaces with the microcontroller and enables the smart meter to be managed in the Home Area Network. It also enable the smart meter to be connected to internet through Wi-Fi technology in the Wi-Fi network.

17.3.12 GSM/3G/LTE Module

GSM module interfaces with the microcontroller and enables the smart meter to be managed in the Wide Area Network with the mobile phone where there is GSM, 3G or LTE coverage. GSM modules like SIM900, SIM800, 5218, 808, 5210, etc. can be used.

17.3.13 LCD Display

LCD display is used to display the voltage that comes from the solar, voltage of the battery and the current of the solar panel. A 16-character and 2-line character LCD display can be used. The first line and the second line can be used to display energy in kWh and power in Watts respectively.

17.4 Proposed Mathematical Model

In Ref. [14] authors proposed Adaptive-Smart Energy Management Tool (A-SEM) for smart home and in Ref. [15] authors present results showing energy saving levels using A-SEM tool. It has a potential to be an affordable smart energy management system in future smart homes. In Ref. [16] authors constructed a discrete time Markov chain, whereby the states are defined by the numbers of on-state meters and request-holding meters, deriving some performance measures. The mathematical model that we are developing in this paper is to be used when computing the energy consumed by the load so that it can be displayed on the LCD display, monitored remotely through a communication technology such as fibre, WI-FI, GSM, 3G, etc. The model starts with a simple equation for energy as below and that is the energy consumed by the load connected to a micro grid.

$$E = \text{Power} \times \text{Time} \tag{17.1}$$

$$\text{or } E = \int_0^T p \, dt$$

E is the actual energy consumed and it is measured in Joules (J). Power is the actual power consumed by the load and it is measured in Watts (W). Time is in seconds (s).

Since the solar panels produce a DC (Direct Current) voltage and DC current, Power is computed using the equation below:

$$P = VI \qquad (17.2)$$

Power is defined as the rate at which energy is consumed. V is the average voltage supplied to the load and I is the average current drawn by the load and combining Equations (17.1) and (17.2), Energy (E) is as below:

$$E = VI \times Time \qquad (17.3)$$

Then V and I can be computed as follows:

$$V = \frac{ADC\,Voltage\,Value * ADC\,sensitivity}{Volt\,sensor\,sensitivity} \qquad (17.4)$$

$$I = \frac{ADC\,Current\,Value * ADC\,sensitivity}{current\,sensor\,sensitivity} \qquad (17.5)$$

Finally, the energy consumed by the load in Joules is calculated as

$$E = \frac{\textbf{ADC Voltage Value} * \textbf{ADC sensitivity}}{\textbf{Volt sensor sensitivity}}$$
$$\times \frac{\textbf{ADC Current Value} * \textbf{ADC sensitivity}}{\textbf{current sensor sensitivity}} \times \textbf{Times(s)} \qquad (17.6)$$

Time is the product of the time delay between the counts of the timer and the value of the timer. It is computed as in the formula in Equation (17.7).

$$Time = Td * Tv \qquad (17.7)$$

Where T_d is the time delay between the counts of the timer and T_v is counter value of the timer. Converting Energy from Joules to kWh and that is accomplished by dividing Joules by a factor of 3,600,000.

$$E = \frac{\text{ADC Value} * \text{ADC sensitivity}}{\text{Volt sensor sensitivity}} \times \frac{\text{ADC Current Value} * \text{ADC sensitivity}}{\text{current sensor sensitivity}}$$

$$\times \frac{Td * Tv}{3,600,000} \qquad (17.8)$$

ADC sensitivity is defined as the minimum voltage the ADC (Analogue to Digital Converter) can sense on its analogue input and it is calculated;

$$\text{ADC sensitivity} = \frac{(\text{VRef max} - \text{VRef min})}{\text{ADC Resolution}} \qquad (17.9)$$

$V_{\text{Ref max}}$ is the maximum voltage reference of the ADC. $V_{\text{Ref min}}$ is the minimum voltage of the ADC, it is usually zero in many application and in this paper, it is considered as such. ADC resolution is the number of quantization levels within the maximum voltage of the ADC and in many application it is referred as 10 bit, 8 bits, 16 bits, etc. where a resolution value of a 10 bit ADC is equal to $2^{10} = 1,024$. Equating $V_{\text{Ref min}}$ to zero, ADC sensitivity is formulated as below.

$$\text{ADC sensitivity} = \frac{\text{VRef max}}{\text{ADC Resolution}} \qquad (17.10)$$

$$\text{Volt sensor sensitivity} = \frac{\text{VRefmax}}{\text{Vin max}} \qquad (17.11)$$

Volt sensor sensitivity is the sensitivity of the voltage sensor and its unit is V/V, $V_{\text{in max}}$ is maximum voltage that can be supplied by the solar panel. Substituting the Equations (17.10) and (17.11) into the Equation (17.8), the energy is formulated as follows:

$$E = \frac{\text{ADC Voltage Value} * \dfrac{\textbf{VRef max}}{\textbf{ADC Resolution}}}{\dfrac{\textbf{VRefmax}}{\textbf{Vin max}}}$$

$$\times \frac{\text{ADC Current Value} * \dfrac{\textbf{VRef max}}{\textbf{ADC Resolution}}}{} \times \frac{Td * Tv}{3600000} \qquad (17.12)$$

Simplifying the Equation (17.12), then simplified model to calculate Energy in kWh is in Equation (17.13)

$$E = \frac{\text{ADC Voltage Value} * \text{ADC Current Value} * \text{VRef max} * \text{Td} * \text{Tv} * \text{Vin max}}{6^2 * 10^5 * (\text{ADC Resolution})^2 * \text{current sensor sensitivity}}$$

(17.13)

17.5   Results

The model was validated by formulated theoretical values, and the values were substituted into the model. In this scenario, solar panel closed circuit 's maximum voltage of 15 V is supplied to a 10-ohm load over a period of 10 h. E, energy consumed by the load, will be computed using the formula below:

$$E = \frac{V^2 \times \text{Time}}{R}$$

$$E = \frac{15^2 * 10}{10} = 225 \text{ Wh,}$$

$$E(\text{kWh}) = 0.225 \text{ kWh,}$$

(17.14)

From the answer that we got in Equation (17.14), our model is validated against the 0.225 kWh of energy that was consumed by the load of 10 Ω over 10 h.

ADC voltage value = 1,023, which is the ADC results after analogue to digital conversion.

ADC current value = 30.72

VRef max = 5 V

Td = 1 s

Tv = 36,000 = 10 h

Vin max = 15 V

Which is solar panel maximum voltage
Current sensor sensitivity = 0.1 V/A
ADC resoulution = 10 bit, which equates to a value of 1,024

$$E = \frac{1023*30.72*5*1*36000*15}{6^2*10^5*(1024)^2*0.1}$$

$$E = 0.22478 \text{ kWh}$$

The error, the difference between the actual and the one calculated from our mathematical model, is 0.0002197. This error can be added to the results of the developed model to improve the accuracy of the results. The model was simulated using Proteus ISIS 8 software where the green energy smart meter circuit was drawn as in Figure 17.5 and accurate results were obtained as illustrated in Table 17.1. In this scenario, a 120 W, 100 RPM DC motor was used as a load, being supplied with a voltage of 12 V from the solar a panel. The resistor divider circuit was used a voltage sensor with a sensitivity of 0.25 V/V, ACS712-20A IC was used as current sensor with a sensitivity of 0.1 V/A. The PIC 16F877A microcontroller was used to sample current values and voltage values with its internal ADC and timer 1 connected to 32.768 kHz oscillator was used to calculate time. Timer1 is a 16-bit timer that counts from 0 to 65535 then it will rollover and when it rolls over it generates interrupt if the interrupt is enabled. So, Timer 1 was configured in software to generate the interrupt every 1 s and every time it generates an interrupt the interrupt flag is set. When the interrupt flag is set, the variable that is declared as an integer will increment by a value of 1. The results of the energy in kilo-Watt-hour are computed by the micro-controller, based on the developed mathematical model, and displayed on the LCD display. The simulation was run for 60 minutes which is equal to 1 hour of time, the total time throughout the energy measurements was sampled at every 5 min and the Figure 17.4 illustrates the flowchart of the source code that was developed and the proposed model was applied. The flowchart also illustrates the systematic steps that must be followed in order to properly apply the proposed model in your applications.

In Ref. [18] the authors provide a way of designing and testing a wire-less monitoring system for measuring the energy consumption of electri-cal devices in the home. The schematic diagram provided in Ref. [18] and other work [19] provided some insights to get to Figure 17.5. In Figure 17.5 the Green Energy Smart Meter circuit diagram is illustrated. In Table 17.1 Energy consumed over time is illustrated.

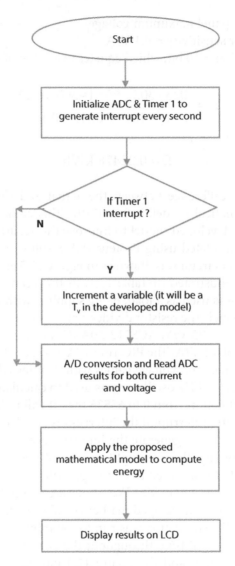

Figure 17.4 Flowchart of mathematical model.

Figure 17.6 represents the time series graph of the energy consumed by the load over a period of time sampled every 5 min interval for 1 h to aid with the interpretation of the results. From the graph, the energy consumed over time indicates a linear graph because of the linearity of the load.

Figure 17.7 represents the time series graph of the power consumed by the load over a period of time sampled every 5 min interval for 1 h to aid

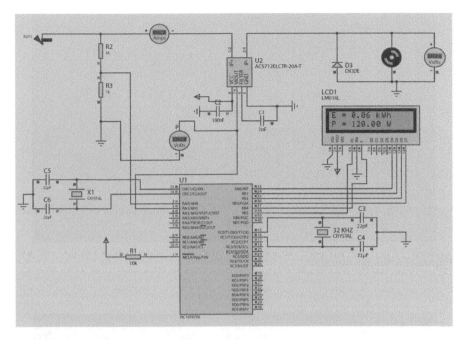

Figure 17.5 Green Energy Smart Meter circuit diagram.

Table 17.1 Energy consumed over time.

Voltage (V)	Current (A)	Time (Min)	Power (W)	Energy (kWh)
12	10 A	5	120	0.01
12	10 A	10	120	0.02
12	10 A	15	120	0.03
12	10 A	20	120	0.04
12	10 A	25	120	0.05
12	10 A	30	120	0.06
12	10 A	35	120	0.07
12	10 A	40	120	0.08
12	10 A	45	120	0.09
12	10 A	50	120	0.10
12	10 A	55	120	0.11
12	10 A	60	120	0.12

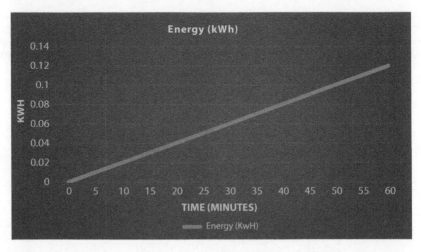

Figure 17.6 Energy over time.

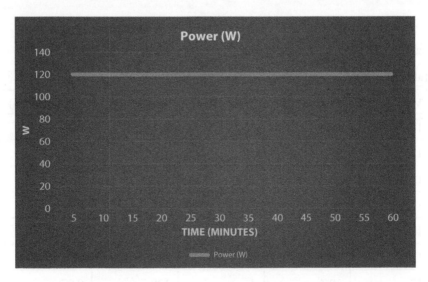

Figure 17.7 Power over time.

with the interpretation of the results. From the graph, it can be noticed that power is derivative of energy as mentioned earlier that energy is integral of power. To bring context, Power = dE/dt and deriving a linear graph produces a constant graph likewise integrating a constant graph produces a linear graph.

Figure 17.8 is a time series graph representing the amount of DC voltage that was supplied to the load over time. The voltage was supplied constantly for 1 h and measured every 5 min.

Figure 17.9 is a time series graph representing the amount of DC current drawn by the load over time. The current was supplied constantly for 1 h and measured every 5 min.

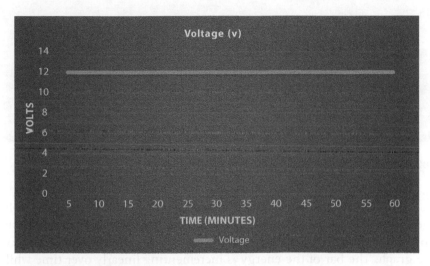

Figure 17.8 Voltage over time.

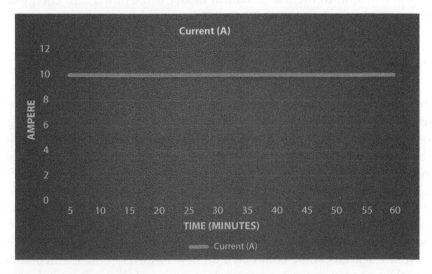

Figure 17.9 Current over time.

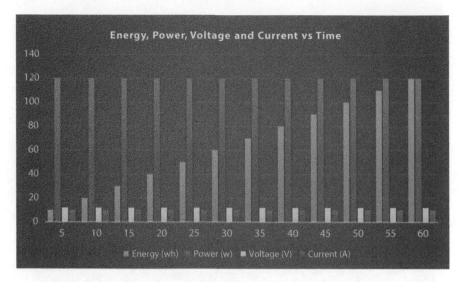

Figure 17.10 Energy, power, voltage and current over time.

Figure 17.10 represents a combination energy, power, current and voltage values in a bar graph easy correlation. Energy values are scaled to watt hour (Wh) rather than kilowatt hour (kWh) for visibility on visibility on the graph. The bar of the energy is incrementing linearly over time while the bars for current, voltage and power remain steady. Current and voltage graphs are input to the mathematical model while power and energy are output graphs from the model.

Conclusion

The mathematical model was developed that can be implemented when designing and developing the energy metering system for green energy sources such as solar in a microgrid environment. Before the model was presented, the paper provided background concepts of renewable energy sources and types. It further provided conceptual diagram of a solar energy charger based on MPPT that has a better power efficiency as compared to series regulator and shunt regulator solar charge controllers. The results that were obtained from testing the model indicated that the accurate energy results can be computed easily using this model. Further research can be conducted on how to develop the mathematical model for energy meter measuring AC power and this makes implementation easy.

References

1. Microchip, Practical Guide to Implementing Solar Panel MPPT Algorithms, Application Note no: AN1415, pp no 1–12.
2. Microgrid, available online: https://energy.gov/oe/services/technology-development/smart-grid/role-microgrids-helping-advance-nation-s-energy-system. [Accessed on 06 January 2017].
3. Solar panel datasheet, available online: http://www.mantech.co.za/Datasheets/Products/SDECOPLUS10-3H.pdf. [Accessed on 06 January 2017].
4. Palacios-Garcia, E.J., Guan, Y., Savaghebi, M., Vásquez, J.C., Guerrero, J.M., Moreno-Munoz, A. and Ipsen, B.S., Smart Metering System for Microgrids, *IECON2015-Yokohama*, pp. no 1–7, 2015.
5. ACS712 current sensor data sheet, available online: https://www.allegro-micro.com/~/media/files/datasheets/acs712-datasheet.ashx. [Accessed on 06 January 2017].
6. Kanchev, H., Lu, D., Francois, B. and Lazarov, V., Smart monitoring of a microgrid including gas turbines and a dispatched PV-based active generator for energy management and emissions reduction.
7. Subudhi, Bidyadhar and Pradhanhen, Raseswari, A comparative study on maximum power point tracking technique for photovoltaic power system, *IEEE Trans. on Sustainable Energy*, vol. 4, pp. 89–98, Jan.2013.
8. Design of charge controller for solar PV systems, Available online: https://www.researchgate.net/publication/305472058_Design_of_charge_controller_for_solar_PV_systems, [accessed on 08 June 2017].
9. Palacios-García, E.J., Guan, Y., Savaghebi, M., Vasquez, J.C., Guerrero, J.M., Moreno-Munoz, A., Ipsen3, B.S., *Smart Metering Systems for Microgrids*, IEEE, 2015.
10. De Smedt, G. and Adonis, M., *Smart meter for renewable energy microgrid island*, IEEE, 2014.
11. Vikas and Bhardwaj, Implementation of advanced energy meter using pic microcontroller, *International Journal of Technical Research (IJTR)*, Vol. 4, Issue 2, July–Aug 2015.
12. Loss, P.A.V., Lamego, M.M., Soma, G.C.D. and Vieira, J.L.F., A Single Phase Microcontroller Based Energy Meter, *Conference Paper in Conference Record—IEEE Instrumentation and Measurement Technology Conference*, June 1998.
13. Sebake, J., *Developing and testing a new generation smart meter for domestic use*, Published UJ MTech dissertation, 2018.
14. Isnen, Maizal & Kurniawan, Sigit & Garcia-Palacios, Emiliano, A-SEM for smart home, 2019, Available online: https://www.researchgate.net/publication/337393325_A-SEM_for_smart_home/citation/download.
15. Isnen, M., Kurniawan, S., Garcia-Palacios, E., *A-SEM: An adaptive smart energy management testbed for shiftable loads optimisation in the smart home*, Vol. 152, February 2020, 107285.

16. Matsuzawa, S., Harada, S., Monden, K., Mathematical Model and Performance Evaluation of AMI Applied to Mobile Environment, *Queueing Theory and Network Applications*, Volume 383, 2016.
17. Ask, K., Singh, N.K., Singh, A.K., Singh, D.K. and Anand, K., Design and Simulation of Smart Prepaid-Postpaid Energy Meter with Alarm and Theft Control, 2018 5th IEEE Uttar Pradesh Section International Conference on Electrical, Electronics and Computer Engineering (UPCON), Gorakhpur, pp. 1–6, 2018.
18. Handhal, Fadhela & Rashid, Abdulmuttalib, Design and building a single-phase smart energy meter using Arduino and RF communication system, *The 3rd International Scientific Conference for Renewable Energy (ISCRE' 2018)*, 2018.
19. Mohammad, A. Barua and Arafat, M.A., A smart prepaid energy metering system to control electricity theft, 2013 International Conference on Power, Energy and Control (ICPEC), Sri Rangalatchum Dindigul, pp. 562–565, 2013.

18

Microgrid Communication

R. Sandhya* and C. Sharmeela

Anna University, Chennai, India

Abstract

The interconnections between energy storage systems, distributed energy resources (DERs), and loads within certain limits that function as a single controllable entity may be characterized by microgrids. When linked to the power network, microgrids are targeted at delivering efficient electrical energy while operating as an island and during the transition between these two systems. The microgrid control system must be secure in three operating modes: network link, island and transitions. Microgrid controls should be made usable for a specified time under island conditions and must have the authority over appropriate infrastructure–power supply, electrochemical or electro-mechanical storage areas, load management facilities, etc. Optimum dispatch is suitable under safe conditions for human or multiple usages. The working of the communications network in a microgrid depends on the size and number of components of the microgrid control device. The deterministic structure of actual regulation requires instant signal transmission. Signals in the communications network are distinguished by the power and location of the system in a microgrid, which may be specified as DER inputs and the signal traffic controls in the opposite direction. This networking infrastructure in microgrid control and monitoring systems examines numerous technical developments related to microgrid.

Keywords: Microgrid, communications, systems, smart grid, Multi-Agent Systems (MAS), IEC 61850

18.1 Introduction

In addition to the state of microgrid connectivity and areas currently subject to growth or design, the implementation of new protocols and

---

*Corresponding author: sandhyalancer@gmail.com

C. Sharmeela, P. Sivaraman, P. Sanjeevikumar, and Jens Bo Holm-Nielsen (eds.) Microgrid Technologies, (471–490) © 2021 Scrivener Publishing LLC

specifications will be explored. Mainly depends on the management priorities and the cost of the installation and maintenance of the installations and protocols for the microgrid communications network [1]. Design criteria include the context in which control systems are placed, the transmission process features, the quantity of data traffic, the degree of consistency required and the number of DERs within the network. Communication arrangements can be divided into three categories: tightly coupled, loosely coupled, and broadcast/multicast communications. Strongly connected connections require full network efficiency, because properties in loose and dispersed networks can function independently. Fully or partly self-reliant, microgrid control schemes integrating local asset management may also be found to have lower output demands. WAN structures are extremely technical and require the use of all microgrid components. Communications of the control signal, the data storage communications will take priority. The incorporation of communication systems is essential to enforce efficient, accurate, secure, functional, and economical microgrid control architecture. This can be done by using an Internet protocol suite [2].

A layered architecture is the protocol suite in which each layer uses one of more interface protocols. Each layer typically has more than a choice of protocol for executing the layer's tasks. The improved performance architecture (EPA), which uses direct communication channels (i.e. no internet), is widely used in Supervisory Control and Data Acquisition (SCADA). The EPA model has fewer alternatives than the OSI model at the cost of less versatility [3]. Microgrid control systems use different protocols to allow communications between power system components and IEDs.

In IEDs, sensor data are gathered, and assets like DERs, energy storage systems, loads and breakers, or intelligent switches are managed. The TCP/IP controller allows the microgrid to connect with an Ethernet under IEC 61850 with IEDs and other parts [4]. An Internet networking software package that can provide routing and switching, guarantees an effective and safe connection of modules. The architecture also includes the interface between person and computers. (HMI) monitoring and control applications, servers for routine system data collection, and event trackers for the identification of predefined events with high-resolution. IEDs capture the data from the DERs and send the data to the microgrid controller as an input to the control system. The IEDs are supplied by the microgrid control on the basis of data, control signals and voltage, frequency, active, and reactive values. The IEDs are, in effect, transmitting DER and load control signals is shown in Figure 18.1. Microgrid communication systems components may have redundancies to increase the efficiency of the communication network. Wired physical networks,

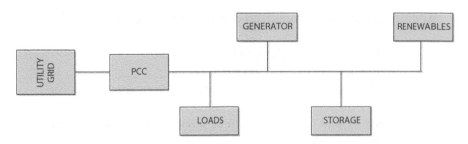

Figure 18.1 Microgrid communication systems.

for example, with wireless links, can be used to increase the availability of communications systems. In order to improve data transfer rates, data transmission can be diverted to the wireless network by reducing traffic congestion over wired connections. Microgrid communication systems components may have redundancies to increase the efficiency of the communication network. Wired physical networks, for example, with wireless links, can be used to increase the availability of communications systems. In order to improve data transfer rates, data transmission can be diverted to the wireless network by reducing traffic congestion over wired connections [5–7].

18.2   Reasons for Microgrids

The standard configuration of the recent large power grid has a wide range of advantages [33]. Large generators are also cost-effective and run with a very limited number of employees. The high voltage integrated transmission network eliminates the reserve requirement for generators. The most economical generation plant is often to be set up, and large power is transported to vast distances with reduced energy losses [8–11, 31, 32]. The delivery network is also designed for single-way power and size flows only to handle client loads. In previous years, however, a number of forces combined to push towards microgrid schemes.

The policy factors for Microgrids:

- Reduction of gaseous emissions (mainly CO_2)
- Energy efficiency, or thermal conservation
- Deregulation or legislation on the competition
- Power source diversification
- Need for the national strength.

Additional focus on commercial consideration, such as:

- Availability of modular production plants
- Smaller generator location room
- Short construction times and lower maintenance costs for smaller installations
- Closer to lead generation can be positioned that will reduce transmission costs
- Microgrids' technological effects on the delivery system
- Adjustment of network voltage and power.

18.3   Microgrid Control

The function of the microgrid depends on the generators control plan. To ensure the precise power-sharing when regulating or directing the frequency of the microgrid and the voltage magnitude of the microgrid, the inverter is regulated. The control technology used as part of the inverters can be communicated or communication-free. The two fundamental control methodologies used by Microgrids in Islanded mode are other than the Single Master Operation (SMO) and Multi Master Operations (MMO) [12, 13]. The voltage and frequency relation are used on the VSI. To monitor voltage and frequency, they use the VSI reference. SMO functions as follows: one act as a key inverter while others function as slaves. If the interruption of power supplies in the slaves is self-sufficient, the voltage reference from the master is regulated. For MMO, not only a few inverters are used as masters, where certain inverters may be attached to the DER or the batteries, but also to the QP. By rethinking another fixed point, the microgrid will change the age trend [3].

18.4   Control Including Communication

As part of the parallel operation of Microgrid converters, the dynamical load sharing method is used. Inverter control depends on communication depending on the data exchange between different Microgrid generators, and diverse inverter data converge to an oriented Microgrid controller under different loading. This enables the microgrid controller to control every individual inverter device in particular. Control mechanisms as below may include communications between the Microgrid controls and inverters:

- Master-Slave Control
- Current Limiting Control
- Circular Chain Control (3C)
- Average Load Sharing Control.

Contact lines for communication systems must be used. Reliability and expandability decrease in the active load sharing process.

Disadvantages with communication involving control methods

1. High bandwidth capacity for dynamic information sharing among the inverter is used by the communication network. It is expensive, and in rural areas, the gap between the inverters is wide and makes it illogical.
2. An inside controller serves as the master control because of one of its failures.
3. Compared to traditional power systems, it is difficult to schedule the dispatch calculation for the Microgrid network's load profile.
4. The quality of the distribution control signal decreases, leading to difficulties in controlling information.

18.5   Control with No Communication

Without communications inverter control, drop control is mainly concerned. In response to the active power (P) and reactive power of the inverter, this scheme modifies the output voltage and frequency [14, 15, 34]. The voltage and frequency of each DG inverter are controllable while the active power and reactive power are exchanged. This technology recognizes the power in (parallel inverter) and injects signals in a decentralization system like that. This signal generates a set of power controls in all situations. It is known that drop-in frequency and voltage techniques in the non-communication network are used for power-sharing. The frequency drop permits the active power and reactive power of each Microgrid generator to be shared with each generator. The droop technique involves no communication between devices, which increases the network stability and reduces costs. The droop technique in today's world is thought to be 40 as a typical microgrid control technology. But for detecting errors of voltage, this droop approach is deficient. A minor power shift in traditional systems is acceptable, but a large power angle can be tolerated with a Microgrid inverter. Due to the absence of a simple load concept, a Microgrid is exposed to certain load conditions. The increasing power demand of each inverter results in low-frequency power-sharing modes [16].

An optimum microgrid operation, control policies involve communication networks or interconnections between the different levels. The communication interfaces must be established to create two-way communication networks, allowing the transmission of information between the different controllers. Generally, data flows in both directions between nodes, i.e., any node can receive and transmit data through links to other nodes or endpoints. The microgrids' nodes are formed by addition to the sub-component or energy resource, providing information and communication capabilities, leading to intelligent electronic devices (IEDs). In order to supply data or execute commands, a microgrid controller may, therefore, communicate with IEDs and others [17]. Predefined procedures or protocols are required for an effective exchange of information between nodes within the microgrid network. The protocol suite consists of a layered architecture in which each layer is assigned to a series of functions using one or more protocols. Multi-level data communication networks typically use ISO-OSI (International Standards Organization/Open Systems Interconnect) interface protocols. This helps the data to be transformed into a form that can be submitted. As far as communications are concerned, the efficacy of the microgrid control and communication network is related to the microgrid control system and its communication architecture. Recently, there has been an increasing movement towards the use of modern communication technologies based on the Internet or the Common Information Model (CIM). The architecture of the Internet is based upon the protocol TCP/IP. TCP/IP is a simple solution to the issue of the end-communication. The TCP/IP protocol suite is used on the Internet. Usually, the TCP/IP stack has four layers: Physical and Data Link layers, Network, Transport, and Application layers. The protocols that have now started being used in electric control systems, and they are seen through innovations in the industrial protocols previously listed for their inclusion in the conventional SCADA, such as Modbus, DNP3, and Profibus, to Modbus/TCP, DNP3 over TCP and Profinet. These protocols take advantage of TCP/IP's features to update. For instance, unwanted events like an incorrect address, a packet failure, illegal function code obtained, etc. have also been recorded for Modbus or Profibus via TCP/IP communication systems. In addition to the listed properties, DNP3 supports time stamps and information on data quality in the messages via TCP/IP. However, the centralized controls in the architectural communication between clients and servers, while these changes cause communication microgrid system inefficiencies, caused by many reasons. The failure of the centralized control point could, on the one hand, result in several faults or could even shut down the entire network. On the other hand, the nodes (slaves) cannot interact with the master themselves. Therefore, data management for a broad number of devices is challenging in time. This can result in inadequate connectivity, bottlenecks, or under-use of network resources. In the future, data management can be challenging. There are major inefficiencies in the communication network used in today's microgrid [18], and the integrated communications needed for the new power grid (smart microgrid (SMG)) are located in the network. Nevertheless, the delivery of energy systems is growing. The incorporation of DERs into the energy network faces many coordination challenges. The network infrastructures must be able to efficiently manage a growing abundance of data transport or service requests and provide real-time monitoring and control of all these nodes in order to take into account more renewable and alternative energy sources.

Current serial communication in SCADA systems refers to a number of obsolete protocols often used for intermittent bit transfer and low data rate applications. As microgrid operation requires timely control steps, a real-time parameter measurement function (RTMP) is required. It is important to know which bandwidth and delay (delay) per microgrid application can be supported, i.e., per the microgrid feature has its own bandwidth and latency requirement depending on the type of response method. This timing must be met by the communication infrastructure in the microgrid because a low bandwidth may lead to bottlenecks, data packets loss, and distortion. In addition, if the time needed for contact is exceeded, the information does not meet its objective, and electrical damage to the microgrid may occur in the worst case. In order to meet, emphasis added, requires time-sensitive data sources, bandwidth, and latency, the underlying communication infrastructure must be configured with network efficiency specifications. Smart microgrid traffic requires the quality of service (QoS) in order to fulfill this network efficiency requirement. The definition of quality of service is the capacity of the network to prioritize communication packages for some important microgrid applications. For distributed control and security microgrid applications that have a severe delay and need to supply information in an appropriate time period, QoS management is important.

For instance, latency (delay), the variability of latency, and packet losses caused by the control network are high-dependencies in the stability of the closed-loop during bilateral load following (with sampling levels typically in the range between 100 and 1,000 ms). There are also packet errors, and low transmission rates suffered as networks surpass their ability to transmit, store, and buffer data. As a consequence of the dense data traffic, QoS is congested in the network.

18.6   Requirements

Throughout the organized activity of distributed power supplies, the microgrid communication network that assumes considerable responsibility for the sharing of information is the foundation. Low communication performance not only results in lower energy efficiency and microgrid service quality but has also posed a potential risk to the grid. The security of the microgrid and optimal operation depend on the several requirements of the communication infrastructure.

18.7   Reliability

The microgrid communications devices rely on sending/receiving messages in the communication backbone in order to maintain stability in the network. Therefore, the timely and efficient exchange of information as a communication backbone is extremely necessary. There are many potential faults, including timeout faults, network failures, and resource failures, which can impact communications reliability.

If the time spent exceeds the time needed, a time loss occurs. If one layer of the communication protocol fails, a network failure occurs. The fault of sending or receiving message refers to a resource error. Noise and interferences with physical media can also affect communication, which in the design process makes it important to enhance the system's reliability.

The coordination mechanism is based on a network of hierarchy regulation that can be separated into three modes of communication [19, 20]: microgrid communication, external communication, dependent on primary levels of control, secondary control and tertiary level.

The cooperation of these three methods of communication will ensure the system's stable and steady operation through the upload of primary control level data and the submission of the secondary/tertiary control level monitoring signal. First, the primary level of data should be properly and thoroughly obtained. In the meantime, data collected should be rapidly transmitted from primary to secondary/tertiary control points.

After the validity of the obtained data has been checked, a secondary/ tertiary control stage of the measurement and energy management algorithm begins to perform a more economical process. Because of various microgrid communications, the efficient and consistent management of these modes of communication is unavoidable. A single coordination standard would, therefore, be conducive to the management of microgrids. Moreover, the contact of the various levels of control will remain their own characteristics by establishing this pattern.

A 184 Smart Power Distribution System should be built based on the advantages and the application of various communication technologies, including costs, applications, and many other factors. The benefit of various communication technologies can be used to the fullest by fair selection and design of the communication system.

18.8 Microgrid Communication

In addition to the increasing energy demand, reduced processing and communication electronics manufacturing costs have generated a new wave of smart devices and applications that challenge the capacity of the associated communications networks. Today's power distribution networks take on an entirely new form: Communication requirements have been expanded by various computational approaches and are historically restricted to transmitting power/voltage and current measurements to an operating center, which measures the "state" of the network [22].

The new services provided by the intelligent microgrid depend on large data transmission. Thus, a central subsystem of the Smart Microgrid is a communication network for supporting the requisite data exchange between the end-users and other grid stakeholders (e.g., operators, aggregators). Although the best layout of such a network is not yet accepted, a typical hierarchy of the network breaks down this subsystem into a Home Area Network (HAN) and a Wide Area Network (WAN) neighbourhood area network.

For each network, several communications technologies were explored [5]. Between them is major electromagnetic interference in the choice of cables, although it appears to be a natural candidate. Wireless networking systems, on the other hand, deliver improved flexibility and are well adapted to many clever microgrid applications at reduced deployment and maintenance costs. Well-established wireless networks, such as wireless services, WiFi, Zigbee, etc., will be integrated into 5 G wireless networks, which will meet the smart grid traffic requirements.

Due to specific connectivity specifications of each microgrid component and implementation, there are differences within the respective connectivity infrastructure architecture. In order to minimize connectivity costs like RS485, and industrial ethernet infrastructure in a smaller, communication node that has no communication node functionality and easy networking, the computer supportive of the simple communication protocol and the common physical communication media effectively serve the needs of microgrid communication.

The large-scale microgrid induced the huge data traffic of the communication system by the increase of the communication nodes and the complexity of the network structure. Optical fiber transmission technology and international standard protocol should be implemented to satisfy the communication criteria in a real-time setting (such as the IEC 61850 protocol). Wireless contact, which can cope with the non-configured wired network, is more versatile in some different microgrids.

The primary task of microgrid communication is to collect and transmit the control signal in time, transmitted through the DG transceiver. DG will send the generated electrical data to the media locally on an on-going basis and will also provide decision information from the control center. Consequently, the microgrid communication needs high real-time bandwidth and good transmission efficiency. In order to implement the reliable, efficient, durable and economic microgrid control architecture, the integration of communications systems is required. The Internet communications protocol package can be used to achieve this.

Due to its high scalability, wireless communication networks are a perfect choice for a microgrid. Wireless networks also need to have a certain amount of wired infrastructure based on access points being accessible or IED wireless power. Development of a microgrid communication network via wireless physical interconnection can simplify the communication network, but the efficiency of the service, bandwidth and latency of the communication points must be taken into account. Examples for microgrid network infrastructure are: IEEE 802.11n, World Mobile Networks, 4G/3G/HSPA, LTE, LTE-A [23, 24]. The functions of the operating mechanism such as reactive power management and power quality control can be enhanced by improving communication systems.

Microgrids can be regarded as the subsystem of the distributed sources and loads of the power system. Such modules are located on the dealer end and can act as smart grid components. The Microgrid Communication Network Connected Mode construction can run under normal operating conditions, but may have to disassociate themselves, act independently of the grid, and meet the requirements of the local load under emergency conditions. This system offers greater local stability and less error in transmission. The microgrid agents exchange information with each other with the access point before sending the data to the centre. The meter nodes exchange data until they are sent for forward transfer to the point of entry. Data from each node is transmitted over a wireless network on the same path. To ensure this, all necessary protocols are used. Collisions between data packets will typically occur while many hosts are attempting to transfer packets through shared communication channels. To order to prevent these threats, a channel access protocol is used to handle the connection to the shared channel. There are two types of access protocols usable for interface, collision-based interface access, i.e. PCF protocol and ii) collision-free channel access, i.e. DCF protocol [25, 26].

18.9   Microgrid Communication Networks

There are three intelligence electronic devices (IEDs) for any safety level of the MG, such as IED estimation, IED breaker control and IED security/control. Since the action of IEDs is defined by a multiagent system, each IED is interpreted as an agent in the network. IEDs are identified in each protection point as local agents and IEDs from each other as remote agents. There are many ways of developing the Microgrid Communication Network (MCN) with Wireless Technologies to create a networking-assisted MG.

18.9.1   Wi-Fi

Wireless communications with a point-to-point connection to the measurement, control and violation agent link to each protection position using the Wi-Fi network [27, 35]. Three municipal authorities connect with each other via the central access point. The central or MGCC officials immediately connect through a Wi-Fi network and tower in the center of the network. The Wi-Fi base station uses a high-value antenna to enhance network efficiency. The data levels and signal intensity of the Wi-Fi network depend however on the distance from the base station to the safety point. Since MG applications have time-sensitive protecting and control information, the lower data rate affects the network latency. Therefore, because of its decreasing distance data rate, Wi-Fi is not ideal for very long distance communication.

18.9.2   WiMAX-Based Network

Wider distance range and adequate data speeds make WiMAX more MG automation-friendly. Especially the WiMAX network would be economical for wide field connectivity than the Wi-Fi network. By comparison to the Wi-Fi network, in each point of security there is no requirement to use the nearest connection point. Both agents are spread across the network and appear like a data point on the island. MGCC and WiMAX base stations may be positioned in the middle of the network in a similar manner to a Wi-Fi network. By comparison to the Wi-Fi network, in each point of security there is no requirement to use the nearest connection point. Both agents are scattered across the network and exist on the island as data points. Base stations MGCC and WiMAX will be put in the center of the network in the same way as Wi-Fi. WiMAX technology is thus a popular means of creating a robust contact network for MG. Higher sampling rate for current and voltage calculation under IEC61850 can also improve the time delay of WiMAX's network. However, depending on the environment, WiMAX equipment can be ineffective.

18.9.3   Wired and Wireless-Based Integrated Network

The router/access point is linked to one wireless router to make contact between multiple agents simpler. The interface of the router is wired and wireless. The wired interface is the interface for communicating between local agents, while the connection between two remote agents is supported by WiMAX. The short-term unavailability of the WLAN has no effect on the algorithm for detection of defects. Even due to the long distance, the data rate does not deteriorate. Electric vehicles can handle more data across this network and improve reliability and an integrated economical approach in the future smart grid environment, such as home automation.

18.9.4   Smart Grids

Smart grids are defined as a smart electric power network of the next century incorporating activities from all linked end-users [28]. The network provides two-way connectivity between the end-user and the grid provider, extending the connection surface to a power device. Consumers such as households and businesses now have wireless connectivity by smart meters across the Widespread Area network through the ICT infrastructures of the delivery system operators (DSOs). Smart grids introduce a new degree of network sophistication that poses new challenges to ensure operating stability and security, in addition to offering improved automation and control capability to transmission and delivery networks. Established systems such as the EMS, the DMS and the Supervisory Control and Data Acquisition (SCADA) are being modified to conform to smart grids and to integrate emerging technologies. Many of these networking infrastructures, like WAN communication, are provided by telephone providers or ISPs. These two cases further show that connectivity networks have become key elements to activate the "intelligent" facets of electricity grids. They have real-time grid information, take decisive action as required and collect data from customers.

18.10   Key Aspects of Communication Networks in Smart Grids

This analyses the infrastructures of connectivity for use of intelligent grids [30] of various domains: end user areas, transmission networks, delivery grids and generation.

18.11   Customer Premises Network (CPN)

The consumer premise networks are made up of big enterprises, medium-sized businesses, industrial buildings, smart buildings and regular home customers, such as new office buildings. The diverse existence of these locations has contributed to the creation of three different networks: Home Area Network (HAN), Business/Building Area Networks (BAN) and Industrial Areas Networks (IAN). The Home Area Network (HAN) handles the power needs of end users on demand effectively. This network aims to link intellectual electrical equipment like TVs, washing machines or energy systems. This network will also incorporate home control devices and energy management systems, and is closely associated with the idea of Smart Home. The Enterprise/Building Area Network, or Business Area Network, is a system that serves the needs of ordinary firms (e.g. office buildings). A HAN group is also regarded as a BAN network. For such a scenario, all contact with one building is included in the network regardless of its scale. The Smart Building idea is specifically connected to the BAN network. The Smart Building Architecture is specifically related to the BAN network. In the end, the Industrial Area Network (IAN), can be described as a connectivity network, facilitating the interconnection and support of all necessary machinery and equipment in a particular industry, including standard ICT software (such as computers, printers and servers) and industrial control systems. "The primary sensor base within the delivery domain is taken into account the buyer with a telephone whose call initiates the return to manage of a field team". Manual switching and activation of electrical substations, energy and suspicious occurrence data is obtained manually. Transmission system Operators (TSO), which is now converted to a better transmission grid, has considerable control over the transmission stage network.

Distribution networks undergo a paradigm change with the advent of smart grids. The distribution networks of major players in the industry are recognized as under considerable strain to meet the requirements of transforming their traditional, static grids into new and fluid smart grids. For the upcoming smart grids, sophisticated technology is awaited on the delivery system. In general, Advanced Distribution Automation (ADA) is the 'special' automation. This is achieved in order to significantly boost the machine stability, Consistency and performance by adjusting the loads in real time, normally without direct operators' interference. A two-way transmission network typically superimposes the power delivery system, requiring functionality such as: automated metering operation, transformer control and substation control, is a last mile connectivity link in the intelligent grid. The networking infrastructures driving this process are: the Neighborhood Area Network (NAN), the Field Area Networks (FAN). Advanced Metering Infrastructure (AMI). The feeder network is the only important transmission system promoting power generation and DER/microgrids. This network aims to share information across the power lines, substation networks and transformer centers with field equipment (such as switches, condenser banks and sensors) and IEDs.

Smart grids have made many improvements to existing power grids, incorporating modern systems and tools, which allow for improved connectivity, delivery, and overall performance. There are other systems that have to be taken into account when evaluating future networks, not specifically connected with communications.

These are

- Failure detection, isolation and repair (FDIR) technologies concentrate on improving delivery network reliability.
- Integrated Volt-VAR (IVVC) control systems are designed to reduce the amount of electrical power loss, increasing the total voltage transfer and safety
- Organic Flash Loop systems (OFC) will theoretically improve thermal energy reservoir power generation.

18.12   Architectures and Technologies Utilized in Communication Networks Within the Transmission Grid

In order to monitor the automation of the transmission grid, different structures and technology are required. Many of these technologies are currently in operation and are critical for transmission grid connectivity [29].

- Distribution Management Systems (DMS) are a collection of systems that are particularly relevant with the introduction of smart grids that are thoroughly managing that regulating the entire delivery network. They include: unbalanced power flow monitoring, delivery state determination, automated volt monitoring, fault and location detection and service recovery. These are augmented by SCADA and EMS systems. In general, they provide the means to enhance the network's management operations and allow operators to run and automate them in real time.
- Energy management systems (EMS) are used for effectively and safely monitoring and running the transmission power grid. Network topology, connection and load conditions (e.g., circuit breakers, switch statuses and equipment condition) can be controlled by operators using this method.
- Control and Data Acquisition (SCADA) systems are communicating with each substation (including HMI and RTU) and the network as a whole. The devices are configured to run, track and manage these substations.

   The SCADA/EMS controls the status of all circuit breakers (open/closed) in order to establish the bus or branch topology of a control network, allowing optimum estimation of control flux, estimate condition, study of risk, failure schedule, voltage and stability test, alarm treatment.

   In addition to these innovations, intelligent grids will deliver numerous innovative services, structures and technology intended to enhance the transmission infrastructure.
- Wide Area Measurement System (WAMS) make use of advanced measurement technologies in order to monitor and control large power grids and super grids.

In order to distribute information efficiently, the deployment of smart grids includes the interconnectedness of different components. Several separate operators belonging to the same network control the power grid. Many produce power, many relay electricity, and some deliver power to end customers. The Standard IEC 60870 describes that knowledge can be shared among the intelligent grid elements to handle everything. While various patent and ad-hoc protocols for the exchanging of information among these elements are in place, it is much more common for actors to share information using uniform protocols with one another, as it is generally simpler and more secure.

The standardized protocols are:

- Inter-Control Center Contact IEC 60870-6.
- RDF System Exchange Format IEC 61698—Common Information System (CIM) for dissemination.
- DF Exchange Model for Transmission, IEC 61670—Standard Knowledge System (CIM).

The established communication system between these network elements (MPLS, PLC, Cable, POTS or Leased Lines) is based on interconnection center communication.

Network interconnection systems and technology Interactions between the production, transmission and delivery realms are complex and typically involve large communication networks that use various specific technology and protocols to respond to the different needs of each segment and region. Therefore, continuity between such intercommunications is fundamental to the assurance of consistency, reliability and protection.

For connectivity between grid parts the IEC 61850 protocol family is specially modified.

The infrastructure of the Internet is dispersed and scalable, no hard-to-point lines are created; links are created by the most efficient means and links to the same target can be made accessible each time from multiple intermediates and contact lines. Additional technical innovations and Protocols began with the introduction of security mechanisms to secure all contact, communications and service delivered over the Internet (e.g., SSL/TLS, mutual authentication, encryption or certificates, point-to-point).

The most suitable ones used for smart grid communications between devices are:

- Internet Protocol (IP): the smart-grid component of the system is expected to be the most common and most critical communication network protocol. The flexibility of this protocol and its open-source implementation enable the exchange between various goods from different manufacturers. Devices can efficiently share data and Control Company and operations using this protocol.

- Multi-Protocol Label Switching (MPLS): is used for encapsulating many network protocols, and for transferring them with short paths to the destination, rather than using a whole long path. This is a scalable protocol which works independently of the transmitted protocol. However, because of its lack of safety controls, this protocol is vulnerable to a wide range of attacks and thus additional security precautions, such as the use of TLS to encrypt the data, are required to insure that the transmitted information or instructions remain important and confidential.

- Distributed Network Protocol (DNP): DNP is a series of networking protocols developed primarily for connectivity between devices part between distributed networks. It is primarily used in SCADA systems for the RTU and IEDS links of the Master Node. It was planned to be secure, but there are no protections.

- IEC 61850: is a standard intended to regulate electrical substation automation processes. This determines the sharing of data between the substation control systems. It involves several essential functions such as data processing, data storage (substitution configuration language, or SCL), fast transmitting events and reporting schemes.

- IEC 60870: specifies the devices necessary for power automation device management and data acquisition. It has been divided into five parts: communication frame types, communication facilities for data links, general software data structure, information element coding concepts and specific software.

References

1. Siow, L.K., So, P.L., Gooi, H.B., Luo, F.L, Gajanayake, C. and N.Vo, Q., Wi-fi based server in microgrid energy management system, in *IEEE Region Ten Technical Conference (TENCON 2009)*, pp. 1–5, Jan. 2009.

2. Siler-Evans, K., Azevedo, I.L. and Morgan, M.G., Marginal Emissions Factors for the U.S. Electricity System, in *Environmental Science & Technology*, no. 46, pp. 4742–4748, 2012.

3. Lopes, J.A.P., Moreira, and Resende, F.O., Microgrids black start and islanded operation, in *Proc. IEEE Power Systems Computational Conference (PSSC'05)*, Liege, Belgium, pp. 1–7, Aug. 2005.

4. Bi, R., Ding, M. and Xu, T.T., Design of common communication platform of microgrid, in *Power Electronics for Distributed Generation Systems (PEDG), 2nd IEEE International Symposium on, Jun. 2010*, pp. 735–738, 2010.

5. Shukla, S., Yi, D. and Mili, L., Construction of a microgrid communication network, in *IEEE Power Engineering Society Innovative Smart Grid Technology Conference (ISGT), 2014*, pp. 1–5, Feb. 2014.

6. *IEEE Standard for Electric Power Systems Communications – Distributed Network Protocol (DNP3)*, IEEE Std. 1815–2010, pp. i–775, 2005.

7. Bruce, A.G., Reliability analysis of electric utility scada systems, in *Power Systems, IEEE Transactions on*, vol. 13, no. 3, pp. 844–849, Aug. 1998.

8. Yongli, Z., Dewen, W., Yan, W. and Wenqing, Z., Study on interoperable exchange of IEC 61850 data model, in *Industrial Electronics and Applications (ICIEA), 2009, 4th IEEE Conference on*, pp. 25–27, May 2009.

9. Cao, J., Ma, M., Li, H., Zhang, Y. and Luo, Z., A survey on security aspects for LTE and LTE-A networks, in *Communications Surveys & Tutorials, IEEE*, vol. 16, no. 1, pp. 283–302, Mar. 2014.

10. Wang, L., Fernandez, J., Burgett, J., Conners, and Liu, Y., An evaluation of network time protocol for clock synchronization in wide area measurements, in *Power and Energy Society General Meeting—Conversion and Delivery of Electrical Energy in the 21st Century, 2008 IEEE*, pp. 1–5, Jul. 2008.

11. Ustun, T.S., Ozansoy, C., and Zayegh, A., Simulation of communication infrastructure of a centralized microgrid protection system based on IEC 61850-7-420, in *Smart Grid Communications (SmartGridComm), 2012 IEEE Third International Conference on*, pp. 492–497, Nov. 2012.

12. Kuznetsova, E., Li, Y., Ruiz, C. and Zio, E., An integrated framework of agent-based modelling and robust optimization for microgrid energy management, in *Applied Energy*, vol. 129, no. 15, pp. 70–88, Sep. 2014.

13. *National Institute of Science and Technology Framework and Roadmap for Smart Grid Interoperability Standards*, 2010.

14. Logenthiran, T., Srinivasan, D. and Wong, D., Multi-agent coordination for DER in microgrid," in *Sustainable Energy Technologies (ICSET), 2008 IEEE International Conference on*, pp. 77–82, Nov. 2008.

15. Abdar, H.M., Chakraverty, A., Moore, D.H., Murray, J.M., and Loparo, K.A., Design and implementation a specific grid–tie inverter for an agent–based microgrid, in *Energytech, 2012 IEEE*, pp. 1–6, May 2012.

16. Ekneligoda, N.C. and Weaver, W.W., Game-theoretic communication structures in microgrids, in *Power Delivery, IEEE Transactions on*, vol. 27, no. 4, pp. 2334–2341, Oct. 2012.

17. Hartono, B.S., Budiyanto, Y. and Setiabudy, R., Review of microgrid technology, in *Quality in Research, 2013 International Conference on*, pp. 127–132, Jun. 2013.
18. Saleem, A., Honeth, N. and Nordstrom, L., A case study of multi-agent interoperability in IEC 61850 environments, in *Innovative Smart Grid Technologies Conference (ISGT) Europe, 2010 IEEE PES*, pp. 1–8, Oct. 2010.
19. Stanciulescu, G., Farhangi, H., Palizban, A. and Stanchev, N., Communication technologies for bcit smart microgrid, in *IEEE Power Engineering Society Innovative Smart Grid Technology Conference (ISGT)*, pp. 1–7, Feb. 2012.
20. Matsuda, S., Watabe, Y., Asrizal, I.I., Katayama, S., Okuno, K. and Kasuga, K., Issues overcome in the design and application of IEC 61850—compliant substation automation systems, in *Advanced Power System Automation and Protection (APAP), 2011 International Conference on*, pp. 198–202, Oct. 2011.
21. Moreira, N., Molina, E., Lázaro, J., Jacob, E., Astarlo, A., Cyber-security in substation automation systems, *Renew. Sustain Energy Rev.*, 54:1552–62, 2016.
22. Short, M., Abugchem, F., Dawood, M., Tunneling horizontal IEC 61850 traffic through audio video bridging streams for flexible microgrid control and protection, *Energies*, 9(3):204, 2016.
23. Lu, Z., Sun, C., Cheng, J., Li, Y., Li, Y., Wen, X., SDN-enabled communication network framework for energy internet, *J. Comput. Netw. Commun.*, 2017.
24. Hare, J., Shi, X., Gupta, S., Bazzi, A., Fault diagnostics in smart micro-grids: a survey, *Renew. Sustain. Energy Rev.*, 60:1114–24, 2016.
25. Wang, W., Xu, Y., Khanna, M., A survey on the communication architectures in smart grid, Comput. Netw., 55(15): 3604–29, 2011.
26. Ren, L., Qin, Y., Wang, B., Zhang, P., Luh, P.B., Jin, R., Enabling resilient microgrid through programmable network, *IEEE Trans Smart Grid*, 2016.
27. Yang, Q., Barria, J.A., Green, T.C., Communication infrastructures for distributed control of power distribution networks, *IEEE Trans. Ind. Inform.*, 7(2): 316–27, 2011.
28. Kantamneni, A., Brown, L.E., Parker, G., Weaver, W.W., Survey of multi-agent systems for microgrid control, *Eng. Appl. Artif. Intell.*, 45:192–203, 2015.
29. Mohan, A., Brainard, G., Khurana, H., Fischer, S., A cyber security architecture for microgrid deployments, In *International Conference on Critical Infrastructure Protection*, Springer International Publishing, p. 245–59, 2015.
30. Sánchez, J., Yahia, and Crespi, N., *POSTER: Self-Healing Mechanisms for Software-Defined Networks*, 2015.
31. P. Sivaraman, D. Gunapriya, K. Parthiban and S. Manimaran, "Hybrid Fuzzy PSO Algorithm for Dynamic Economic Load Dispatch", *Journal of Theoretical and Applied Information Technology*, Vol. 62, No.3, pp. 794-799, April 2014.
32. P. Sivaraman, S. Manimaran, K. Parthiban and D. Gunapriya, "PSO Approach for Dynamic Economic Load Dispatch Problem", *Int. Journal of Innovative*

Research in Science, Engineering and Technology, Vol. 3, No.4, pp. 11905-11910, April 2014.

33. Sivaraman, P., and Sharmeela, C. (2020). Introduction to electric distribution system. In Baseem Kahn, Hassan Haes Alhelou & Ghassan (Eds.), *Handbook of Research on New Solutions and Technologies in Electrical Distribution Networks*, (pp. 1–31). Hershey, PA: IGI Global.

34. P. Sivaraman, C. Sharmeela and D. P. Kothari, "Enhancing the voltage profile in distribution system with 40 GW of solar PV rooftop in Indian grid by 2022: a review" 1st International conference on Large scale grid integration renewable energy in India, September, 2017, New Delhi, India.

35. P. Sivaraman and C. Sharmeela, (2020). IoT Based Battery Management System for Hybrid Electric Vehicle. In Chitra A, Sanjeevikumar Padmanaban, Jens Bo Holm-Nielsen and S. Himavathi, *Artificial Intelligent Techniques for Electric and Hybrid Electric Vehicles*, Scrivener Publishing.

19

Placement of Energy Exchange Centers and Bidding Strategies for Smartgrid Environment

Balaji, S.* and Ayush, T.

IIT Kanpur, Kanpur, India

Abstract

The clustering scheme has been implemented so that the energy exchange centers are optimally placed, and bidding strategies have also been developed with the help of different bi-level and relaxation algorithms. The simulation case shows that the proposed algorithms can effectively solve the equilibrium strategy of interaction between microgrid and prosumers, which can not only improve their individual monetary benefits, but also achieve mutual benefit and win-win, and more effectively use the resources of prosumers.

Keywords: Prosumers, game theory, nash equilibrium, supply–demand function, energy exchange clusters

19.1 Introduction

19.1.1 Overview

The Concept of Smart grid brought with it the vision for smart cities and energy trading markets. Distributed energy resources are used to improve power quality and majorly for improvement in reliability of power distribution systems [21–23]. With the integration of distributed energy resources and storage technologies into the conventional electrical grid [24], the consumers evolved into prosumers who can consume as well as produce

Corresponding author: balajisriram15@gmail.com

C. Sharmeela, P. Sivaraman, P. Sanjeevikumar, and Jens Bo Holm-Nielsen (eds.) Microgrid Technologies, (491–520) © 2021 Scrivener Publishing LLC

using renewable energy resources and advocate an energy sharing market to encourage energy exchange.

In this chapter two major concerns in the smart grid environment are dealt along with relevant simulations to help the reader understand:

- The notion of Local energy exchange centers for prosumers
- Energy markets and bidding strategies based on an approach driven by game theory

Firstly, we will get into the details of what local Energy Exchange Centers (EECs) are and their significance in the smart grid environment. Later in the chapter we will discuss the energy bidding strategies.

19.1.2   Energy Exchange Centers

In order to control the flow of electricity at distribution level, the Power sector came up with the idea of Local energy markets to facilitate prosumers [25]. In this Market, energy is traded between prosumers and distributed generators. As usual, the prosumers with energy deficit pay the system operator (S.O.). The system operator pays the Scheduling coordinators (prosumers or generators who contribute to net energy production). Local energy exchange centers (EEC) facilitate the energy trade. For this purpose, an unsupervised-learning based clustering algorithm is presented. The Simulation results and the proposed algorithm that guarantees optimal placement of energy exchange centers (EEC) such that it verifies the distribution fairness and maximum coverage with the lowest number of EEC.

The next-generation power grid is envisioned to be a smart grid architecture driven by a growing demand for higher energy efficiency, reduced greenhouse gas emissions and improved power quality and reliability [26, 27]. This evolution is enabled by innovations and continuing developments in distributed generation and energy storage, advanced power electronics and modern communication technologies. With these changes in the conventional electrical grid, the traditional electricity consumers are also getting transformed into prosumers who actively take part in energy conservation, demand response management, energy trading and are much more informed than before.

As stated previously, prosumers can consume as well as produce electricity using renewable energy resources in the modern power electric systems [24]. As the number of prosumers increases, In order to control the power flow in microgrid and to avoid power quality and reliability issues at distribution level, few electric power companies such as the Korea Electric Power Corporation (KEPCO) has introduced the concept of Local Energy Market which allows electricity trading among prosumers.

A Local Energy Market consists of prosumers, distributed energy generators and a Local Power Exchange center. In this market, a prosumer who needs electricity can request electricity from the local energy market. Then, prosumers with surplus electricity can auction and submit their bidding values to local power exchange centers. Here, the local power exchange center acts as an aggregator for electricity trading. The job of a local power exchange center is to determine the winning bid and pricing for the electricity trading.

In [1], reduce the cost of energy production and make the flow of electricity efficient in the microgrid. For this purpose, they proposed a geometric local market clustering scheme based on Unsupervised Learning algorithm concepts.

19.1.3   Energy Markets

Electricity has become an integral part of everyone's life. It is very hard nowadays to imagine life without electricity [28, 29]. The power blackout of 2012 in India has raised several questions about the conventional methods of power generation. The dependency on coal-based plants has been successfully limited by adopting generation techniques based on renewable energy resources. Also, the installation of self-generation units at the consumer end has restructured the entire power system which had ensured the stability and reliability in the power supply. This has brought endless opportunities for the power distribution companies but at the same time has become more challenging due to the shift in this retail electricity market.

The consumers having the facility of self-generation are termed as Prosumers. These generation capabilities of the prosumer ranges from Kilowatts to few Megawatts. These electricity-producing resources or controllable loads that are connected to a local distribution system or to a host facility within the local distribution system are termed as Distributed Energy Resources (DERs) [30–32]. DERs include solar panels, combined heat and power plants, electricity storage, small natural gas-fueled generators, electric vehicles and controllable loads, such as HVAC systems and electric water heaters. In this chapter we have mainly focused on 3 entities namely (i) Prosumers, (ii) Distribution system operator (DSO), & (iii) Utility companies. A Distribution System Operator (DSO) securely operates and develops an active distribution system comprising networks, demand, generation and other flexible distributed energy resources (DERs).

In Ref. [4], the proposed algorithm focuses on efficient double auctions along with proportional allocation of electricity among its buyers. Double auctions are mechanisms involving both buyers and sellers which simultaneously participate in the bidding process and are allocated individual shares of the resource. It proposes a double-auction mechanism which includes one set as buyers and another set as sellers. It also assumes the presence of a separate mediating agent called the aggregator whose role is to (i) receive monetary bids from the buyers and available energy for trade from the sellers; (ii) proportionally allocate energy to the buyers; (iii) iteratively converge to the market clearing price. Double-sided auction can readily minimize the loss of efficiency arising from price anticipation as compared to single-sided auction. It does consider the proportional distribution of electricity among its buyers. But it does not consider the distribution fairness of the electricity based on the geometrical locations and thus it might result in electricity monopolies.

In Ref. [5], an auction mechanism is proposed under the consideration of the Stackelberg game theory. The study presents the economic benefits of a fully distributed energy trading among microgrids by analyzing its hierarchical decision-making scheme as a multi-leader multi-follower Stackelberg game. The proposed mechanism turns out to be cost-effective, reliable and efficient for energy trading. But, the Stackelberg model applies to monopolistic conditions.

Cintuglu and Mohammed in Ref. [6] proposed the reverse auction architecture based on a second price Vickrey auction for truthful bidding. However, since the market environment in Ref. [6] consists of one buyer and multiple sellers, it is not suitable for a local energy market consisting of multiple buyers and sellers.

In Ref. [7], it proposes auction mechanisms for energy trading in a smart multi-energy district, in which the district manager sells electricity, natural gas, and heating energy to users and meanwhile trades with the outer energy network. The auction scheme guarantees the properties of economic efficiency, truthfulness and individual rationality and thus, users are incentivized to participate in the auction with fairness. Thus, the paper proposes the VCG auction mechanism with a linear problem. its truthfulness is mathematically proven with real data. However, the bidding has been done by the buyer in Ref. [7], while the bidding is done by the seller in the present context.

This chapter emphasizes on the fact that prosumers need to maximize their revenue, distribution system operator (DSO) need a market clearing mechanism in this version of electricity market whereas the utility companies face a challenging task of this grid integration. Hence an innovative approach

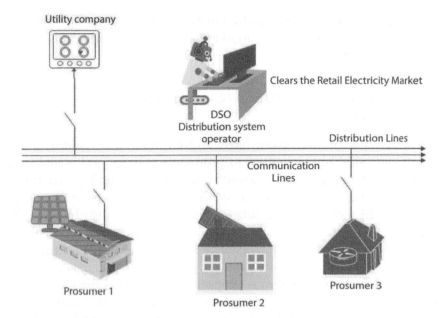

Figure 19.1 Smart grid Environment.

based on game theory has been developed for this Microgrid environment with the help of different algorithms and functions. Hence to interpret the competition among various players present in the retail electricity market, supply function equilibrium (SFE) model, function based on Nikaido Isoda model, algorithms based on bilevel and relaxation have been implemented.

The basic topology of a smart grid system is as shown in Figure 19.1. In Section 19.3 we will elaborate on the above summary. This will involve in-depth mathematical reasoning and explain analysis results based on MATLAB simulations.

19.2   Local Energy Centers and Optimal Placement

In this section we have introduced a modified K-means clustering algorithm which is like that of geometric local market clustering [1]. The modified K-means algorithm proposed is simple and would help the reader clearly understand the process of clustering.

This clustering scheme clusters all the prosumers based on the location when the number of clusters is given. Clusters are created considering the geometrical distance from the distributed energy generators and the local power exchange center ensuring the distribution fairness.

The key idea and strategy involved in the proposed clustering algorithm for organizing the local energy market based on Unsupervised Learning concepts are as follows.

19.2.1   Problem Formulation (Clustering of Local Energy Market)

Power systems of the future have evolved from the traditional PS. Consumers would have evolved to prosumers and the grid would have locally distributed generators, avoiding long distance bulk power transmission. These advanced power systems would require local energy exchange (EE) centers (like substations) for power distribution. The efficiency of these exchange centers solely relies on their geographical location which determines the distance to the connected prosumers and generators. Now, to tackle the problem of optimal placement of energy centers a clustering algorithm is proposed. Which takes the locations of prosumers and generators as input and outputs the optimal location of EE centers and the corresponding prosumers & generators to whom the EE centers will be connected to.

We also iterate the number of clusters (EE centers) to find how many EE centers would yield the optimal solution. The criteria of optimization are to minimize Distortion measure function (DMF) which is the sum of distances between each cluster center (EE center) and the corresponding players (prosumers as well as generators) assigned to them [2].

19.2.2   Clustering Algorithm

The Algorithm modified K-means algorithm for clustering is as follows:

- Iterate for number of clusters between 1: Max. number of clusters
  - Assign random X–Y coordinates for each cluster center
  - DMF = infinity
  - Start K-means clustering
    - ❖ Calculate distances between each prosumer and each cluster center
    - ❖ Calculate distances between each generator and each cluster center
    - ❖ For each cluster center, assign the closest prosumers and generators
    - ❖ to that cluster.

❖ Assign the X–Y coordinates of each cluster center as the mean coordinate of the prosumers and generators (in specified ratios) in that cluster.
- Repeat the above 4 steps, until the clusters converge (convergence criteria: less than 3% change in the coordinates of the cluster center)
- Calculate DMF
- End of iteration process for number of clusters
- Display: The number of clusters, the coordinates of the cluster centers and the prosumers & generators assigned to each cluster will have the optimal values for which DMF is minimum.

19.2.3   Test Cases

There are 3 test cases considered, and are as shown below

- **Number of prosumers = 1,000, number of generators = 07**
- **Number of prosumers = 2,000, number of generators = 15**
- **Number of prosumers = 2,000, number of generators = 25**

1.) Number of prosumers = 1,000, Number of generators = 7

Figures 19.2(a), (b) represent the scatter of prosumers and generating units in a specific area where the number of prosumers and generators is 1,000 and 7 respectively.

2.) Number of prosumers = 2,000, Number of generators = 15

Figures 19.3(a), (b) represent the scatter of prosumers and generating units in a specific area where the number of prosumers and generators is 2,000 and 15 respectively.

3.) Number of prosumers = 4,000, Number of generators = 25

Figures 19.4(a), (b) represent the scatter of prosumers and generating units in a specific area where the number of prosumers and generators is 4,000 and 25 respectively.

The prosumers and generators are scattered in a fashion such that the distribution of players in the area is close to the practical scenario. The generators are randomly distributed (Uniform distribution) in the given area.

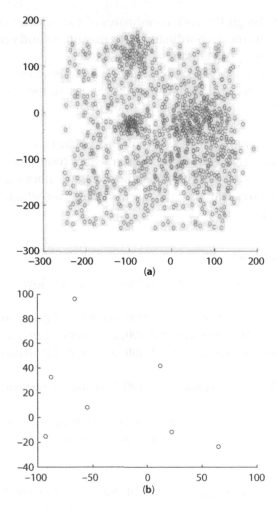

Figure 19.2 (a) Scatter plot of prosumers. (b) Scatter plot of generators.

Whereas the prosumers are distributed in a superimposed fashion (Random normal distribution superimposed on uniform distribution). The shape and scale parameter are chosen at random to simulate ideal scenario.

For all the scatter plots of prosumers and generators considered above the corresponding clustering results and discussions are shown below.

19.2.4 Results and Discussions

For the reader to understand segmentation of clusters each cluster has been identified using a unique color. The cluster centers represent the optimal

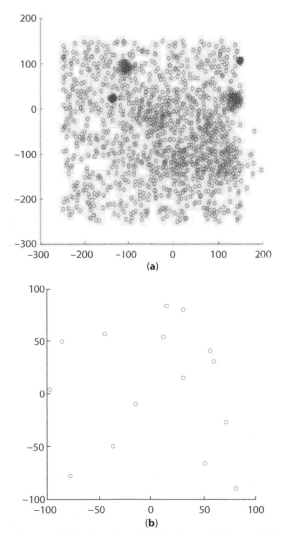

Figure 19.3 (a) Scatter plot of Prosumers. (b) Scatter plot of generators.

location of energy exchange centers (EEC). These centers are represented in the figure by an "O" symbol. The generators are represented by "X" and the prosumers are represented by "*" in the cluster plot shown below.

1) Number of prosumers = 1,000, Number of generators = 7

In Figures 19.5(a), (b) the plot of DMF for case 1 and the corresponding optimal cluster plot (optimal no. of cluster = 4 arrived from DMF plot) has been shown.

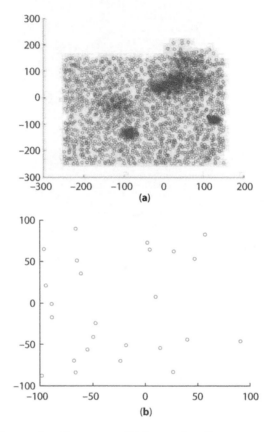

Figure 19.4 (a) Scatter plot of prosumers. (b) Scatter plot of generators.

2) Number of prosumers = 2,000, Number of generators = 15

In Figures 19.6(a), (b) the plot of DMF for case 2 and the corresponding optimal cluster plot (optimal no. of cluster = 7 arrived from DMF plot) has been shown.

3) Number of prosumers = 4,000, Number of generators = 25

In Figures 19.7(a), (b) the plot of DMF for case 3 and the corresponding optimal cluster plot (optimal no. of cluster = 7 arrived from DMF plot) has been shown.

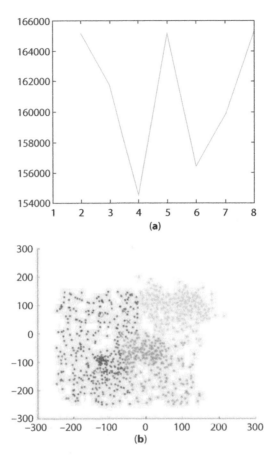

Figure 19.5 (a) Plot of DMF for Np = 1,000, Ng = 7. (b) Cluster plot for optimal case.

19.2.5   Conclusions for Simulations Based on Modified K Means Clustering for Optimal Location of EEC

Results from the above clustering algorithm suggests that:

1. The clustering results have been shown in Figures 19.4, 19.5, 19.6 for the optimum number of clusters.
2. In the optimum number of clusters, we have maximized the coverage with least number of energy exchange centers possible. This will indirectly reduce the distribution losses and provide more uniformity in the system.
3. The proposed clustering algorithm is very effective for identifying the optimal number of EE centers (optimal number of clusters) considering the distribution Fairness of distributed

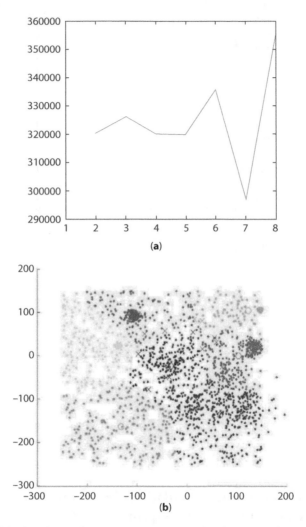

Figure 19.6 (a) Plot of DMF for Np = 2,000, Ng = 23. (b) Cluster plot for optimal case.

energy generators in the local energy market. The clustering scheme is based on unsupervised learning concepts implemented using MATLAB platform.

4. The proposed method can be used to identify the locations of prosumers and distributed energy generators corresponding to each cluster (Coordinates).

The MATLAB/Octave code for the proposed algorithm is provided in the appendix.

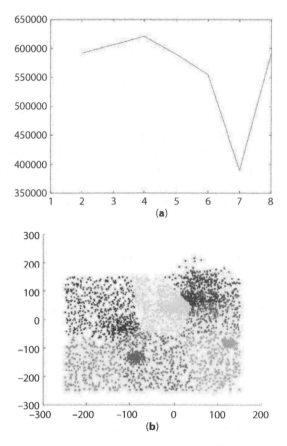

Figure 19.7 (a) Plot of DMF for Np = 4,000, Ng = 25. (b) Cluster plot for optimal case.

19.3   Local Energy Markets and Bidding Strategies

It is a must to understand that smart grids would have an oligopo-listic market where there are many competitors for energy trading. Distribution system operators will face challenges in the retail electric-ity market.

Hence to tackle these challenges, a strategy based on game theory has been used for prosumers using bi-level algorithms consisting of Nikaido Isoda function and relaxation algorithms. These functions help in achiev-ing a greater number of prosumers with reasonable computational time and convergence rate.

19.3.1   Prosumer Centric Retail Electricity Market

The proliferation of distributed wind, solar power and energy storage have been endowing traditional "pure" consumers with capability of generation, precipitating the advent of prosumers. Prosumers not only consume but also produce energy in a prolific manner. Hence, they can either choose to buy or sell energy while participating in the energy market which provides the option of energy exchange while improving social efficiency. This section proposes a simple but effective mechanism based on game theory-based bidding strategy for prosumer centric retail distribution market. Distribution energy resources (DERs) play an important role in restructuring the conventional power system network and ensure reliability in power supply.

DERs also help in reducing carbon emissions using RES units, trigeneration which is otherwise termed as combined cooling heat and power (CCHP) which can further help in increasing the overall efficiency of the distribution system. The concept of prosumers comes from the fact that the conventional consumers have become smart and they proactively participate in the energy exchange process. However, they may have a partial or total conflict of interest with others. Hence a well-defined strategic bidding mechanism is needed to maximize the revenue of operation of prosumers, Game theory is one such tool which can help in comparing the relationship between prosumers in proposed distribution systems.

This section elaborates the game theory approach which helps in establishing a connection between different prosumers in the distribution system with AC power flow constraints. In this section power quality and system reliability is not included. An innovative game theoretic based approach has been done where the retail electricity market is modelled with the help of bi-level algorithms.

This section is summarized as:

- Prosumers in the retail electricity market are identified and modelled with the help of bi-level algorithms.
- An approach based on Game theory is applied to interpret the competition within the players (prosumers and generators) during bidding.
- An optimal bidding strategy has been identified for maximizing the revenues of prosumers.
- Extensive simulation has been performed and results are illustrated to validate the proposed theory.

Non cooperative game theory can be used to analyze the strategic decision-making processes of several independent entities, i.e., players, that have partially or totally conflicting interests over the outcome of a decision process which is affected by their actions. Non cooperative does not always imply that the players do not cooperate, but it means that any cooperation that arises must be self-enforcing with no communication or coordination of strategic choices among the players.

Cooperative games on the other hand allow one to investigate how one can provide an incentive for independent decision makers to act together as one entity to improve their position in the game. Cooperative game theory in both of its branches provides tools that allow the players to decide on whom to cooperate with and under which term can be given several cooperation incentives.

Nikaido-Isoda function which serves as a merit function, vanishing only at the first-order stationary points of each player's optimization problem, and provides error bounds to a stationary Nash point. Gradient descent is shown to converge sub linearly to a first-order stationary point of the GNI function. For the case of bilinear min-max games and multi-player quadratic games, the Nikaido-Isoda function is convex. Hence, the application of gradient descent in this case yields linear convergence to a Nash Equilibrium.

In Ref. [8], a game-theoretic approach is utilized to study the dynamic interaction among the prosumers in a distribution system subjected to AC power flow constraints. But the authors didn't consider a unique bidding strategy for the prosumers in the retail electricity market. An approach based on game-theory is exploited in order to simulate the nature of these players (distributed electricity generators and prosumers). Distribution Locational Marginal Price (DLMP) concepts are also considered to facilitate tempo spatial cost signals to all market participants without considering the system power quality, AC power flow constraints and System reliability issues into consideration.

19.3.2   System Modeling

19.3.2.1   Prosumer Centric Framework

The prosumer market of the future will be tri-component: (a) Prosumers (b) Utility companies & (c) Distribution system operator (DSO).

19.3.2.2   Electricity Prosumers

Prosumers have local generation in the form of wind, solar and energy storages like batteries to generate or store their own power. They are self-sufficient and may have surplus power to sell to the grid.

$$C_{gi} = a_i P_{gi}^2 + b_i P_{gi} + C_i + M_{servicei} \tag{19.1}$$

i = Index of prosumer
a_i = Generation cost coefficients of i-th prosumer ($/MW²h).
b_i = Generation cost coefficients of i-th prosumer ($/MW h).
C_i = Generation cost coefficients of i-th prosumer ($).
$M_{servicei}$ = The constant subscription fee paid by the ith electricity prosumer to the utility company

The locational marginal price of the ith electricity prosumer is given by

$$lmp_i = \frac{dC_{gi}}{dP_{gi}} = 2a_i P_{gi} + b_i \tag{19.2}$$

The bidding function for prosumer is given by:

$$\rho_i = k_i lmp_i = k_i (2a_i P_{gi} + b_i) \tag{19.3}$$

The payoff function of the i-th electricity prosumer is:

$$Max\ R_i = C_{retaili} \sum_{i=1}^{N_i} (P_i - P_{di}) - \sum_{i=1}^{n} C_i \tag{19.4}$$

$$P_i = P_{gi} + P_{ri}$$

$$St.\ P_{i,min} \le P_i \le P_{i,max}$$

$$C_{retaili} = \beta_i - \alpha_i \sum_{i=1}^{N_i} (P_i - P_{loss}) \tag{19.5}$$

P_i = Total active power generation by the ith prosumer
P_{ri} = Renewable power generation of the ith prosumer
P_{di} = Power demand of the ith prosumer
α_i = Electricity price coefficient of the i-th prosumer
β_i = Electricity price coefficient of the i-th prosumer
C_i = Cost of the i-th prosumer ($)
$P_{i,min}$ and $P_{i,max}$ are the lower and upper bounds of the ith prosumer

19.3.2.3   Modeling of Utility Companies

Utility company helps in ensuring Power System Reliability and provide power to the prosumers who are incapable of generating power. The payoff function of utility companies is

$$U = C_{retaili} P_{utility} + \sum_{i=1}^{N_i} M_{servicei} \qquad (19.6)$$

$P_{utility}$ = Power supplied by the utility company;
$C_{retailu}$ = Market clearing price of the utility company
R_i = Revenue of the i-th prosumer ($).

19.3.2.4   Modeling of Distribution System Operator (DSO)

The DSO minimises the market price to benefit the normal consumers (without any form of generation) subjected to bids and power flow constraints. The location marginal price is defined as:

$$Min \sum_{i=1}^{N_i} \rho_i P_i \quad \forall i \in [1, N_i] \qquad (19.7)$$

$x \in R$ = Auxiliary matrix

$y \in R$ = Auxiliary matrix

19.3.2.5   Supply Function Equilibrium

The supply function equilibrium (SFE) model comprises of (N_{i+1}) players, i.e. N_i competing prosumers and one DSO. The consumer's demand is given by the demand function $D(p)$ which depends on the market price p such that it is a decreasing function of price. In this model at the beginning of the Game period, every prosumer submits it's bidding function to DSO; which must be a piecewise differentiable non-decreasing function of price. The DSO formulates a market wide supply function based on the minimization of the market price.

19.3.2.6　Constraints

The simplified AC power flow is applied here. The expression of real, reactive powers and voltages are as follows:

$$P_{K+1} - P_K = p_k - r_k \frac{\left(P_k^2 + Q_K^2\right)}{V_K^2} \qquad (19.8)$$

$$Q_{K+1} - Q_K = q_k - r_k \frac{\left(P_k^2 + Q_K^2\right)}{V_K^2} \qquad (19.9)$$

$$V_{k+1}^2 - V_k^2 = -2(r_k P_k + x_k Q_k) - \left(r_k^2 + x_k^2\right)\frac{\left(P_k^2 + Q_K^2\right)}{V_K^2} \qquad (19.10)$$

r_k = Resistance of the distribution line connecting node k and node k + 1 (Ω).
x_k = Inductance of the distribution line connecting node k and node k + 1 (Ω).

The power losses are very small and compared to branch power so they can be neglected and $V_k = V_0$

$$P_{k+1} - P_k = p_k$$

$$Q_{k+1} - Q_K = q_k$$

N_i = Number of prosumers
N_k = Number of bus node
m = Number of lower level constraints
N = Number of iteration parameters

$$V_{k+1} - V_k = \frac{(r_k P_k + x_k Q_k)}{V_O} \qquad (19.11)$$

V_0 = Bus voltage magnitude at the slack bus (kV)

The voltage range should be within the limit

$$V_{min} \leq V_k \leq V_{max}$$

The total active power loss can be calculated as

$$P_{loss} = \sum_{k=1}^{N_k} P_{lossk} = \sum_{k=1}^{N_k} r_k \frac{\left(P_k^2 + Q_k^2\right)}{V_k^2} \approx \sum_{k=1}^{N_k} r_k \left[P_k^2 + Q_k^2\right] \qquad (19.12)$$

Power balance:

$$\sum_{k-1}^{N_i} (P_{di} + P_{loss} + P_{base}) = \sum_{i=1}^{N_k} (P_l + P_{utility}) \qquad (19.13)$$

P_{base} = Base load of the system except prosumers (MW)
V_{min} = Lower bound of bus voltage magnitude (kV)
V_{max} = Upper bound of bus voltage magnitude (kV)
θ_{min} = Lower bound of weighting term
θ_{max} = Upper bound of weighting term

19.3.3   Solution Methodology

Flowchart explaining the steps pertaining to the solution methodology of the problem is shown in Figure 19.8.

19.3.3.1   Game Theory Approach

Let N_i players participate in one game, where vector x_j denotes the action taken by the jth player, j = 1,2, 3...,N_j. Therefore, a collective action set x = x_1, x_2,x_{Nj} is formed when all the players act at the same time. Moreover, ϕ_j represents the jth player's profit, earned from setting its own strategy when other strategies are settled. The payoff function ϕ_j is the difference between sale revenue and the cost of electricity production and facilities.

$$\Phi_j = R_j - C_j,$$

R_j represents the revenue of the jth participants
C_j denotes the cost functions for the jth participants

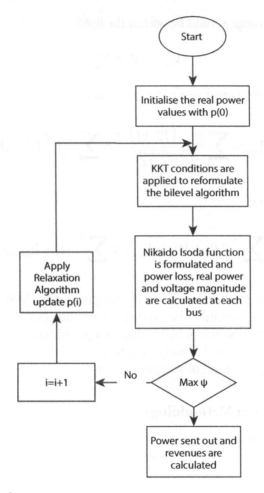

Figure 19.8 Flowchart.

Nash equilibrium point

$$\emptyset_j(x*) = max_{(x_j/x*)\in X}\emptyset_j(x_j/x) \qquad (19.14)$$

By Nikaido Isoda function

$$\psi(x,y) = \sum_{j=1}^{N_j}[\phi_j(y_j/x) - \phi_j(x)] \qquad (19.15)$$

Nash equilibrium problem can be solved by

$$Z(x) = arg\ max_{y \in \tilde{X}}\ \psi(x, y)x, Z(x) \in X \qquad (19.16)$$

19.3.3.2   Relaxation Algorithm

The reformulated single-level optimization problem is solved iteratively via relaxation algorithm until the solution converges to the Nash equilibrium point. It is implemented as follows:

$$X^{m+1} = (1 - \theta_m)x_m + \theta^m Z(x^m)\ 0 \le \theta_m \le 1 \qquad (19.17)$$

$\theta_m = 0.5\ \forall\ n \in R$ Weighing term of mth iteration

$$max_{(x^m, y) \in \tilde{X}}\ \psi(x^m, y) \le \grave{o} \qquad (19.18)$$

19.3.3.3   Bi-Level Algorithm

The objective function of the prosumers (i.e. Maximizing their revenues) is the upper level function, represented as F(x, y), subjected to the maximum and minimum generating capabilities of these prosumers, represented in the form of G(x, y)< = 0

The bi-level algorithm is represented as:

$$\text{Maximum Limit: } min[-F_{up}(x, y)] \qquad (19.19)$$

$$\text{s.t.} \qquad G_{up}(x, y) \le 0$$

$$\text{Minimum Limit: } min[-F_{low}(x, y)] \qquad (19.20)$$

$$\text{s.t.} \qquad g_{low}(x, y) \le 0$$

where F_{up} and G_{up} represents the maximum limits and f_{low} and g_{low} represents the minimum limits.

Reformulated single-level problem using KKT (Kuhn Tucker conditions) is

$$min_{x \in \tilde{X}, y}[-F(x, y)]$$

s.t.

$$G(x, y) \le 0 \tag{19.21}$$

$$g(x, y) \le 0 \tag{19.22}$$

$$\lambda_i \ge 0; \forall i \in [1, n] \tag{19.23}$$

$$\lambda g_i(x, y) = 0, \forall i \in [1, n] \tag{19.24}$$

$$\nabla y L(x, y, \lambda) = 0 \tag{19.25}$$

$$\text{where } L(x, y, \lambda) = f(x, y) + \sum_{i=1}^{N_i} \lambda_i g_i(x, y) \tag{19.26}$$

19.3.3.4   Simulation Results

The model of IEEE 33 bus system has been shown in Figure 19.9. All the transformers, switches, and voltage regulators are ignored.

The data corresponding to active and reactive powers at each node and resistances and reactances between the two nodes have been taken from Refs. [19] and [20]. Using the equations from (19.1) to (19.28) the data of three prosumers is shown in Table 19.1.

The coefficients of the prosumers' cost functions, a_i and b_i, are listed and the corresponding fee must be 'n' times output power where n is an integer, to be considered within limits of b_i and additionally considering that every C_i is costless.

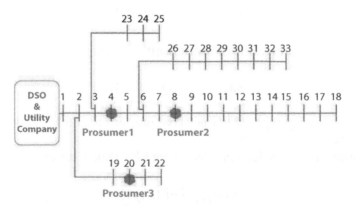

Figure 19.9 IEEE 33 Bus System [20].

Table 19.1 Prosumer parameter values.

Parameters	1st prosumer	2nd prosumer	3rd prosumer
a_i($/MW2h)	10.9508	6.6455	0.0435
b_i($/MW h)	14.8738	37.358	26.2789
k_i	2.3	2.124	1.3
α_i	8	9	10
β_i	330	338	305
Capacity (MW)	10.8	9.48	7.345

19.3.3.5   Nikaido-Isoda Formulation

To implement Nikaido-Isoda function, the ith prosumer changes its output from p_i to p_i^{new}, while other prosumers stick to their previous generation. Then, the differences in the payoff values are evaluated for each prosumer and then added up.

The p_i^{new} for which this function maximizes can be derived to obtain the following expression:

$$\frac{\partial \Psi}{\partial P} = 0 \qquad (19.27)$$

This further gets reduced to

$$\frac{(\beta_i - b_i) + \alpha_i(P_{loss} + P_{di}) - \alpha_i(P_t - P_i)}{2(\alpha_i + a_i)}, \quad \forall_i \in [1, N_i] \qquad (19.28)$$

Nikaido Isoda algorithm for single iteration in MATLAB is provided in the Appendix.

19.3.4   Case Study

Since the demand curve and bidding strategies are similar for all the prosumers, they generate almost the same amount of power. The revenue of the third prosumer is less due to the payoff coefficient as shown in Table 19.2. The magnitude of voltages at all the buses are between 0.9 and 1.1 pu.

Table 19.2 Power and revenue of prosumers.

Variables	1st prosumer	2nd prosumer	3rd prosumer
P_i, MW	6.9538	8.2145	6.7493
Revenue, $/h	1168.9133	1123.5472	461.9081

Also, the total active Power loss is 0.247 MW, which is about 1.2% of the total active power generated by the prosumers.

19.3.4.1   Plots

The resulting voltage profile at each bus and the active power loss are as shown in Figures 19.10(a) and (b) respectively. The simulations are done using MATLAB and Wolfram alpha online widget.

19.3.4.2   Anti-Dumping

Dumping corresponds to reducing price on identical goods to improve sales. Here 3rd prosumer bids at nearly 30% cost as shown in Tables 19.3 and 19.4. In this regard, the DSO diminishes energy share to retain a stable market.

Prosumers are 14 in number for iteration process.

19.3.4.3   Macro-Control

Macroeconomic regulation and control serve to reduce the heat of the economy. It is operated by the system operator. For the prosumers ranging from 2–4, a sensitivity study has been made. Since 3rd prosumer is out of the market, 1st and 2nd prosumers can compete and sell their excess energy. The increasing bid of prosumer 3 is as shown in Table 19.5.

19.3.4.4   Sensitivity Analysis

For the prosumers ranging from two to four, a sensitivity study has been made. Since 3rd prosumer is out of the market, 1st and 2nd prosumers can compete and sell their excess energy in the market. Convergence rate of these two prosumers is also higher than three prosumers. The expected payoffs of the first two prosumers are as shown in Table 19.7.

No. of iterations with three prosumers = 14
No. of iterations with four prosumers = 47 (Convergence rate is slower).

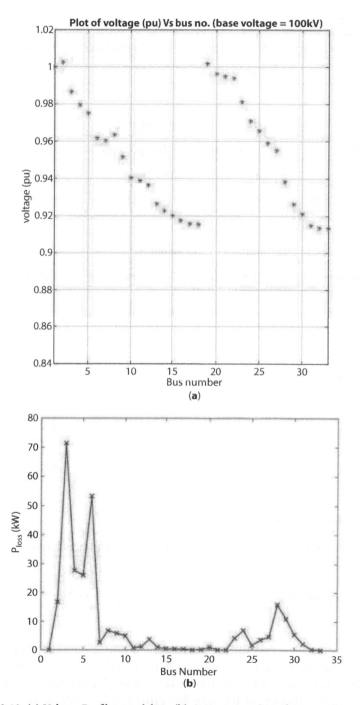

Figure 19.10 (a) Voltage Profile at each bus. (b) Active power loss plot.

Table 19.3 Bids of three prosumers.

Bidding Strategy	1st prosumer	2nd prosumer	3rd prosumer
k_i	2.1023	2.1045	2.3037

Table 19.4 Updated power and revenue of prosumers.

Variables	1st prosumer	2nd prosumer	3rd prosumer
P_i, MW	8.0311	8.7321	1.1445
Revenue, ($/h)	1566.8391	1652.2364	3.1996

Table 19.5 Hiking the bid price of 3rd prosumer.

Parameters	1st prosumer	2nd prosumer	3rd prosumer
k_i	2.1	2.2	50
β_i	320	338	337

Table 19.6 Expected payoff of three prosumers based on updated bidding strategy and demand parameters.

Variables	1st prosumer	2nd prosumer	3rd prosumer
P_i, MW	2.2101	2.3494	0.4912
Revenue, $/h	915.4671	999.6875	67.488

Table 19.7 Power and revenue in two prosumer case.

Variables	1st prosumer	2nd prosumer
P_i, MW	8.3628	9.0741
Revenue, $/h	1656.5289	1775.0273

In the case of 4 prosumer market, the bidding strategy used and the expected payoff for each prosumer is provided in Tables 19.8 and 19.9 respectively. Hence, in addition to less computational effort, the approach based on game theory for bidding has proved to be fruitful.

Table 19.8 Strategic bid for the four-prosumer case.

Parameters	1st prosumer	2nd prosumer	3rd prosumer	4th prosumer
k_i	2.1	2.1	1.5	1.7
β_i	320	330	300	250

Table 19.9 Power and revenues of four prosumers.

Variables	1st prosumer	2nd prosumer	3rd prosumer	4th prosumer
P_i, MW	4.8864	5.1281	4.8812	2.5307
Revenue ($/h)	1152.542	1101.589	569.519	181.380

Conclusion

An innovative approach based on game theory has been implemented for this prosumer centric retail electricity market. Bilevel algorithms and Nikaido Isoda functions have been used effectively to maximize the profit of prosumers. Bidding strategies were observed to be genuine when cross checked with multi-player simulations that use bilevel algorithm and relaxation algorithms. It was also observed that the rate of solution convergence is better than other approaches.

Energy exchange centers (EEC) play a vital role in determining energy flow in a smart grid environment. Hence to satisfy the necessity of optimal EEC placement, a machine learning clustering approach has been used to place the energy exchange centers (EEC) subject to minimizing DMF. This has resulted in a system whose clusters have evolved to provide maximum coverage with the least number of energy exchange centers (EEC).

The prosumers and the generators in the smart grid environment have been selectively identified and mapped to each cluster to optimize the topological connectivity. In the future, the bidding strategy can be developed considering dynamic load variation. Also, a proper scheduling mechanism can be incorporated for the prosumers, Energy storage resources and for V2G and G2V applications. Another future work could be incorporation of congestion management mechanism in the distribution system in presence of a huge number of prosumers.

References

1. Park, L., Jeong, S., Kim, J. and Cho, S., Joint Geometric Unsupervised Learning and Truthful Auction for Local Energy Market, in *IEEE Transactions on Industrial Electronics*, vol. 66, no. 2, pp. 1499–1508, Feb. 2019, doi: 10.1109/TIE.2018.2849979.

2. Kanungo, T., Mount, D.M., Netanyahu, N.S., Piatko, C.D., Silverman, R. and Wu, A.Y., An efficient k-means clustering algorithm: analysis and implementation, in *IEEE Transactions on Pattern Analysis and Machine Intelligence*, vol. 24, no. 7, pp. 881–892, July 2002.

3. Arefifar, S.A., Mohamed, Y.A.I. and El-Fouly, T., Optimized multiple microgrid-based clustering of active distribution systems considering communication and control requirements, *IEEE Trans. Ind. Electron.*, vol. 62, no. 2, pp. 711–723, Feb. 2015.

4. Faqiry, M.N. and Dad, S., Double-sided energy auction in microgrid: equilibrium underprice anticipation, *IEEE Access*, vol. 4, pp. 3794–3805, Jul. 2016.

5. Lee, J., Guo, J., Choi, J.K. and Zukerman, M., Distributed energy trading in microgrids: A game-theoretic model and its equilibrium analysis, *IEEE Trans. Ind. Electron.*, vol. 62, no. 6, pp. 3524–3533, Jun. 2015.

6. Cintuglu, M.H. and Mohammed, O.A., Behaviour modeling and auction architecture of networked microgrids for frequency support, *IEEE Trans. Ind. Inf.*, vol. 13, no. 4, pp. 1772–1782, Sep. 2017.

7. Zhong, W., Xie, K., Liu, Y., Yang, C. and Xie, S., Auction mechanisms for energy trading in multi-energy systems, *IEEE Trans. Ind. Inf.*, vol. 14, no. 4, pp. 1511–1521, Apt. 2018.

8. Chen, T., Pourbabak, H., Su, W., A game theoretic approach to analyze the dynamic interactions of multiple residential prosumers considering power flow constraints, In: *Power and Energy Society General Meeting, 2016 IEEE*, pp. 1–5, 2016.

9. Zhang, N., Yan, Y., Xu, S., Su, W., Game-theory-based electricity market clearing mechanisms for an open and transactive distribution grid, In: *Power and Energy Society General Meeting, 2015 IEEE*, pp. 1–5, 2015.

10. Council, E.C.R., *The economic impacts of the August 2003 Blackout*, Washington, DC, 2004.

11. Zhang, N., Yan, Y., Xu, S., Su, W., A distributed data storage and processing framework for next-generation residential distribution systems, *Electric Power Systems Research*, 116, pp. 174–181, 2014.

12. Hatziargyriou, N., Asano, H., Iravani, R., Marnay, C., Microgrids, *IEEE Power and Energy Magazine*, 5, (4), pp. 78–94, 2007.

13. Liang, Z., Alsafasfeh, Q., Jin, T., Pourbabak, H., Su, W., Risk-constrained optimal energy management for virtual power plants considering correlated demand response, *IEEE Transactions on Smart Grid*, 2017.

14. Saad, W., Han, Z., Poor, H.V., Basar, T., Game-theoretic methods for the smart grid: An overview of microgrid systems, demand-side management, and smart grid communications, *IEEE Signal Processing Magazine*, 29, (5), pp. 86–105, 2012.
15. Molzahn, D.K., Dörfler, F., Sandberg, H., Low, S.H., Chakrabarti, S., Baldick, R., *et al.*, A survey of distributed optimization and control algorithms for electric power systems, *IEEE Transactions on Smart Grid*, 8, (6), pp. 2941–2962, 2017.
16. Du, Y., Wang, Z., Liu, G., Chen, X., Yuan, H., Wei, Y., *et al.*, A cooperative game approach for coordinating multi-microgrid operation within distribution systems, *Applied Energy*, 222, pp. 383–395, 2018.
17. Du, Y., Li, F., Kou, X., Pei, W., Coordinating multi-microgrid operation within distribution system: A cooperative game approach, In: *Power & Energy Society General Meeting, 2017 IEEE*, IEEE, pp. 1–5, 2017.
18. Kristiansen, M., Korpås, M., Svendsen, H.G., A generic framework for power system flexibility analysis using cooperative game theory, *Applied Energy*, 212, pp. 223–232, 2018.
19. Ansari, B., Simoes, M.G., Distributed energy management of PV-storage systems for voltage rise mitigation, *Technology and Economics of Smart Grids and Sustainable Energy*, 2, (1), pp. 15, 2017.
20. Liang, Z., Su, W., *Game Theory Based Bidding Strategy for Prosumers in a Distribution System with a Retail Electricity Market*, 2017.
21. C. Sharmeela, Sivaraman, P., and S. Balaji (2020). Design of Hybrid DC MiniGrid for Educational Institution: Case Study, Lecture Notes in ElectricalEngineering, 580, pp. 125-134.
22. P. Sivaraman and C. Sharmeela, "Battery Energy Storage System Addressing the Power Quality Issue in Grid Connected Wind Energy Conversion System" 1st International conference on Large scale grid integration renewable energy in India, September, 2017, New Delhi, India.
23. R. Mahendran, P. Sivaraman and C. Sharmeela, "Three Phase Grid Interfaced Renewable Energy Source using Active Power Filter" 5th International Exhibition & Conference, GRIDTECH 2015, April, 2015, pp. 77-85, New Delhi, India.
24. Sivaraman, P., and Sharmeela, C. (2020). Power quality problems associated with electric vehicle charging infrastructure. In Sanjeevikumar Padmanaban, C. Sharmeela, Jens Bo Holm-Nielsen, *Power Quality in Modern Power Systems*, Elsevier.
25. Sivaraman, P., and Sharmeela, C. (2020). Existing issues associated with electric distribution system. In Baseem Kahn, Hassan Haes Alhelou & Ghassan (Eds.), *Handbook of Research on New Solutions and Technologies in Electrical Distribution Networks*, (pp. 1–31). Hershey, PA: IGI Global.
26. Sivaraman, P., and Sharmeela, C. (2020). Power Quality and its Characteristics. In Sanjeevikumar Padmanaban, C. Sharmeela, Jens Bo Holm-Nielsen, *Power Quality in Modern Power Systems*, Elsevier.

27. Sivaraman, P., and Sharmeela, C. (2020). Power System Harmonics. In Sanjeevikumar Padmanaban, C. Sharmeela, Jens Bo Holm-Nielsen, *Power Quality in Modern Power Systems*, Elsevier.
28. P. Sivaraman, D. Gunapriya, K. Parthiban and S. Manimaran, "Hybrid Fuzzy PSO Algorithm for Dynamic Economic Load Dispatch", Journal of Theoretical and Applied Information Technology, Vol. 62, No.3, pp. 794-799, April 2014.
29. P. Sivaraman, S. Manimaran, K. Parthiban and D. Gunapriya, "PSO Approach for Dynamic Economic Load Dispatch Problem", Int. Journal of Innovative Research in Science, Engineering and Technology, Vol. 3, No.4, pp. 11905-11910, April 2014.
30. Sivaraman, P., and Sharmeela, C. (2020). Solar Micro-Inverter. In J. Zbitou, C. Pruncu, & A. Errkik (Eds.), *Handbook of Research on Recent Developments in Electrical and Mechanical Engineering* (pp. 283–303). Hershey, PA: IGI Global.
31. Sivaraman, P., and Sharmeela, C. (2020). Introduction to electric distribution system. In Baseem Kahn, Hassan Haes Alhelou & Ghassan (Eds.), *Handbook of Research on New Solutions and Technologies in Electrical Distribution Networks,* (pp. 1–31). Hershey, PA: IGI Global.
32. P. Sivaraman, C. Sharmeela and D. P. Kothari, "Enhancing the voltage profile in distribution system with 40 GW of solar PV rooftop in Indian grid by 2022: a review" 1st International conference on Large scale grid integration renewable energy in India, September, 2017, New Delhi, India.

Index

Also of Interest

Check out these other related titles from Scrivener Publishing

Green Energy: Solar Energy, Photovoltaics, and Smart Cities, edited by Suman Lata Tripathi and Sanjeevikumar Padmanaban, ISBN 9781119760764. Covering the concepts and fundamentals of green energy, this volume, written and edited by a global team of experts, also goes into the practical applications that can be utilized across multiple industries, for both the engineer and the student. *DUE IN SPRING 2021*

Progress in Solar Energy Technology and Applications, edited by Umakanta Sahoo, ISBN 9781119555605. This first volume in the new groundbreaking series, Advances in Renewable Energy, covers the latest concepts, trends, techniques, processes, and materials in solar energy, focusing on the state-of-the-art for the field and written by a group of world-renowned experts. *NOW AVAILABLE!*

Energy Storage 2nd Edition, by Ralph Zito and Haleh Ardibili, ISBN 9781119083597. A revision of the groundbreaking study of methods for storing energy on a massive scale to be used in wind, solar, and other renewable energy systems. *NOW AVAILABLE!*

Nuclear Power: Policies, Practices, and the Future, by Darryl Siemer, ISBN 9781119657781. Written from an engineer's perspective, this is a treatise on the state of nuclear power today, its benefits, and its future, focusing on both policy and technological issues. *NOW AVAILABLE!*

Zero-Waste Engineering 2nd Edition: A New Era of Sustainable Technology Development, by M. M. Kahn and M. R. Islam, ISBN 9781119184898. This book outlines how to develop zero-waste engineering following natural pathways that are truly sustainable using methods that have been developed for sustainability, such as solar air conditioning, natural desalination, green building, chemical-free biofuel, fuel cells, scientifically renewable energy, and new mathematical and economic models. *NOW AVAILABLE!*

Sustainable Energy Pricing, by Gary Zatzman, ISBN 9780470901632. In this controversial new volume, the author explores a new science of energy pricing and how it can be done in a way that is sustainable for the world's economy and environment. *NOW AVAILABLE!*

Advanced Petroleum Reservoir Simulation, by M.R. Islam, S.H. Mousavizadegan, Shabbir Mustafiz, and Jamal H. Abou-Kassem, ISBN 9780470625811. The state of the art in petroleum reservoir simulation. *NOW AVAILABLE!*

Sustainable Resource Development, by Gary Zatzman, ISBN 9781118290392. Taking a new, fresh look at how the energy industry and we, as a planet, are developing our energy resources, this book looks at what is right and wrong about energy resource development. This book aids engineers and scientists in achieving a true sustainability in this field, both from an economic and environmental perspective. *NOW AVAILABLE!*

The *Greening of Petroleum Operations*, by M. R. Islam *et al.*, ISBN 9780470625903. The state of the art in petroleum operations, from a "green" perspective. *NOW AVAILABLE!*

Emergency Response Management for Offshore Oil Spills, by Nicholas P. Cheremisinoff, PhD, and Anton Davletshin, ISBN 9780470927120. The first book to examine the Deepwater Horizon disaster and offer processes for safety and environmental protection. *NOW AVAILABLE!*

Biogas Production, Edited by Ackmez Mudhoo, ISBN 9781118062852. This volume covers the most cutting-edge pretreatment processes being used and studied today for the production of biogas during anaerobic digestion processes using different feedstocks, in the most efficient and economical methods possible. *NOW AVAILABLE!*

Bioremediation and Sustainability: Research and Applications, Edited by Romeela Mohee and Ackmez Mudhoo, ISBN 9781118062845. Bioremediation and Sustainability is an up-to-date and comprehensive treatment of research and applications for some of the most important low-cost, "green," emerging technologies in chemical and environmental engineering. *NOW AVAILABLE!*

Green Chemistry and Environmental Remediation, Edited by Rashmi Sanghi and Vandana Singh, ISBN 9780470943083. Presents high quality research papers as well as in depth review articles on the new emerging green face of multidimensional environmental chemistry. *NOW AVAILABLE!*

Bioremediation of Petroleum and Petroleum Products, by James Speight and Karuna Arjoon, ISBN 9780470938492. With petroleum-related spills, explosions, and health issues in the headlines almost every day, the issue of remediation of petroleum and petroleum products is taking on increasing importance, for the survival of our environment, our planet, and our future. This book is the first of its kind to explore this difficult issue from an engineering and scientific point of view and offer solutions and reasonable courses of action. *NOW AVAILABLE!*

Printed and bound by CPI Group (UK) Ltd, Croydon, CR0 4YY

27/10/2024

14580467-0005